The Royal Commission on Legal Services

Chairman: Sir Henry Benson GBE

FINAL REPORT

Volume One

Chapters 1–28

The Library
Exeter College
Oxford.

Presented to Parliament by Command of Her Majesty
October 1979

LONDON
HER MAJESTY'S STATIONERY OFFICE
£12 net
(2 parts not sold separately)

Cmnd. 7648

The Report of the Royal Commission on Legal Services

VOLUME I REPORT

VOLUME II SURVEYS AND STUDIES

The estimated total expenditure of the Royal Commission is £1,245,606. Of this sum £189,751 represents the estimated cost of printing and publishing this report.

ISBN 0 10 176480 4*

THE ROYAL COMMISSION ON LEGAL SERVICES
REPORT
Volume One
Cmnd 7648

ISBN 0 10 176480 4

CORRECTIONS

Page 57, end of Table 5.1
Delete "Total cost of the scheme"

Page 96, sub paragraph 9.21(a), second line
For "please" read "pleas"

Page 133
R12.12
Delete "12.57–12.58" and insert "12.66–12.67"
R12.13
Insert "legal" after "Civil"
Delete "12.59" and insert "12.68"

Page 167, paragraph 15.3, sixth line
For "Common" read "Commons"

Page 221, sub paragraph 1(d)(iii), first line
Delete "cases" and insert "centres"

Page 279, paragraph 21.95, fourth line
For "usually" read "unusually"

Page 375, R27.4
Delete "24.14" and insert "27.14"

Page 376, R27.10
Delete "27.41" and insert "27.42"

Page 550, paragraph 37.26, fourth line
For "practice" read "practise"

Page 675, running heading
After "NORTHERN IRELAND:" delete "LEGAL SERVICES" and insert
"INTRODUCTORY"

Pages 677–688, running headings
After "NORTHERN IRELAND: LEGAL" delete "PROFESSION" and insert
"SERVICES"

Page 718, R42.28
Delete "42.10" and insert "42.100"

Page 728, sub paragraph B3(j)
Delete "renewed" and insert "reviewed"

Page 735, section G.1, second paragraph
Delete "agreed" and insert "argued"

Page 761,
R12.12
Delete "12.57–12.58" and insert "12.66–12.67"
R12.13
Delete "12.59" and insert "12.68"

Page 776, R27.10
Delete "27.41" and insert "27.42"

Page 832, index
Under "Barristers—
cab rank rule—"
delete "relaxation" and insert "retention"

Page 858, index
Insert new entry "Real Property Commission report, 21.5"
between "Race discrimination" and "Recommendations"

Page 860, index
Delete "Royal Property Commission report, 21.5"

October 1979

LONDON: HER MAJESTY'S STATIONERY OFFICE

THE ROYAL WARRANTS

ELIZABETH R.

MARGARET.
 (*Signed on behalf of Her Majesty*)

ELIZABETH THE SECOND, by the Grace of God of the United Kingdom of Great Britain and Northern Ireland and of Our other Realms and Territories QUEEN, Head of the Commonwealth, Defender of the Faith, to Our Trusty and Well-beloved:

> Sir Henry Alexander Benson, Knight Grand Cross of Our Most Excellent Order of the British Empire;

> Sir Sydney William Templeman, Knight, Member of Our Most Excellent Order of the British Empire, one of the Justices of Our High Court of Justice;

> Peter Goldman, Esquire, Commander of Our Most Excellent Order of the British Empire;

> Ralf Dahrendorf, Esquire;

> Leonard Firby Edmondson, Esquire;

> Joseph Thomas William Haines, Esquire;

> Thomas Patrick Shirley Harper, Esquire;

> Mark Littman, Esquire, one of Our Counsel learned in the Law;

> Agatha Susan Marsden-Smedley;

> William Marshall, Esquire;

> Peter Morris Oppenheimer, Esquire;

> Sally Ramsden;

> Alwyn Roberts, Esquire;

> David Joseph Seligman, Esquire;

> William Maxwell Harries Williams, Esquire,

Greeting!

WHEREAS We have deemed it expedient that a Commission should forthwith issue to inquire into the law and practice relating to the provision of legal services in England, Wales and Northern Ireland, and to consider whether any, and if so what, changes are desirable in the public interest in the structure, organisation, training, regulation of and entry to the legal profession, including the arrangements for determining its remuneration, whether from private sources or public funds, and in the rules which prevent persons who are neither barristers nor solicitors from undertaking conveyancing and other legal business on behalf of other persons:

Now Know Ye that We, reposing great trust and confidence in your knowledge and ability, have authorised and appointed, and do by these Presents authorise and appoint you the said Sir Henry Alexander Benson (Chairman); Sir Sydney William Templeman; Peter Goldman; Ralf Dahrendorf; Leonard Firby Edmondson; Joseph Thomas William Haines; Thomas Patrick Shirley Harper; Mark Littman; Agatha Susan Marsden-Smedley; William Marshall; Peter Morris Oppenheimer; Sally Ramsden; Alwyn Roberts; David Joseph Seligman and William Maxwell Harries Williams, to be Our Commissioners for the purposes of the said inquiry:

And for the better effecting the purposes of this Our Commission We do by these Presents give and grant unto you, or any eight or more of you, full power to call before you such persons as you shall judge likely to afford you any information upon the subject of this Our Commission; to call for information in writing; and also to call for, have access to and examine all such books, documents, registers and records as may afford you the fullest information on the subject and to inquire of and concerning the premises by all other lawful ways and means whatsoever:

And We do by these Presents authorise and empower you, or any of you, to visit and personally inspect such places as you may deem it expedient so to inspect for the more effectual carrying out of the purposes aforesaid:

And We do by these Presents will and ordain that this Our Commission shall continue in full force and virtue, and that you, Our said Commissioners, or any eight or more of you, may from time to time proceed in the execution thereof, and of every matter and thing therein contained, although the same be not continued from time to time by adjournment:

And We do further ordain that you, or any eight or more of you, have liberty to report your proceedings under this Our Commission from time to time if you shall judge it expedient so to do:

And Our further will and pleasure is that you do, with as little delay as possible' report to Us your opinion upon the matters herein submitted for your con¯sideration.

Given at Our Court at Saint James's the Twentieth day of July 1976; In the Twenty-fifth Year of Our Reign

By Her Majesty's Command,
ROY JENKINS

Notes: Mr. Marshall resigned in October 1976.
In November 1978 Sir Sydney Templeman was appointed a Lord Justice of Appeal.

ELIZABETH R.

ELIZABETH THE SECOND by the Grace of God of the United Kingdom of Great Britain and Northern Ireland and of Our other Realms and Territories QUEEN, Head of the Commonwealth, Defender of the Faith, to Our Trusty and Well-beloved:

Darwin Herbert Templeton, Esquire, Commander of Our Most Excellent Order of the British Empire,

Greeting!

WHEREAS by a Warrant under Our Royal Sign Manual bearing date the twentieth day of July 1976 the Royal Commission on Legal Services was constituted:

AND WHEREAS We have deemed it expedient to appoint a further member of the said Commission in the place of Our Trusty and Well-beloved William Marshall, Esquire, who has resigned:

Now KNOW YE that We, reposing great trust and confidence in your knowledge and ability, have appointed and do by these Presents appoint you the said Darwin Herbert Templeton to be a member of the said Commission.

GIVEN at Our Court at Sandringham the sixth day of January 1977; In the Twenty-fifth Year of Our Reign

By Her Majesty's Command.

MERLYN REES

WARRANT appointing Darwin Herbert Templeton, Esquire, CBE to be a member of the Royal Commission on Legal Services.

ROYAL COMMISSION ON LEGAL SERVICES

Report

To the Queen's Most Excellent Majesty

MAY IT PLEASE YOUR MAJESTY

We, the undersigned Commissioners, having been appointed by Royal Warrant
"To inquire into the law and practice relating to the provision of legal services in England, Wales and Northern Ireland, and to consider whether any, and if so what, changes are desirable in the public interest in the structure, organisation, training, regulation of and entry to the legal profession, including the arrangements for determining its remuneration, whether from private sources or public funds, and in the rules which prevent persons who are neither barristers nor solicitors from undertaking conveyancing and other legal business on behalf of other persons"

HUMBLY SUBMIT TO YOUR MAJESTY THE FOLLOWING REPORT.

CONTENTS

Volume I

PART I—INTRODUCTORY

Chapter 3 The Legal Profession

PART II—LEGAL SERVICES

Chapter 4 The Need for Legal Services

Chapter 5   The Provision of Legal Services: Principles and Methods

Chapter 6   The Organisation of Legal Services
Introduction

Chapter 7   General Advice and Citizens Advice Bureaux

Chapter 13 Legal Advice and Assistance and Civil Legal Aid: the Administrative Aspects

Chapter 14 Criminal Legal Aid

Chapter 18   Rights of Audience

Chapter 19 Restrictions on Practice and Competition

Chapter 20 Employed Lawyers

Chapter 21   Conveyancing

Chapter 22   Quality of Service

Chapter 23   Protection of the Client: Solicitors

Chapter 24 Protection of the Client: Barristers

Chapter 25 Discipline: Solicitors

Chapter 26   Discipline: Barristers

Chapter 27   Information for the Public

Chapter 28 The E E C

PART IV —THE LEGAL PROFESSION

Chapter 31   Legal Executives

Chapter 32   The Structure and Organisation of the Profession: Barristers

Chapter 33   Practising arrangements: Barristers

Chapter 34 Barristers' Clerks

Chapter 35 Discrimination

Chapter 36 Remuneration

Chapter 37   Lawyers' Charges

Chapter 38   Legal Education

Chapter 39   The Future of Legal Education

PART V   NORTHERN IRELAND

Chapter 40   Northern Ireland—Introductory

Chapter 41   Legal Services in Northern Ireland

Chapter 42   The Legal Profession in Northern Ireland

PART VI THE FUTURE

Chapter 43 Matters outside our Terms of Reference

Chapter 44 A Programme for the Future

PART VII   CONCLUSIONS

Summary of Conclusions and Recommendations

PART VIII   NOTES OF DISSENT

INDEX

TABLES

FIGURES

Volume II

Part A   Lists of Those Who Assisted the Commission

LIST 1   Individuals and organisations who gave written and/or oral evidence to the Commission.

LIST 2   Individuals and organisations who provided information or who assisted the Commission.

LIST 3   The Commission's consultants.

Part B   Surveys and Studies

Definitions of statistical and accounting terms used.

PART I

Introductory

CHAPTER 1

The Commission and its Work

Meetings

1.1   The names of the members of the Commission were announced in Parliament on Tuesday 30th June 1976 and we held our first full meeting on Thursday 2nd July 1976. The full Commission met on 74 occasions.

1.2   We set up committees, numbering as a rule three or four members, to look into needs for legal services and their provision, conveyancing, the speed and cost of legal proceedings, education and training and lawyers' fees and charges. The function of these committees was to assemble and analyse the information available on each topic and present it for consideration by the full Commission. The committees held a total of 67 formal meetings and met informally on numerous other occasions. In addition, a large number of visits were paid by individuals or groups of us. These are described in paragraph 1.24.

Progress report

1.3   We published a progress report in April 1977 (Cmnd. 6770), containing information concerning our enquiries and consultations which it is not necessary to repeat in detail.

Ascertaining the facts

1.4   Our first task was to ascertain the facts which we had to take into account in reaching our conclusions. Accordingly, we set about obtaining this information in a number of ways. We issued circulars and advertisements asking for evidence in general terms. We formulated detailed questionnaires addressed to a wide variety of persons and organisations, within the legal profession and outside it. We prepared and carried out a number of surveys and enquiries. All these are described in more detail below.

Circulars and advertisements

1.5   In our first circular, intended as a general consultative document, we invited evidence under six main headings, divided into a total of approximately 40 subheadings. In the course of our work we found that some of the topics set out in this way were absorbed by others, and that new topics emerged, but the general pattern remained unchanged. Over 3,000 copies of the circular were sent out to those from whom we sought evidence and to those who offered to submit evidence.

3

1.6   However long our address list, we could not expect to reach the public at large by sending out circulars. Therefore, in the autumn of 1976, with the assistance of the Central Office of Information, we placed advertisements in the national press and in certain local papers, inviting anyone who wished to give evidence to get in touch with us.

Questionnaires

1.7   In cases where a witness had knowledge and experience which we thought likely to be of use to us, we did not invite evidence in general terms. Instead, we sent to each such witness a questionnaire setting out in detail the points on which we sought information. The questionnaires addressed to the governing bodies of the legal profession in England and Wales and Northern Ireland and to a number of organisations within it contained over 300 questions requesting statistical data, evidence both of fact and opinion and statements of intention or of policy. We sent other questionnaires in similar, but usually shorter, form to over 130 persons and organisations. We cross-checked the answers given and where these indicated that further information was required, supplementary questions followed. The research effort involved placed a considerable burden on those to whom our enquiries were addressed, but it laid the foundation of our own work. The material obtained makes up a collection of knowledge about the profession and the provision of legal services in this country which has not hitherto been available.

Surveys and enquiries

1.8   The research undertaken by the Commission was not confined to enquiries of the kind just described. We undertook a number of surveys and studies which ranged from relatively minor exercises to a survey carried out on a nationwide basis among a sample of 16,000 members of the adult population; this survey will be referred to in this report as the Users' Survey. In Volume II we include as appendices to this report the results of a number of these projects which are of general interest.

1.9   We also made use of research undertaken by others. At the outset of our work we sent consultation papers to upwards of 90 universities, colleges and polytechnics and to organisations such as the Association of Law Teachers and the Society of Public Teachers of Law. We also asked for details of relevant studies and research known to be in progress. The Institute of Advanced Legal Studies supplied us with a list of titles of post-graduate theses and other current legal research and we wrote to those whose work was relevant to our enquiries.

1.10   While in this way we made use of research conducted by others and commissioned research of our own, we also became aware of certain constraints and limitations which had to be borne in mind. Perhaps the most important was the conflict between the time required for basic research and the need to complete our work without undue delay. Moreover, since little prior data were available for the purpose of making comparisons with different periods or with other relevant activities, there was a likelihood that research conducted under these limitations would be of a "snapshot" variety. We also recognised that in research there is a point, not always easy to detect, beyond which increased sophistication does not yield a proportional improvement in material on which to base decisions. At various places in this report we emphasise the need for continuing research activity by existing bodies and by new institutions the establishment of which we recommend. This we believe to be essential to the development of an effective and responsive legal service.

1.11 We would like to express our gratitude to all those who helped us by making available to us, often in advance of publication, the results of their work. We are also indebted to centres of study such as the Institute of Judicial Administration at Birmingham University and the Centre for Socio-legal Studies at Oxford University, for their interest and assistance.

Enquiries abroad
1.12 We made enquiries about legal services in a number of Commonwealth and European countries and the United States of America. Considerable attention is now paid to the provision of legal services throughout the world, and the topic is frequently discussed at international gatherings, such as the conference organised by the Council of Europe on European Law held at Leyden in March 1976, whose published records provided useful material. We were able to supplement such material with information obtained by correspondence and discussion. Many visitors from abroad called at our offices and assisted us by giving information themselves or by putting us in touch with sources of information. We are particularly grateful for the assistance given to us by members of the American College of Trial Lawyers.

1.13 A number of us who individually travelled abroad for other purposes pursued enquiries on behalf of the Commission in the course of their journeys. Members of the Commission and its secretariat visited Australia, Belgium, Canada, India, the Republic of Ireland, Israel and the United States of America. It proved unnecessary for the Commission as a whole to undertake any foreign visits.

Evidence
1.14 There was a large and widespread response to our requests for evidence. Nearly 3,500 persons and organisations wrote to us to express their views or relate their own experiences. We have divided this evidence into two categories.

1.15 The first comprises letters from private persons relating their personal experiences. Over 2,000 people in this category wrote to us. We analysed the information contained in these letters, and deal with the results in Chapter 22.

1.16 The second came from persons and organisations who gave us information or views about the provision of legal services, and made suggestions for change or improvement. We include in this category the evidence given in answer to the questionnaires mentioned above. We received over 900 submissions of evidence of this description, ranging from short papers of half a page in length to documents of several hundred pages. All those who gave evidence or information are listed in Volume II.

1.17 We wish to record our appreciation of the response to our requests for evidence and information. Foreign visitors to whom we spoke of our work expressed astonishment that we were able to make any progress without the power to compel the attendance of witnesses and the production of documents. If such a power had been available to us, we would have gained little by exercising it. The detailed information given to us included material relating to private meetings, extracts from confidential papers and financial accounts. In spite of its confidentiality, such material was made available to us freely and without hesitation.

1.18 Most of the evidence we received was in written form. We considered it preferable to obtain evidence in this way if possible. Where appropriate, however, we heard oral evidence to enable witnesses to develop the points they had made in writing, and to provide the members of the Commission with an opportunity to test these by question and answer. One hundred and fifty-three witnesses gave oral evidence; and they are marked accordingly in the list in Volume II. Oral evidence was taken in England and in Belfast.

Publication of evidence
1.19 In deciding whether or not to make public the evidence submitted to us we had to hold a balance between the interests of the witnesses, in particular private individuals who gave us information of a personal character, and the interest of the public in having access to the material before us.

1.20 The witnesses in our first category, who wrote to tell us of some personal experience, gave evidence which involved disclosure of their private lives. A number of them were anxious that what they told us should not be made public. We decided that all evidence of this character should be regarded as submitted in confidence, and none of it has been published. The analyses which appear in Chapter 22 and Volume II should provide sufficient information for all practical purposes.

1.21 With regard to evidence in the second category, which was of a general rather than personal character, we took the opposite view, namely that it should be published if possible for the information of the public and for the benefit of scholarship and research. Accordingly, when we received any such evidence we wrote to the witness to suggest its publication. We enclosed with our letter a list of newspaper correspondents and agencies who had expressed an interest in seeing any material submitted to us; we also told the witness that, with permission, we would put a copy of the evidence he had submitted in the files kept available in our office for public inspection. Most of the witnesses in this category made their evidence publicly available and are marked accordingly in the list in Volume II.

1.22 Witnesses who gave oral evidence were sent a copy of the transcript for checking and were asked to agree to its publication. They were told that if they regarded any passage as confidential they should mark it, and that such passages would be omitted from the transcripts made public at that stage, though we reserved the right to quote from any oral evidence given to us, or to append extracts from it to our report. A number of witnesses marked passages as confidential and in two instances, at the request of the witnesses, the whole of their evidence was withheld from publication.

1.23 All the records of the Commission have been deposited in the Public Record Office and the Public Record Office of Northern Ireland. They include a complete set of the evidence now publicly available, as described in paragraphs 1.20 – 1.22, which will be available for examination in the usual way. Arrangements have been made to deposit further sets of this evidence in the Bodleian Library Oxford, the library of the Middle Temple, the universities of Cambridge, Durham, Kent, Manchester, Newcastle-upon-Tyne, Warwick, the Queens' University, Belfast, the University College of Wales, Aberystwyth, University College, Cardiff, the University of Wales Institute of Science and Technology, the South Glamorgan Institute of Higher Education, the London School of Economics, the Institute of Judicial Administration at Birmingham University, the Centre for Socio-legal Studies at Oxford and the Institute of Advanced Legal Studies in London.

Meetings and visits

1.24 As a Commission we visited Belfast, Birmingham, Cardiff, Liverpool, Manchester and Newcastle-upon-Tyne where we met members of the profession and others engaged in the provision of legal services. The majority of us are not lawyers and before joining the Commission had a limited knowledge of legal practice and the way in which lawyers work. To remedy this as far as possible, we went, individually and in small groups, in all parts of the country to solicitors' offices, barristers' chambers, courts, tribunals, the Inns of Court, law centres and legal advice centres, citizens advice bureaux, building societies, schools of law, polytechnics, colleges, local authorities, the Land Registry and other government offices. Members of the Commission also visited prisons to study legal services available to prisoners.

1.25 We were struck by the friendliness with which we were greeted in the course of all our visits and the openness with which all our enquiries were answered. We are indebted to all those who helped us in this way, often at cost to themselves in loss of working time.

The Royal Commission on Legal Services in Scotland

1.26 The Royal Commission on Legal Services in Scotland, appointed with terms of reference similar to our own, started work in October 1976. The two Commissions exchanged minutes and papers and maintained informal but close contact. The appointment of members of the Royal Commission on Criminal Procedure was announced in February 1978. We also kept in touch with this Commission and exchanged information of mutual interest.

Reports from other bodies

1.27   A great deal has been written in recent years about legal services and the legal profession. We have already mentioned material that came from abroad. In this country a large number of commissions, committees and inquiries have reported on these topics from both outside and within the profession: in its evidence the Senate of the Inns of Court and the Bar listed 17 reports, all but one delivered in the last ten years and all relevant to the structure or work of the profession. We return to this point in Chapter 3, and at this stage wish to record our appreciation of the work of all those who have gone before us.

Form and content of the report

1.28   Our report is published in two volumes. Volume I contains the main text, with our conclusions and recommendations and a full index. Some chapters in this volume have annexes containing statistical or other material which is necessary for a full understanding of the text. Volume II contains detailed reports of surveys and studies which we have commissioned or carried out. Unless published in this way, these would not be readily available for the purpose of scholarship and research. For ease of reference, a list of the contents of Volume II, showing where each item may be found, follows the table of contents of this volume.

1.29   The text of Volume I is divided into eight parts. Part I contains introductory material and deals in general terms with legal services and with the history and character of the legal profession. Part II concerns the need for, the means of providing and the organisation of legal services. It includes chapters on legal aid and alternatives to legal aid, law centres, general advisory services, duty solicitor schemes and related topics. Part III concerns the work of lawyers. Its opening chapter is on fusion, an issue which has to be dealt with at the outset of any treatment of the work of the legal profession. This part also includes chapters on rights of audience, conveyancing, quality of service, the protection of the client, lawyers' discipline, information available to potential clients and the European Economic Communities. Part IV deals with the structure and organisation of the profession, its practising arrangements, its employment of staff, its remuneration and education. Part V relates to Northern Ireland. In Part VI we set out, for consideration by others, a number of matters raised in evidence submitted to us which deserve attention but which fall outside our terms of reference and we set out a programme for the future. In Part VII we bring together all the recommendations which we have made. This is followed by Part VIII which contains notes of dissent on certain issues in this report.

1.30   Throughout the report we deal with the subject matter, as far as possible, in layman's terms. In dealing with present arrangements for the provision of legal services, we describe them from the viewpoint of a lay client. It will be found that there is some duplication of material in the text of Volume I. This is deliberate. Facts and argument relevant to more than one topic are repeated when appropriate.

Terminology

1.31   We should mention three matters of terminology. First, throughout our report we try to avoid expressions which suggest discrimination between the sexes. However, it is not possible without laborious circumlocution always to avoid expressions of this character. Constant use of "he or she", "him or her" and "his or her" is cumbersome, and so we follow convention in using the masculine alone. As we said in our progress report, it should not be inferred from this that we have chosen to ignore half the population.

1.32   The second relates to the expression "private practice". To lawyers, a person in private practice is one who offers services, for a fee, to the general public. In some professions this is described as "public practice". We have adopted the expression "private practice" in this report, as it is the one normally used by the legal profession.

1.33   The third concerns the term "layman", which arises from time to time in the text, mainly in connection with service on committees. We use the term to describe a person who is not a member of the legal profession. It should not be taken to imply ignorance of legal matters: we are aware that many of the laymen now serving on committees concerned with legal matters have developed a wide general knowledge of the topics which come before them.

Reservations

1.34   Our conclusions and recommendations number about 370. In the text of this report many points of view are explored. As is to be expected in a Commission with broad terms of reference, comprising fifteen people drawn from a wide variety of backgrounds and persuasions, we take different views on some matters and on points of detail and emphasis. But we have done our best to avoid notes of reservation or dissent and though we may not personally subscribe to every expression of view in the text, we are in broad agreement, save when specifically stated, on our conclusions and recommendations. Matters upon which there is disagreement between us are set out in the notes of dissent at the end of this volume.

Acknowledgements

1.35   We received assistance from so many people, in so many ways, that it is invidious to single anyone out. However we record our gratitude, first, to all those who took the trouble to respond to our requests for evidence and to our advertisements. We also thank all those abroad who, although they had no direct interest in the results of our work, nevertheless gave us valuable help. We list in Volume II a number of persons and organisations abroad for whose help we wish to record our thanks.

1.36   The officers, council members and staff of the governing bodies of both branches of the profession responded with willingness and goodwill to our requests for evidence and information. They co-operated in our survey work and consulted us in connection with their own surveys of remuneration and other matters. In spite of the pressure of their regular day-to-day work, they gave attention to all our requirements, though the resulting additional burden of work and the financial cost was heavy. We would not have been able to complete our work with ease or despatch without their cooperation, for which we here express our gratitude.

1.37   We conclude this chapter by expressing warm thanks to all members of the secretariat who have served the Commission during the last three years. Exacting demands were made upon them; they worked as a team, often for long hours under pressure of time, and never failed to meet the tasks we set them. We reserve a special measure of appreciation for the Commission's Secretary, John Heritage. The high quality of his work, his untiring energy, judgment and sense of humour made an outstanding contribution which all members of the Commission gratefully acknowledge.

CHAPTER 2

Legal Services

Background

Meaning
2.1   In some parts of the English-speaking world, notably the United States of America, the expression "legal services" is taken to mean legal advice and assistance made available, free or at reduced rates, to people without adequate means. In our terms of reference, we construe the expression as having a wider meaning, and have taken it to include services which should be available to any person or organisation requiring advice or assistance of a legal character, whether payment for the service is made from public or private funds.

2.2   There can be no precise definition of the extent of legal services. Lawyers in private practice may be found who are willing to give advice on a wide variety of matters which have no close connection with the law, but about which previous experience has given them expert knowledge. It is entirely a matter for any professional adviser personally to decide to what extent he is willing to give advice for which he accepts professional responsibility. For our purposes, however, we regard legal services as being concerned with advice, assistance and representation which is required by a person in connection with rights, duties and liabilities of a legal character. We describe in the following paragraphs some of the means by which services of this kind may be provided.

2.3   What is thus described covers services available not merely from members of the legal profession in private practice, but from lawyers employed in commercial and industrial organisations, in national and local government, in trade unions and other private associations and in a large number of advisory organisations, some supported by private, others by public, funds. In succeeding chapters we assess the merits and deficiencies of the present system of legal services. In this chapter we give a brief summary of the present position.

Lay advice
2.4   When a person encounters a problem (which, although a legal problem, may not at the outset be recognised as such) he is likely in the first instance to consult someone whose judgment he trusts; this may be a relative, friend, priest or minister, neighbour, employer, trade union official, bank manager, Member of Parliament, councillor or anyone in whom he is willing to confide. Anyone consulted in this way and giving advice about what is a legal problem might be said to provide a legal service. A large amount of such advice is given. The Users'

Survey, the report on which may be found in Volume II section 8, showed that, of those who consulted a solicitor in 1977, 27 per cent had previously sought advice on their problems from non-lawyers. This source of legal assistance is to be distinguished from services available from the legal profession and advisory organisations with which we deal in this report.

2.5 Apart from consulting a trusted acquaintance, a person may obtain advice otherwise than by going to a solicitor's office. He may get advice from a person whose work is not connected with any advisory service or from an organisation which is set up for an entirely different purpose. For example, informal advice may be given in offices of national or local government, in community centres and public libraries. Advice about a legal problem is often given by members of other professions. Accountants, architects, bankers, brokers, estate agents, insurers, social workers, surveyors and many others give advice which may incidentally include a legal element. A large source of advice may be found in organisations whose function it is to assist their members in this way. There are two main sub-divisions in this category: organisations concerned with a specific class of problem, such as tenants' associations and those concerned with a particular pursuit or occupation, such as the motoring associations and the trade unions. Finally, of considerable importance in this field, are the organisations which offer an advisory service to the general public. Most prominent among these are the citizens advice bureaux (CABx), but there are many others.

2.6 The advice given in the way described above is large. For example, the National Association of Citizens Advice Bureaux (NACAB) supplied us with information showing that in 1977/78 its bureaux, of which there are about 750 in the United Kingdom and in which some 9,000 people work, handled over 3 million cases; it was estimated that in one third of these, advice of a legal character was required. Consumer advice centres are a more recent creation than the CABx. In the financial year 1977/78, their advice was sought in over 700,000 cases.

2.7 We were given information also by 66 of the legal advice centres, believed to number about 120, now in operation. These 66 centres dealt with over 95,000 cases in 1976; they employed 49 full-time and 56 part-time workers and over 1,000 volunteers.

2.8 The Trades Union Congress (TUC) told us in its evidence that, in 1974, 37 unions (representing 35 per cent of all union members), who received some 50,000 accident forms forwarded on behalf of potential claimants, between them recovered £33 million in damages in personal injury and employment claims on behalf of about 35,000 members. It is common practice for union officials to represent their members in national insurance and industrial tribunals. Although their main concern is with legal matters connected with employment, of the kind we have just described, a number of unions offer a general legal advisory service and it appears from the TUC's evidence that this is a growing trend.

2.9   Some organisations do not fall precisely into the categories we mentioned in paragraph 2.5. These are the agencies which are designed to promote reform or are formed for a charitable purpose or for the purpose of comradeship and which develop expertise in certain types of case work for individuals. For example, Justice (the British branch of the International Association of Jurists) and the National Council for Civil Liberties have as their main purpose the improvement of the law and of legal and administrative procedures and are concerned with matters of general policy, but both organisations deal with individual cases. They offer a service of value to people who turn to them when other sources of help have failed. In a different category, the Royal British Legion provides for former servicemen and their families a comprehensive service of representation in the Pensions Appeal Tribunals.

2.10   Many of the agencies we have mentioned are concerned with the legal problems of the poor and the low-paid. These problems relate to what has come to be called " social welfare law ". This branch of the law is concerned largely with social problems such as housing (including evictions, public health and the rights of tenants and landlords), claims for social security benefits, problems involving family relationships, loss of employment, environmental problems, and, in some areas, juvenile crime and some forms of adult crime. It is a feature of cases of this type that legal problems do not arise in isolation and that in many instances, although a legal element exists, personal and social problems predominate and call for appropriate skill and knowledge in those who deal with such cases.

2.11   We do not interpret our terms of reference as requiring us to investigate all the numerous sources of advice mentioned above for the purpose of con-sidering whether and, if so, what changes are desirable in the way in which they are organised or in which they provide legal or para-legal services as part of their work. It is necessary, however, to consider the means by which the legal profession can develop systematic means of contact with these organisations, in order to help them in their work and so that the individuals who consult them may get readier access to professional legal advice. We deal with these points in Chapters 7 and 8.

2.12   Although our remit does not require us to deal with all the advisory organisations now in operation, it is necessary for us to refer in particular to the functions of the CABx as a first-tier general advisory service and means of access to professional legal advice and also to the role of advisory organisations in relation to representation before tribunals. We return to these points in Chapters 7 and 15 respectively.

Services provided by the legal profession

2.13 The work done by the legal profession in courts of law is not the largest component of its total work, but it appears to attract the most publicity. In annex 2.1, we set out the names of the various courts in England and Wales, their composition and functions and the numbers of civil proceedings commenced and of defendants dealt with, in criminal proceedings, in 1977. For the purpose of comparison, information is given in annex 2.2 about tribunals and the number of cases of which they disposed.

Litigation: the courts

2.14 It will be seen from annex 2.1 that in England and Wales the heaviest caseload is in the magistrates' courts where, with the exception of a small proportion of stipendiary magistrates, the bench consists entirely of laymen. The next heaviest caseload is that of the county courts which have a limited jurisdiction in civil matters. More serious civil and criminal business is dealt with in the Supreme Court. This comprises the three divisions of the High Court, which hear the weightier civil cases and also certain appeals from the lower courts; the Crown Court, in which the more serious criminal cases are tried; and the Court of Appeal, which hears appeals from the High Court and Crown Court as well as from the county courts and certain other courts and tribunals. Juries are not used in appeal cases, and, in England and Wales, are now rarely required for civil cases. They function almost exclusively at criminal trials in the Crown Court. The House of Lords is the final court of appeal. In both magistrates' and county courts, barristers and solicitors have the same right of audience. In the Crown Court in England and Wales, barristers alone have a right of audience save for certain limited exceptions, mentioned in Chapter 18, under which solicitors are entitled to appear as advocates. The position is different in Northern Ireland, however, where solicitors have more extensive rights of audience (see Chapter 42). In the Supreme Court and House of Lords, barristers alone, save for certain limited exceptions mentioned in Chapter 18, have a right of audience.

2.15 Only a small proportion of civil cases in which proceedings are started reach final judgment. In 1978, of 143,577 actions commenced in the Queen's Bench Division, 102,909 were claims under various heads for debt, and in these cases summary judgment or judgment by default was entered in 48,246. Cases set down for hearing numbered 9,625, of which 1,793 came to trial. The investigations of the Royal Commission on Civil Liability and Compensation for Personal Injury published in March 1978 (Cmnd. 7054 Volume II paragraph 394) showed that less than 2 per cent of cases in which an attempt was made to recover damages for personal injury reached the stage of a hearing in court.

Tribunals

2.16 There is an increasing number of tribunals with functions akin to those of the courts, though some bear little resemblance to an ordinary court and are not intended to do so. Representation is permitted before nearly all tribunals but in some, legal representation is not encouraged, though, so far as we are aware, it is forbidden only before the service committees which hear complaints against National Health Service practitioners.

2.17 We deal in Chapter 15 with legal services in relation to tribunals. At this stage, we remark only that our evidence shows that, whatever the tribunal and however informal its procedure, representation, whether by a lawyer or skilled layman, in the majority of cases confers an advantage on the represented party. There may be no need for representation where the nature of the proceedings or the composition of the tribunal is such that neither party is at a disadvantage through not being represented and where the parties conduct the case on equal terms. However, the second condition is not satisfied where one party (even though not legally represented) regularly appears before a particular tribunal and so develops expertise in the class of case handled; in such circumstances, the other party to the proceedings, if he is an unassisted layman, will be at a disadvantage.

Non-contentious business
2.18 The volume of work done in connection with proceedings before courts and tribunals on disputes between two parties which never reach the stage of court proceedings is, although large, only part of the total work of the profession. Advice is given, negotiations are conducted and documents are prepared in relation to property, matrimonial and family matters, trusts, probate, consumer problems, company and commercial matters, taxation, planning applications, industrial property rights, shipping and other matters too numerous to mention. In conveyancing, while the exact number of transactions is nowhere recorded, we estimate, on the basis of the Users' Survey, that in 1977 over a million people consulted a solicitor about a domestic conveyancing matter. In 1978 there were 253,868 grants of representation in the estates of deceased persons of which approximately 78 per cent were taken out by solicitors.

The Work of the Legal Profession

The nature of the work
2.19 The work undertaken by the members of the legal profession is wide in extent and in some cases highly specialised. Traditionally, some barristers specialise in one or other of the sub-divisions of the law but some solicitors also concentrate on particular branches of the law. For example, some solicitors working in the City of London have an internationally recognised expertise in commercial matters.

2.20 Like other people, lawyers may be asked for advice on matters wholly outside their professional field. Many solicitors, particularly from country districts, told us that they were accustomed to being consulted by their clients on all kinds of personal and social problems, whether or not they had anything to do with the law. They expressed regret that this tended to happen less often nowadays. We think it is inevitable that the solicitor's role of informal adviser will decline, for two reasons. The first is that people are able to obtain advice of all kinds—in relation to financial and consumer problems, marital difficulties and many others—from the advisory organisations which are now numerous and from local authority departments, both of which have developed appropriate knowledge and expertise. The second is that, as time goes on, it becomes less and less easy, for economic reasons and through pressure of work, for solicitors in private practice to offer an informal advisory service in matters which do not relate to the law.

Unpaid work

2.21 Lawyers do not always make their services available only in return for their full fees. Many lawyers undertake voluntary unpaid work or work for reduced fees. For example, about 120 legal advice centres are now in operation, and many of them depend on the services of lawyers, usually given without charge, in the evenings after their normal working day is over. In 1976, some 3,300 solicitors were involved, on a rota basis, in providing legal advice, free of charge in CABx and we were told that the number has since increased. By August 1978, 75 lawyers, barristers and solicitors, were working in law centres for salaries lower than they might have been earning in other forms of salaried employment or in private practice.

Law centres

2.22 The lawyers who work in law centres have exercised an influence in recent years out of proportion to their numbers. They deal largely with cases relating to social welfare law in which, at present, the services of the profession in private practice are inadequate. Their experience has emphasised the need for training in this branch of the law, both for newcomers to the profession and established practitioners. We obtained information about the structure, manning and finances of law centres which is set out in Volume II section 3. In Chapter 8 we make recommendations for the improvement of publicly funded law centres in respect of their organisation, pay and working methods so as to enlarge their contribution to the provision of legal services.

Voluntary service

2.23 The voluntary services of lawyers are in demand for various public purposes. Their knowledge and training are regarded as apt for the commissions and inquiries which are set up for a wide variety of purposes. Voluntary service is necessary also for the purpose of running the legal profession. Both branches of the profession employ permanent staff, but a number of lawyers in private practice have to devote a considerable part of their working and leisure time to service on the governing bodies and their committees. The work involved is not merely concerned with the interests of the profession itself: for example, the civil legal aid system is dependent on practitioners up and down the country who give time to reading papers and attending area and local committees. The profession is regularly consulted on matters of law reform. Practising lawyers are well represented on the law reform committees and rules committees. An indication of the voluntary service given by the solicitors' branch of the profession is contained in the following extract from the evidence of the editor of the Solicitors' Journal.

> Today, the Law Society is expected by the Government and other non-members to supply a considerable amount of information and expressions of view in assisting the administration of justice to the Lord Chancellor's Office and others, and to the Law Commission and Committees concerned with law reform, as well as to make representations to the Inland Revenue and other Government Departments on proposed and enacted amendments to the law . . . It is doubtful whether the public at large appreciate the collective efforts made by or on behalf of solicitors in these activities.

Lawyers in employment
2.24 We should also mention the contribution of lawyers who are not in private practice but are employed in the government service, both national and local, and in industry, trade and commerce. We deal further with their special position in paragraph 3.22.

Lawyers in politics
2.25 Lawyers have always played a large part in political life. For many years, the proportion of lawyers in the House of Commons has been about one-fifth of the total number of members. Prominent members of all the political parties have legal qualifications. The head of the Bar, in the person of the Attorney General, is a member of the House of Commons and of the government. The Lord Chancellor, the head of the judiciary, is a senior minister in the Cabinet and is Speaker of the House of Lords.

Increased demands for legal services
2.26 In recent years there has been a rapid increase in the demand for legal services. The number of lawsuits, civil and criminal, rose to peaks in 1975 and 1976, and the number of civil legal aid certificates issued, in 1977. In annex 2.3 are shown the trends in litigation. There has also been a steady increase in non-contentious work and cases dealt with under the legal advice and assistance scheme. Every year there are more practising lawyers.

Summary
2.27 In this chapter we have given no more than a brief review of the present position. Our conclusions from the evidence we have received and the studies we have made are that the legal profession makes its services available in all those areas in which it has traditionally functioned, but that, as we shall later show, gaps and deficiencies have arisen.

2.28 A society in which all human and social problems were regarded as apt for a legal remedy or susceptible to legal procedures would not be one in which we would find it agreeable to live. But at present there are too many people whose rights, for want of legal advice and assistance, go by default. The improvements we propose are intended to remedy this, without creating an over-litigious society.

ANNEX 2.1

TABLE 2.1

Courts in England and Wales and their Workload, 1978

(paragraph 2.13)

Description of Court	Composition as at 1st January 1979	Main Functions	Civil: Proceedings commenced in 1978	Criminal: Defendants dealt with in 1978
House of Lords[1] (Appellate Committee)	Lord Chancellor, 9 Lords of Appeal in Ordinary	Appeals from the Court of Appeal and in certain cases direct from the High Court	83	55[6]
Court of Appeal	Master of the Rolls, 17 Lords Justices	Appeals from:— the High Court and county courts in civil cases the Crown Court in criminal cases	1,401	6,056[6]
High Court: Chancery Division	Lord Chancellor, Vice-Chancellor and 11 High Court judges	Civil cases at first instance	13,745	—
		Appeals and special cases from county courts and tribunals	47	—
Queen's Bench Division	Lord Chief Justice and 47 High Court judges	Civil cases at first instance	143,577	—
		Appeals on point of law from, principally, magistrates' courts, the Crown Court and tribunals	572[2]	—
Family Division	President and 16 High Court judges	Family proceedings at first instance and grants of probate	254,808	—
		Appeals from magistrates' courts on domestic matters	247	—

19

TABLE 2.1 (*continued*)

(paragraph 2.13)

Description of Court	Composition as at 1st January 1979	Main Functions	Civil: Proceedings commenced in 1978	Criminal: Defendants dealt with in 1978
High Court: (continued) Restrictive Practices Court	3 judges of the High Court, 1 judge of the Court of Session[3], 1 judge of the Supreme Court of Northern Ireland[4] and not more than 10 lay members	Applications under the Restrictive Trade Practices Act 1956	10	—
Court of Protection	Lord Chancellor, judges and officers of the Court of Protection	Administration of the affairs of persons suffering from mental disorder	4,253	—
Employment Appeals Tribunal	Presiding judge and other judges from the High Court and the Court of Appeal	Appeals from industrial tribunals	700	—
Crown Court (90 court centres)[5]	High Court judges, Circuit judges (305), Recorders (271), Certain lay magistrates	Trials of serious crime on indictment	—	78,835
		Committals for sentence from magistrates' courts	—	17,253
		Appeals from magistrates' courts against conviction and/or sentence	—	15,002
		Civil cases in some licensing matters	204	—
		Appeals from magistrates' courts and local authorities in certain non-criminal matters	1,156	13,858
County courts (320)[5]	Circuit judges (305), Registrars (144)[5]	Civil cases and small claims	1,692,211	—

20

TABLE 2.1 (continued)

(paragraph 2.13)

Description of Court	Composition as at 1st January 1979	Main Functions	Civil: Proceedings commenced in 1978	Criminal: Defendants dealt with in 1978
Magistrates' courts (700)[5]	Lay magistrates (24,000)[5], Stipendiary magistrates (52)	Minor criminal cases	—	2,075,820[6]
		Committal proceedings in serious criminal cases	—	86,127[6]
		Proceedings in family and other non-criminal matters	60,000[5]	—

[1] Also has jurisdiction in Scotland and Northern Ireland.

[2] This figure includes some criminal matters.

[3] The equivalent in Scotland of the High Court.

[4] The equivalent in Northern Ireland of the High Court.

[5] Approximate figure.

[6] 1977 figures.

Sources: Lord Chancellor's Department.
        Home Office.

21

ANNEX 2.2

TABLE 2.2

Selected Tribunals in England and Wales and their Workload, 1978

(paragraph 2.13)

Description of Tribunal	Composition	Main Functions.	Number of Centres	Cases disposed of in 1978
Supplementary Benefit Appeal Tribunals	Chairman and 2 members.	Appeals on Supplementary Benefit and Family Income Supplement (non-contributory benefit)	105	63,281
National Insurance Local Tribunals	Chairman and 2 members	Appeals on sickness cases and unemployment benefit (contributory benefit)	179	39,798
Industrial Tribunals	Chairman and 2 members	Appeals on redundancy payments, unfair dismissal, discrimination and equal pay	55	39,118
Mental Health Review Tribunals	Legally-qualified president, 1 medically-qualified member and 1 other member	Review of compulsory detention of mentally disordered patients in hospital	108	707
Immigration Appeal Tribunal	1 adjudicator	Appeals against decisions by Home Secretary	8	8,443
	Legally-qualified chairman and 2 other members	Appeals from adjudicators	1	446
Medical Appeal Tribunals	Legally-qualified chairman and 2 medically-qualified members	Appeals on National Insurance awards where medical issues are involved	22	15,730

22

TABLE 2.2 (*continued*)

(paragraph 2.13)

Description of Tribunal	Composition	Main Functions	Number of Centres	Cases disposed of in 1978
Rent Tribunals	1 legally-qualified member	Cases at first instance on valuation and security of tenure	15	5,976
Rent Assessment Committees	1 valuer and 1 other member	Appeals on fixing of 'fair rents' by rent officers	15	9,145
Pensions Appeal Tribunals:		Appeals on war pensions decisions by Department of Health and Social Security	9	
Entitlement Appeal Tribunals	Legally-qualified chairman, 1 medically-qualified member and 1 other member	Entitlement appeals		1,327
Assessment Appeal Tribunals	Medically-qualified chairman, 1 medically-qualified member and 1 other member	Assessment appeals		963

Note: Unless otherwise stated, no particular qualification is required of any chairman or member of the above tribunals.

Source: Council on Tribunals.

23

ANNEX 2.3

TABLE 2.3

Numbers of practitioners, of cases before the courts and of legally-aided cases in England and Wales, 1960–78

(paragraph 2.26)

Year	The legal profession[1]		Court proceedings[2]		Legal aid		
	Barristers in private practice	Solicitors with practising certificates	Proceedings commenced in the civil courts ('000s)	Criminal defendants proceeded against ('000s)	Civil legal aid[3] certificates issued ('000s)	Criminal legal aid orders made ('000s)	Cases under[3,4] legal advice and assistance scheme ('000s)
1960	1,919	19,069	1,670	896	23	16	13
1961	1,935	19,438	1,883	1,045	39	20	25
1962	1,964	19,790	1,882	1,278	76	24	46
1963	2,073	20,269	1,746	1,340	91	33	57
1964	2,118	20,683	1,720	1,398	97	43	61
1965	2,164	21,255	1,741	1,439	99	47	58
1966	2,239	21,672	1,796	1,519	106	56	60
1967	2,333	22,233	1,878	1,664	112	74	63
1968	2,379	22,787	1,790	1,665	128	99	73
1969	2,448	23,574	1,969	1,702	135	142	76
1970	2,584	24,407	2,132	1,777	147	172	83
1971	2,714	25,366	1,874	1,796	159	187	84
1972	2,919	26,327	1,986	1,942	204	217	114
1973	3,137	27,379	1,872	2,040	187	244	111
1974	3,368	28,741	2,241	2,051	180	293	109
1975	3,646	29,850	2,525	2,111	200	336	199
1976	3,881	31,250	2,325	2,210	208	362	253
1977	4,076	32,812	2,292	2,162	211	395	301
1978	4,263	33,864	2,109	na[5]	149	na[5]	323

[1] At 1st October. At 1st January 1979 there were 4,363 barristers in private practice. At 30th April 1979 there were 34,090 solicitors with practising certificates

[2] Civil and criminal appeals and defendants committed for trial and sentence are not included in this table, to avoid double counting.

[3] Civil legal aid figures relate to financial years ending in the calendar year shown.

[4] The figures for 1960–73 relate to the forerunner of the present scheme.

[5] Not available.

Sources: Judicial Statistics.
Criminal Statistics.
Legal Aid Annual Reports. } for the appropriate year.
Evidence of the Bar.
Evidence of the Law Society.

24

CHAPTER 3

The Legal Profession

Background

The Bar

3.1　The Senate of the Inns of Court and the Bar places the origin of the legal profession at the close of the thirteenth century when clerics were forbidden by canon law from appearing in secular causes and when one of the Royal Courts, the Common Bench, was established at Westminster. The profession's connection with what are now the Inns of Court dates from the early fourteenth century when, on the dissolution of the crusading order of the Knights Templar, its buildings were occupied as tenants by the lawyers who had previously lived in lodgings and hostels about Holborn. By the end of the fourteenth century the four societies still in existence had formed, the Inner and Middle Temples, Lincoln's Inn and Gray's Inn.

3.2　For some centuries the legal profession was not divided. Barristers (under their earlier names of "professors" or "apprentices" in the law) received the lay client without any intermediary. If, however, as frequently occurred, the client appointed an agent or "attorney" to act for him, instructions would be taken from the attorney.

3.3　In 1608, by Royal Charter, the Inner and Middle Temples were granted ownership of the land which they had occupied as tenants for the previous 250 years. The purposes for which the land was granted were "to serve for the accommodation and education of the students and professors of the law aforesaid residing in the same Inns forever". In the same period the right to practise as an advocate in the Royal Courts became restricted to members of the Inns of Court and serjeants-at-law.

3.4　At about the time of the Restoration, it was established that barristers' services were not delivered by virtue of any legally binding contract and therefore that barristers might not sue for their fees. In the nineteenth century, the practice was finally established of accepting instructions to appear in court only from a solicitor acting for the lay client. It also became the practice, when leading counsel (a serjeant or Queen's Counsel) was retained in a case, always to employ junior counsel with him.

3.5　In the early nineteenth century the standard of legal education at the Bar, which had been low ever since the time of the Civil War, became a scandal and in 1852 the Council of Legal Education was set up to put matters right.

The Library
Exeter College
Oxford.

3.6   In 1875 the Order of Serjeants was abolished. We will not deal here with the history of this Order, but one effect of its abolition calls for mention. The serjeants-at-law were the most senior members of the practising Bar and had their own Inn of Court, Serjeants' Inn. It was the practice to appoint judges of the superior common law courts from the ranks of the serjeants-at-law. Every common law judge was a member of Serjeants' Inn, having resigned from his former Inn on appointment as a judge or serjeant. Until 1875, therefore, these judges took no part in the government or management of the Inns to which all the practising profession except the serjeants belonged, though by virtue of their judicial office they exercised discipline over both branches of the profession. After 1875, the judges and serjeants returned to their former Inns, where they took their places as benchers, and thus became directly concerned in the management of the practising profession.

3.7   The Bar Committee, as it was then called, was created in 1883. In 1894 the Bar at its annual general meeting recommended that the functions of the Bar Committee should include, effectively, all matters relating to the functions, control and discipline of the profession. The Inns did not accept this, and the General Council of the Bar (usually known as the Bar Council) came into being in 1895 with its functions circumscribed so as not to "interfere with the property, jurisdiction, powers or privileges of the Inns." Disciplinary powers remained vested in the Inns, but the rulings of the Bar Council on matters of professional etiquette were in practice accepted by the Bar as a whole.

3.8   In 1966, the Senate of the Four Inns of Court was set up by resolutions of the four Inns and of the General Council of the Bar. Its purpose was to speak with one voice on behalf of all these bodies on matters upon which a common policy was regarded as essential. On 27th July 1974 the Senate of the Inns of Court and the Bar took over the functions of the former Senate. Its constitution is more fully described in Chapter 32.

3.9   In 1901, there were 1,147 practising barristers in England and Wales. In 1954, there were 2,010. The number fell to 1,919 in 1960 but since then it has more than doubled. On 1st January 1979 there were 4,363 barristers in private practice, not including pupils.

Solicitors
3.10   By the end of the seventeenth century some formal divisions in the legal profession had come into existence. Apart from the barristers, there were attorneys, solicitors, notaries, scriveners and proctors. The attorney has already been mentioned; he was the representative and adviser of his client for many purposes. Solicitors were associated particularly with matters relating to land. Proctors were concerned with ecclesiastical law which in those days included matrimonial affairs. The functions of solicitors, attorneys and proctors were merged by the Judicature Act 1873 and the title "solicitor" generally adopted.

That title is now, by statute, reserved exclusively to those qualified as solicitors. From an early period, solicitors have been regarded as officers of the court and the Supreme Court is still responsible for ensuring that they maintain a high standard of conduct. The Master of the Rolls (who presides over the Civil Division of the Court of Appeal) has since 1933 had the function of approving the rules of practice and conduct of the solicitors' branch of the profession. This reflects the link between solicitors and the court.

3.11 Until 1831, the leading professional association of solicitors was the Society of Gentlemen Practisers but in that year a Royal Charter was granted which created the Law Society. A second Charter granted in 1845 defined the objects of the Society as "promoting professional improvement and facilitating the acquisition of legal knowledge". These remain its objects today. The powers of the Law Society are derived from legislation and in the past 150 years considerable responsibilities have been imposed on it by Parliament.

3.12 Like the Bar, the solicitors' branch of the profession has increased in numbers. In 1900 practising certificates were issued to 16,063 solicitors. By 1960 the number had grown to 19,069, and at 30th April 1979 the number was 34,090. By contrast with barristers, who are required to practise as individuals, solicitors may form partnerships and employ fee-earning staff who may, but need not, be qualified solicitors. In April 1979, over 6,500 firms were in private practice. More detailed information is given in Chapters 29 and 31.

The future strength of the profession

3.13 The total number employed in any capacity in the provision of professional legal services in England and Wales is around 140,000. The growth which has taken place in the total number of barristers in chambers and solicitors with practising certificates is illustrated in annex 2.3. The trends there shown are significant and prompt the question as to what is the likely or desirable size of the profession in the future. Experience has shown that precise estimates of the future strength or requirements of a particular occupation are unreliable. It will, however, be necessary for the profession to make the best possible regular estimates of future requirements in order to form its policies. In our view, among the factors to be taken into account are the steady flow of new law in the form of legislation, case law and EEC law, changes in the rates of crime and detection and, if our recommendations are adopted, the greater availability of legal aid and legal services. The overall effect of these factors will in our view involve a long-term increase in the demand for the services of lawyers.

Inquiries into the legal profession

3.14 We have been conscious throughout our work of the long history and achievements of both branches of the legal profession. They occupy an important place in our history, and their members have played a leading part in developing a system of law which has spread to many parts of the world. Our contacts abroad have left us in no doubt that the standing of our legal profession is high in the eyes of the rest of the world.

3.15 It is common experience that any institution or organisation, however venerable, will at certain times benefit from the process of independent investigation and analysis and from a study of the potential value of changes in its structure and practices. The attitude of the profession throughout our inquiry has been that all its present practices are open to examination and review so as to establish whether or not, in modern conditions, they are justified in the public interest. We desire to record that the attitude of the profession in this respect has eased our work and has been most helpful to us.

3.16 There have been a large number of inquiries of various kinds in recent years which have, directly or indirectly, affected the profession. Particulars of some of these inquiries and of their reports since 1960 are set out in Table 3.1.

3.17 If our recommendations are implemented, some inquiries will still be needed, notably in relation to fees and court procedures. But when the necessary decisions and action on our recommendations have been taken, a process of quiet and orderly consolidation will be needed to enable the profession to develop its service to the public without interruption and changes of course.

Characteristics of a Profession

The main features

3.18 We summarise below what appear to us to be the five main features of a profession, with particular reference to the legal profession.

(a) *Central organisation.*

A profession is more than an aggregation of individuals. A governing body (or bodies) represents a profession and is formally recognised as doing so; it has powers of control and discipline over its members.

(b) *Functions.*

The primary function of a profession is to give advice or service in a specialised field of knowledge. This requires not only the period of education and training mentioned in (c), but also practical experience and continuing study of developments in theory and practice. In the case of the legal profession there is an added function which is not required of other professions, namely a direct responsibility to the court for the proper administration of justice.

(c) *Admission.*

Entry as a student is restricted to those with a certain standard of education. Admission to full membership of a profession is dependent upon a period of theoretical and practical training in the course of which it is necessary to pass examinations and tests of competence.

TABLE 3.1

Inquiries and reports affecting the legal profession since 1960

Description	Date	Reference Number
Government		
Business of the Criminal Courts (Streatfield Committee) ..	1961	Cmnd. 1289
Remuneration of Solicitors (National Board for Prices and Incomes)	1968	Cmnd. 3529
Royal Commission on Assizes and Quarter Sessions (Beeching Commission)	1969	Cmnd. 4153
NBPI Report No. 134 (standing reference)	1969	Cmnd. 4217
Restrictive Practices in the Professions (Monopolies Commission)	1970	Cmnd. 4463
Legal Education (Ormrod Committee)	1971	Cmnd. 4595
NBPI Report No. 164 (standing reference)	1971	Cmnd. 4624
Distribution of Criminal Business (James Committee) ..	1975	Cmnd. 6323
Lay Observer's First Report	1976	HOC 332
Second Report	1977	HOC 375
Third Report	1978	HOC 454
Two-Counsel Rule (Monopolies and Mergers Commission) ..	1976	HOC 512
Restrictions on advertising by Solicitors (Monopolies and Mergers Commission)	1976	HOC 557
Restrictions on advertising by Barristers (Monopolies and Mergers Commission)	1976	HOC 559
Other		
Special Committee on the Examination of the Circuit System (Gardiner Committee)..	1964	
Committee of the Four Inns on Legal Examinations (Heald Committee)	1964	
Partnership at the Bar (Templeman Committee)	1969	
The Silk System (Arnold Committee)	1970	
Complaints against Lawyers (Justice)	1970	
Joint Committee on the Ormrod Report (Cairns Committee)	1971	
The Organisation and Finance of the Bar and Subsequent Reports leading to Senate Regulations (Pearce Committee)	1972–74	
Admission, Organisation, Conditions and Needs of Pupils (Wilmers Report)	1975	
Lawyers and Social Welfare Law (Peter Webster QC) ..	1976	

(d) *Regulation and standards.*

A profession is given a measure of self-regulation so that it may require its members to observe higher standards than could be successfully imposed from without. In order to protect its clients and provide a service of the necessary standard, a profession must impose on its members high standards of conduct and performance, above those required by the general law, and it must see that these standards are observed. A rule of conduct or practice and any restriction should stand or fall on its capacity to protect the interests of, or to enhance the level of service to, the public.

(e) *Duty to the client.*

A professional person's first and particular responsibility is to his client. In the case of lawyers this professional duty of maintaining the client's interests is paramount, subject only to their direct responsibility to the court. The relationship between a professional person and his client is in our view the most important of the characteristics here described. Most people who seek a professional service are at a disadvantage; they know little of the technicalities surrounding their problems, and are often suffering from physical, emotional or financial difficulties. The client's case should receive from the adviser the same level of care and attention as the client would himself exert if he had the knowledge and the means.

3.19   The characteristics of a profession were summarised in somewhat similar terms in the evidence given to the Monopolies Commission by the Law Society in 1968.

> The learned professions have not suddenly come into existence, but have developed over the centuries as a result of needs generated in all advancing societies. Before any profession can emerge, circumstances must exist in which the general public require protection; ... At first the practitioners in each sphere operated independently. Gradually they came to group together with the object of extending their knowledge by the sharing of skills and they undertook the training of their successors. In order to maintain their own repute and understanding and to retain public confidence in their abilities, these groups imposed upon themselves a discipline and adopted ethical rules and restrictions, sometimes to their own personal disadvantage but always designed to establish their probity and competence in the eyes of the public . . . When a profession is fully developed it may be described as a body of men and women (a) identifiable by reference to some register or record; (b) recognised as having a special skill and learning in some field of activity in which the public needs protection against incompetence, the standards of skill and learning being prescribed by the profession itself; (c) holding themselves out as being willing to serve the public; (d) voluntarily submitting themselves to standards of ethical conduct beyond those required of the ordinary citizen by law; (e) undertaking to accept personal responsibility to those whom they serve for their actions and to their profession for maintaining public confidence.

The cab-rank rule

3.20   There is one rule of professional practice, affecting barristers in England and Wales, which should be mentioned in this context. It is that a practising barrister's freedom to refuse to act for a client is limited. This principle is expressed in *Conduct and Etiquette at the Bar* by Sir William Boulton in the following terms.

> Counsel is bound to accept any brief in the courts in which he professes to practise at a proper professional fee dependent on the length and difficulty of the case, but special circumstances may justify his refusal, at his discretion, to accept a particular brief.

This principle is commonly known as "the cab-rank" rule. The profession attaches great importance to it; in the view of the Senate, it "secures for the public a right of representation in the court which is a pillar of British liberty". We consider it right to ensure that when the services of a barrister are required, he should be selected for his capacity to handle the case without regard to any other considerations and should accept a case without regard to his personal views, whether about the client, the nature of the case or, in the case of crime, the offence charged. Although this rule is generally observed in Northern Ireland, it is not formally laid down. In paragraph 42.28 we recommend that it should be.

Types of professional service

3.21 Members of a profession can usually be divided into two categories. The first comprises those who are in private practice. A number of solicitors, particularly in their early years of practice, are salaried employees of firms of solicitors in private practice and, for this purpose, we regard them as being in the same category as their employers. The second category comprises those who are employed in industry, trade and commerce, national and local government services and other fields.

Employed lawyers

3.22 In considering the work of the legal profession, the distinction between those in private practice and those in employment does not lie in the work they do, which in the case of solicitors may be identical, and certainly not in the standards of professional conduct and integrity to which they are required to adhere. So far as the law is concerned, the position of the salaried legal adviser has been described in this way.

> [Salaried legal advisers] are regarded by the law as in every respect in the same position as those who practise on their own account. The only difference is that they act for one client only, and not for several clients. They must uphold the same standards of honour and of etiquette. They are subject to the same duties to their client and to the court. They must respect the same confidences. They and their clients have the same privileges.
>
> *Alfred Crompton Amusement Machines Limited* v. *Commissioners of Customs and Excise* [1972] 2 All E.R. 353 at p. 376, per Lord Denning, M.R.

3.23 The distinction lies in the fact that the lawyer in employment has only one client, the employer: this puts him in a different position from that of the lawyer in private practice, and sometimes in a more difficult position. He must be sensitive to the employer's interests and policies. He must have regard to the opinions and attitudes of those in the office hierarchy who have authority over him. In some organisations it may not be possible to offer advice directly to the client employer, whether a board of directors, a council or an individual, but only through a senior executive who is not himself a lawyer. Members of some organisations may tend to be influenced by their loyalty to the organisation rather than loyalty to any external body. Accordingly, the employed lawyer may face a practical difficulty in reconciling loyalty to his employer with loyalty to his profession and with the need to maintain an independent and objective attitude.

3.24 By contrast, the lawyer in private practice is not committed to a sole client on whom alone he depends for remuneration and advancement; accordingly, he escapes pressures by which the impartiality and objectivity of his work may be called in question. These characteristics of private practice are of particular value to the client. However, the tradition of independence derived from private practice benefits all lawyers however employed. The Legal Section of the Association of First Division Civil Servants, a civil service trade union, said in its evidence:—

> As the legal profession has hitherto established its standards on the basis of independence, so we see our value to our employer as being founded on a recognition of the value of that professional independence . . . We earnestly hope that, in its Report, the Royal Commission will acknowledge the value to our society of an independent legal profession . . .

Summary

3.25 We think that the characteristics outlined above collectively provide the profession with a sense of corporate indentity and independence which is of value not only to its members but to the public at large. It is founded on the ability of its members to speak with knowledge and authority in a particular field of learning; the right to express professional opinions free from external pressures or fear of reprisals; the power to regulate their affairs so as to enhance the prestige and standing of their calling not only nationally, but internationally; the sense that its members are directly serving the public to whom they are answerable for their actions; their dependence for their livelihood and advancement on their own talents and abilities; the importance of high standards, beyond those required by the law, voluntarily set and maintained; a commitment to providing voluntary services in many spheres. We attach importance to the need for independence in the legal profession and the attitude of mind and outlook it involves. It has been emphasised, in one form or another, in the submissions of a very large number of witnesses; so far as it is compatible with the public interest we recognise it in the recommendations made in this report.

3.26 It must also be recognised that provision of a service by a privately practising profession can have disadvantages. Independence and self-regulation can breed insularity and complacency and a narrow attitude of mind. These characteristics may be accentuated in the case of a small and closely-knit profession. A further difficulty is that, although a profession's services should be available in all areas of its operation and to clients of all kinds, the members of a profession whose income depends on fees paid by clients may be unable to work in certain areas, or for certain classes of client, because the work would show a profit insufficient to enable them to earn a reasonable living.

The Image of the Profession

The principal factors

3.27   In recent years, lawyers have faced criticism, sometimes severe, particularly in the press and other media and in political and academic circles. Many lawyers are engaged in work which makes heavy demands and have to cope with constant changes in the law resulting from the large volume of legislation enacted each year and from developments in case law. Even so, most lawyers provide a service which their clients find satisfactory. They therefore feel that these criticisms are unjust. We sympathise with this feeling. Our investigations, including the Users' Survey, showed that much of the criticism publicly expressed is ill-founded or exaggerated. However, this criticism is a symptom of unease with the standards of the profession and it must be accepted by the profession as a whole that, for reasons which are complex and often long-standing, its image is not satisfactory.

3.28   Amongst the reasons are the following. First, it is the temper of our times to subject all institutions and organisations to close scrutiny, and to require justification for all their practices. Unless they are seen manifestly to serve the public interest, they come under attack. Secondly, the law in many of its aspects is a contentious business. In any lawsuit there will be a losing party, and this can mean a dissatisfied client.

3.29   A third reason for the unsatisfactory image of the legal profession arises from the complexity of the law itself. We mention elsewhere in this report the enormous output of Acts of Parliament in recent years, to which is added an even greater quantity of delegated legislation. We have received much evidence to show that the public and the legal profession are oppressed by the present volume of legislation and by the difficulty of keeping up-to-date with its provisions. There is irritation at the difficulty of understanding and interpreting the wording used. Criticism of this state of affairs is unfairly directed at practising lawyers.

The cost of legal services

3.30   Fourthly, lawyers have the reputation of earning large incomes and the level of fees in individual cases is often the cause of indignation and complaint. In fact, the level of lawyers' earnings taken overall is not, in our view, excessive. The subject is dealt with in our remuneration surveys and comparative studies, discussed in Chapter 36. As to the level of fees, one witness has pointed out a possible reason for the indignation often expressed at lawyers' bills, that it is only rarely that most of us encounter professional fees in the course of our private lives.

3.31   To some extent a lawyer's charges fall into perspective if compared with the cost of such things as repairing a motor car, buying furniture, carpeting a room or having the outside of a house painted. It is, however, easier to judge whether a garage, a furnisher or a decorator has given value for money. The amount and nature of the work involved in, and the benefit resulting from, a professional service are hard for a layman to assess and if the charge made is higher than expected, it will be thought excessive. We recommend in Chapter 37 certain measures by which to avoid this source of dissatisfaction. But whatever may be done in this way, it is necessary to accept that the provision of legal services, which calls for the expenditure of time by skilled people, cannot be cheap.

3.32   It is important for practising lawyers to recognise the anxiety with which clients regard mounting costs. It is their responsibility to use all proper means of reducing costs consistent with providing the level of service required for the work in hand. This is not an easy principle to apply. In the face of potential complaints of inefficiency or even of claims for negligence, the natural impulse is to do more than is necessary in order to avoid the risk of doing less than professional duty requires. We deal further with these matters in Chapter 37.

3.33   An onus rests also on those responsible for the administration of justice to assist the legal profession in reducing the cost to the public of the services it renders. In Part VI of this report we list a number of proposals the purpose of many of which is to enable litigation to be dealt with more cheaply. Cost cannot be reduced below a certain point without lowering the quality of legal services and of justice which we are entitled to expect. But existing procedures could and should be reviewed, for the purpose of adopting the most economical methods of disposing of judicial business, having regard to the importance and value of different classes of case.

Delay

3.34   A dominant feature of the complaints against lawyers which we received related to delay. Much of the evidence which was submitted to us commented specifically on this point and made suggestions for improvement. In this con-nection the present court procedures, referred to above, appear to us to be partly responsible. We think that the slow-moving nature of some of these procedures, and of legal proceedings as a whole, has been a factor in harming the image of the legal profession. We believe that, in the future, both branches of the legal profession should concentrate their efforts on reducing delay in the conduct of legal business. Insofar as delay is not dependent on court procedures, the remedy lies in the hands of the profession itself; the governing bodies of both branches should, we think, take note of the various causes of delay and make recommendations, or set standards, for their members. Sug-gestions are made in Chapter 22 which provide a basis for this work. Insofar as delay is a result of court procedures, the governing bodies should, preferaby jointly, make it their business to get changes made. The material set out in Part VI of this report provides a starting point for this purpose.

Other criticisms

3.35 Another matter which causes resentment is difficulty in finding a lawyer willing to act in proceedings against another lawyer. This may not happen often, but when it does it arouses strong ill-feeling. This problem is linked with that of maintaining standards of competence with which we deal in Chapter 22. We think that, hitherto, the public has felt that not enough has been done to prevent or to reprimand indifferent standards of work and we believe it is the responsibility of the profession itself to remove this impression. We make recommendations about this in Chapter 25.

3.36 It has been said that sections of the public find lawyers remote and un-approachable. This may occur in two ways. A lawyer may find it difficult to communicate with his client or may, for other reasons, give an impression of remoteness. It may also happen that a person who requires legal advice does not approach a lawyer because he regards all lawyers as being remote and unapproachable. The citizens advice bureaux have found that some clients are reluctant to approach solicitors directly and have set up rota schemes to bridge the gap. The Users' Survey showed, however, that the most frequently mentioned cause of satisfaction with the services of a solicitor was that he was approachable and easy to talk to. When it occurs, the impression of remoteness is, we think, partly explained by the function of the legal profession. Most subjects on which advice is sought generate emotion; the task of a lawyer is to strip a problem of emotion so that the legal issues can be assessed dispassionately. In some cases it is difficult to do this while maintaining the confidence of a client that he is receiving the singleminded support he desires. Failure to maintain the client's confidence, whether or not resulting from want of care or sensitivity, will lead him to think that his lawyer is cold, unsympathetic or inattentive.

3.37 It is more difficult to establish whether persons who refrain from approaching a lawyer do so for the reason given above. The Users' Survey showed that the main reason why persons who mentioned that they had a problem requiring legal attention refrained from approaching a lawyer was their fear of the probable cost. The TUC said in evidence that it was important not to ignore the reluctance which some people have to approaching unfamiliar offices and to involvement in the legal process and the degree of apprehension about the cost involved in legal procedures.

3.38 Another ground of criticism is that there is an area of the law in which the majority of lawyers are not yet sufficiently skilled or knowledgeable. This is social welfare law, in which there has been a considerable volume of legislation in recent years which affects a large body of citizens in every facet of daily life —housing, social security, matrimonial problems, child care and welfare and related matters. Those who deal with these matters feel that there are insufficient lawyers available to give advice and help on the legal issues concerned. In some measure we find this to be true and in later chapters we suggest how this need can be met in the future. The shortage in numbers and in the requisite skills has had its effect on the public image of lawyers.

Improving the image of the profession

3.39 We know that the governing bodies of the profession have given thought to its image in the public mind. They may not agree with our assessment of that image, but would no doubt agree that time and money are worth spending if thereby the standing of the profession can be enhanced. The publication of this report and the action which the profession and others take as a result will, we hope, bring about a gradual change in the public image of the profession and make it less subject to criticism.

3.40 Great effort will be needed to bring about a transformation; for any major change, careful planning and preparation are indispensable and take time. Moreover, in all professions, the legal profession being no exception, events tend to move slowly. Even after the need for change has been detected, it takes time to bring it home to members of the profession and to persuade them that traditional methods and procedures must be abandoned or altered. We therefore regard this as a task not only for those now engaged in the profession. As students join the profession year by year in future it should be emphasised to them, in the course of their formal training and education and during service under articles or in pupillage, that the responsibility for bringing about and maintaining this change rests in their hands.

Conclusions and Recommendations

Paragraphs

Future of the profession	R3.1	The demand for the services of lawyers will grow; the profession should plan accordingly.	3.13
	R3.2	When the decisions arising out of this report have been taken and implemented, the profession should have a period of orderly development free, so far as possible, from external interventions.	3.17
Image of the profession	R3.3	In the light of the comments made in the text, the legal profession should wherever possible take measures to remove the causes of its indifferent public image.	3.27–3.40

PART II

Legal Services

CHAPTER 4

The Need for Legal Services

Background

4.1   In the census of 1901 the population of England and Wales stood at 32.5 million. In 1901 3,593 civil cases were disposed of in the higher courts, 799,930 judgments were entered in the county courts; 10,793 criminal defendants appeared at assizes and quarter sessions, 781,622 in the magistrates' courts. In 1977, when the population stood a little short of 50 million, 11,564 cases were disposed of in the superior civil courts, 943,736 judgments were entered in the county courts; 78,835 criminal defendants appeared in the Crown Court, 2,161,947 in magistrates' courts of whom 1,222,028 were charged with motoring offences. The number of cases per head of population has increased by no more than 32 per cent. The total volume of cases, however, has increased by 100 per cent.

4.2   It is clear from the figures given that, since the turn of the century, the demand for legal services in the courts has risen considerably. We know that it rose sharply in the criminal courts in the late nineteen fifties, when the criminal legal aid scheme took effect. There also have been increased demands for services in other areas. Demands for conveyancing services, for example, have increased with the growth of owner-occupation. In 1901, about 10 per cent of dwellings were owner-occupied. The figure in 1978 was 53 per cent. There has in this period been a rise and fall in matrimonial cases. The volume of matrimonial business greatly increased as a result of the legislation of the nineteen thirties and war-time conditions, but the procedure in uncontested cases has been so simplified by recent legislation that there is no longer thought to be any need in most cases for legal representation.

4.3   The past 100 years have seen a change from a *laissez faire* society to one in which it is regarded as right for the state to take a large and active continuous responsibility for maintaining individual welfare. This has reflected changing attitudes about morality and social relationships, in particular the view that a person who needs help should receive it as a matter of legal right, rather than as an act of charity. One outward sign of this change is the enormous increase in legislation which is intended to improve the life and welfare of the population. The impact on the amount and character of legal services demanded has been correspondingly great. Revenue law has increased greatly in extent and complexity. Wholly new branches of the law have come into existence such as those relating to planning and industrial relations.

4.4 There has been a striking growth in the numbers and case-load of tribunals. These vary widely in their constitution and procedure but nearly all have some of the attributes of the judicial and adversary processes, two sides arguing the issues and a decision being made by persons independent of both sides, based on the evidence of fact and the arguments which they have heard. The courts of law have an inherent jurisdiction over the conduct of quasi-judicial proceedings of this kind and a dissatisfied party may in certain circumstances apply to the court to quash the decision of a tribunal even where its decision is stated to be final.

4.5 One purpose of arranging for certain issues to be determined by a tribunal created for the purpose, rather than by a court of law, is to secure the use of simple procedures, devised for the specific purpose, which enable a person without legal training to deal with a case on his own or with the assistance of another layman. This purpose is not realised in practice because many tribunals have to apply complex legislative codes and unravel complicated issues of fact. Non-lawyers working for organisations representing their members and others before tribunals have developed expertise in this field. Even so, many of those appearing before tribunals would have found it advantageous to use the services of a lawyer, but were unable to afford them and legal aid was not available. Although at present lawyers are retained in only a minority of tribunal cases, the total volume of such work is large, being comparable with the case-load of the civil courts. The development of tribunals in the course of the present century, therefore, has made a substantial addition to the work load of the profession which, on present trends, is likely to increase rather than diminish in the future.

4.6 Elsewhere than in tribunals a number of the additional demands described above have been met not only by lawyers but by other professions and institutions. Much advisory work on revenue law is undertaken by accountants. Banks deal with the administration of estates. The task of negotiating mortgages on behalf of a client, once an important part of the solicitor's function in conveyancing, has in many cases been replaced by a direct transaction between client and building society. In areas where by law or practice a qualified lawyer alone has the right to perform certain functions, notably in advocacy and conveyancing, there is pressure to abolish the restrictions so as to enable non-lawyers to undertake these functions.

4.7 The need for the services of lawyers has been called in question in a number of connections. In family disputes, for example, it is argued that legal intervention, because of its adversarial nature, may exacerbate problems rather than solve them. In problems affecting individuals it is sometimes thought that, although the services of a lawyer may be needed, the personal disadvantage of retaining a lawyer may outweigh the advantage. We were told in evidence of such a situation in which it was most desirable that a certain person should make a will, but she was not advised to see a lawyer for this purpose because those involved wished to avoid worrying her by any implication that death might be approaching.

4.8   The value of the law as a means of resolving disputes is also questioned on general grounds. It is argued that in certain areas there are matters best resolved by negotiation between individuals, groups and the state rather than by the judicial determination of issues in a court of law. Not all new legislation, though concerned with the resolution of disputes, attempts to achieve this purpose through the use of legal procedures. Controversy at present centres over the question of the extent to which industrial relations are a proper subject for legal procedures.

4.9   In some areas legislation has provided procedures which are an alternative or a supplement to legal action by an aggrieved person. For example, both a duty of conciliation and a power of legal enforcement in matters relating to sex or race discrimination has been given to the Equal Opportunities Commission and the Commission for Racial Equality. The Advisory, Conciliation and Arbitration Service (ACAS) exercises similar functions in the field of industrial relations. None of these bodies, however, stands apart from the action of the law and the Chief Executive of the Commission for Racial Equality stressed to us the continuing importance of access by an aggrieved individual to the courts.

4.10   Pointing to these facts and to the trends we have described above, some commentators have described the situation as "a flight from the law". It is not necessary for our purposes to decide whether this is an accurate description of the present situation. What we have found is that there is a wide demand for legal services of certain kinds which is at present inadequately met. It does not appear to us that the trend of events since the beginning of this century, taken as a whole and including recent experience, suggests that demand will be moderated by any reluctance on the part of the public to seek legal remedies or of Parliament to provide them where needed for the purpose of securing rights and benefits.

4.11   When dealing with changes in the law and in the nature of legal services for which there is a public demand, we think it important to bear in mind the special responsibility which lies on the solicitors' branch of the profession. Solicitors are responsible for all day-to-day work on their clients' cases. Barristers are involved (if at all) only at certain stages. It is true that these may be crucial points for the client but barristers are not continuously engaged in work on cases for lay clients nor are they directly available to them. The result is that a limited number of barristers experienced in a given class of work can satisfy the needs of a large number of clients for specialist advice and representation in that field. It is part of a solicitor's responsibility to know or find out which barristers have the necessary expertise for his client's purposes. Solicitors are approached directly by members of the public and the majority of them like to

41

offer their services in a wide range of work. This is shown in the legal aid solicitors lists (see paragraph 27.9). For this reason the solicitors' branch of the profession is of particular importance in meeting changing needs for legal services and in acquiring the necessary knowledge and expertise to do so. It requires special effort to achieve this in a profession the members of which are in offices widely spread through the country and whose practices are general in nature.

Size of the profession

4.12 Bearing in mind the changing and additional demands which have been made on the services of the profession since the beginning of this century, it is remarkable that the numbers of both barristers and solicitors in practice (set out in paragraphs 3.9 and 3.12) showed little increase for the first half of it. In spite of the rapid growth of the profession in the past few years, the number of lawyers in practice in relation to the size of the population, which in 1901 was one to 1,900, is today one to 1,300. There are indications in the figures now available to us that the recent rate of growth is declining. In the case of the Bar, where the proportion of young practitioners is particularly high, the growth was for a time sustained by an increase in the volume of criminal business which at the same time has considerably increased the dependence of a large part of the profession on earnings from public funds. We think it likely that growth in the solicitors' branch of the profession has been sustained by earnings from conveyancing, which provides nearly half the total volume of solicitors' earnings, and to a lesser extent by earnings from legally-aided work.

Response to change

4.13 In adapting to the changes which have occurred in the course of this century, the performance of the profession has varied. In the spheres of commerce and property, and particularly in its willingness to expand its business internationally, the profession has done well. Our enquiries suggest that its performance has earned respect at home and in other parts of the world. In other spheres it has adapted imperfectly. It has been criticised for failing to take a sufficient interest in the problems of the legal needs of the less well-to-do. Our survey of conveyancing work and charges (Volume II sections 5 and 6) showed that the majority of solicitors derived between 40 per cent and 60 per cent of their income from conveyancing. Our Users' Survey (Volume II section 8) showed that households the heads of which were in non-manual occupations (37 per cent of the total) accounted for 49 per cent* of all users, while households the heads of which were in manual occupations (55 per cent of the total) accounted for 43 per cent* of all users. To the extent that services for those in the latter socio-economic group are less readily available, this in part is a consequence of the fact that it has not proved possible for most practitioners to undertake work of this character and make a living at it. Until fairly recently legal services for poor people continued to be provided, as in previous centuries, on an unsystematic and charitable basis.

---

* 8 per cent of users did not fall into either category.

4.14   Recent years at home and abroad have been a time of change and experiment. There has been much discussion in academic and professional circles throughout the world about the part lawyers should play in society. A number of practical, innovative measures have been taken to improve legal services and their availability. For example, in the United States, there have been developments such as the growth of public interest law firms. In this country, a number of law centres employing salaried lawyers have been established; practising solicitors, through their local organisations, have set up duty solicitor schemes to assist those appearing on criminal charges. An important part of the work of this Commission has been to assess innovations of this kind in order to make recommendations about their future development.

4.15   In connection with the changing nature of lawyers' work, a point should be mentioned which relates to the image of the profession dealt with in Chapter 3. With the change in the types of work undertaken by a lawyer, there has been a change in the nature of his clientele. In the nineteenth century, except in criminal cases, a lawyer's work was closely connected with property and the few who had it. Only a small minority of the whole population ever consulted a lawyer. Today, according to our Users' Survey, 22 per cent of the adult population of England and Wales have consulted a lawyer in the previous two years. But use of a lawyer is, in most cases, not repeated or continuous. It is no longer true that the client himself can largely ensure from the start that he is well served by his lawyers, for he may not know what he is entitled to expect. This appears to us to be a source of potential dissatisfaction and complaint. We make recommendations in this connection in subsequent chapters of this report.

Nature of legal services
4.16   A legal service may be described as any service which a lawyer performs for his client and for which professional responsibility rests on him. No precise definition has been put to us and none is needed for our purposes. We have been mainly concerned with the interests of the individual citizen and the services provided to him, alone or in association with others, to enable him to make use of the benefits and protection conferred by the law. We have treated the law-making process and the administration of justice as being outside our terms of reference.

4.17   Services which are "legal", in the sense that a lawyer would perform them in the ordinary course of practice, may also be performed by non-lawyers. In some instances a person may act on his own behalf without seeking the support either of a lawyer or another layman. Among the examples we have in mind are the citizen who takes a small claims case to arbitration, the defendant who represents himself in person in a criminal case, the person who draws up his own will or who does his own conveyancing. We believe on the one hand that the right of every citizen to act on his own behalf in such circumstances, even although it may be less effective than the employment of a professional adviser, is a fundamental right which should be preserved. On the other hand, no-one

43

should be forced to act for himself against his will and best interests because necessary professional services are not available or are beyond his means.

4.18 Services of a legal character may be provided by those who are not lawyers by profession and whose primary function is to provide a social or community service. In our chapters on citizens advice bureaux and on tribunals we touch upon the legal services provided by several such organisations. We do so with diffidence, because we do not wish to appear to be passing judgment on the general performance of such organisations or on the non-legal services they provide, but their importance as a means of access to legal services makes it necessary to mention them.

4.19 In many cases, in order to assert a legal right or pursue a claim, it may be thought appropriate to resort to some other form of service, rather than to seek advice from a lawyer or bring an action before the courts.

4.20 In respect of some matters the State provides legal services for individuals as a matter of public policy. For example, an individual case may be taken up by an officer of a public authority, such as a local authority's trading standards officer, or by a statutory body such as the Commission for Racial Equality, the Equal Opportunities Commission or the Health and Safety Executive. Although the primary purpose of such bodies is to promote certain policies for the good of the public at large, the service they provide to individuals may be similar to those provided by lawyers. In some cases they retain the services of lawyers to pursue individual cases.

Extent of need for legal services
4.21 The need for legal services may be estimated in a number of ways but its extent cannot be precisely quantified. The evidence before us is nevertheless clear that, however restricted is the definition of need for legal services, such services are, in some areas and for certain classes of society, not available. In respect of some types of business, there is no complaint. The evidence received from industrial and commercial interests shows that their needs are met and that they are for the most part well satisfied with the service received. In conveyancing there is no shortage of legal services, though there are criticisms of their cost and quality and questions as to their necessity with which we deal in Chapter 21. Nearly all defendants charged with serious crimes who appear before the Crown Court have legal aid for representation. There are criticisms of the adequacy of this service, to which we refer in Chapter 22, but there is no doubt that it is generally available. But in other areas, even allowing for the improvements in legal aid which took effect in April 1979, legal services are seriously inadequate.

4.22 The inadequacy to which we refer appears in two main forms. First, certain classes of people who need the assistance of lawyers but cannot afford it are not eligible for financial assistance, and in certain classes of case where legal aid is desirable, as in certain tribunals, it is not available. It is easy to discern the remedies for this form of inadequacy, which are to raise or remove the limits of eligibility and to extend legal aid to new classes of legal work. It is more difficult to establish the principles indicating whether and to what extent the nation's resources should be allocated for these purposes. We return to this point in Chapter 5.

4.23 Inadequacy of legal services in its second form is more complex and difficult to analyse. It is to be found in particular among the poorer part of the population where the limits of eligibility for legal aid do not act as a barrier to obtaining legal services. Among the reasons why legal services are deficient in these areas are the following.

(a) There may be lack of knowledge: the effect will be that a person with a problem will not realise that it arises from infringement of a legal right or breach of a legal duty, and that it may be resolved with legal advice or by means of a legal process.
(b) The necessary resources may not be available; no lawyers may practise locally or, if they do, there may be a lack of lawyers with appropriate knowledge and training to deal with the problem.
(c) There may be a lack of information about the availability of suitable lawyers and the means of getting in touch with them.
(d) There may be reluctance to consult a lawyer for fear of what is involved, in particular the cost.
(e) The public image of the legal profession conveyed to some sectors of society, which we have discussed in Chapter 3, may inhibit approaches to lawyers.

Lack of knowledge
4.24 The rights and duties of the citizen are contained in a large number of legal rules and principles to which Parliament adds in every session. Most of us are unaware of the exact extent of these rights and obligations. Many will fail to appreciate that a problem may be resolved by seeking legal advice or resorting to legal action. The principle is always followed in our courts that no-one may plead ignorance of the law as a defence or answer, but the corresponding principle that a person should be entitled to know when the law is able to help him is not observed with any consistency.

4.25 We recognise that this problem can never wholly be overcome. It can be reduced by a variety of means, for example by devising a pattern of organisation that is not prohibitively expensive, which is able to inform the citizen of his rights and which can direct him to those who can assist him to obtain the remedies to which he is entitled. Other means include ensuring that schools provide some knowledge and understanding of the law as part of their regular curricula and that there is much wider publicity for legal services, including advertising by the profession.

45

Teaching law in schools

4.26 In recent years there has been increasing support in professional and academic circles for the teaching of some knowledge of law in schools. We know of no better means of reducing ignorance about rights and duties under the law which acts as an unseen but impervious barrier in many cases to achieving legal entitlements and justice itself. Little is done involving others in our daily lives which is unaccompanied by considerations of legal rights and duties and yet no instruction in them is provided as a regular part of education. We make many detailed recommendations in the chapters following which are intended to improve the availability and quality of legal services, to bring them to public attention and to cover the cost of them when necessary. But, unless accompanied by some knowledge of the law itself, none of these measures can be effective in working into the roots of deprivation of the law and above all will not promote in relation to problems of a legal nature that confidence and self-reliance which members of the public increasingly expect to be able to acquire in dealing with their own affairs.

4.27 We are aware of the pressure on schools always to enlarge their curricula and of their reluctance to make changes due in part to the difficulty of finding staff with the requisite knowledge. If the need for instruction in the law is acknowledged, we believe the means to provide it can be found. The legal profession is willing to help and the Law Society now runs a programme of support for the teaching of law. If there is a temporary shortage of professional teachers in the subject, we believe that members of the practising profession should supply the deficiency where it arises. Those who have done this have found the experience of value to themselves as well as to their pupils.

Shortage of solicitors

4.28 A large number of witnesses have pointed to the uneven distribution of solicitors. In 1971 (the year of the last census) there was one solicitors' office for every 4,700 people in England and Wales. Their distribution varied from approximately one office for every 2,000 people in Guildford and Bournemouth to one for 16,500 in the London Borough of Tower Hamlets, one for 26,000 in Salford, one for 37,000 in Bootle and one for 66,000 in Huyton.

4.29 Of greater relevance to the problem of unmet need is the distribution of solicitors who are willing to undertake work of the kind covered by the legal aid scheme. In 1977/78, 8,421 solicitors' offices (including branch offices) received payments out of the legal aid fund in respect of legal advice and assistance, civil legal aid or criminal legal aid in the magistrates' courts. An analysis, on a county basis, of solicitors' offices appearing in the Law Society's first legal aid solicitors list, shows that in November 1975 there was a wide variation between counties in the ratio of offices willing to undertake work covered by the legal aid scheme to population. The national average was one office to 7,000 people, but county figures varied between one to 3,800 for the Isle of Wight to one to 11,900 for County Durham. Furthermore, the spread of legal aid work over the offices available to do it is uneven, as can be seen from the following table taken from the 28th Legal Aid Annual Reports [1977–78].

TABLE 4.1
Analysis of payments made to solicitors during the year 1977/78

Total[1] payments in ranges	Offices receiving payments[2]		Items[4]		Payments	
	Number	%	Number[3]	%	Total[3]	%
£					£	
1–500	1,836	21.80	6,994	0.90	302,693	0.53
501–2,000	1,756	20.85	31,880	4.08	2,019,150	3.51
2,001–5,000	1,711	20.32	84,658	10.84	5,782,431	10.04
5,001–10,000	1,389	16.49	137,980	17.67	9,937,041	17.26
10,001–20,000	1,043	12.39	199,367	25.53	14,722,873	25.58
20,001–40,000	504	5.98	182,441	23.37	13,883,255	24.12
40,001–60,000	126	1.50	75,069	9.61	5,984,771	10.40
60,001 and over	56	0.67	62,431	8.00	4,930,196	8.56
All ranges	8,421	100	780,820	100	57,562,410	100

[1]Includes disbursements and VAT where applicable.
[2]A firm may have more than one office to which payments are made.
[3]Columns 4 and 6 comprise payments in respect of work done relating to legal aid certificates, legal advice and assistance and criminal legal aid orders.
[4]The total amount due in respect of a certificate may consist of more than one payment and each such payment is counted as a separate item.
Source: 28th Legal Aid Annual Reports [1977–78] Appendix 17.

4.30   This table relates to payments to solicitors' offices, including branch offices. The payments cover work done under the headings of legal advice and assistance, civil legal aid and criminal legal aid in the magistrates' courts. It shows that of the 8,421 offices receiving payments, over 1,800 offices received not more than £500 in payments in the year in question; they constituted nearly 22 per cent of all offices who did legal aid work, but they accounted for less than one per cent of the items of work and only half of one per cent of the amount paid out. At the other end of the scale, 686 offices received payments in excess of £20,000, accounting for 41 per cent of the items of work and 43 per cent of the payments made.

4.31   In January 1977, the National Association of Citizens Advice Bureaux (NACAB) sought the views of individual bureaux on the availability of legal services in their areas. NACAB told us that, nationally, 88 per cent of bureaux who replied considered that there were enough firms of solicitors within reach of their enquirers. In Greater London, however, over a quarter of all bureaux considered that there were not enough solicitors within reach. NACAB also commented that some bureaux covered wide areas and that there might be neighbourhoods within these areas which were not well served. Furthermore, there were many areas where there was no CAB service. NACAB also drew our attention to the fact that 51 per cent. of bureaux agreed with, or did not dissent from, the statement that there were too few firms of solicitors with expertise in the fields of law which concerned their enquirers and gave details of 101 cases drawn from the whole country over a two-week period where bureaux had difficulty in finding an appropriate solicitor to whom to refer an enquirer.

Reasons for the shortage of solicitors

4.32   As we have indicated previously, there appears to be no shortage of solicitors available to provide legal services for commercial clients or services such as conveyancing. The Lord Chancellor's Legal Aid Advisory Committee drew our attention to a study by its special consultant which suggested that the regional distribution of solicitors corresponded more closely with the distribution of owner-occupied property than with the distribution of population.

4.33   It is said that one reason for the concentration of solicitors in certain areas and in certain types of work is that many find these preferable to working in deprived areas or concentrating on certain kinds of work. The most likely reason, however, for the lack of enthusiasm on the part of many solicitors for legally-aided contentious work is the present level of remuneration for such work. We have received evidence that work in the criminal or matrimonial field can at present only be made profitable when dealt with in volume by what may be described as mass production methods and that a solicitor who deals with this kind of work on any other basis can afford to do so only by subsidising it from other and more profitable forms of work. In areas of social deprivation there is often little such work. It follows that, so long as work provided under the legal aid scheme is less remunerative than other types of work, the location of solicitors will largely be determined by the availability of other forms of more remunerative work. It is for this reason that, in paragraph 13.68, we stress that work performed under the legal aid scheme should be adequately remunerated and it is why we look to salaried lawyers in citizens' law centres to complement the services provided by private practitioners.

Lack of information

4.34   Our Users' Survey (Volume II section 8) showed that most people knew how to set about finding a solicitor, once they knew that they needed one. It is less certain, however, that in all cases they would quickly find a solicitor willing and able to provide the legal services they required. We discuss this problem in detail in Chapter 27 in which we recommend that solicitors should be permitted to advertise and inform the public of their specialisms.

Cost of legal services

4.35   We have received evidence that potential clients are deterred from consulting a solicitor for fear of incurring substantial costs. We believe that this fear, even when unjustified, is a very real one and everything possible should be done to allay it. Accordingly, in Chapters 36 and 37 we put forward a number of proposals designed to overcome this problem and in Chapter 13 we suggest that an initial period of advice lasting half an hour should be provided without charge to any client, whatever his means, under the legal aid scheme.

Special needs

4.36 We have received evidence from several quarters about forms of need which call for special measures. We have been told, for example, of the difficulties which face the deaf in some courts and tribunals. The housebound are at a disadvantage in obtaining legal advice, as in other respects. There are organisations which give the housebound regular assistance for many purposes but we are not aware of any systematic arrangements to provide legal advice and assistance when needed. Members of ethnic minority groups, particularly first generation immigrants, may face particular difficulties in identifying a legal problem, finding a source of advice and communicating with an adviser.

4.37 Practical remedies can be proposed for the problems described above. The use of experienced workers with the deaf as translators, the use of institutional advertising to encourage those assisting the housebound to obtain information about the availability of a solicitor's services from local law societies, the granting of permission to firms to indicate in advertisements that their members speak a minority language or that they can provide interpreters, would all reduce these difficulties. These are, however, only examples of problems arising in the provision of legal services, many of which may not have been reported to us. A body such as this Commission, set up to investigate within a limited duration specific matters at a certain time, cannot provide remedies for all future needs nor anticipate them. It is for this reason that we attach importance to the appointment of a standing body as recommended in Chapter 6.

Future research

4.38 There is growing interest in social needs and the provision of legal services and some able research has been done in this field. In general, however, the level of research has not been high in the past and a number of witnesses and research institutes have expressed the need for more substantial future research programmes. We have no doubt that such a need exists. We commissioned certain items of research as part of our investigations; the main results are set out in Volume II. This should be regarded as no more than a beginning. There are other projects of future interest and value, some requiring a continuing programme of study over a period of years, which should be undertaken. Much of the information we have acquired should be regularly updated. This applies in particular to information gathered by the profession. We have made use of such information as was available or could reasonably be obtained within the time-scale of our work. There remains a need for a co-ordinated programme of research in the future, to meet which we make the recommendation in Chapter 6, to which we here add emphasis, that the standing body whose appointment we propose should have an adequate research capacity.

CHAPTER 5

The Provision of Legal Services:
Principles and Methods

Background

Introduction

5.1 There are a great number of legal rights and duties affecting us all which are changed and extended in every session of Parliament. In exercise of one of the longest established functions of a civilised state, the government maintains a system of courts throughout the country to which there should be equal access. Citizens will not have equal access to the courts nor enjoy the full benefit of rights and safeguards provided by the law without the provision of adequate legal services.

Legal aid

5.2 The introduction of legal aid in England and Wales in 1950 brought legal services within reach of a large number of the population. It established the principle that legal services should be made available to those who need them but cannot afford to pay for them. Until 1950 legal services for many people had been available only in limited classes of case and usually on a charitable or semi-charitable basis. The system of legal aid has now been with us for a generation. There have been developments, notably the introduction in 1973 of the present system of financial support for advice and assistance (the "green form" scheme) which made legal aid more readily available for non-contentious business. But the present position is that a large number of people are not obtaining adequate legal services when they are needed and, for financial reasons, have limited access to the civil courts. We consider in the following paragraphs the principles on which and the means by which legal services should in future be made available at public expense.

Principles

Assistance for individuals

5.3 Financial assistance out of public funds should be available for every individual who, without it, would suffer an undue financial burden in properly pursuing or defending his legal rights.

Corporations

5.4 As a general rule, corporations are formed for the purpose of conducting a trade or business. Legal costs are regarded as part of their overhead expenses and are allowable for tax purposes. We have had no evidence to suggest that legal aid should be available for corporate bodies, whether trading or non-trading, and we consider that assistance from public funds under the system of legal aid should remain, in accordance with its original intention, available for the assistance of individuals alone. This is not to say that assistance from public funds should never be available to any form of association: we deal with this point in Chapter 12.

Equal treatment

5.5   All those who receive legal services are entitled to expect the same standard of legal service irrespective of their personal circumstances. In order that those who receive legal services at public expense should have the same standard of services as those who pay for them, a lawyer undertaking such work should not be expected to do so for less than a reasonable rate of remuneration. The system as a whole should not depend on lawyers working for less than a fair return, but this is not to say that the extensive voluntary work of lawyers provided in CABx, in legal advice centres, in the administration of legal aid and in many other ways should in any way be discouraged. It is a valuable expression of the profession's desire to serve the public.

Freedom of choice

5.6   It is said that every citizen should have the right to be represented by the lawyer of his choice. In criminal cases, this right is embodied in the European Convention of Human Rights which, in Article 6(3), provides that:—

> Everyone charged with a criminal offence has the following minimum rights ... to defend himself in person or through legal assistance of his own choosing.

We have been informed that the European Commission has held that this provision is satisfied by the provision of an assigned lawyer in cases in which the services of a lawyer are provided at public expense. We consider that the principle stated requires that the client, whether supported out of public funds or fee-paying, should always have a free choice among available lawyers and should not be required to retain an assigned lawyer. This is consistent with the principle enunciated in the previous paragraph that the client is entitled to expect the same service whatever his circumstances.

Means of Providing Legal Services

A national legal service

5.7   One means of securing a wide distribution of legal services would be to institute a national legal service of salaried lawyers, employed by the government or an agency of the government to perform all publicly-funded legal work. Although this would be one means of organising publicly-funded legal services, the proposal has had scarcely any support in the evidence submitted to us and the majority of witnesses, including all the main political parties, are strongly opposed to the concept. The main objection of principle is that legal services are required more and more by private individuals who are in dispute with authority in one of its many forms and to protect the interests of clients in such cases, the independence of the legal profession is of paramount importance. If all the lawyers available to assist an individual at public expense depended on the authorities for position and advancement, there would be a risk that an individual's case might be conducted not in the way which best served his interests or complied with his wishes, but in a way which avoided causing difficulties and gave least offence to those in authority.

5.8   It might be argued that a national legal service should operate in a specific sector of the law. In criminal cases, for example, with few exceptions, the lawyers on both sides are paid out of public funds. If they were employed in a salaried service, the lawyers involved would be assured of an income, and the administrative costs of arranging for the assessment and taxation of the fees would be avoided. It is, however, necessary not only that the client should be able to obtain advice and representation from a lawyer he chooses (as indicated in paragraph 5.6 above) but that there should be no doubt as to the independence of that lawyer from the state. It follows, therefore, that it would be inappropriate for a whole section of the law, such as criminal work, to be the preserve of salaried lawyers.

The salaried sector

5.9   Because a national legal service is rejected, it does not follow that there should be no salaried sector. Such a sector exists at present in the law centres. These not only provide legal services in areas where there is a shortage of solicitors in private practice but also provide some services which would be uneconomical for such solicitors. Law centres, therefore, have and will continue to have some advantages which cannot be matched by solicitors in private practice; they are here to stay. The use of such a salaried service is essential to remedy present deficiencies and we make proposals for this purpose in Chapter 8.

5.10   At present the number of solicitors employed on a salary to provide a legal service to the public at large is a minute proportion of the total number of solicitors who hold practising certificates: approximately 75 out of 34,000. There is room for considerable expansion of the salaried sector without creating any of the disadvantges of a salaried national legal service. Moreover, a regular interchange of lawyers between the two sectors is desirable but is at present inhibited by the income and working conditions of salaried lawyers in the public sector. We deal with this point in Chapter 8.

Equality of service

5.11   If public funds are to be equitably distributed for the purpose of providing legal services, such services should be available to all who require them, whether supplied by the fee-earning or salaried sector. At present there are gaps and deficiencies in the provision of services under legal aid. Some of these deficiencies are met by the law centres now in operation, but law centres can provide only for the needs of those who live within reach of them and they are not numerous or widespread.

A free or contributory service

5.12   Legal aid is available only beneath a certain limit of eligibility, determined by the income and capital of the applicant. An applicant with an annual disposable income (as defined in paragraph 12.12) greater than £3,600 is not entitled to civil legal aid. If his disposable capital (as defined in paragraph 12.12) is greater than £2,500, he will be refused legal aid unless his disposable income is less than £3,600 per year and his case is likely to cost more than the maximum contribution which he could be expected to pay. If an applicant is eligible, a contribution is payable according to his means. An applicant will be required to make a contribution if his disposable income exceeds £1,500 a year or his disposable capital exceeds £1,200.

5.13   There are three main issues which concern us here: whether the publicly-funded service should be wholly free in all cases; if not, what the financial limits of eligibility should be; and the basis on which the contribution should be fixed.

A free service

5.14   It has been proposed that legal aid should be available to individuals for the purpose of litigation without contribution or tests of financial eligibility. It is emphasised that litigation, particularly in the High Court, is so expensive that it cannot be contemplated by anyone unless his resources are very large. Against the argument that a free system is vulnerable to abuse, it is pointed out that the legal aid committees would continue to ensure that support was given only when justified. By analogy with experience in medicine and education it is said to be likely that those who can afford to provide their own legal services would do so; but if they do not, the wealthy are assumed and expected to contribute to the cost by means of taxation and should be equally entitled to the benefits which are publicly available. It is not part of this argument that the free system should be used for business purposes and it is assumed that appropriate regulations should be drafted and administered to prevent such use.

A contributory service

5.15   Some services provided out of public funds are free at the point of use and in others there is a means-tested contribution. In either case, there may be difficulties. Against free services, it can be argued that they are more costly and open to abuse; against contributory services, that they may deter those who have a right to use them and they may operate inequitably. It is said that there is a risk that a free litigation service would tempt people to engage in litigation too readily and to pursue proceedings without sufficient regard to economy; a legal aid committee, properly concerned only with reasonable prospects of success and taking a broad approach to its work, could not and should not exercise the degree of control which would be required to reduce excessive litigation.

5.16 There is also the question whether a free service would be a proper use of public resources. Litigation may be a means of asserting essential rights, or of gaining personal or financial advantage over an opponent. It is easy to say that the first purpose should be served without regard to means, and that the second should be contributory. In practice, however, there is no clear dividing line. It is also possible to propose a range of legal needs in respect of which the service should be free; but apart from the difficulty of settling on appropriate areas of need, this ignores the fact that in the cases falling within each area there is a range of need and that some litigants merit support while others do not.

Summary

5.17 The choice between a free and contributory system is a matter partly of principle, partly of experience and partly of resources. As things stand at present, Parliament has decided in principle in favour of a contributory system which has been in operation since 1950. The resources available for legal services would have to be considerably increased if a free service for litigation were to be brought into operation. There is at present no basis of experience upon which to determine whether the introduction of a free service would bring with it the abuses that are predicted. In these circumstances, we favour a system in which contributions are required but accept that the system may in future years be varied by reason of decisions of principle, experience and the resources available.

The proposed system

5.18 Whilst favouring a contributory system, we are satisfied that if an individual's resources are below certain levels, no contribution should be sought from him. To do otherwise would create hardship and, in any event, the contribution assessed would, in practice, prove to be irrecoverable. We do not feel that it is desirable, as is at present the case, to set an upper limit of resources beyond which legal aid is not available to the citizen. We believe that the principle to be observed is that legal aid should be available to all, but that above minimum levels the contribution to be sought should increase by reference to the size of the individual's resources. The contribution assessed should be such that it will not place an undue financial burden upon him.

Legal Aid

The forms of legal aid

5.19   At present, legal aid is available in three forms, for criminal cases, for civil litigation and for legal advice and assistance. Suggestions have been made to us in evidence that there should be special forms of legal aid for a variety of purposes: for example, that there should be a special system for tribunals, another for environmental inquiries and others for various purposes. We do not favour this and consider that the number of schemes should be reduced rather than increased. We accept that a separate system is required for the purpose of criminal legal aid. The circumstances in which applications arise, the way in which they fall to be considered, the criteria and the requirements as to contributions all differ from those relating to civil cases and the simplest course is to maintain a separate system; we deal with this subject in Chapter 14. The same distinctions do not arise in respect of civil legal aid and legal advice and assistance, which in our view should be assimilated. Our proposals in this connection are set out in Chapters 12 and 13.

Administrative arrangements

5.20   The administrative arrangements of the civil legal aid scheme are complex. The tests of eligibility include a number of refinements which call for detailed investigation and assessment which are undertaken by the Supplementary Benefits Commission (SBC). As a result, it takes time to process an application for civil legal aid, and the administrative cost of doing so is appreciable. The system of legal advice and assistance under the green form scheme has the advantage that the tests of eligibility are simpler than those for legal aid for civil litigation, and can be dealt with by the solicitor consulted without reference to the SBC. We consider that initially all contributions payable, other than for criminal work, should be assessed in the same way.

5.21   If the method of assessment is simplified by reducing the number of factors taken into account, it will become less precise and less capable of adjustment to individual circumstances. It will be a serious disadvantage for applicants, on the borderline of liability, to pay a contribution; this will, therefore, only be acceptable if the levels of income and capital at which a contribution becomes payable are raised to a point at which, even in borderline cases, no significant hardship would result from its payment. Proposals for simplification must, in our view, be linked with a more generous allocation of benefits.

General Issues

Advisory services

5.22   So far we have dealt only with needs for specifically legal services. The majority of those who need advice, however, do not necessarily require legal advice in the first instance. As we have remarked in Chapter 2, there is a clear need for a general advisory service, which might be provided by a number of agencies, from which anyone requiring assistance may find out more about the nature of his problem and possible solutions, and can have access to legal services if they are required. It is not our function to make recommendations concerning advisory services in general, but the service which they offer, and in particular the service offered by citizens advice bureaux, is so important a factor in the provision of legal services that we deal with their position in more detail in Chapter 7.

Preventive services

5.23 It is better to prevent a problem arising than to provide a legal remedy for it after it has arisen. Our terms of reference require us to have regard only to the provision of legal services. The fact that we are bound to concentrate on this topic should not be taken to indicate that we consider preventive services to be of lesser value. The benefits which follow from effective accident prevention, marriage counselling and similar endeavours may be greater and more widespread that those to be gained from a system of legal remedies and legal services.

Cost

5.24 In order that the background to our recommendations may readily be understood, the following table sets out the gross and net cost of the various forms of legal aid during 1977/78 in England and Wales.

TABLE 5.1
Cost of legal aid schemes in England and Wales, 1977/78

	£	£	£
Civil Legal Aid			
Gross expenditure		38,661,974	
Less			
Contributions retained	3,642,346		
Costs recovered	8,833,552		
Damages retained	1,740,370		
Other receipts	89,005	14,305,273	24,356,701
Costs of successful unassisted parties			70,211
Criminal Legal Aid in Magistrates' Courts			
Gross expenditure		20,942,142	
Less			
Contributions received	876,587[1]		
Costs received	12,241	888,828	20,053,314
Criminal Legal Aid in Higher Courts			
Gross expenditure		23,643,438	
Less			
Contributions received		457,321	23,186,117

Legal Advice and Assistance		£	£
Gross expenditure		6,399,771	
Less			
Fees		255,962	6,143,809
Administration			
Gross expenditure of Law Society		7,356,783	
Less			
Miscellaneous receipts		25,188	7,331,595
Total cost of the Scheme..			81,141,747

Total cost of the scheme

[1]Including £152,933 collected in the higher courts in respect of proceedings in the magistrates' courts.

The costs incurred by the Supplementary Benefits Commission in assessing eligibility and contributions amounted to approximately £3,322,000. The total costs incurred by the courts in administering the criminal legal aid scheme are not recorded separately.

Sources: Lord Chancellor's Department.
Home Office.

5.25   If all our recommendations are implemented they will add significantly to the cost of providing legal services in this country. But the evidence is clear that public provision of such services has been inadequate for many years. We attach a summary of expenditure in the United Kingdom in the 1977/78 financial year, the latest year for which such detailed figures are available, showing the amounts spent on legal services, compared with other forms of expenditure.

TABLE 5.2
Summary of public expenditure in the United Kingdom, 1977/78

Programme	£m	£m
Social security		13,220
Defence, overseas aid and other overseas services		8,358
Education		8,513
Health and personal social services		7,841
Housing		4,709
Roads and transport		2,718
Environmental services		2,913
Law, order and protective services		
excluding legal aid	1,858	
legal aid	94[1]	
total		1,952
Northern Ireland		1,806
Trade, industry, energy, employment, fisheries, food and forestry..		2,607
Other expenditure on programmes		1,567
Total public expenditure on programmes		56,204
Debt interest		1,986
Total public expenditure		58,190

[1]This figure includes Scotland but does not include legal aid in Northern Ireland which is recorded under the heading Northern Ireland. The inclusion of Scotland explains the difference between this figure and the total shown in Table 5.1.

Source: HM Treasury.

5.26   These figures are not quoted so as to suggest that as much should be spent on legal services as on other forms of national expenditure. But they show that, even by comparison with the amount spent on law and order, the proportion of public expenditure devoted to the provision of legal aid is small.

5.27   When the government announced its intention of appointing this Commission, the news was welcomed in Parliament. This was in part because it was expected that we would investigate abuses and inefficiencies and propose remedies. But we believe that the main hope was that we would be able to recommend an improved system of legal services which would bring them within reach of the great majority of the population.

5.28   We have subjected the legal profession and the conduct of its work to careful scrutiny, and have made numerous detailed recommendations in the following parts of this report. We have recorded in Part VI a large number of proposed improvements in legal procedures which have the same purpose. But however efficiently the legal profession is organised and however carefully legal procedures are devised, the fact remains that legal services call for highly skilled and time-consuming work which cannot be cheap. In the last analysis, therefore, it is for Parliament to decide the extent to which legal services are to be provided at public expense to meet the needs of the majority of the population. But, unless legal services are provided, the full benefit of our legal rights and safeguards cannot be realised.

CHAPTER 6

The Organisation of Legal Services

Introduction

Background

6.1   Until recently, the organisation and work of the legal profession and the provision of legal services were the subject of intermittent inquiry but came under no regular or continuous review. In the last 30 years the number and frequency of such inquiries has increased considerably, as appears from Table 3.1. There is much to be said for reducing the number of such inquiries in the future, in order to allow for a period of orderly development of legal services on the lines we recommend. At the same time account must be taken of strong public and Parliamentary interest in legal services, the provision of which on the scale we propose would call for a substantial increase in public expenditure. For these reasons it is necessary to consider the nature of the responsibilities for the provision of legal services, where they should rest and how, on behalf of the public, they should be kept under review.

Ministerial responsibility

6.2   The minister with general responsibility for legal services is the Lord Chancellor, for whom the Attorney General answers in the House of Commons. Responsibility for legal aid is at present divided between the Lord Chancellor and the Home Secretary. The Lord Chancellor is responsible for the legislation and administration relating to legal advice and assistance (the "green form" scheme), which covers both civil and criminal business, and for legal aid in civil proceedings. The Home Secretary is responsible for the legislation and administration relating to legal aid in criminal proceedings in all courts. Expenditure on legal advice and assistance, civil legal aid and criminal legal aid in magistrates' courts is borne on the Lord Chancellor's Vote; that for criminal legal aid in the higher courts on the Home Secretary's Vote.

6.3   The result of these arrangements is that the Lord Chancellor is responsible to Parliament for expenditure on criminal legal aid in the magistrates' courts, but has no direct control over it: his only function is to pay the bills which are assessed by the Law Society in accordance with regulations made by the Home Secretary. The Home Secretary is answerable to Parliament for the administration of the magistrates' courts, where the Lord Chancellor pays for legal aid, while the Lord Chancellor answers for the administration of the higher courts, where the Home Secretary pays for legal aid in criminal cases but where the costs involved are taxed by officials of the Lord Chancellor's Department.

6.4   Neither the nature of the legal aid scheme nor the level of expenditure involved (roughly £81 million in England and Wales in 1977/78) justifies so complex a distribution of ministerial responsibility. We have received evidence criticising the present arrangements, and have ourselves reached the view that they are undesirable. We make suggestions for simplifying the present structure in Chapter 11.

A Minister for Justice

6.5 It was suggested to us in evidence that the political head of the department responsible for the provision of legal services should be not the Lord Chancellor but a minister in the House of Commons. This proposal is connected with the suggestion that the name of the responsible department should be changed to "Ministry for Justice" or a similar title. Against this, we received evidence supporting the present arrangements and pointing out that they have evolved over the years in a way which meets the particular needs of this country in the administration of justice. We wish to draw attention to the fact that these arguments have been addressed to us. We have not however enquired into this matter because it was not necessary to do so in order to fulfil our terms of reference.

6.6 There is an alternative to a general change in ministerial responsibilities, to which we should draw attention. The Lord Chancellor already carries a heavy burden of work and our proposals, if implemented, will increase that burden. In order to help him discharge these duties, the Lord Chancellor might find it convenient to ask the Prime Minister to appoint a junior minister to assist him with his administrative and Parliamentary business in the same way as other departmental ministers of Cabinet rank. If this minister sat in the House of Commons, it would meet one of the criticisms of the present arrangements.

Responsibilities of the profession

6.7 It is in the interests of the profession, as well as of those of the public at large, not merely to maintain systems of training and discipline which ensure that adequate standards of competence and probity prevail but also to accept much of the responsibility for ensuring that the supply of lawyers is sufficient to meet public needs. We readily acknowledge the difficulty of forecasting future requirements but, if the profession wishes to retain the primary responsibility for the practical task of providing this need, it must accept the function of forming policies to maintain the provision of legal services and to increase them where they fall short. A number of policies need to be considered in fulfilling these responsibilities; these are dealt with in appropriate chapters of this report.

6.8 The Law Society has an additional and unique responsibility for the administration of the civil legal aid scheme. No other private organisation exercises public responsibilities of this character. The Society acts in effect as the agent of the government for this purpose.

6.9 Although there have been criticisms of the operation of the legal aid scheme, the evidence we have received is that the Law Society has exercised its responsibilities well. Submissions have been made to us that some other organisation should take over the work of administration from the Law Society; other submissions propose that there should be no change. The feeling in the profession, as expressed by the Senate and Law Society, is strongly in favour of retaining the present responsibilities. We have reached the view that it would not be in the public interest to change the present arrangements and that the Law Society should remain responsible for the administration of legal aid, other than in criminal cases, to the same extent as at present, subject to compliance with any directives that may be issued by the Lord Chancellor (see paragraph 13.48). We consider there are certain measures which may be taken to assist it and with these we deal below in paragraphs 6.32 – 6.37 and elsewhere in this report.

Investigation and supervision by external bodies
6.10   As pointed out earlier, the profession has been subject to investigation by external bodies on a number of occasions in the recent past. In 1968 the National Board for Prices and Incomes reviewed the remuneration of solicitors, and repeated the study in 1969 (under its standing reference) and in 1971. Investigations of this character are undertaken from time to time for reasons of national policy which prevail over other considerations, but they are open to the criticism that they are intermittent and have not in the past enabled the government of the day, and the profession, to develop agreed policies on such matters as scale charges and remuneration from public funds. To improve the present position, we propose in Chapter 37, the creation of a standing advisory body on fees and charges.

6.11   The Monopolies Commission has jurisdiction to investigate professional practices and, in the case of the legal profession, has done so on three occasions. The Monopolies Commission derives its authority from the Fair Trading Act 1973 which conferred jurisdiction on the Commission, rather than on the Restrictive Practices Court, to investigate practices in the learned professions and certain other service occupations. The sole function of these procedures, whether of the Restrictive Practices Court or the Monopolies Commission, is to eliminate undesirable practices. They do not provide any means by which positive policies for legal services can be proposed or developed. This is the main need, and for this purpose a body of a different character is required.

6.12   The Lay Observer is a recent creation. The first occupant of this post completed a period of service of nearly four years in 1978. We deal with the future of this office in Chapter 25 and for our present purposes draw attention to the fact that the remit of the Lay Observer is limited to keeping under review the way in which the Law Society handles complaints against solicitors.

6.13   The Master of the Rolls has the duty of supervising the rules of conduct and discipline made by the Law Society. New rules may not be brought into effect without his consent. This enables him to influence the policies of the

61

Society affecting the protection of the client but he is not in a position to promote policies concerning the future provision of legal services. We deal further with his functions in Chapter 25.

A Council for Legal Services

The present position

6.14 The Lord Chancellor's Legal Aid Advisory Committee has been established for nearly 30 years. In its early years its impact was not considerable but in recent years it has made a significant contribution to progress in the field within its terms of reference, namely the provision of legal aid and advice and assistance in civil matters. It has succeeded in bringing together a large number of diverse interests and in promoting public discussion. It has reported, year by year, in clear and uncompromising terms, on the deficiencies of the present system. The public, Parliament and the responsible minister rightly attach importance to what it says. The question we have to consider is whether such work should be expanded.

6.15 We draw attention in this report to a number of instances where the provision of legal services has not in our view been adequate or even on the right lines. Gaps and deficiencies are apparent and there is a lack of coordination. We do not imply that there has been anything approaching a breakdown in the provision of legal services. But the long term policies based on adequate data and coherent planning which are necessary to build up an orderly and consistent system have not always been clearly formulated. If the necessary policies are not clearly understood by all concerned, it is difficult to ensure that the separate and independent organisations, on which a public service of this character must rely, are well coordinated and operating at maximum efficiency. We have reached the conclusion that there is a strong case for setting up a body with a wider remit than the Legal Aid Advisory Committee. To distinguish the new body from the existing committee and from the range of other organisations which have been proposed to us under the name of a Legal Services Commission, we propose that it should be known as the Council for Legal Services.

The task of the Council

6.16 We are satisfied that, if it is to operate satisfactorily, it should be the task of the Council for Legal Services to have regard not merely to work done under legal aid or otherwise paid out of public funds, but to legal services of every description. We consider therefore that the Council should keep under review the provision of all forms of legal services.

Composition of the Council

6.17 The composition of the present Legal Aid Advisory Committee provides a useful guide to the composition of the Council. On this basis, the membership would include representatives of the legal profession, of other organisations involved in the provision of legal services and of the public. If it is composed in this way, the members of the Council would necessarily be part-time, though we believe that it would be essential for the chairman to spend a large part of his or her working time on the business of the Council. If it is to command the same respect as the present Committee, the members of Council would have to be representative, of acknowledged standing and impartial in their approach.

Functions of the Council

6.18   So far as the working of the Council is concerned, we recommend that it should report at regular intervals to the responsible minister, should deliver occasional or special reports as required on specific topics and, when necessary, should propose plans and policies for the more effective provision of legal services.

6.19   Different views have been expressed on the nature and functions of the Council. A number of models have been proposed to us, and there are arguments and counter-arguments about their virtues and defects. Such proposals are usually couched in terms of the distinction between an "advisory" body and one with "executive" functions. Proposals range from a purely advisory body, concerned, like the present Legal Aid Advisory Committee, only with publicly-funded legal services, to a Legal Services Commission with wide executive powers and authority to determine the allocation of all public funds provided for legal services.

6.20   We have examined these proposals carefully and considered many arguments. For reasons which we shall give presently, we have come to the conclusion that the remit of the Council for Legal Services should be:—

(a)   to review, and carry out research on, the provision of legal services and to report to the Lord Chancellor;

(b)   to prepare, for the consideration of the Lord Chancellor, proposals for the more effective provision of legal services of any description;

(c)   where proposals are accepted by the Lord Chancellor, to keep under review their implementation by whatever body is made responsible or, if so requested by the Lord Chancellor, to accept direct responsibility for implementing them;

(d)   to carry out such other executive functions as are allocated to it by the Lord Chancellor.

6.21   An overall advisory function is essential to this remit, and there is no disagreement on its need. Somewhere, legal services as a whole have to be considered, so that gaps can be identified, priorities tested, and proposals for change put in context. This is a necessary condition of considered action by both government and the profession. It is also a considerable task, as we ourselves have found in our work.

6.22 In order that the Council may discharge its responsibilities effectively from the outset, we consider that it should be given a research capacity and that its administrative arrangements and budgets should enable it to combine research with running pilot and experimental projects.

6.23 There are arguments for extending the remit of the Council further and including in it functions which are executive in the sense of involving not merely proposals, but decisions on needs and priorities as well as the disbursement of funds. These arguments fall into a number of categories. There is concern that a council which is confined in its functions to advising others may lack the authority which is needed for it to be effective. It is argued that the overall view developed by a council might well be lost in the process of implementation, unless the council itself participates in this process. There is particular concern about the need for innovation and the desirability of having the same body involved in the design and implementation of new schemes. It is argued that both government and the profession may be reluctant to get involved in new schemes, whereas an independent council would have no such reluctance. Specific services ancillary to the legal aid scheme, such as citizens' law centres and a scheme for giving assistance at tribunals, are cited as tasks for a council. In more general terms, it is said that the detailed tasks involved in planning and coordinating legal services would be best performed by a body independent of a government department.

6.24 Arguments against an extension of the functions of the Council into the executive field are equally numerous. There is concern both about the independence of the profession and the reduction of accountability involved in setting up such a council. It is argued that detailed supervision and implementation of schemes would in fact detract from the task of developing an overall view of legal services. It is argued that executive tasks are performed well by existing bodies, this being notably true of the administration of legal aid by the Law Society (though not all schemes for an executive council would transfer this function to it). There are doubts whether a council with a wide remit could operate without setting up an administration of considerable size. Tension would be built up by the fact that such a council would have the power to promote and influence policies in the public sector which might be detrimental to the private sector.

6.25 The Commission has considered these and other arguments carefully. We were impressed by some, not by others. While we are by no means certain that the distinction between "advisory" and "executive" functions is as clear as it appears to be, our decision (as expressed in the remit in paragraph 6.20 above) is un-ambiguous: the Council for Legal Services should have above all advisory functions. Nothing should be done that would detract from its ability to develop an overall view. These functions include however not only a research capacity, but also the ability to initiate pilot schemes and experiments. Moreover, the Council would be able to carry out such other executive functions as are allocated to it by the Lord Chancellor. We do not expect these to be functions which are at present dealt with effectively by other bodies. Finally, we feel strongly that its composition and remit must be such that the Council has sufficient authority to command respect with government, the profession, and the general public.

The Legal Aid Advisory Committee

6.26   Our proposals for a Council for Legal Services owe much to the work in recent years of the Legal Aid Advisory Committee. When the Council is established, it will absorb the work done at present by the Committee, and no purpose would be served by keeping the Committee in existence.

Relations between the Council and Other Bodies

The governing bodies of the profession

6.27   A good relationship between the Council for Legal Services and the governing bodies of the two branches of the profession is essential. The level of cooperation which we have enjoyed shows that no problem need arise. One observation should, however, be made. Our own enquiries have cost the profession heavily in time and money. It cannot fairly be expected to give immediate attention to new demands, nor to sustain the same scale of activity as was involved in the exceptional effort it has made in the past three years to meet all our requirements. Moreover, the profession will need a reasonable period in which to study the full implications of the report and to put its recommendations into effect.

The Fees Advisory Committee

6.28   We recommend in Chapter 37 the appointment of a Fees Advisory Committee. This is to be a small body of experts in the costing and evaluation of professional work. Its purpose will be to advise the government on the appropriate levels of fees for all classes of work in respect of which several different rules committees at present specify the levels or bases of charges. This is not a function for which the Council for Legal Services would be appropriate, having regard to its intended composition and purposes. On the other hand, there is an intimate and complex relationship between the system of fees and charges, the provision of legal aid, the nature and extent of legal services and the remuneration of the profession. It will be essential for each body to pay careful regard to the work of the other and for their secretariats to maintain close contact.

The body to administer citizens' law centres

6.29   In Chapter 8, we propose the creation of a small body, operating separately from any government department, to administer citizens' law centres. It will be for the responsible minister to provide whatever financial authority is required to open a new centre or expand an existing centre. This body will have the 'establishment' functions, to recruit staff, administer their pay and conditions of service, rent premises and supervise the efficient and impartial operation of all citizens' law centres in accordance with the guidelines in paragraph 8.32. We do not advise making this body an offshoot of the Council, for this would prejudice the power which the Council should have to review and if necessary, to criticise the provision of services by law centres as well as by the privately practising profession.

The body to review procedures
6.30   In Part VI, we propose that civil court procedures as a whole should be reviewed either by an enlarged Law Commission or by a small body of experts of a similar kind, appointed for the purpose. It will be called on to take some decisions which will have a considerable impact on the conduct of legal proceedings. We consider that it would be suitable to arrange for at least one of the lawyer members of the Council for Legal Services to be a member also of the appropriate working party of the Law Commission or any other body set up for the purpose.

The Council on Tribunals
6.31   We deal with the functions of the Council on Tribunals in Chapter 15. We wish here to emphasize the need for close coordination of policies and proposals between the Council for Legal Services and the Council on Tribunals. Here again, it may prove convenient to appoint one person to be a member of both bodies.

Regional Arrangements for Legal Services

The need for a regional organisation
6.32   A number of witnesses, including the Legal Aid Advisory Committee, the Law Society and the Legal Action Group told us that there was a need for better coordination, on a regional basis, between those who provide legal services. We agree and consider that regional committees, as defined in the paragraphs below, should be established which can speak for the public at large as well as for barristers and solicitors in private practice, law centres, citizens advice bureaux, social workers, probation officers and local authorities. It would be helpful if members of the court service and, where appropriate, representatives of the prison service, served on these regional committees.

Regional committees
6.33   In our view the functions of regional committees should include:—

(a) assessing the needs for legal and para-legal services in their regions and recommending how they should be met;

(b) coordinating regional services and agencies.

6.34   To perform these functions effectively, each committee should be provided with a full-time liaison officer, the cost being borne out of legal aid funds. These officers should be appointed by the Lord Chancellor but should be responsible to the regional committees.

6.35   Good collaboration is important because the provision of adequate services depends on cooperation between the legal profession and many other agencies and interests. The function of the committees will be to stimulate proposals for improvements and to promote collaboration between all those involved in the provision of legal and para-legal services, identifying and co-ordinating their responsibilities and relating them to local need.

6.36   Regional committees should report annually, and more often if necessary on specific issues. Reports should be submitted to the Lord Chancellor and to the Council for Legal Services and should also go to the various interest groups, local and national, from which the committee members are drawn. The regional liaison officers should maintain close contact with the secretariat of the Council.

6.37   There is no electorate by which regional committee members could be elected. The most practical arrangement would be for the Lord Chancellor to prescribe the composition of the committees and for interest groups named by him to appoint their own representatives, by whatever method seems suitable to each, to fill the places prescribed for them. The Lord Chancellor should appoint the chairman in each case and should have the power to appoint additional members. It will, we think, be convenient for there to be one committee for each of the fourteen legal aid areas. Smaller groupings, may, in the light of experience, prove to be desirable, at least for the discussion of some issues.

The Manchester experiment

6.38   Our views are strengthened as a result of an experiment recently made in the Greater Manchester area. In 1977 a Legal Services Committee was set up, comprising approximately 20 members representing organisations which are concerned with the provision of legal services to the community. The Manchester Legal Services Committee differs in composition from the committees proposed in paragraph 6.37 in that it was set up by the Legal Aid Committee of the Law Society with the assistance of the No. 7 (North Western) Legal Aid Area Committee. The objectives are, however, similar to those which we propose in this report. We have visited Manchester, and have studied the Committee's first annual report; we consider that it is serving a valuable purpose and that it provides an example which should be followed.

Overall responsibility

6.39   While the Council for Legal Services, with its research capacity, will no doubt employ increasingly sophisticated methods of assessing needs, the overall responsibility for assessing the need for legal services in all regions and the extent to which legal services are available to meet them will continue to rest with the Lord Chancellor. In order that he may meet this responsibility we consider, as recommended in Chapter 11, that certain functions should be transferred to him from the Home Secretary and we doubt whether the task can be performed effectively unless this transfer is made. The Lord Chancellor will, we think, be assisted not only by the reports and advice of the proposed Council for Legal

Services but also by the work of the regional committees, in the way proposed above.

Conclusions and Recommendations

Paragraphs

Responsibility for civil legal aid	R6.1	The Law Society should remain responsible for the administration of civil legal aid	6.9
Council for Legal Services	R6.2	A Council for Legal Services should be appointed, with the functions proposed in paragraph 6.20, replacing the Legal Aid Advisory Committee.	6.15–6.26
	R6.3	The Council for Legal Services should maintain close contact with the other bodies mentioned in the text, in some cases sharing members.	6.27–6.31
Regional organisation	R6.4	Committees, with full-time liaison officers, should be set up to co-ordinate legal services in each of the fourteen legal aid regions.	6.32
Overall responsibility	R6.5	The overall responsibility for assessing needs and the services available to meet them should remain with the Lord Chancellor, advised by the Council for Legal Services and the regional committees.	6.39

CHAPTER 7

General Advice and Citizens Advice Bureaux

General Advice

The need for generalist advice agencies

7.1   In making our recommendations about access to legal services we have had regard to the barriers which we enumerated in paragraph 4.23. We have reached the conclusion that the primary need is for a competent and accessible national network of generalist advice agencies which offer initial advice or information to citizens on any problem and sift out for them those problems which have a legal element and may call for a legal remedy. We believe that the availability of such advice agencies is an essential ingredient in a successful policy for providing legal services.

7.2   In the simpler cases, whether or not they have a legal content, these agencies should be able to provide a solution themselves, by advice, correspondence, negotiation or help in form-filling. Where the advice or assistance of a solicitor is needed, the agencies should be able to assist in the selection of a solicitor who is willing and competent to handle the particular problem. They should be able to provide information about cost and eligibility for legal aid, and help their enquirers overcome any inhibitions against going to a solicitor. Special arrangements will be needed in those areas where solicitors are not available to do the work; we deal with these in Chapter 8.

The essential features of generalist advice agencies

7.3   The essential features of generalist advice agencies are the following.

(a) *Generalist approach*. These agencies are available to give initial help in connection with any problem. They provide access to legal services but are not predominantly legal agencies.

(b) *Competence*. The staff are expected to have a sufficient level of skill, based on formal training, to enable them to interview applicants effectively, to give accurate advice and to make appropriate referrals to other agencies.

(c) *Information*. An efficient agency requires a comprehensive information service, covering the whole range of the problems it encounters, which is regularly up-dated.

(d) *Independence*. Members of the public expect to be advised solely on the basis of their own interests and in confidence. Accordingly, they wish for advice from agencies free from bias or external influence.

A national generalist advice service

7.4   Our terms of reference do not require us to examine advice services generally and we have not found it necessary to do so. There are many such advice services, some of a local or a specialist nature, which have differing objectives and are of varying quality. We have however taken note of the generalist advice services which are available and have identified a particular national advice service, provided by the citizens advice bureaux (CABx), which together form the largest and, in our view, the best placed organisation to provide a primary or first tier service.

7.5   We agree with the recommendation of the National Consumer Council in its review of local advice services *The Fourth Right of Citizenship* that the CABx should provide the basic local general practitioner or first tier service; we also agree with its reasoning, namely, that it would be perverse to ignore what already exists and that no other organisation can rival the CABx in organisation and experience. The views of the National Consumer Council are supported by a significant volume of other evidence which has been put before us. Although the CABx are more widely known and used than any other advice agency, they are conscious of the need to ensure that they are accessible and acceptable throughout the community. Later in this chapter, therefore, we make suggestions concerning the organisation of the CABx and the conditions which we think are appropriate for receipt of public funds.

The citizens advice bureaux

7.6   The membership of the National Association of Citizens Advice Bureaux (NACAB) in March 1978 comprised 676 CABx in England and Wales, 27 in Northern Ireland and 53 in Scotland. Each bureau is a local self-governing unit with an independent management committee representing local interests and voluntary and statutory bodies. Day-to-day administration is the responsibility of an organiser; less than a quarter of the organisers are full-time and paid. Bureaux vary in the number of their staff, who may be employed full or part-time and may be either paid or voluntary. Some 9,000 people work in CABx throughout the United Kingdom, of whom over 90 per cent are volunteers. The service offered by most bureaux has the important advantage that it is supported by the NACAB information service and by the Citizens Advice Notes Service provided by the National Council of Social Service. All bureaux are required to comply with the national standards in their operation and to conform to the training requirements laid down by NACAB.

7.7   NACAB told us that its bureaux handled over 3 million enquiries in 1977/78. A survey which it carried out for us in England, Wales and Northern Ireland in 1976 showed that one-third of enquiries had a legal component. It appeared that about 250,000 enquiries a year were referred from bureaux to solicitors. The following table gives a breakdown of the problems handled in 1977/78 by all the bureaux linked to NACAB.

TABLE 7.1
CAB enquiries, 1977/78

	Number (000s)	%
Family and personal	631	20·3
Consumer, trade and business	526	17·0
Housing property and land	514	16·6
Administration of justice	268	8·7
Employment	264	8·5
Social security	262	8·5
National and international..	129	4·2
Health	127	4·0
Travel, transport and holidays	103	3·3
Taxes and duties	93	3·0
Leisure activities	80	2·5
Education	55	1·8
Communications	27	0·9
Immigration and nationality	21	0·7
	3,100	100·0

Source: NACAB Annual Report 1977/78.

The Role of Citizens Advice Bureaux

Lay advice on legal matters
7.8   Not all problems with a legal component need to be referred to a lawyer. It has been found that a trained and experienced lay adviser can, in many cases, provide the guidance that is needed and can also pick out those cases where professional assistance is required. It is sensible and economical to make use of lay services in cases which can adequately be handled without the intervention of a qualified lawyer. It avoids expense to the client and to the public purse, and avoids taking up the time of a lawyer unnecessarily. We regard as important the part which can be played by a para-legal service, based on laymen with common sense, training and experience, of the kind provided by the CABx and similar agencies.

Referrals
7.9   For the purposes of their work, CABx have to refer their clients to a wide range of specialist agencies such as consumer advice centres. In many districts, agencies are available to give specialised advice in relation to consumer problems, financial matters, social security benefits, housing, matrimonial problems and others. Much of the work done by these agencies falls outside our terms of reference, but we would not give a complete picture of local advisory services without mentioning them.

7.10   There has been some debate whether one kind of service is to be preferred to another. In this connection we agree with the approach suggested by the National Consumer Council in its report *The Fourth Right of Citizenship*.

> It is not a question, as it has sometimes in the past been considered to be, of whether we should have one kind of advice service or the other. What is wanted is a proper balance between the two. A fundamental aim, therefore, of local strategic plans should be the achievement of a proper mix of specialist and voluntary services and of working links and effective referral systems for the handling of people's problems where more than one agency needs to be involved.

Referrals to solicitors

7.11   In order to refer clients to suitable agencies, CABx need a good knowledge of the specialist services available. One of their functions is to assist clients in finding a local solicitor who is willing and able to handle their legal problems. In doing this they can act as a bridge between the individual and the lawyer.

7.12   Referral to solicitors in private practice depends for its success both on the availability of solicitors and on the following considerations.

(a) CAB workers need to have at their disposal adequate records and information to enable them to advise clients on a suitable choice of solicitor. The Law Society's legal aid solicitors lists (see paragraph 7.13) provide one starting point for such a body of information.

(b) Clients are more likely to take up an appointment with a solicitor if they know before they leave a CAB that they can obtain a first interview with a solicitor free of cost, or at a fixed fee, and are aware of the terms on which they will be eligible for legal aid if their case proceeds beyond an initial interview.

(c) It will often be best if the initial interview with a solicitor can take place in the office of a CAB which operates a rota scheme (see paragraph 7.16).

7.13   The CABx have two main sources of information about the availability of solicitors willing and able to undertake certain kinds of work. These are the Law Society's legal aid solicitors lists (formerly known as referral lists) and their own local knowledge. The Law Society already publishes lists for the whole of England and Wales, which show solicitors' firms and the types of work they are prepared to do under legal aid. The cost of preparing and issuing these lists is met from the legal aid fund. In Chapter 27, we recommend ways in which the extent and quality of the information available from the lists might be improved; we also recommend that solicitors should, in due course, be able to indicate certain specialisations. These changes will provide the CABx with more information from official sources than they have at present and should increase the usefulness of the lists.

7.14 On the other hand, local and background knowledge are of great value and are unlikely to be replaced by any formal system of published lists. Whatever information is provided in the legal aid solicitors lists and other official publicity, every bureau will find it indispensable to use its personal knowledge of local firms; it can be expected to make use of both sources for identifying solicitors to whom it can refer cases.

7.15 At the same time the legal profession has a responsibility for ensuring that solicitors are available to whom clients may be referred by the CABx in any given area. The profession should find out the types of work required and should try to ensure that an appropriate service is provided. Each CAB needs to have available one or more solicitors whom it can consult informally for advice on day-to-day problems and to have in its area one or more solicitors to whom it can turn in an emergency to take a case at short notice. We have been told that CAB workers are inhibited from approaching a solicitor informally, because they know that they will have to ask him to help them at his own expense. We therefore consider that, in appropriate cases, retainers should be paid. Responsibility for arranging that a proper service is provided to CABx in the above ways should rest with the Law Society or local law societies.

Rota schemes

7.16 When a client is reluctant to go to a solicitor or it is probable that his problem can be dealt with in one interview with a solicitor, it is helpful to make use of advisory sessions which are provided in many CABx. Under these schemes local solicitors, on a rota basis, provide advice on the understanding that, where necessary, they can subsequently accept an enquirer as their own client. We understand that, in February 1977, some 40 per cent of CABx in England, Wales and Northern Ireland had such schemes and over 3,300 solicitors participated in them. This number has increased as further schemes have been established, but precise figures are not available. These schemes are much to be commended, not least because they provide an opportunity for solicitors to become more aware of the range of problems which arise in their locality. We urge that solicitors and barristers should assist in establishing them and take part in them on a regular basis so as to become familiar with the needs of CABx and their clients, and should take part in training sessions organised by CABx.

7.17 NACAB is keen to extend the rota schemes and it will be for the Law Society and NACAB in cooperation to establish them in all places where it is appropriate to do so. It is primarily the task of the CABx to formulate their needs in this respect and, within the limits of what the profession can offer, to determine the manner in which these needs can best be met. There should be regular contact between the CABx and local societies and, if difficulties arise which cannot otherwise be resolved, they should be reported to the regional committees whose appointment we have recommended in Chapter 6.

Financial support for the CAB service

7.18   Local CABx are financed in the main by local authority grants. NACAB and its network of area advisory offices are funded by central government. In addition NACAB was, until recently, in receipt of a national development grant from central government amounting to some £2.75 million over five years. This was used to improve central services and to make special grants to support the establishment of new bureaux and the improvement of existing ones. This five-year grant came to an end in March 1979. However, on 16th November 1978, the government announced that it would continue to provide financial support to NACAB, at no less than the level of that provided during 1977/78, for a further two years. The form of support thereafter would depend on a review of advice services generally following our report.

7.19   The organisation and funding of the CAB service is outside our terms of reference but we draw attention to certain broad considerations which will, we think, be of importance if the CABx are to provide an adequate primary service as a basis for the provision of professional legal services.

Conditions for financial support

7.20   NACAB indicated to us certain deficiencies in its service and said that there were wide variations in the quality of the service provided by different bureaux; in many areas there is no CAB at all. Nevertheless, we take the view that the CABx are the most appropriate means now available of providing the first tier advisory service. For this service to be provided effectively, the CABx must receive adequate support from public funds and the public has the right to expect that any agency financed in this way maintains high standards. We think, therefore, that the following conditions may reasonably be proposed for the provision of public finance.

(a) The aims and policies of NACAB should specify what is expected of all bureaux in connection with the provision of advice services generally, including legal services.

(b) The CABx national training arrangements should make provision for para-legal work, including, where appropriate, tribunal representation services.

(c) There should be a programme agreed between NACAB and the government to establish new bureaux in areas where they are needed but are not now available.

(d) High standards in staffing should be maintained and all bureaux should, as at present, be required as a condition of receiving support to comply with detailed standards prescribed by NACAB, relating to management, the provision of premises of a suitable kind, staff training and all other necessary matters.

7.21   We recognise that NACAB is already fully committed to improving CAB standards generally and is taking steps to that end. It has recently submitted a major development plan: see paragraph 7.23 below. We think it may prove necessary to increase the proportion of paid staff, for example the full-time bureaux organisers; nevertheless we consider it important to maintain the valuable element of voluntary service which is given by many people in the course of their work for the CABx.

7.22   In the oral evidence which representatives of NACAB gave to us, we sensed some uncertainty as to the range and scope of the future programme of activity of the CAB service based, in part, on doubts as to the funds which would be made available. Although it is clear, as we have pointed out earlier, that the service will require to be financed out of public funds, it is not part of our function to suggest what proportions of finance should come respectively from central and local government. It is suggested by some that the funds provided by central government should be borne on the Lord Chancellor's Vote. We do not think that this would be appropriate because the CABx provide a generalist advice service and this should not be the responsibility of the Lord Chancellor. If, as would seem right to many, part of the funds are to continue to be provided by local authorities, we think that this should be on the basis of a statutory duty.

The scope of the CAB service
7.23   The CAB service accepts that its work is not static and must be adjusted to changing conditions. As more social legislation is introduced, the CAB service has to expand to give advice to citizens who are unaware of the new provisions or are unable to interpret them. In a similar way, the CABx have in recent years undertaken the provision of legal advice and representation for citizens in tribunals in various parts of the country. If it is decided that this work is to be expanded in CABx on a national scale, extra funds will be required. A necessary prerequisite for any funding programme will, therefore, be the preparation of coordinated long term plans, with supporting budgets of expenditure, defining the future scope of the CAB service both as regards its geographical spread and the range of work it will cover. We have noted that NACAB has recently submitted a detailed development plan to the responsible minister. We have not regarded it as part of our function to consider the details of this plan but we have no doubt that it will be given urgent and careful consideration in the light of our comments.

7.24   Before any development plan is implemented, the functions to be fulfilled by the CAB service will need to be defined with care. There is sometimes a tendency for a generalist service to expand into the specialisms with which it is in daily contact. If this were to happen in the case of the CABx, they would lose their primary purpose as first tier advisory agencies; there would be duplication of effort, waste of public money and, in all probability, deterioration in the quality of the specialist advice provided.

7.25   As regards legal services, the division of function between the para-legal work of the CAB service and the use of professional lawyers has hitherto been established on a sensible and practical basis and it should continue in this way. We do not think that a CAB should build up, as part of its staff, a team of lawyers to give legal advice to individuals. It would be better to preserve the general advisory character of the CABx, and to look for legal advice to the professional legal services which are already available from solicitors in private practice and from the citizens' law centres (CLCs) to which we refer in the next chapter.

Salaried lawyers in CABx
7.26   This is not to say that there would be no place for salaried solicitors in some of the larger CABx, or in a group of CABx. Salaried solicitors employed by the citizens' law centre service should where necessary be seconded to a CAB or group of CABx. Such solicitors would act as internal advisers to the staff of the bureaux and, amongst other functions, would assist in the drafting of technical material and the training of CAB staff. They might be called on, from time to time, to provide legal advice to an individual CAB client; such individual service should not be ruled out, but we think that it should be the exception and not the rule. The routine provision of legal services to individual clients is best carried out by private practitioners or by CLCs.

Alternative Advice Services

Salaried solicitors in local government
7.27   Some local authorities employ salaried solicitors to provide legal services to individual members of the public. While this may work adequately in certain cases, we do not favour it as a general arrangement. A large number of the problems which face members of the public concern the individual's relationship with his local authority. If the solicitor giving advice is employed by the local authority his independence in such matters is inevitably impaired.

Legal advice centres
7.28   Apart from the established law centres there are about 130 voluntary legal advice centres manned by solicitors and barristers who give up their time to provide this free service. Over half of them are in London. Most of the centres have been founded in the last ten years in response to a need which has been discovered during this period but some have been providing an important service for many years. They are usually open for one or two evenings a week to provide legal advice, write letters and refer clients to private practitioners. The problems presented to them cover a broad range, but tend to concentrate on the fields of family law, housing, employment, consumer and debt problems, accidents and some criminal cases. Few legal advice centres provide representation in court. Apart from a small number of centres which have full-time staff, the overheads are modest and are met from small grants from public funds or charitable sources, or, in a few instances, from donations from clients.

7.29 It is, in our view, appropriate for advice facilities to be provided by those who are willing to give the time and effort to the task and who can raise the necessary finance. We believe, however, that the strengthening of the CABx on the lines we have proposed, backed up by close liaison with the practising profession and the establishment of CLCs, will diminish the need for separate legal advice centres, and that the considerable, and valuable, voluntary work which is now put into advice centres might with advantage be made available to rota schemes for CABx or advisory sessions at CLCs. It may, however, be necessary for the voluntary legal advice centres to continue to operate as at present, on an interim basis, in those areas where no first tier centre has been established or where such a centre is insufficiently developed to provide for the needs of its clients.

Conclusions and Recommendations

Paragraphs

Generalist advice agencies	R.7.1	A competent, accessible, independent national network of generalist advice agencies is needed.	7.1–7.3
Citizens advice bureaux	R.7.2	The citizens advice bureaux should provide the basic generalist advice service.	7.4
Referrals	R7.3	The CABx should be backed up by a variety of advisers and agencies to whom cases can be referred.	7.9–7.10
	R7.4	Local law societies should ensure that every CAB is properly serviced by solicitors to whom CABx can refer their clients.	7.15
Rota schemes in CABx	R7.5	Rota schemes of solicitors and barristers should be established in CABx wherever needed.	7.16
Funding of CABx	R7.6	CABx should be financed out of public funds.	7.20
	R7.7	As a condition of receiving public funds, CABx should:—	
		(a) be required to maintain high standards;	7.20
		(b) draw up long-term plans defining the scope of the work to be undertaken, with supporting budgets.	7.23–7.24

77

Paragraphs

Provision of services

R7.8   Legal services for individual clients of the CAB service should be provided by solicitors in private practice or by citizens' law centres.   7.25

R7.9   Salaried lawyers should be seconded where necessary to CABx to act as internal advisers.   7.26

CHAPTER 8

Law Centres

Background

The growth of law centres

8.1   Law centres are a recent development. The first law centre came into operation in North Kensington in 1970; it was set up by a group of lawyers and laymen and was funded from charitable sources. In succeeding years law centres were established at a steady rate, averaging about four a year, mostly, at the outset, in London. Their spread has been random, depending on local initiative and voluntary action.

8.2   The possibility of setting up a legal service of this character was envisaged in the Legal Advice and Assistance Act 1972, which was consolidated in the Legal Aid Act 1974. This contained provisions to enable the Law Society to employ salaried solicitors for the purpose of providing a service directly to members of the public. In the event, no financial provision was made to implement this part of the legislation, which has not yet been brought into force and the Law Society has not, therefore, itself set up any law centres, though one or two in recent years have been promoted on the initiative of local law societies.

8.3   In the early years law centres were regarded at times with suspicion and hostility by some members of the profession, who feared that they would lose work to an organisation providing a service without charge and entitled to advertise its existence to the public. Problems also arose over the terms of the waiver from the strict professional rules as to advertising and touting without which law centres could not bring their services to the attention of those for whom they were intended. Eventually, after lengthy discussions, a standard waiver was agreed in August 1977 setting out the nature of the legal work that might be performed by law centres. We were told that there have been no complaints of breaches of the guidance note issued by the Law Society and that it has helped to foster good relations between law centres and solicitors in private practice. It is now thought that a law centre is more likely to stimulate than to reduce the business of firms working in its locality.

Present position

8.4   We carried out a survey of law centres in August 1978, at which time there were 27 of which 17 were in Greater London and the remainder were in Belfast, Birmingham, Cardiff, Coventry, Liverpool, Manchester, Merthyr Tydfil and Newcastle. Between them they had a staff of upwards of 250 people of whom 75 were lawyers. The full results of the survey are set out in Volume II section 3. The picture is one of considerable diversity in structure, finance and functions.

8.5   All the centres employed at least one lawyer full-time; three centres employed five. A number of centres also employed full-time or part-time paid staff, and made use of the services of volunteers.

8.6   The forms of management vary between centres, but all of them have, or intend to have, a management, advisory or planning committee. Sometimes these committees may be self-appointed, at any rate in the early stages, sometimes they are elected by a membership of local subscribers and sometimes they consist of nominees of local government, the profession and local or national groups and organisations. The function of committees of this kind appears not to be to take direct responsibility for the professional work of the lawyers in the centres, but rather to enable the policies of the centre to develop in a way that is sensitive to local opinion. The intention is to give the local community, for whose benefit the law centre is intended, a sense of participation in its work.

Finance

8.7   The data in Volume II section 3 show the wide range of sources of funds of existing centres. In the early years centres depended to a great extent on charitable funds. It is possible for centres to earn some income from legal aid, in particular from the green form scheme, but in only one case in the survey was it found that a centre obtained more than one-fifth of its income in this way. Most centres are now heavily dependent on grants from local authorities, from the Department of the Environment under the Urban Programme and from the Lord Chancellor. Most law centres are accustomed to facing financial difficulties. These have become more acute in recent years, when a number of the payments out of public funds have been in the nature of rescue operations rather than of planned support based on long-term policies.

Functions

8.8   Law centres have different approaches to their functions and the type of work which they undertake. Some deal with individuals on a case-by-case basis, others prefer to undertake activities intended to benefit their local communities. The Law Centres Working Group pointed out in oral evidence that, with limited resources, it is more effective to concentrate on the source of a problem rather than to attempt to alleviate its effect by legal action in individual cases. Accordingly, some law centres have assisted groups campaigning against bad housing, unemployment and other problems, sometimes by direct participation, sometimes, quite properly, by giving legal advice. In either case, association with such campaigns has sometimes given rise to controversy and some sponsoring authorities have cut off funds or have threatened to do so.

8.9   It has been questioned whether the activities of some law centres are directed to the provision of legal services. As we remarked in Chapter 2, there is no settled definition of legal services and lawyers in private practice accept professional responsibility for activities which would not normally be categorised as legal services. Some law centres, whose staff undertake work which is not directly connected with legal rights, duties and liabilities, argue that in the case of law centres a definition of legal services should be applied which is broader than the conventional meaning of the words.

8.10 We were told that some law centres refused to act for certain classes of client, for example, private landlords. As the movement has got under way this attitude has changed and the law centres themselves have told us that in principle they are willing to act for any type of client. The question is whether, if law centres are financed out of public funds, the nature of their work and clientele should be settled by those providing the funds or their delegates, by reference to local opinion or by those who work in each centre according to their own views. We give our views in paragraph 8.32.

The impact of the law centres
8.11 The impact of law centres has been out of all proportion to their size, to the number of lawyers who work in them and to the amount of work it is possible for them to undertake. The volume of work they have attracted has shown how deep is the need they are attempting to meet. It has dispelled the possibility of complacency over the institution of the legal aid scheme, has emphasized the importance of a wider distribution of legal services and has shown the desirability of enabling and encouraging lawyers to take up work elsewhere than in their traditional areas of activity and types of practice. The Lord Chancellor's Legal Aid Advisory Committee summed up informed opinion thus in its evidence.

> ... we think that law centres are, and should be, here to stay and that they are making a vital contribution to legal services.

Main considerations
8.12 The last decade has been a period of development and experiment. In this period, diversity of approach has been an advantage, enabling various models to be tested. A great deal of valuable work has been done, some within the normal ambit of legal services, some outside. It is not our purpose to put a stop to further experiment but it must now be decided on what basis public money, voted for the provision of legal services, should be used in the funding of law centres and how centres supported out of public funds should work and be organised.

8.13 We consider that the time has come to move forward from a period of experiment to one of consolidation, characterised by continuity, orderly development, adequate resources and proper administrative and financial control. The purpose of our recommendations is to combine the achievement of these objectives with the preservation of the special qualities which have marked the formative years of law centres, their dedication, imagination and commitment to meeting local needs and to ensuring that the rights of citizens are upheld.

The characteristics of law centres

8.14 The success of law centres shows clearly that they have favourable characteristics both for their clients and those who work in them. They enjoy a psychological advantage in the fact that they offer their services, as a rule, without charge and are regarded as operating with the sole purpose of providing a benefit for the local population. In fact, those working in law centres, like any others, must earn a living but this obtrudes less than in the case of those working in private practice. The fact that workers in law centres are salaried rather than fee-earning enables them to deal with cases with which, although legal aid may be available, it would be uneconomic for a private practitioner to deal, at present levels of remuneration for legally-aided work. This benefit is offset by the heavy workload of some centres which, as we have remarked, has caused them to give individual case work, which is time-consuming, a low priority. It is a particular advantage of law centres that they can operate at present in areas of work which a private practitioner could only undertake on behalf of a client who did not have the means to pay him if he were willing and able to do such work without remuneration. Finally, law centres have become clearly identified as a source of help for those at any kind of disadvantage and as being willing to side with citizens against authority.

8.15 Some of the disadvantages of the privately-practising profession by comparison with the law centres will be reduced to a considerable extent if there are improvements in fee structures and in the extension of legal aid in the way we recommend in later chapters. But, in some classes of work which are time-consuming, a salaried service will continue to have certain advantages and the services of private practitioners will, therefore, need to be supplemented in certain areas by salaried lawyers deployed in law centres.

8.16 Existing law centres operate under a number of disadvantages. Each centre must find its own funds from a variety of sources, such as government departments, local authorities, charitable agencies and legal aid work. There is no coordination between these sources and whether a centre can obtain enough for its purposes in any year is a matter partly of chance and partly of the aptitude of its staff and supporters for fund-raising. Because their distribution is haphazard and because they are under-financed, they are unable to offer as comprehensive a service as they would wish. Furthermore, lack of resources does not permit them either adequately to remunerate their staff or to provide for their pensions. There is no career structure for legal staff in law centres, with the result that most of the lawyers in such centres are young and at an early stage in their careers. Many go from law centres into private practice but there is very little movement from private practice into law centres. It is therefore scarcely surprising that professional standards vary widely between law centres. In addition, the present system of management has not in all cases prevented poor internal administration. Law centres differ in their constitutions, which range from that of a company limited by guarantee to an unincorporated association or a trust. Some are registered charities, while others are not.

Citizens' Law Centres

General

8.17 At present there are certain classes of legal work for which legal aid is not available. There are also certain areas of the country where the shortage of lawyers is acute. Our recommendations on legal aid should, in time, remedy the first deficiency. The second deficiency, in the availability of lawyers, cannot be expected to be removed in a short time, and it is likely that it will never be wholly overcome in some areas. We have already remarked on the heavy workload of law centres which gives an indication of the lack of services which are needed in their localities. We consider, therefore, that the efforts of private practitioners will need to be supplemented in certain areas by salaried lawyers, deployed in law centres. We propose that this service should be provided by a system of law centres, financed out of public funds and built on the experience of existing law centres in a way which preserves the advantages and overcomes the defects of the present system. In what follows we refer to the centres which would be established by the new service as "Citizens' Law Centres" (CLCs) in order to distinguish them from the law centres as at present organised.

The purpose of the new service

8.18 The main purpose of a CLC should be to provide legal advice, assistance and representation to those in its locality. It should receive clients directly or on referral from the CABx and other agencies. It should lay particular emphasis on work in areas of the law where there is a deficiency in existing legal services, in particular in the areas of social welfare law.

8.19 A distinction should be drawn between providing legal services in the way described and in carrying out general community work. At present some law centres concentrate on community work and, for this purpose, employ one or more community workers, without legal training or qualifications. These centres like to work for the community at large or sections of it, rather than for individuals. They often seek to attack the roots of problems by organising groups to bring pressure to bear on landlords, local authorities and central government either to improve working, housing or living conditions or to urge changes in priorities of public expenditure so as to meet urgent needs or to promote changes of a similar character. They become a focus in the neighbourhood for campaigns on behalf of the community.

8.20 Whatever opinion is held as to the value of work of this kind, we firmly believe that if it is to be carried on, it should be funded from a suitable source such as Urban Aid and carried on by local or national groups, by political parties or by members of the local authority. We consider that this type of work is not appropriate for a legal service for the following reasons.

(a) The purpose of the service is to bring legal advice and assistance within reach of all those in its area who otherwise would not receive them.

(b) Community action tends to involve a centre with only one sector of the local population, whereas it should act, and be seen as willing to act, for anyone who needs its services.

(c) A CLC cannot be expected to maintain the position that it provides an independent service if it is seen as a base from which campaigns are run.

8.21   While we consider it inappropriate for a law centre to devote its resources to taking part in political or community activities, there can be no objection to a law centre providing advice and assistance on legal matters to individuals on how best to proceed, whether or not they are connected with such activities. The existing law centres provide legal advice and assistance to groups and attach considerable importance to this aspect of their work. We agree that such services are important and we deal with this point in paragraphs 12.57 – 12.65. It is also within the scope of a law centre to provide legal support to CABx, housing aid centres, consumer advice centres and other legal agencies. But the centre should not itself be involved in action of the kind described in paragraph 8.19.

8.22   We consider that the arrangements between lawyers in a law centre and their clients should be the same as that between a solicitor in private practice and a client in receipt of legal aid. Those who obtain legal services in law centres should be expected to make the same financial contributions as they would have made had they sought similar services from a solicitor in private practice. As in the case of private solicitors, there should be a system of contribution-free diagnostic interviews (see paragraph 13.5).

The management of CLCs
8.23   A number of considerations, some conflicting, must be taken into account when deciding what management structure is best suited to the new service. It is essential, first, that while the lawyers in CLCs may work independently of the government service, there is proper accountability for the use of public funds. It is necessary to establish a coherent system across the country for the appointment, training, promotion and movement of legal staff, to provide an effective career structure and to promote interchange between the salaried and the privately practising profession.

8.24   At the same time, it is essential that a CLC should maintain close contact with the community it serves and be sensitive to its particular needs. We mentioned in paragraph 8.6 the importance attached by existing law centres to the appointment of advisory, management or policy committees for these purposes. It is also of assistance to have a law centre situated near a CAB, not only for the convenience of clients referred from one to the other, but also because the staffs of the centre and the bureau are in regular contact.

Central agency for citizens' law centres

8.25 In our view the requirements set out above can best be met by establishing a new central agency, appointed by government but independent of it, both to finance and to manage the new service. The agency should comprise a small part-time committee and a secretariat appointed by the Lord Chancellor and financed by grant in aid paid out of his Vote.

8.26 We have considered whether the new central agency should simply be a source of funds to independent CLCs, with no management functions. We appreciate that, where, as in the past, funds for law centres have come from a variety of sources, it has been necessary to establish separate management committees to provide independence from a funding agent whose interests might conflict with those of the clients of a centre. It will be the responsibility of the new agency to establish a professional service in specialized fields of legal work and in areas which are not adequately served by solicitors in private practice. If high standards, continuity of service and an adequate career structure are to be achieved then in our view the new agency should be responsible for managing as well as for financing the centres and we suggest in paragraph 8.32 the subjects which might be covered in guidelines used by this central agency. Moreover, we do not think it right for people who have no knowledge of the law or the handling of legal problems and possibly little experience of managing an office, to be expected to assume direct responsibility for the professional work of a CLC. But law centres are a matter of strong local interest. We propose therefore that each CLC, or group of CLCs, should have a local committee composed of residents and representatives of organisations in the area. This local committee should ensure that the law centre is sensitive to local circumstances and in a position to meet the needs of the community and its views should be taken into account by the central agency when staff are appointed or moved.

8.27 Many of the existing law centres are at present financed by their local authorities, and in some cases the local authority was instrumental in setting up the centre. However, we regard the need for a CLC to be, and to be seen to be, free from any possibility of a local authority's influence or pressure as of overriding importance. Cases have occurred where a funding agency has attempted to put pressure on a law centre, and, in one or two cases, centres have been deprived of funds. We recommend, therefore, that central government through the new agency, rather than local authorities, should fund and manage CLCs. Local authorities should, however, be represented on local committees. Local authorities and any other agency such as a charitable trust may, if they wish, maintain any organisation which they regard as of benefit to the inhabitants in their areas but this would not form part of the CLC service.

Existing centres

8.28 We are aware that existing law centres value their independence but we hope that they will wish to become constituent parts of the new agency which is devised to provide independence from central and local government and, on matters other than professional standards and discipline, from the professional bodies. The independence of the service, together with its continuity and efficiency, will, we consider, best be guaranteed if there is one national agency responsible rather than an increasing number of separate local entities operating with differing procedures and administration, sources of finance and professional standards.

8.29 We recommend that all new law centres should take the form of CLCs under the oversight of the agency we have proposed. Existing law centres should be invited to become part of the new agency. Financial provision for their up-keep by central government out of funds provided for legal services should in future be conditional on their doing so and on their complying with the guide-lines specified in paragraph 8.32 below.

8.30 Some law centres are at present financed under the Urban Programme. Where a law centre and its local authority wish it, and the responsible govern-ment department and local authority are prepared to maintain the contribution, existing arrangements will no doubt continue; but the centre will not form part of the CLC service.

Solicitors employed by the Law Society
8.31 We have mentioned that the Legal Aid Act 1974 already empowers the Law Society to employ salaried solicitors. We do not think that this arrangement would provide what experience has shown to be needed for CLCs. It is acknow-ledged, for example, to be too limited in the scope of work it covers. Moreover, it does not provide for the employment of barristers, several of whom work in existing law centres. Our general approach is that the Law Society should con-centrate its efforts on the administration of legal aid, in ensuring that the best use is made of practitioners' services in providing a referral and a rota service to the CABx, and in establishing and extending duty solicitors schemes.

Guidelines for CLCs
8.32 It will be for the new national agency we have recommended to lay down detailed working guidelines for CLCs. We limit ourselves in what follows to indicating the matters which the guidelines should cover. They should not duplicate or conflict with the rules of the professional bodies, to which solicitors and barristers employed in CLCs will be subject.

Careers, salaries and pensions
(a) There should be a career structure, national salary scales and a national pension scheme.

Internal responsibility
(b) Each centre should have a senior lawyer answerable for the work done, including that done by volunteers, and the management of the centre.

Training

(c) There should be adequate arrangements for the training of lawyers and of unqualified staff. In practice, training schemes for the lawyers involved might be run in conjunction with, or as part of, schemes run by the Law Society or the Senate or other bodies, such as the Legal Action Group, for private practitioners.

Work to be done

(d) The type of work that may be carried out by CLCs should be clearly prescribed and should be based upon the standard waiver referred to in paragraph 8.3 above. Individual CLCs could be authorised by the central agency to give priority to certain types of work depending on local needs but such arrangements should be reviewed regularly. It should be made clear that a CLC should not discriminate between different types of client in the area of practice. Under no circumstances should a single centre act for both parties to a dispute.

Referral

(e) CLCs should encourage referrals to them from CABx or other referral agencies.

(f) In order to enable a centre to concentrate on its work as prescribed under (d) above, clients should if necessary be referred to solicitors in private practice. Whether this is appropriate will depend on the ability and willingness of such solicitors to undertake the work, the wishes of clients and the nature and urgency of the problem.

Educational Work

(g) Arrangements should be made for the CLC staff to take part, within limits defined by the agency, in training in CABx and other agencies and in educational work in schools and community groups.

Premises

(h) Standards should be laid down for office premises and the times of opening. Wherever possible offices should be sited adjacent to a CAB.

Records and books

(j) CLCs should keep uniform daily and other records as prescribed by the central agency.

(k) The records kept should have regard to the need for analysing information for research purposes.

(l) CLCs should keep uniform accounts, suitable for management purposes. There should be a central accountancy system so that as far as possible individual CLCs are concerned only with day-to-day client accounting and petty cash.

Insurance

(m) The central agency will need to examine whether indemnity and fidelity insurance will be required and to make the necessary arrangements.

Reports

(n) CLCs should make annual reports to the central agency and should make such other periodic reports as are required by it. The agency should report annually to the Lord Chancellor and a copy should be sent to the Council for Legal Services.

Secondment to CABx and other agencies

(o) As we indicated in paragraph 7.26, legal staff from CLCs may be seconded on occasion to a CAB or groups of CABx, to act as resource lawyers. We consider that the use of resource lawyers should not be confined to CABx but that they should be employed whenever an agency can make effective use of such a source of internal advice to improve the quality and extent of its para-legal service.

Waivers of professional rules

8.33 The Solicitors' Practice Rules, made by the Council of the Law Society under section 31 of the Solicitors Act 1974, forbid solicitors to advertise or to share professional fees with non-lawyers. The Law Society has, however, the power to waive these rules in particular cases. Since law centres have had to advertise in order to make themselves known to their local communities and since most law centres are run by management committees which include non-lawyers, it has been necessary for them to obtain waivers from the Law Society. These have been granted to law centres on an individual basis subject to the fulfilment of certain strict criteria.

8.34 Waivers from the Bar's normal rules of conduct are required by barristers who work in law centres in order that they may be released from the prohibition against employed barristers conducting a practice and from the requirement to comply with the "cab rank" rule (see paragraph 3.20). The Senate has accordingly drawn up special rules of conduct which apply to all barristers working in designated law or advice centres. In evidence to us, the Senate proposed their replacement by a revised set of rules. The Senate has voiced its concern that some law centres might discriminate against certain types of clients; it is therefore reluctant to grant waivers from the "cab rank" rule. We are conscious of this danger; hence our recommendation in paragraph 8.32(d) that such discrimination should not be permitted.

8.35 We believe that, if the law centres are to provide an adequate professional service, it is essential that the professional conduct of lawyers employed in law centres should remain the responsibility of their professional bodies. Waivers from some of the standard rules of conduct will, therefore, continue to be required. At present, the Senate has to consider, in relation to each application for a waiver, whether it is needed for the purpose of providing professional services in a law centre.

8.36 If a system of the kind we propose is set up, working under approved guidelines, individual waivers should be unnecessary: the central agency, the Law Society and the Senate should agree to a general waiver which should apply to all lawyers working in CLCs. If agreement cannot be reached between the agency and the professional bodies, the matter should be determined by the Lord Chancellor.

Number of CLCs required

8.37 The 26th Report of the Legal Aid Advisory Committee listed the areas identified in a survey by the Lord Chancellor's Department as having the greatest unmet need for legal services. We have not thought it necessary to repeat the survey two years after it was completed and we think that, initially, particular regard should be had to the areas mentioned in the list, which were as follows:—

North East	*Midlands*
Newcastle	Birmingham
Sunderland	Wolverhampton
Gateshead	Leicester
South Tyneside	Nottingham
Middlesbrough/Stockton-on-Tees	
North West	*Yorkshire and Humberside*
Liverpool	Sheffield
Knowsley (Huyton and Kirkby)	Leeds
Salford	Bradford
Sefton (Bootle)	Kingston-upon-Hull
	London
	Hammersmith
	Southwark

The areas with the next most intense need appear (subject to further local enquiry) to be Bolton, Brighton, Bristol and Cardiff.

Since the survey was carried out law centres have been opened in Birmingham and Southwark.

8.38 Needs for legal services exist not only in the big cities identified in paragraph 8.37. They are also prevalent in rural areas, among a more widely-scattered population. Such areas have suffered from the loss of a number of services, in particular public transport and of advice facilities generally. Solicitors' offices tend to be found only in the towns and are not always accessible to those who have need of their services. The solution to the problem of rural needs is, however, unlikely to be found in the establishment of a CLC, though there may on occasion be scope for salaried lawyers to be seconded from the CLC agency to work full-time with agencies, such as CABx, which operate in rural areas. The geographical areas in which such salaried lawyers might have a role to play, and the means by which this should be achieved, should be examined by the regional legal services committees referred to in Chapter 6. We think that solicitors should also be encouraged to open in practice in such areas with the assistance of the scheme which we recommend in Chapter 16.

8.39 On 8th February 1979, the Lord Chancellor announced that existing funds would be made available both to support existing law centres and to establish new ones. We welcome this development and we recommend that detailed discussions should be held with local bodies and with the regional legal services committees, as soon as these are set up, to identify the most suitable locations for new CLCs.

Conclusions and Recommendations

Paragraphs

Citizens' law centres	R8.1	There is a need in many localities for a legal service which should be provided by a system of law centres.	8.15
	R8.2	Law centres operate at present under a number of disadvantages; in future, this form of service should be provided by citizens' law centres (CLCs).	8.16–8.17
The work of CLCs	R8.3	The main purpose of a CLC should be to provide legal advice, assistance and representation to those in its locality, with special emphasis on social welfare law.	8.18
	R8.4	It is not appropriate for a CLC itself to undertake community work and campaigns, but it may give legal advice to individuals in respect of such matters.	8.19–8.21
	R8.5	Clients of CLCs should pay for the services they receive on the same basis as legally-aided clients of private practitioners.	8.22

Paragraphs

Administration and finance

R8.6   There should be a small central agency appointed by government, but independent of it, to finance and manage CLCs.   8.25

R8.7   There should be a local advisory committee for each CLC or group of CLCs.   8.26

R8.8   CLCs should be financed wholly out of funds provided by central government.   8.27

R8.9   Funds voted for the provision of law centres should be available only to CLCs which are managed by the central agency.   8.29

R8.10   For the purpose of providing a high standard of administration and of professional service, guidelines should be laid down as set out in the text.   8.32

Waivers

R8.11   The Senate and the Law Society should retain responsibility for the professional standards of lawyers employed in CLCs; any necessary waivers of professional rules should be agreed between the central agency and the professional bodies.   8.35–8.36

Needs

R8.12   In setting up CLCs, regard should be had initially to the deprived areas mentioned in paragraph 8.37. Measures should also be taken to meet rural needs.   8.38

CHAPTER 9

Duty Solicitor Schemes

The Present Position

Origin and development of duty solicitor schemes

9.1   The first duty solicitor scheme in the United Kingdom was set up in Glasgow in 1964. The first schemes in England and Wales were set up in Bristol and Cardiff in 1972 by the Bristol Law Society and the Cardiff Law Society in order to provide legal assistance for unrepresented defendants in the Bristol and Cardiff magistrates' courts. By 1st April 1979, a total of 107 duty solicitor schemes were in operation and had been granted waivers by the Law Society from the practice rule that prohibits touting. The Law Society told us that it hopes that schemes will, in due course, be established in every magistrates' court which hears a substantial number of cases.

Nature of duty solicitor schemes

9.2   The essence of the duty solicitor scheme is that solicitors in private practice are available on a rota basis, to give assistance to defendants in the magistrates' court. This may include:—

(a)   advising the defendant before the hearing;

(b)   applying for bail;

(c)   applying for legal aid;

(d)   applying for an adjournment if time is needed to prepare the case;

(e)   making a plea in mitigation.

A further function which does not exist at present but which will appear if our proposals later in this chapter are implemented, is:—

(f)   advising a suspect when he is taken into custody.

9.3   A wide range of assistance is provided to defendants in these ways. They are, however, intended only to provide a first-aid service like a casualty station; they are not designed to provide legal assistance for the whole conduct of a case. Most schemes enable the client to instruct the solicitor who has advised and assisted him under the scheme to conduct his case to its conclusion, but the client can subsequently instruct another solicitor or represent himself if he so wishes.

9.4   The total number of defendants assisted by duty solicitor schemes and the extent of the assistance provided cannot be precisely established since detailed records and statistics are not maintained in respect of all schemes. Figures provided by the Law Society, as part of a survey in August 1976, showed that during the previous two months, one scheme had enabled over 800 cases to be dealt with, two schemes over 300 cases each, twelve schemes over 100 cases each and a further thirteen schemes over 50 cases each. Such information as is available suggests that a substantial number of defendants, who might otherwise have received no help at all, have been assisted by duty solicitors.

Weaknesses of duty solicitor schemes

9.5 Duty solicitor schemes have been strongly encouraged by the Law Society and by the Lord Chancellor but their success in practice has depended on the efforts of local law societies and their members. As might be expected of a recent voluntary development, these schemes do not yet provide full national coverage and the range and quality of services available are variable.

9.6 The schemes in operation differ widely, in particular in the following respects:—

(a) the manner in which contact is made between the duty solicitor and the defendant;

(b) the manner in which the scheme is brought to the notice of defendants and is publicised in the courts and elsewhere;

(c) the extent to which the service is offered to defendants not in custody;

(d) the extent to which non-lawyers (for instance CAB workers or social workers) are used as receptionists to contact such defendants;

(e) the extent and nature of the service offered to juveniles;

(f) the availability of a twenty four hour emergency service;

(g) the basis used for claiming remuneration;

(h) the arrangements for recording statistics;

(j) the number of solicitors who participate in the rota and in the frequency of participation; and

(k) the requirements, if any, as to the experience or competence of a solicitor who wishes to go on the rota.

The justification for duty solicitor schemes

9.7 One effect of the duty solicitor scheme is to distribute criminal work among all the solicitors who take part in it. It has been suggested that this is the dominant motive for participating. If this is so, it is no discredit to self-employed people who must find work in order to earn a living. In any case, we are satisfied that these schemes are indispensable in a number of ways: they provide pre-trial advice to defendants who are often confused or ignorant and who have not previously obtained it, they encourage the adequate preparation of bail applications and help to reduce the number of ill-advised pleas, whether of guilt or innocence, and the number of remands required.

9.8   We are satisfied that, although there are at present certain weaknesses to be overcome, it is in the public interest that duty solicitor schemes should, as soon as possible, be available in some form in all magistrates' courts. In the smaller courts this may not involve the attendance of a solicitor at the court every day that the court sits, but it will, at least, involve his being on call to attend at short notice, should the need arise.

Suggested Improvements

Setting standards
9.9   In our view it is the responsibility of the Law Society to settle requirements and standards for duty solicitor schemes and to ensure that schemes are set up. These requirements, when approved by the Lord Chancellor, should be observed in any scheme supported by the provision of public funds. The standards laid down should be specific and should cover all the matters set out in paragraph 9.6 some of which we elaborate below. The Law Society should continue to include a report on duty solicitor schemes in its annual report to the Lord Chancellor on legal aid. If voluntary methods should prove unsuccessful in providing this essential service where needed, consideration should be given to the introduction of a system based on the employment of salaried lawyers.

Information and access
9.10   The provision of a duty solicitor scheme alone is not enough. Members of the public should be aware that the scheme exists and of the services which are provided; and they must be given this information at the time when it is most needed. Consequently, arrangements should be made to enable those in custody or awaiting a hearing to be told that a duty solicitor is available in sufficient time to enable them to make the best use of the service.

9.11   In this context, we stress three points. First, a person detained in custody should have a right to immediate legal advice. We accept that this right may have to be restricted in certain cases for the purposes of the detection or prevention of crime, but the onus of establishing the need for restriction lies on those who seek it. The point was emphasised during the inquiry by Sir Henry Fisher into the Confait case. His report drew attention in chapter 2 paragraph 23 and in chapter 17 to the requirement of principle (c) of the preamble to the Judges' Rules:—

> that every person at any stage of an investigation should be able to communicate and consult privately with a solicitor. This is so even if he is in custody provided that in such a case no unreasonable delay or hindrance is caused to the investigation or the administration of justice by his doing so.

The report pointed out that this provision will not protect persons in custody unless steps are taken to ensure that solicitors are available and willing to attend at police stations. Even then, the system will operate in the way which we think is desirable only if the provisions of the Judges' Rules are interpreted and enforced by the court on the basis of the principles discussed in this chapter.

9.12 These issues are at present under examination by the Royal Commission on Criminal Procedure and it is the responsibility of that Commission to recommend at what stage and in what circumstances a suspect or detainee should have access to legal services; we have drawn its attention to our views. It is our responsibility to recommend arrangements which will ensure that solicitors are available when needed. For this purpose, we regard a twenty four hour emergency service as a necessary part of a properly organised duty solicitor scheme.

9.13 Our second point relates to access by duty solicitors to defendants held in custody in a court. In our view, a duty solicitor should have direct access to unrepresented defendants who are in custody in the precincts of the court. As we have pointed out above, there is no point in providing a service unless those in custody know of its availability and have ready access to the duty solicitor.

9.14 We have been informed that defendants held in custody are more likely to make use of the services of a duty solicitor if approached in person than if invited to do so by means of a notice or by the police or the court staff. We consider, therefore, that, unless good reason can be shown to the contrary, duty solicitors or intermediaries, such as CAB workers, should be permitted to approach every defendant in the cells directly and duty solicitors should adopt this practice. As before, the aim of establishing the need for any restriction falls upon those seeking it.

9.15 In order that prisoners held in the cells may not be deterred from retaining the duty solicitor, there should also be a notice in each cell indicating that the duty solicitor will call to explain his functions. In explaining his functions, the duty solicitor should at the outset make it clear to each defendant why he has come and should stress that he has no connection with the prosecution, the police or the court. We recognise that this might give rise to anxiety about touting. We therefore recommend that there should be a code of practice for duty solicitors governing their approach to, and dealings with, defendants on the lines proposed above. This code of practice, breach of which would be a disciplinary offence, should be drawn up by the Law Society.

9.16 The third point is that in all the larger magistrates' courts there should be an easily identifiable information point, preferably at the main entrance to the court, indicating where defendants not held in custody but seeking the services of a solicitor can find the duty solicitor or the person acting as his contact. We have been told that in at least one court this information point is manned by staff from the local CAB and that the duty solicitor wears a badge which enables him easily to be identified. We regard these as sensible arrangements which could with advantage be adopted elsewhere.

9.17 Experience has shown that it is undesirable for court staff, police officers, ancillary staff or those supervising the cells to recommend particular solicitors or their firms to accused persons. Such a practice can lead to touting and corrupt practices. If a duty solicitor scheme is operated as proposed above, it becomes unnecessary for public officials to give guidance as to the choice of a solicitor, and in such circumstances it should be forbidden.

Financial considerations

9.18 Under present arrangements, solicitors who provide assistance to defendants under duty solicitor schemes usually act without charging a fee, unless the assistance given is covered by the legal advice and assistance (green form) scheme, or unless the defendant is granted legal aid by the court. In some cases solicitors do not collect contributions required under the green form scheme, nor do they make a charge to defendants who are not entitled to legal aid.

9.19 The first objection to the present arrangements is that the solicitor handling a case may not be fairly remunerated. The second is that legal services may be obtained on different terms by those who retain a solicitor before the hearing and by those who make use of the services of a duty solicitor at the time of hearing. The second objection will largely be removed if our proposals for criminal legal aid in Chapter 14 are accepted.

9.20 The Law Society proposed to us that the work of duty solicitors should be remunerated out of the legal aid fund at an hourly rate and should not depend on the number and personal circumstances of the defendants who are advised. Taking account of the fact that the duty solicitor scheme is like a legal first-aid post in which the solicitor is on stand-by duty, we agree that payment on an hourly or sessional basis is more appropriate than payment on a case-by-case basis. Such payment should be made only for attendance at times and places specified by the appropriate legal aid authority. Where a twenty four hour emergency service is maintained, in accordance with the recommendations made above in paragraphs 9.6(f) and 9.12, we consider that enhanced remuneration should be paid for work done at times or places giving rise to unusual difficulty or inconvenience.

Duty Solicitor Schemes and Legal Advice in Prisons

Needs for legal services

9.21 Persons on remand or serving sentences in prisons are at a disadvantage when seeking legal services, because they cannot visit solicitors and there may be some restrictions on their correspondence. Persons in prison may need or wish to seek legal advice in a variety of circumstances, in particular the following:—

(a) in relation to bail and legal aid applications, for representation at trial and for please in mitigation;

(b) in relation to a possible appeal against conviction and/or sentence and for representation at an appeal hearing;

(c) in relation to ordinary legal problems, unrelated to the offence for which a prisoner is in prison—problems concerned, for example, with a prisoner's marriage, the care and custody of children, housing, hire-purchase, wills and business affairs;

(d) in relation to matters internal to the prison, including complaints about staff or conditions, or in connection with disciplinary proceedings.

9.22   A prisoner, especially on remand, may have greater difficulty in getting in contact with a suitable solicitor than a person who is on bail. He may not know of a solicitor from whom he can obtain advice. If he does know a solicitor, he may practise at a considerable distance from the prison. The same difficulty may arise in any of the circumstances mentioned in the preceeding paragraph. In Chapter 14, we recommend procedures which should ensure that following conviction all persons receive advice about the possibility of an appeal. This alone will not overcome the problems described above which may result in many prisoners failing to obtain the legal advice to which they are entitled. In the following paragraphs we recommend means by which these needs might be met.

Duty solicitors in prisons
9.23   One means of meeting the need for legal services in prisons would be for salaried solicitors to be employed, or solicitors in private practice to be retained, by the prison authorities in order to provide legal advice to prisoners. We do not favour the employment of salaried solicitors for this type of work; it would not be satisfactory that the only readily available source of advice was a lawyer employed by the authorities. The lawyer might be exposed to conflicts of responsibilities, and his potential clients could suffer loss of confidence if he was not seen to be independent.

9.24   We recommend, therefore, that a rota of duty solicitors drawn from private practitioners in the locality should be set up in each prison. These rotas should operate on the same basis as rotas in the courts, in that they should be administered by the local law society in accordance with the guidelines laid down by the Law Society and the solicitors should be paid on a sessional basis out of the legal aid fund. Should it prove difficult to establish a rota because, for example, the prison is in an isolated area, it would be necessary to obtain assistance from the regional legal services committee which we described in Chapter 6. In such cases, it might be necessary for the legal services committee to arrange for payment of a special fee to cover the time spent travelling and staying overnight. The Home Office indicated in evidence that it would not object in principle to the establishment of lawyers' surgeries or duty solicitor schemes within prisons, provided that prisoners' access to them was subject to the existing controls and that they were subject to supervision in accordance with the Prison Rules. We discuss the question of restriction on access to legal services in paragraphs 9.27–9.29 below.

Designated officers for legal aid and appeals

9.25 The main link, at present, between prisoners and outside solicitors is a prison officer who is responsible for interviewing prisoners on their arrival in prison, for dealing with enquiries about how to obtain legal advice and with processing application forms for legal aid. He is described in the prison service as the "designated officer for legal aid and appeals". Although these officers have no professional qualifications, they receive training at a regional level and are provided with written reference material to help them in their job. The amount and quality of both training and written material varies from region to region. Designated officers are usually experienced, with a good knowledge of their responsibilities; although officially they do not provide advice, in practice they frequently help confused or inarticulate prisoners to apply for legal aid and to understand the purpose of the legal aid solicitors lists.

9.26 During our visits to a number of prisons, we met several designated officers and were impressed by the conscientious way in which they carried out their duties. It is clear that these officers play an important role in bringing legal services to prisoners and that, without them, prisoners' unmet needs would be substantially greater. We consider that there will continue to be a role for such officers after the introduction of duty solicitor schemes, because these officers are on the spot and are readily available to prisoners. They will also be able to act as a filter and continue to resolve minor problems themselves. In order that they may operate to their full capabilities, we recommend that a system of training and refresher courses should be set up and centrally coordinated to provide the information and instruction required. Reference books and similar material should be available and regularly updated centrally.

Restrictions on legal services

9.27 There are, at present, a number of restrictions on the access to legal services by prisoners. They apply in particular in respect of complaints against the prison authorities or individual prison officers and in disciplinary matters. The discipline and management of prisons are outside our terms of reference and we have made no study of them. We are, however, concerned with the provision of legal services and wish to offer some observations on the principles we regard as important.

9.28 As a matter of principle we consider that anyone should have access to the services of a lawyer if he thinks it necessary. Accordingly, we consider that a prisoner should be permitted to send letters without restriction to any solicitor whom he wishes to instruct on his behalf but that, for reasons of security, such letters should not be exempt from examination by the prison authorities. If confidential communication between client and solicitor is necessary, it should take place by way of oral consultation subject to such restrictions as are necessary for the purpose of security and the prevention of crime.

9.29 A prisoner charged with a disciplinary offence is not entitled to legal representation before a board of visitors or the prison governor. A governor may award a total loss of remission of up to 28 days; a board of visitors may award loss of remission of up to 180 days. Consecutive awards are possible. We regard a loss of remission as equivalent to an extended loss of liberty. In general, we consider that no one should face the risk of loss of liberty without the opportunity of legal advice and representation, though accepting that strict application of this principle in prisons should not impede disciplinary arrangements in relatively minor cases. Accordingly we think that there are good reasons against imposing a penalty involving loss of remission on any prisoner unless:—

(a) he has been given the opportunity of being legally represented; or

(b) the period of loss of remission awarded is seven days or less; or

(c) in circumstances such as those now prevailing in Northern Ireland, the Secretary of State on security grounds prescribes alternative arrangements.

Conclusions and Recommendations

Paragraphs

Standards	R9.1	The Law Society should take responsibility for introducing duty solicitor schemes, based on uniform and acceptable standards, in all magistrates' courts.	9.9
Information and access	R9.2	Persons in custody or awaiting a hearing should be informed in good time that a duty solicitor is available.	9.10
	R9.3	Persons taken into custody should, as a general rule, have immediate access to a solicitor.	9.11
	R9.4	Duty solicitors should normally have unrestricted access at the court to prisoners in the cells.	9.13
	R9.5	A code of practice for duty solicitors should be drawn up by the Law Society.	9.15

Paragraphs

R9.6   There should be an information   9.16
point in all magistrates' courts which
should, *inter alia,* indicate how duty
solicitors can be contacted.

R9.7   Court staff and police officers should   9.17
not recommend particular solicitors
to accused persons.

Remuneration   R9.8   Duty solicitors should be properly   9.20
remunerated and there should be
enhanced pay for work involving
special inconvenience.

Prisons   R9.9   Duty solicitors schemes should be   9.24
established in prisons.

R9.10   Designated officers in the prison   9.26
service should be provided with the
necessary training and information
under a centrally-organised scheme.

R9.11   Legal representation should be avail-   9.29
able to prisoners in future in certain
disciplinary proceedings.

CHAPTER 10

The Historical Background to Legal Aid

Civil cases from the fifteenth century to 1914

10.1 From early times special arrangements have been made to enable poor people to have access to the courts. The first formal provision for legal representation for the poor is a statute of Henry VII, passed in 1495, entitled "an Act to admit such persons as are poor to sue *in forma pauperis*". By this Act, a poor person was enabled to obtain a writ without payment, and the court dealing with such a case assigned counsel, attorneys and others to pursue the resulting proceedings; they gave their services without charge. The Act did not apply, in the common law courts, to defendants; and by the mid-eighteenth century a plaintiff had, at his own expense, to produce counsel's opinion as to the merits of his case.

10.2 In 1883 the statutory basis was changed by the Statute Law Revision and Civil Procedure Act, but the procedure remained that laid down in 1495, as subsequently amended and interpreted by the courts, and the principle of aid was still that (subject to tests of means) solicitors and counsel were assigned to a case by the court and thereafter made their services available free of charge.

Civil cases 1914–45

10.3 By 1914, in which year 99 applications were presented, the provision for poor persons in civil cases was plainly unsatisfactory. New rules for civil legal aid were therefore introduced and became known as the "poor persons' procedure". There was established for the first time a form of administration, known as the Poor Persons' Department. This department referred applications to a panel of reporting solicitors; if they reported favourably on an applicant's prospects of success, solicitor and counsel were appointed to act for him from a list of those willing to do so. Provision was to have been made for the expenses of lawyers so engaged to be paid out of a fund, financed out of public monies. In the event, this fund was never established and litigants had to meet the out-of-pocket expenses of their lawyers themselves. Apart from this, the lawyers were unpaid.

10.4 The 1914 arrangements were not a success. Civil legal aid was the subject of inquiries by separate departmental committees which reported in 1919, 1925 and 1928. The 1919 and 1925 committees were mainly concerned with the lack of solicitors to cope with poor persons' work. The 1919 committee proposed that the rules of financial eligibility should be tightened so as to reduce the number of cases and this was done. It also proposed amendments to the rules so as to ensure that no profit could be taken by a solicitor, the intention being to make the work more respectable from the point of view of solicitors of good standing. This failed to increase to a sufficient extent the number of solicitors participating.

10.5   The 1925 committee was faced with the same problem. Its leading proposal was to transfer the whole administration of poor persons' procedure to the Law Society. It recommended this on the ground that a system based on gratuitous legal services rendered by the profession must have the goodwill of the profession. This recommendation was implemented and for the next 12 years the arrangement proved reasonably successful in ensuring that work coming within the scheme was done.

10.6   The 1928 committee made two recommendations. First, no new arrangements were needed for legal advice save to encourage the system of poor man's lawyers, and the administrative organisation of this service should not be maintained by state subsidy. Secondly, legal aid should not be extended to county court cases unless the case had been remitted from the High Court. The two main reasons given for this recommendation were that "any scheme which might tend to make people more litigious should be deprecated" and that, in the absence of state-employed lawyers (an arrangement not acceptable in principle), there would not be enough solicitors to do the work. The recommendations of the committee were accepted.

10.7   The poor persons' procedure began to break down after the Matrimonial Causes Act of 1937 had increased the volume of divorce business. Applications doubled between 1929 and 1939. In the latter year the law societies of Wales resolved to withdraw from the scheme. They were bearing a large part of the burden of poor persons' work and they insisted that a reasonable fee should be paid to any solicitor conducting such cases. This ran counter to the prevailing policy of the Law Society. The government's response was to set up a committee but its work was cut short by the declaration of war and it never reported.

10.8   War-time conditions led both to a shortage of solicitors and to an increase in matrimonial problems, for which legal advice was difficult to obtain. This was thought likely to affect the morale of the fighting forces. In 1942 the Law Society established a department to improve the position, which was financed by government and employed salaried solicitors to conduct servicemen's divorces. The scheme was later extended to civilians and continued after the war in a reduced form, until 1962.

Criminal cases until 1930
10.9   In criminal cases before 1903, accused persons who could not afford to pay normal fees were dependent on representation by dock briefs, an arrangement by which the defendant was entitled to pick counsel to represent him from amongst the barristers who chose to remain in court for selection. The fee paid

was small—at its highest not more than two guineas for counsel and half a crown for his clerk. No solicitor could be appointed to assist in the preparation of a case on a dock brief and, as a rule, only the most junior counsel or the least employed made themselves available for this kind of work. In 1903 the Poor Prisoners' Defence Act made provision for legal aid in trials on indictment. This was supplemented in 1907, when the Criminal Appeal Act of that year made legal aid available for appeals in the Court of Criminal Appeal. No further changes took place until 1930.

Criminal cases 1930–45
10.10 The Poor Prisoners' Defence Act 1930 removed the requirement in criminal cases to disclose the defence to the lower court before legal aid was granted for trial in the higher courts. It also made provision, in serious cases, for legal aid for committal proceedings and for summary cases. Legal aid for appeals from magistrates was introduced by the Summary Jurisdiction (Appeals) Act 1933.

The general nature of legal aid until 1945
10.11 The characteristic of all measures for representation of poor people until the end of the second world war was either that they required lawyers to act as a matter of charity without making a charge, or that the fees which might be paid (often on a fixed scale) were inadequate and involved working at a loss.

The post-war changes
10.12 In 1944 a departmental committee was appointed under Lord Rushcliffe to inquire into the existing facilities for giving legal aid and advice to poor persons and to make recommendations. The leading recommendations of the Rushcliffe Report, which appeared in 1945, were that civil legal aid should be available in all courts and in all tribunals where lawyers had a right of audience; that it should be available not only to the poor but also to people of moderate means; that those who could not afford to pay anything should receive it free, and there should be a scale of contributions for those who could afford to pay something; that it should be administered by the Law Society; that solicitors and counsel should be paid reasonable remuneration for the work done; and that legal advice should be available in each centre of population to all those who could not afford to pay for it in the ordinary way, the advice to be provided by solicitors employed by the Law Society for the purpose.

10.13 All these recommendations were given statutory force by the Legal Aid and Advice Act 1949. Their implementation has been gradual but legal aid is now available for most proceedings before all the civil courts. The provision for representation before tribunals is not yet in general operation. Arrangements were made in 1959 for legal advice to be provided by solicitors in private practice. Improved arrangements were made by the Legal Advice and Assistance Act 1972 which introduced the "green form" scheme.

10.14 The Rushcliffe Committee recommended that legal aid should be available in all cases in criminal courts where this was desirable in the interests of justice, and that any doubt should be resolved in favour of the applicant. Solicitors and counsel were to have fair remuneration. The scheme was to be administered by the courts. These recommendations were all embodied in the 1949 Act although their implementation was not completed until 1963. In 1966 further recommendations were made in relation to criminal legal aid by a committee under the present Lord Chief Justice, then Mr. Justice Widgery, concerning, amongst other matters, the criteria for the grant of criminal legal aid and arrangements for contributions by an assisted person to the costs of his case. The latter arrangements were given statutory form in 1967.

10.15 In considering legal aid, both civil and criminal, and legal services generally, we have had regard to the valuable work which has already been done. This includes the 28 annual reports of the Law Society and of the Lord Chancellor's Legal Aid Advisory Committee on civil legal aid, the report of the Departmental Committee on Legal Aid in Criminal Proceedings referred to in the previous paragraph and the recommendations of the Legislation Working Party and the Financial Provisions Working Party which were commissioned by the Lord Chancellor's Advisory Committee and are annexed to its 25th to 27th reports. We have adopted as our own many of the recommendations of these bodies and here acknowledge the value we have found in their work.

CHAPTER 11

The Organisation of Legal Aid

The Present Systems of Legal Aid

Introduction

11.1 Legal aid takes three forms. First, there is legal advice and assistance in civil and in criminal matters, normally excluding representation in court proceedings; this is commonly known as the "green form" scheme. The second form of legal aid covers representation in civil proceedings and the third covers representation in criminal proceedings. Each of these types of legal aid has its own application forms, administrative arrangements and financial conditions. In this chapter we outline the general organisation. In subsequent chapters we indicate the changes in financial conditions and in administration which we suggest should be made.

The green form scheme

11.2 This scheme, which is administered by the Law Society, provides the quickest and simplest means of obtaining legal aid for limited purposes. The scheme covers legal advice and the assistance of a solicitor (and of counsel if needed) in writing letters and negotiating on a client's behalf , or in preparing legal documents such as contracts, wills or transfers of property. The scheme does not at present provide for representation in court or before a tribunal; however the Legal Aid Act 1979 empowers the Lord Chancellor to prescribe types of proceedings in respect of which representation may be provided under the green form scheme.

11.3 To obtain assistance under the green form scheme, the applicant goes direct to a solicitor. He provides details of his means, from which the solicitor himself determines whether the applicant comes within the financial limits of the scheme and, if so, whether any contribution is required from him.

11.4 When a solicitor has assessed his client as eligible for legal advice and assistance subject to a given maximum contribution, he presents his bill to the client in the normal way unless the amount exceeds the client's maximum contribution. When this occurs the solicitor bills the client for his maximum contribution and claims the balance from the Law Society's legal aid area committee on the green form from which the scheme takes its name. When the maximum contribution is small, many solicitors forgo it.

11.5 Contrary to popular belief, there is no limit to the amount of work which a solicitor may do under the green form scheme. It is, however, necessary for him to obtain authority from the legal aid area office before incurring costs in excess of £45 in matrimonial cases when these include the work necessary to file a divorce petition and £25 in other cases.

11.6   In 1977/78 some 300,000 cases were handled under the green form scheme in the following categories.

						%
Matrimonial and family	..	..	..	..		60
Criminal	..	..	..	..	..	15
Landlord and tenant		..	..	..	..	5
Employment	..	..	..	..	..	2
Hire purchase and debt	..	..	..	..		3
Accidents and injuries	..	..	..	..		3
Others	..	..	..	..	..	12
						100

The above figures are based upon a sample of 226,320 cases.

11.7   In some 26 per cent of cases, steps were taken, following the advice given, to apply for legal aid to cover representation in court proceedings. Payments to solicitors amounted to £6,399,771 and averaged £21 per case, while contributions were collected from assisted persons in about nine per cent of cases and totalled £255,962.

Legal aid in civil cases
11.8   This scheme provides for the conduct of litigation in civil cases and for representation in court by a solicitor or barrister. It is available only to individuals and not to firms or corporate bodies. An applicant may choose his own solicitor but the assessment of the client's means and the decision whether he is to have legal aid are not dealt with by the solicitor, as in the green form scheme. The decision whether or not to grant legal aid is made by or on behalf of one of the Law Society's legal aid area or local committees and the assessment of means is carried out by the Supplementary Benefits Commission on a basis more detailed than that of the green form scheme. The limits for financial eligibility and the method of assessing contributions are also different from those used for the green form scheme. They are set out in detail in Chapter 12.

11.9   As well as satisfying a test of financial eligibility, the applicant must establish that his case is one which it is reasonable to pursue. This is decided by the legal aid local or area committee, depending on whether the proceedings are at first instance or on appeal. These committees consist of practising lawyers who assess from their own knowledge and experience whether the applicant's case is one which a person in the litigant's position, able to pay the cost from private funds, would think it worthwhile to pursue. The right to grant but not to refuse legal aid is delegated to the committee's secretary.

11.10   In 1975/76 some 208,000 civil legal aid certificates were taken up by individual citizens. 178,000 or 87 per cent of these related to matrimonial and family matters. In 1977/78, following the abolition of legal aid for undefended divorce proceedings, some 149,000 civil legal aid certificates were taken up of which 111,000 or 74 per cent related to matrimonial and family matters. In 1977/78 solicitors' and barristers' charges amounted to some £33 million, and their other expenses totalled some £6 million. The average cost to the legal aid fund of each matrimonial proceeding in the High Court and the county courts was £101, and of each civil proceeding (mainly family and matrimonial) in the magistrates' courts was £64. The average cost, case by case, to the legal aid fund of other proceedings in the High Court was £562. Contributions retained came to £3.6 million. The Law Society's administrative costs in connection with all forms of legal aid amounted to £7.3 million, while those of the Supplementary Benefits Commission in connection with the making of assessments came to some £3.3 million.

Legal aid in criminal cases

11.11   The test of financial eligibility in criminal cases is different from that in civil cases, as is the contribution system. The decision whether to grant legal aid is made by the court. In practice the clerk of the court may grant legal aid on his own authority but must refer the application to the court if he considers that it should be refused.

11.12   In criminal cases anyone whose immediate resources do not exceed £75 (£120 in the case of married applicants) or who is on supplementary benefit, is eligible on financial grounds. Anyone else, however large his means, is eligible provided that it appears to the court that his means are such that he requires assistance in meeting the costs which he may incur. The court may, after a case has been disposed of, order the defendant to pay a contribution towards his costs. The court may also, when making the order, demand a down-payment on account which is refunded if no contribution order is subsequently made. There is no fixed scale, save that contributions must be reasonable, having regard to the assisted person's resources and commitments. The means of the applicant are assessed by the court but it may, and at the request of the defendant shall, ask the Supplementary Benefits Commission to make an assessment. The basis of assessment used by the court is normally that used in the civil legal aid scheme. The administrative costs of the criminal scheme are not known.

11.13   In 1977, 297,000 legal aid orders were made for representation in criminal cases in the magistrates' courts and 97,000 orders for representation in the Crown Court. Gross expenditure on representation in the magistrates' courts in the financial year 1977/78 amounted to some £20.9 million, and in the higher courts to £23.6 million. In 1977/78 £1.3 million was ordered in contributions in respect of all criminal proceedings.

The Present Administration of Legal Aid

The green form scheme and civil legal aid

11.14 It is the responsibility of the Law Society to ensure that advice and assistance and civil legal aid are available in accordance with Part I of the Legal Aid Act 1974. The Law Society's functions are discharged by its Council (in consultation with the General Council of the Bar) and, more particularly, by the Society's Legal Aid Committee which includes not less than three representatives of the Bar and a nominee of the Lord Chancellor. Two laymen participate in the work of the committee. These functions are exercised under the general guidance of the Lord Chancellor to whom the Law Society makes an annual report. The Lord Chancellor is advised by a statutory advisory committee, called the Legal Aid Advisory Committee, the members of which are appointed because of their knowledge of the work of the courts and social conditions. This committee advises the Lord Chancellor on particular matters which he may refer to it and comments on the Law Society's annual report. Its comments and recommendations are laid before Parliament, with the Law Society's report, by the Lord Chancellor.

11.15 England and Wales are divided for the purpose of civil legal aid into 14 areas, each with an area committee appointed by the Law Society. Within each area there are local committees appointed by the area committee. Area and local committees consist of practising solicitors and barristers. The Law Society employs area secretaries and local secretaries together with supporting staff to administer the civil scheme and service the committees.

11.16 The main function of local committees is to consider the legal merits of applications and determine whether it is reasonable for legal aid to be granted. The applicant must show both that he has a reasonable prospect of success and that it is reasonable for him to have the support of public funds. Where a local committee refuses, on legal grounds, to grant an application for civil legal aid (other than for civil proceedings in magistrates' courts), or attaches conditions to a grant, the applicant has a right of appeal to the area committee.

11.17 A determination by the Supplementary Benefits Commission as to the applicant's financial eligibility and the subsequent decision by a local or area committee on the financial terms on which legal aid is to be offered are final. Unless found to be entitled to free legal aid, an eligible applicant is asked to enter into a contractual arrangement under which he will pay a contribution based on his income during the 12 months following. If, however, his financial circumstances subsequently change he may apply for a re-determination of his means by the Supplementary Benefits Commission and, if his means increase substantially during the 12 months following the grant of the certificate, he may be required to submit to a reassessment.

11.18 The evidence we have received shows a high level of confidence in the Law Society's administration of legal aid and in the manner in which it has discharged its stewardship since the inception of the scheme. It has combined humanity in the handling of individual cases with prudence in the control of public funds. It is right to place on record the significant contribution thus made in the provision of legal aid over a long period.

Criminal legal aid
11.19 Applications for criminal legal aid are made either to magistrates' courts, or to the Crown Court, the Court of Appeal (Criminal Division), or the House of Lords. There is not, as there is in the case of civil legal aid, one agency, working through regional offices, which is responsible for administering the system as a whole. Because immediate decisions are necessary in criminal cases and bearing in mind our proposals about ministerial responsibility for legal aid in paragraph 11.22 and about criminal legal aid in Chapter 14, we consider it undesirable to create any such agency.

Ministerial responsibility
11.20 Ministerial responsibility is divided; indeed, so far as responsibility to Parliament for expenditure is concerned, it is fragmented. The Lord Chancellor is responsible for legislation and administration relating to the green form scheme (which covers both civil and criminal business) and to legal aid for civil proceedings. The Home Secretary is responsible for legislation and administration relating to legal aid for criminal proceedings in all courts.

11.21 The Lord Chancellor's Vote carries expenditure on the green form scheme, civil legal aid in all courts and criminal legal aid in the magistrates' courts. The Home Secretary's Vote carries expenditure on criminal legal aid in the higher courts. Thus the Home Secretary is responsible to Parliament for the administration of the magistrates' courts, in which the cost of both civil and criminal legal aid is borne on the Lord Chancellor's Vote, while bills for criminal legal aid are assessed by the Law Society in accordance with regulations laid down by the Home Secretary. The Lord Chancellor answers for the administration of the higher courts and while the expenditure on criminal legal aid is borne on the Home Secretary's Vote, the costs involved are taxed by officials of the Lord Chancellor's Department.

11.22   We are satisfied that the present complex division of ministerial responsibility for what is a comparatively modest programme, a net expenditure of £81 million in 1977/78, cannot be justified. There is a good case, from the point of view not only of the public and the legal profession, but also of good government and control of public expenditure, for vesting responsibility for legal aid in one minister; this is strongly supported by responsible witnesses who have given evidence to the Commission on this topic. We recommend therefore that, as we have already stated in Chapter 6, there should be one minister responsible for all forms of legal aid and that this should be the Lord Chancellor.

11.23   The two departments concerned, the Lord Chancellor's Department and the Home Office, have submitted evidence to us upon this point. They acknowledge that it can be argued that civil and criminal legal aid are best administered as a single system, but point out that it would lead to difficulties if the responsibility for criminal legal aid were separated from responsibility for the adminstration of criminal justice. We consider that another principle is of importance in this connection, namely that ministerial responsibility for framing and enforcing the criminal law should be kept separate from ministerial responsibility for the administration of criminal justice. It follows therefore that in recommending the transfer of responsibility for criminal legal aid from the Home Secretary to the Lord Chancellor we accept that this increases the strength of the case for transferring to the Lord Chancellor responsibility also for the administration of magistrates' and juvenile courts and for rules of procedure in all criminal courts.

The division between civil and criminal legal aid
11.24   By the same token it might be thought that there should be a single system of civil and criminal legal aid, administered locally by one agency. This is not, however, possible because the two systems differ in nature. For civil purposes it is essential to conduct an investigation of the applicant's case in order to determine whether it is reasonable for him to be granted legal aid. To ensure that the grant or refusal of legal aid does not affect the outcome of the case in any way, it is essential that this investigation be conducted by a body other than the court or tribunal which is to hear the case. In criminal cases, on the other hand, the applicant's eligibility is determined not by the merits of his case but by the seriousness of the charge brought against him. This can best be dealt with by the court before which the applicant appears. Separate systems of civil and criminal legal aid will therefore continue to be needed. In subsequent chapters we consider who should be eligible for legal aid, and under what conditions, and suggest changes in the way the schemes are administered.

Conclusions and Recommendations

Paragraphs

Ministerial responsibility	R11.1	The Lord Chancellor should be responsible for all forms of legal aid.	11.22
Division between civil and criminal legal aid	R11.2	Separate systems of criminal and civil legal aid will continue to be necessary.	11.24

CHAPTER 12

Legal Advice and Assistance and Civil Legal Aid: Financial Considerations

Nature of the scheme

12.1 The intention of the Rushcliffe Committee in recommending that a civil legal aid scheme be set up for individual litigants, was that such a scheme should benefit not only the poor but also those of moderate means. It was not however contemplated that the scheme should be of universal application. The scheme set up on the Committee's recommendations imposes financial limits on eligibility for assistance and on the levels of contributions.

12.2 The civil legal aid scheme is open-ended, in the sense that no limit can be imposed on the level of demand from those eligible. When the scheme first began there were, therefore, introduced both a requirement that the reasonableness of the proceedings should be assessed and an elaborate apparatus for means-testing. It was reasonable at the time to take such precautions, because there was no dependable prior experience of such a scheme in this or any other country. Thirty years have now passed and the experience gained suggests that the arrangements for means-testing are over-elaborate. They are strongly influenced by the nature of the financial provisions, with which we shall deal in this chapter.

Factors to be considered

12.3 Two main factors have to be kept in mind when considering the provision of civil legal aid.

(a) *Eligibility.* It is necessary to decide who is intended to benefit from the scheme. The extent of the scheme is controlled by imposing limits related to the applicant's income and capital and by excluding certain classes of persons such as corporate bodies. It is affected also by the level of contributions required of assisted persons, for high contributions act as a deterrent.

(b) *Scope.* It is possible to restrict the scheme to specific classes of legal business, or to exclude certain categories of business from its operation. Initially its scope was limited, but it is now so wide that it is more easily discussed in terms of what is excluded. We deal with this in Chapters 13 and 15.

Background

Growth of the scheme

12.4 We traced in Chapter 10 the growth of the civil legal aid scheme. This has been achieved in two ways. The number of courts and proceedings in which legal aid is available has increased steadily, starting with the High Court and Court of Appeal in 1950 and adding, in succeeding years, the county courts, appeals to the House of Lords, certain civil proceedings in the magistrates' courts and the Lands Tribunal. The number of legal aid certificates issued increased substantially over the years, mainly as a result of growth in litigation, in particular concerning divorce. In the full first year of operation, about 38,000 legal aid certificates were authorised. In the year 1976/77 the total was 211,337. This number included undefended divorce cases, which ceased to be eligible for legal aid on 1st April 1977. In 1977/78 the number of certificates authorised fell to 149,455.

Changes in the numbers eligible for legal aid

12.5 By contrast with the growth we have just described, there was, until early 1979, a steady decline in the number of those eligible for legal aid. It has been calculated that the proportion of the population eligible for legal aid on income grounds in 1950 was over 80 per cent. The proportion actually eligible was smaller because a number of those eligible on income grounds would have had sufficient capital to render them ineligible. By 1973 the proportion of the population eligible on income grounds alone is estimated to have declined to 40 per cent. This decline would have been even greater but for an increase in the proportion of old age pensioners and single parent families in the population. Between 1964 and 1974 the proportion of households with children eligible for legal aid on income grounds is estimated to have declined from 60 per cent to 23 per cent and no more than an insignificant fraction of such households were eligible for legal aid free of contribution. This decline in eligibility reflects the fact that, whereas the financial limits for legal aid kept pace with changes in the retail price index, they did not keep pace with the rise in average net earnings of the population.

12.6 The decline appears to have been arrested and partly reversed for a time after 1974, in a period when prices rose faster than average net earnings. It is estimated that in 1976 some 30 per cent of households with children were eligible for legal aid on income grounds. The decline probably resumed when average net earnings again started to increase faster than prices. The proportion of population and of households eligible for legal aid has, however, increased sharply, as a result of the changes in financial limits introduced in April 1979. These are described in subsequent paragraphs.

Assessment of means

12.7 As we explained in Chapter 11, an applicant for legal aid is subject to a test of means. The present method of assessment varies as between the scheme for legal advice and assistance (the green form scheme) and the scheme for civil legal aid, which is used largely for representation in civil litigation, both in court and in the preparation of a case for hearing. In both schemes, if the income and capital of an applicant are below certain limits, he is entitled to

113

legal aid without any contribution. If either income or capital is above other higher limits, no legal aid is at present available. Between the limits, the applicant is required to pay a contribution.

Legal advice and assistance – the green form scheme

12.8 In order to be eligible for free legal advice and assistance under the green form scheme, an applicant's disposable income, during the seven days preceding his application, must not have exceeded £35. If his disposable income during that week amounted to £75 or less, he would be eligible for legal advice and assistance subject to a contribution. 'Disposable income' in this context is defined as gross income from all sources after the deduction of tax, national insurance contributions and certain allowances in respect of dependants. An applicant in receipt of supplementary benefit or family income supplement is eligible provided that his capital is within the prescribed limit. In order to qualify for advice and assistance, an applicant must have not more than £600 of capital, apart from his principal dwelling house and its contents. The effect of dependants' allowances is to increase this figure, so that for a married man with two children it is £980.

12.9 Contributions range from £5 for those with a disposable income for the week in question exceeding £35 but not exceeding £40, to £56 for those with a weekly disposable income between £72 and £75.

12.10 The maximum contribution payable in respect of legal advice and assistance under the green form scheme is limited to a proportion of the disposable income of the preceding week, not merely because the scheme is thereby simple to operate but principally because the cost of such advice and assistance is itself limited in amount. We pointed out in paragraph 11.5 that a solicitor must seek the authority of the legal aid area office to incur costs greater than £45 in matrimonial work where it is intended to petition for divorce and £25 in other cases. Such applications are increasing but are made in only a minority of cases; in 1977/78 the average cost per case of legal advice and assistance, after deducting contributions charged, was £21.

Civil legal aid – the eligibility limits

12.11 Since April 1979 an applicant has been eligible for civil legal aid if his estimated disposable income, as defined in paragraph 12.13 below, during the twelve months following his application, does not exceed £3,600. Should his disposable capital be in excess of £2,500, however, he will be refused legal aid unless his disposable income is below £3,600 and his case is likely to cost more than the maximum contribution which he could be required to pay. The assessment of both disposable income and disposable capital is at present made by the Supplementary Benefits Commission.

Disposable income and capital

12.12 Disposable income is calculated on a more detailed and generous basis for the purposes of civil legal aid than for legal advice and assistance. From

114

gross income there are deducted income tax, national insurance contributions, allowances in respect of dependants (set out in Table 12.1), rent or mortgage payments together with rates, the cost of travelling to and from work, certain other expenses connected with employment and the first £208 of income derived from capital. Prior to April 1979 there was also an allowance of £104 for hire purchase commitments which was increased to the full amount of such commitments if they exceeded that sum. This allowance is no longer to be made after April 1979. Instead, a discretionary allowance may be given for large hire purchase commitments for essentials. To calculate disposable capital, there is deducted from gross capital the value of the principal dwelling house, the tools of the applicant's trade and, save in exceptional cases, household furniture and effects. Before April 1979 further allowances against capital were given in respect of dependants. When the limits were substantially increased, these allowances were abolished.

Table 12.1

Civil legal aid: allowances for dependants against gross income

Dependants							Allowances before 6.4.1979	Allowances as from 6.4.1979
							£	£
Spouse	..	..	..	..	..	..	504	909
Child under 5	..	..	..	..	..	..	229	344
Child 5–10 ..	..	..	..	..	..	..	276	414
Child 11–12 ..	..	..	..	..	..	..	341	511
Child 13–15 ..	..	..	..	..	..	..	413	620
Child 16–17 ..	..	..	..	..	..	..	497	745
Dependant over 18	..	..	..	..	..		647	971

Source: Lord Chancellor's Department.

12.13 The allowances made for these purposes have an important effect on the scope of legal aid. For example, the more generous the dependants' allowances, the greater the number of households with children brought within the scope of the scheme.

Free limits and eligibility limits

12.14 Below certain levels of disposable income and capital, no contribution is required from an assisted person. We refer to these levels as the 'free limits'. Above certain levels of income and capital, legal aid is not available save in the circumstances mentioned in paragraph 12.11. We call these levels the 'eligibility limits'. Between the 'free limits' and the 'eligibility limits', contributions from income or capital are payable. Table 12.2 sets out changes made in the limits with effect from April 1979. The second column shows the limits applicable before that date, and the third, the limits applicable thereafter; where appropriate the figures in the second column have been adjusted to include the allowance of £104 for hire purchase commitments (see paragraph 12.12) in order to place them on a basis comparable to those in the third column.

115

TABLE 12.2

Financial conditions for civil legal aid

Free and eligibility limits of disposable income and capital	Equivalent disposable limits before 6.4.1979	Disposable limits as from 6.4.1979
	£	£
Income limits		
Free limit (below which legal aid is free) ..	919 pa[1]	1,500 pa
Eligibility limit (above which legal aid is not available)	2,704 pa[1]	3,600 pa
Capital limits		
Free limit	365[2]	1,200
Eligibility limit	1,700[2]	2,500

[1]Adjusted as stated in paragraph 12.15, last sentence.
[2]Before the inclusion of capital allowances for dependants (see paragraph 12.12).
Source: Lord Chancellor's Department.

Civil legal aid–the contributions

12.15 An applicant whose annual disposable income exceeds £1,500 but does not exceed the eligibility limit of £3,600 is therefore required to make a contribution towards the cost of his case. The maximum contribution amounts to one-third of his annual disposable income in excess of £1,500. In April 1979 the Lord Chancellor announced that he intended to reduce to one-quarter the proportion of an applicant's annual disposable income in excess of £1,500 that would be payable as a contribution. At the time of writing this change has not taken effect. The applicant is also required to make a contribution from capital equivalent to the amount by which his realisable capital exceeds £1,200, exclusive of the value of his principal dwelling house and its contents.

The amount of the contributions

12.16 The following table shows the contributions from income and capital which were required for legal aid before 6th April 1979 and those now prevailing.

TABLE 12.3

Civil legal aid: maximum contributions required from disposable income and capital

	Before 6.4.1979	After 6.4.1979
	£	£
Income		
Free limit	919 pa	1,500 pa
Eligibility limit	2,704 pa	3,600 pa
Contribution of income in excess of the free limit ..	one-third	one-quarter[1]
Capital		
Free limit	365[2]	1,200
Eligibility limit	1,700[2]	2,500
Contribution of capital in excess of the free limit ..	the whole	the whole

[1]Not in force at the time of writing.
[2]Dependants' capital allowances affected the level of capital limits before 6th April, 1979: see the text, paragraph 12.12.
Source: Lord Chancellor's Department.

12.17 An applicant's disposable income is based on an estimate of his gross income for the year following the date of the application, after making the deductions referred to in paragraph 12.12. The contribution is expressed as a proportion of the excess of his disposable income for that year over £1,500. The contribution represents the applicant's maximum liability. It is not dependent on the length of the case and, accordingly, no adjustment is made if the case lasts for less or more than one year. The contribution is normally collected by monthly instalments over a period of one year.

12.18 The expression 'free limit' in Table 12.3 represents the net income which would be left in the hands of a single person without dependants after deducting from his gross annual income the items specified in paragraph 12.12. The net income of married persons with or without children is higher than their disposable income and that of a single person because of the dependants' allowances which are built into the computation. The following table makes this clear.

TABLE 12.4

Relation between disposable, net and gross income, by family status of litigants

	Single person	Married no children	Married two children aged 4 & 8	Married four children aged 4, 8, 12 & 14
	£	£	£	£
Annual disposable income	1,500	1,500	1,500	1,500
Allowances for dependants	—	909	1,667	2,798
Annual net income after taxation and after the outgoings below	1,500	2,409	3,167	4,298
add				
Outgoings[1]	577	654	689	766
Taxation[2]	404	593	780	1,170
Gross annual income	2,481	3,656	4,636	6,234

[1]For the purpose of this table outgoings comprise national insurance and a notional sum of £8 per week in respect of rent, rates, mortgage and other payments (see paragraph 12.19).
[2]Taxation is calculated on the basis of the allowances announced by the Chancellor of the Exchequer in April 1979.
Source: Supplementary Benefits Commission.

12.19 Levels of eligibility and rates of contribution are expressed in terms of disposable income. Table 12.5 illustrates the approximate gross annual income of a single person, of a married couple and of a married couple with two children aged four and eight, with various disposable incomes. The allowances used in the calculations are those in force at 6th April 1979 save for the tax allowances which are those announced by the then Chancellor of the Exchequer in April 1979 but not yet brought into force. A notional sum of £416 a year is included for rent, rates and other allowable expenses. It must be appreciated that the gross income required to achieve the disposable income in column 1 will vary according to the particular circumstances of the applicant concerned. Thus, if the applicant pays more than £416 a year in respect of rent, rates, mortgage and other payments, as many do, his gross income, relative to his disposable income will be higher. The table therefore gives an impression, but cannot give a precise indication, of actual gross incomes.

TABLE 12.5

Comparison of disposable and gross incomes

Disposable income	Gross income		
	Single person	Married couple	Married couple with 2 children 4 & 8
£	£	£	£
1,500 ..	2,481	3,656	4,636
1,750 ..	2,894	4,070	5,052
2,000 ..	3,308	4,484	5,466
2,250 ..	3,722	4,898	5,880
2,500 ..	4,133	5,311	6,292
2,750 ..	4,546	5,724	6,702
2,900 ..	4,796	5,971	6,999
3,000 ..	4,960	6,135	7,116
3,250 ..	5,374	6,548	7,521
3,500 ..	5,787	6,962	7,896
3,600 ..	5,954	7,117	8,043
3,750 ..	6,200	7,340	8,266
4,000 ..	6,614	7,714	8,461
4,500 ..	7,399	8,460	9,386
5,000 ..	8,145	9,206	10,138
5,500 ..	8,891	9,985	10,971
6,000 ..	9,704	10,831	11,870
7,000 ..	11,530	12,755	13,932
8,000 ..	13,706	15,078	16,385
9,000 ..	16,366	17,880	19,433
10,000 ..	19,583	21,418	23,203

Source: Supplementary Benefits Commission.

12.20 The estimated average gross earnings of men in full-time employment in April 1978 was £4,650 per year. The figures at April 1979 have not yet been compiled but we are informed that they are likely to fall in the region of £5,200 to £5,300.

Criticisms of the system

12.21 The main criticism of the system, as it was up to 6th April 1979, made forcefully to us in evidence, was that the eligibility limit was too low. Only the poorest received legal aid in civil cases. Those of moderate means were not eligible. We have traced the reasons for this in paragraphs 12.5—12.6. The criticism has to some extent been met by the improvements introduced in April 1979. We believe, however, that concentration on the levels of the eligibility limit has distracted attention from the question whether in principle it is desirable to have any egibility limit.

12.22 The levels of contribution have been criticised because they act as a deterrent. There is evidence that a number of persons eligible for legal aid do not take it up because the contributions required from income and capital are more than they are able or willing to pay. The Law Society has provided us with figures showing that in the month of January 1979, of those offered legal aid subject to a contribution, 14 per cent of those whose contributions were less than £50 failed to take up the offer. When the contribution exceeded £50, about one-third of the offers were not taken up. This raises a question of general principle whether a contribution should be payable at all and, if so, on what basis. We deal with this point further in paragraph 12.32.

12.23 The extent of the present scheme is said to be insufficient because it does not cover tribunals, with which we deal in Chapter 15, nor certain classes of action such as defamation, with which we deal in Chapter 13. Other features of the present scheme which call for attention are referred to either later in this chapter or in Chapter 13.

The Future

Financial and statistical information
12.24 Since legal aid was first introduced its scope and extent have, as we pointed out in paragraph 12.5, been greatly enlarged. The changes made in April 1979 have been widely welcomed and have improved the position materially. We emphasise, however, that these changes served mainly to correct a long decline in the proportion of the population which was eligible for legal aid. Whatever further changes are made, we feel that it is essential to ensure that a similar decline does not occur again in the future. Increases in the financial limits which kept roughly in line with the retail price index proved not to be satisfactory and led to a substantial fall in the number of those eligible for legal aid. Therefore there should be regular revisions based wholly or largely on average net earnings and, in view of the many factors which enter into the cost of legal aid, we believe that it will be necessary to devise a special formula for the purpose of calculating the changes required.

12.25 Before considering what further changes, if any, are needed in the financial provisions of the civil legal aid scheme since the new proposals came into force on 6th April 1979, we comment on certain limiting factors.

12.26 The public funding available for legal services depends on the financial resources which the government of the day is in a position to allocate to them in the face of competing demands such as education, health, defence and many others. There are also competing or conflicting demands within any allocation of funds that is made for the provision of legal services. Rapid growth of expenditure on civil legal aid might lead to cuts or restrictions on criminal legal aid or on the provision of law centres; alternatively, the introduction of legal aid for tribunals, which is already a pressing need, might have to be deferred. Decisions must often depend on the relative cost of one scheme against another.

12.27 We emphasise that if there is to be proper provision for legal services in the future and balanced decisions are to be made, a regular flow of information concerning needs and the estimated cost of different options will be required. It will be necessary for the operation of the publicly-funded legal services to be constantly monitored and there should be a continuing programme of research into these subjects.

Further changes in the financial provisions
12.28 We expressed the view in paragraph 5.18 that the principle on which legal aid should be based is that no assisted person should suffer an undue financial burden. What constitutes an undue financial burden must ultimately rest on an empirical judgment after study of relevant financial and statistical data. We feel that this principle should be considered in relation to four main areas:—

(a) eligibility limits;

(b) free limits;

(c) contributions;

(d) alterations in the methods of calculating disposable income and disposable capital.

Eligibility limits
12.29 The present financial limits are based on the principle adopted by the Rushcliffe Committee that legal aid should be directed both to the poor and to those of moderate means. In observing this principle, imposing an upper limit of eligibility has the advantage that those of more than moderate means can with certainty be excluded. But this is not necessarily desirable. People with higher incomes pay higher taxes and should, in principle, be entitled to benefit when need arises from schemes provided out of public money. They may need less help than others. If so, an adjustment in the legal aid scheme can be made by appropriate levels of contribution. It does not follow that they should have no help at all.

12.30　An upper limit of eligibility is arbitrary and may operate unfairly. A person whose resources fall above the line is denied assistance of any kind. It is true that a person whose resources fall just below the line may be required to make a substantial contribution. Nevertheless he will still enjoy a considerable benefit as compared with someone who is ineligible for assistance, because the fixed nature of the contribution operates as a limitation on his liability regardless of the outcome of the case and its total cost. Even when the contribution is large, the benefit of the security provided by such an arrangement is considerable.

12.31　This advantage is most marked in litigation. Elsewhere we recommend measures by which the legal profession may operate with greater efficiency and economy. We advocate a review of all procedures and administrative arrangements to simplify and speed up the administration of justice. But even when all measures of this kind have been taken, we are satisfied that the cost of any substantial piece of litigation will be formidable and beyond the pockets of nearly all private individuals.

12.32　We are satisfied that, as long as eligibility limits exist, the effect will, in some cases, be to create unfairness and to expose some individuals to a choice between abandoning their legal rights and accepting the risk of suffering an undue financial burden. The eligibility limits for both capital and income should, therefore, be abolished.

12.33　Criticism has been voiced of the arrangement whereby there are separate methods of assessing contributions and computing disposable income for the green form and the civil legal aid schemes. The assessment of the income contributions on the basis of the previous week's income in the case of the green form scheme and on the estimated income during the twelve months following the application in the case of civil legal aid, inevitably gives rise to anomalies. It can be accepted that, when the general limits of eligibility are low, there are sound reasons of policy for providing advice and assistance at advantageous rates. If however the principle is adopted that no assisted person should suffer an undue financial burden, we see no reason why levels of contribution assessed in accordance with that principle should not apply to every form of legal service.

12.34　It would be convenient in many ways to assimilate the financial provisions in the schemes of advice and assistance and of legal aid. This would make it more straightforward to calculate the effects of changes in levels of eligibility and contributions and to put them into operation. Both solicitors and those advising in generalist advice agencies such as the CABx could more readily explain to inquirers the effect of a single set of financial provisions. In a case which did not stop at advice and assistance but in due course required representation under legal aid, the assisted person would know from the outset his maximum liability under the scheme. While we therefore favour assimilation of the financial provisions, we note that under present arrangements, although contributions under the green form scheme are lower, the provisions for calculating disposable income are less favourable to the applicant than those of the civil legal aid scheme. This is because the advice and assistance scheme assumes the provision of a smaller range of services at lower cost. If the financial provisions were assimilated on present levels of eligibility and contribution, a number of persons who can now obtain the benefit of the advice and assistance scheme would have to pay substantially more by way of contribution. We recommend therefore that the financial provisions of the two schemes should be assimilated at the time when measures are taken to improve the levels of eligibility and contribution as proposed in this chapter. We discuss the procedure to be followed in making the assessment in Chapter 13.

The free limit — income

12.35   In the early stages of our work, fixing with precision the right level for the free limit of legal aid was not an important consideration. By universal consent, the limits of eligibility for legal aid were far too low, and what appeared to be required from us was a strong recommendation that a substantial increase was necessary, with a broad indication, based on available information, as to the level thought desirable. At a time when our work was approaching completion, new levels for limits of eligibility were announced, making an appreciable increase over earlier limits. It then became desirable to give, if possible, a more precise indication of the proper level for the free limit. This is important not only in itself but in its effect on contributions which are payable by all assisted persons whose resources are above that limit.

12.36   We have already stated the principle which should be applied, namely, that no undue financial burden should be imposed on an assisted person. What constitutes an 'undue' burden is in the last analysis a matter of personal impression, but different factors must clearly be taken into account at different levels of income. On the one hand, an undue burden cannot fairly be defined in terms of excess of available income over a basic minimum subsistence level. Although certain essential items of expenditure such as housing are covered by the method of calculating disposable income, nearly everyone is committed to other items of expenditure which cannot be categorised as mere luxuries and would experience hardship if required to reduce them substantially. On the other hand, a person whose income is above the average may be able to raise money at need, repaying it over a period of time, without suffering undue hardship.

12.37   Our studies of data relating to family expenditure support the view that a family with children is under appreciably greater financial pressure than a single person or a couple with no dependent children. We take account also of the fact that the Users' Survey (Volume II section 8 table 4) showed that the time of life at which couples are setting up house and starting a family appears to be the period of the highest demand for legal services. These factors confirm us in the view that, in framing the allowances and levels of eligibility, particular attention should be paid to households with children. We shall relate the discussion in the paragraphs following to the household comprising a husband, wife and two children.

12.38   Table 12.5 shows the relationship between disposable income and gross income for different types of household, making certain assumptions throughout in respect of outgoings such as rent, rates and travel. In practice, the calculation of disposable income is based on the expenditure of each applicant on these items and not on fixed figures. We appreciate, therefore, that it is more convenient to base limits of eligibility on disposable rather than gross income, and we are aware that the Financial Provisions Working Party considered but rejected the possibility of basing limits on gross income. We intend however to express our own view on the desirable level of the free limit in terms of gross income because proposals made in terms of disposable income are difficult for the ordinary reader to equate to his own experience of earning and spending.

12.39   Although, as we point out in paragraphs 12.26 – 12.27 more research and data are required for the purpose of making a fully-informed decision, it is in the last analysis a matter of subjective judgment to decide what constitutes an unfair financial burden. We think it right that we should record our own judgment as to the appropriate level for the free limit.

12.40   Making the same assumptions as to level of expenditure for the purpose of calculating disposable income as are made in Table 12.5, we are in broad agreement that for a married couple with two children the right level for arriving at the free limit should be based on a gross income of £7,000 a year at April 1979 levels of earnings. This is more than the average earnings of adult males in April 1979, but we are informed that it is in the region of the average household income for a married couple with two children in April 1979. A gross income of £7,000 a year for a married couple with two children would represent on this basis a disposable income of £3,000 a year. Some of us would have preferred a higher limit; others consider that below a disposable income of £3,000 a modest contribution should be payable.

The free limit – capital
12.41   The present free limit of disposable capital is £1,200 as shown in Table 12.3. It is arrived at after deducting from the gross capital the value of the principal dwelling house, the tools of the trade and, save in exceptional cases, household furniture and effects. All applicants are treated on the same basis and no deductions are made for married couples, children or other dependants. The whole of the applicant's capital above the free limit is required as a contribution and it is normally paid in a single lump sum.

12.42   We have no reliable information as to the disposable capital which might now be held, or have been accumulated, by the bulk of the population and the circumstances of the applicants are in any event likely to be widely different.

Sometimes capital assets are the result of a windfall, sometimes, with increasing frequency, the result of a redundancy payment. The thrifty applicant who has saved all his spare income is required to contribute the whole of his savings above a disposable figure of £1,200 up to the eligibility limit of £2,500. The applicant who has spent up to the limit of his income and made no effort to put savings aside will not be required to make any contribution from capital because he will have none available. There is unfairness in this situation. Other inequalities are likely to arise, depending on whether the applicant is married or single because the calls on resources of married couples with children are greater and they have less opportunity for saving. If, however, both spouses are in work and there are no children, the opportunity for saving is greater. The age of the applicant is also a factor which can be expected to have a bearing on the capital available because those in the higher age brackets will have had more opportunity for saving and may have inherited some assets on the death of parents or relations.

12.43 There are the same difficulties in making an assessment of the appropriate free limit of capital as there are in the case of income limits. It must be borne in mind that disposable capital includes not only cash in hand but also assets such as motor cars and insurance policies whose cash value can be realised; also that experience has shown that the overall contribution from capital is very small. Bearing these factors in mind, we think it right, as before, to give our own view of the appropriate free limit. We consider this to be £10,000.

The contributions – general
12.44 There is evidence that, in the past, the level of contribution required of assisted persons has operated as a deterrent (see paragraph 12.22). A large proportion of those eligible did not pursue proceedings with the assistance of legal aid because they were unable or unwilling to pay the contribution required. Even though the position has been improved by the changes made in April 1979, it will be necessary to make a further study of contribution rates because, in the absence in the future (if our recommendations are adopted) of any eligibility limits, the level of the contribution and the way it is assessed will have an important effect on the extent and use of legal aid.

12.45 It is argued that a contribution serves a number of purposes. Levels of contribution can be arranged so as to enable resources to be used where needs are greatest. Those in greatest need can be provided with a free service. Those able to meet the expense of minor legal services can be required to pay for them in full but can be helped, when they most need it, in facing unusually heavy costs. Since legal services in the civil courts may be used not only to protect essential rights, but also to gain some personal or financial advantage, it is reasonable that there should be payment according to means.

12.46 It is arguable that for certain classes of legal proceedings no contribution should be required. It is proposed, for example, that no contributions be levied in personal injury litigation on the practical grounds that it is not financially worthwhile to do so. However, provided the free limits are fixed at realistic levels, we consider that, as a general principle, all who receive legal advice or assistance subsidised out of public funds, for litigation or other purposes, should do so on the same terms and that a contribution should be required in all cases above certain levels of income and capital.

Contributions — income

12.47   The contribution out of income is at the time of writing one-third, but in April 1979 Lord Elwyn-Jones, then Lord Chancellor, said that he intended to reduce it to one-quarter. This figure of one-quarter would apply to disposable income in excess of £1,500 up to the eligibility limit of £3,600. It will be recalled that we have recommended earlier that the eligibility limit be abolished.

12.48   The proposed reduction from one-third to one-quarter is a welcome relief, particularly in the light of the weight of evidence that one-third is too high and gives rise to hardship. In our view, however, a contribution of one-quarter is still too high a proportion to exact in the circumstances of many contributors, on whom it is likely to impose an undue financial burden. If a single level of contribution is required we suggest that it be reduced to one-fifth. But we believe that a better method of assessing the contribution, where upper limits of eligibility are removed, is to base it on a sliding scale. This should start at a relatively low figure of 10 per cent and increase by 1 per cent for each £200 of disposable income up to a maximum of 25 per cent in order that it may fall progressively more heavily on those with large incomes who have less need of financial support.

12.49   For the purpose of illustrating our recommendations concerning the free limit and the levels of contribution we set out in the following table against annual disposable income (which we assume to be calculated in the same way as in Table 12.5) the levels of contribution which would be required under present arrangements, and under a free limit of £3,000 on the basis of a straight one-fifth contribution and on the basis of a sliding scale starting at 10 per cent.

125

TABLE 12.6

Contributions from income

Disposable income[1]	Gross income married couple 2 children 4 & 8[2]	Maximum contribution		
		¼ disposable income above £1,500	1/5 disposable income above £3,000	sliding scale above £3,000
£	£	£	£	£
2,000	5,466	125	nil	nil
2,500	6,292	250	nil	nil
3,000	7,116	375	nil	nil
3,500	7,896	500	100	54
4,000	8,461	625	200	120
4,500	9,386	750	300	223
5,000	10,138	875	400	290
6,000	11,870	1,125	600	510
7,000	13,932	1,375	800	760
8,000	16,385	1,625	1,000	1,010
9,000	19,433	1,875	1,200	1,260
10,000	23,203	2,125	1,400	1,510

[1]The equivalent gross income for a single person and for a married couple with no children are set out in Table 12.5.

[2]On the basis set out in paragraph 12.19.

Contributions — capital

12.50   Until April 1979 the contribution of capital was the whole of the capital above the free limit of £365, up to the eligibility limit of £1,700; certain dependants' capital allowances were added to these figures. The present contribution is the whole of the capital above the free limit of £1,200 up to the eligibility limit of £2,500.

12.51   Amongst the majority of the population, disposable capital arises wholly or mainly from savings. The evidence we received showed that the previous contribution, which took the whole of the applicant's capital above the free limit, gave rise to great hardship and very often absorbed the bulk of his hard-won savings accumulated over many years. The changes proposed in April 1979 raise the free limit to £1,200 but still require the contribution to be the whole of the capital above that figure. We feel that this requirement is harsh and that it is too large a proportion to exact from what, in most cases, represents the applicant's savings. If an undue financial burden is to be avoided we think that further relief is justified.

12.52   If, as we recommend, the upper eligibility limit is abolished it will in any event be necessary to reconsider what contribution should be payable above the free limit. We suggest, as in the case of the contribution from income, that although it might be a flat rate of one-fifth above the free limit, it would be better calculated on a graduated scale. We suggest a contribution beginning at a relatively low figure of 10 per cent and rising by steps of 5 per cent per £5,000 of disposable capital to a maximum contribution of 25 per cent. This would have the effect that all those with a substantial fund of capital would, other than in exceptional cases, bear the whole of any legal costs for which they might become liable.

12.53   In order that the reader may appreciate the effect of the foregoing recommendations we set out in the table below the maximum contribution that would be payable if the free limit of disposable capital was fixed at £10,000.

TABLE 12.7

Contributions from capital

Disposable capital				Maximum contribution	
				1/5 disposable capital above £10,000	sliding scale above £10,000
£				£	£
10,000	..	..	..	nil	nil
12,500	..	..	..	500	250
15,000	..	..	..	1,000	500
17,500	..	..	..	1,500	875
20,000	..	..	..	2,000	1,250
25,000	..	..	..	3,000	2,250
30,000	..	..	..	4,000	3,500
40,000	..	..	..	6,000	6,000
50,000	..	..	..	8,000	8,500
75,000	..	..	..	13,000	14,750
100,000	..	..	..	18,000	21,000

Calculation of disposable income
12.54   We set out in paragraph 12.12 the method of calculating disposable income. We have no recommendations to make in this respect save that we think that the allowances for children could with advantage be amended. It will be seen from Table 12.1 that these vary according to the age of the child. We think that it would simplify the scheme and add little or nothing to the cost if the allowance for each child up to the age of 18 was £550.

Calculation of disposable capital
12.55   Whilst agreeing with the present provisions for calculating disposable capital, we recommend that, in making this calculation, any sum arising from damages for personal injury should be excluded. We draw attention also to the increase in the frequency and amount of redundancy payments which are intended to provide compensation for loss of income. We recommend that further study should be made of the possibility of excluding capital arising from such payments and similar sources in appropriate cases. We recommend also that double assessment should be avoided where possible. When capital is brought into charge, the income derived from it should be excluded. This will simplify the calculation, for there will be no need to take into account investment income, in respect of which a deduction is now made, subject to a limit of £4 a week.

Combination of capital and income

12.56 Under the present scheme, if an applicant's resources fall above the contribution-free income limit and below the contribution-free capital limit, a contribution from income alone is made. If his resources are below the income free limit but above the capital free limit a contribution is made only from capital. If the applicant's resources fall above both income and capital free limits a contribution is made from both sources. We agree with this arrangement and consider that it should remain in force.

Supplementary Points

Legal services for groups

12.57 Since it was first introduced, the purpose of legal aid has been to provide assistance to individuals. We think it important, as a matter of principle, that this purpose should be preserved. If it is not, it would in practice be impossible to prevent the use of legal aid by a variety of associations, partnerships, companies and corporations, many of whom would be financially self-sufficient and able to charge the cost of most legal expenses against revenue for tax purposes.

12.58 We consider that this principle should be relaxed where a number of individuals in a locality form a group because they have a common interest or a common problem. Frequent examples are to be found in tenants' groups or associations, formed to deal with inadequate services from a landlord or his oppressive conduct, and residents' groups formed by people affected by developments in their neighbourhood. Groups so formed may be loose aggregations of individuals, constantly changing in composition, or more formal associations. Such groups may serve a number of useful purposes. Views can be put with greater force. Work in a group causes people to feel more able to help themselves and to influence events. Groups can cope with modern bureaucracy more effectively than most individuals. Such groups often need legal advice in order fully to understand the legal implications of a situation and the legal remedies available. In any event, time and expense can be saved if legal advice and assistance is given to a group rather than to its members individually.

12.59 Under present arrangements, legal advice and assistance is available to each of the persons in a group in his individual capacity, if he is entitled to it under the regulations. A legally-aided service may also on occasions be made available for a group as a whole, but the principles on which this can be done are not defined and there is no settled practice. Before considering how the problem of groups should be approached, a distinction must be drawn between legal advice and assistance and legal aid for the purposes of civil litigation.

12.60 Legal aid is available only in rare cases for groups involved in litigation. It is possible for a single plaintiff or defendant to represent others in a representative action, when it is desired to assert or defend a right on behalf of, or against, a large and possibly fluctuating body of persons: the example often given of such a group is that of the commoners in a certain district. It has not

128

been suggested to us that the present arrangements by which legal aid may be granted in such cases should be changed. Further developments in this area of the law, if they are thought desirable, depend on changes in the rules of court, a matter outside our remit. In what follows, therefore, we are concerned with legal aid for the purpose of providing advice and assistance to groups.

12.61   We consider that the rules relating to legal aid should enable legal advice and assistance to be made available to groups either by CLCs or by solicitors in private practice. A simple recommendation to that effect would not, however, be satisfactory. Unless the nature of the groups which are to receive legal advice and assistance is carefully defined, the result of such a recommendation would be to open the gate too widely. It would be impossible to apply an effective means test and many wholly unjustified claims for legal advice and assistance would become admissible.

12.62   In summary, we have come to the conclusion that:—

(a) legal advice and assistance should be made available for groups but the groups which would be entitled to receive it should be carefully defined as proposed below;

(b) no change is necessary to the principle that, for the purpose of civil litigation, legal aid should be confined to individuals save in representative actions as described in paragraph 12.60.

12.63   We suggest the following provisions should be adopted to identify the groups which would be entitled to legal advice and assistance.

(a) Groups may be constituted on a formal or informal basis, but the minimum requirements are that:—

(i)   a register should be maintained of the names and addresses of the individuals comprising the group and regularly updated;

(ii)   the members of the group should have a personal interest in the purpose of the group;

(iii)   a secretary should be appointed;

(iv)   the purpose of the group should be recorded in writing in the register;

(v)   the register should be available for inspection by an interested party.

(b) The group would not be entitled to legal advice and assistance if:—

(i)   it is carrying on a trade or business or operating for profit;

(ii)   it carries on party political activities;

(iii) it has access to adequate funds.

(c) The only purpose for which legal advice or assistance should be available should be to protect the members of the group in respect of their legal rights, duties and liabilities.

(d) A group should be entitled to four hours' advice and assistance without contribution if two-thirds of its members are entitled to legal aid without contribution.

(e) Initially the solicitor or law centre instructed by the group should determine whether advice may be given without charge. This determination should be based not on a means test of all members but on a statement supplied by the secretary, combined, when applicable, with personal knowledge of the group or the locality.

(f) If more than four hours' advice and assistance is required, the legal aid area committee should be given the available information about the group through its secretary. It should be within the discretion of the area committee to decide, in the light of all the circumstances, whether further legal aid should be available and on what terms as to contribution.

12.64 The proposals made above must be tested in practice and will need refinement in the light of experience; guidelines will need to be issued to legal aid area committees, and updated as necessary, to ensure consistent treatment of groups throughout the country. We believe nevertheless that an arrangement on these lines will fulfill the need for this form of legal advice and assistance which is at present lacking in many communities.

12.65 Under these proposals, legal advice and assistance would be available only in respect of legal rights, duties and liabilities. On occasions a public inquiry is set up which may be of importance to a group but does not at that stage directly involve issues relating to legal rights, duties or liabilities of the individual members, for example a road scheme inquiry. We consider that such inquiries are not appropriate for the legal aid scheme but that, in future, the legislation which authorises the inquiry should specify the manner in which the various parties affected by the inquiry should be represented and the way in which funds for this purpose are to be provided. If public funds are provided in this way, a CLC should be entitled to accept instructions to appear in the same way as lawyers in private practice.

Use of legal aid for business purposes

12.66 At present there is no restriction preventing an individual using legal aid for the purposes of trade or business. This conflicts with the principle, which we regard as important, that legal aid should not be available to corporations. The reason is that if corporations require legal services for business purposes, the cost ranks as a business expense against taxation, and it is not, in our view, appropriate to grant legal aid when the equivalent expense is allowed as a charge for taxation purposes. When the limits of eligibility for legal aid were low, no serious anomaly arose. On humanitarian grounds, it was not desired to deny legal aid to a self-employed worker in a small way of business, for example a jobbing gardener or a small shopkeeper. If eligibility limits are removed and further changes are made, as we propose, in the levels of contribution, it may become possible for persons running substantial business enterprises as individuals to make use of legal aid for business purposes. If this is permitted, there is no reason why corporations also should not have it. We recommend therefore that legal aid for this purpose should not be available. Any expense in obtaining legal services which is allowable as a charge for tax purposes, either as a charge against revenue or by way of capital allowances, should be excluded from legal aid.

12.67   This recommendation could cause hardship for those we have mentioned, in a small way of business. They have until now been entitled to legal aid, and we do not wish to make their position worse. It is not a serious breach of the principle to allow legal aid in such cases. We consider therefore that the recommendation made in the preceding paragraph should be qualified to the extent that a person entitled to legal aid without contribution (that is, with disposable income and capital below the free limits) should receive it, whether for a business or a private purpose.

Use of legal aid for conveyancing

12.68   We do not, however, consider it appropriate that the resources of the scheme should be used to assist those buying and selling houses. The cost of conveyancing services is a small part of the total cost of such a transaction and we do not consider that it creates an undue financial burden; the transfer cost is, or should be, taken into account by a purchaser when considering how great a total cost he can afford and by a seller, when estimating how much his sale will realise. If it is desired to confer a benefit on those buying and selling houses, consideration should be given to reducing stamp duty rather than providing legal aid. If, however, a transaction is not concerned with buying and selling houses, although it might be categorised as conveyancing, we do not consider that legal aid should be withheld. In the rare cases where litigation arises in the course of a sale and purchase of a house, we consider that legal aid should be available as at present on the usual terms.

Effect of increased benefits and simplification

12.69   Increased benefits, by reducing hardship in marginal cases, enable a broader and simpler approach to be adopted. The improvements in benefits made in April 1979 were accompanied by measures to simplify the scheme which will enable an interview by the Supplementary Benefits Commission to be dispensed with in most cases. The improvements in benefits which we propose will enable the conditions and methods of assessment to be further simplified on the lines set out in Chapter 13.

Conclusions and Recommendations

			Paragraphs
General principles	R12.1	The financial provisions of legal aid should be regularly updated in future to avoid the long downward drift which took place up to April 1979.	12.24
	R12.2	Reliable financial and statistical information concerning publicly funded legal services is necessary.	12.27
	R12.3	The principle underlying the provision of legal aid should be that an assisted person should not suffer an undue financial burden in pursuing his legal rights.	12.28
	R12.4	The eligibility limits should be abolished.	12.32
	R12.5	The green form scheme and civil legal aid should be assimilated when the financial provisions applicable to legal aid are improved.	12.34
Free limits	R12.6	The free limit of disposable income should be increased to £3,000.	12.40
	R12.7	The free limit of disposable capital should be £10,000.	12.43
Contribution	R12.8	The contribution from income and from capital above the free limits should be reduced to one-fifth, or preferably calculated by reference to a sliding scale.	12.48 and 12.52
Allowances	R12.9	Children's allowances against income should be simplified.	12.54
	R12.10	The method of calculating disposable capital should be revised as stated in the text.	12.55

Paragraphs

R12.11 Legal aid should be available to groups on the basis set out in the text.   12.62–12.63

Scope   R12.12 Legal aid should not be used for business purposes, except to the limited extent stated in the text.   12.57–12.58

R12.13 Civil aid should not be available for legal charges relating to buying and selling houses.   12.59

CHAPTER 13

Legal Advice and Assistance and Civil Legal Aid: The Administrative Aspects

Introduction

13.1 In the previous chapter, we examined the different levels of eligibility, the rates of contribution and the methods of calculating contributions for the green form and civil legal aid schemes and recommended ways of removing certain anomalies. In this chapter, with the aim of effecting further improvements, we consider means of simplifying the general administration of both the green form and civil legal aid schemes and reducing administrative costs. We also examine the procedures for assessing and collecting contributions and for determining whether assistance is merited in any given case. Finally we consider the scope of the schemes and suggest ways in which they should be extended. The administration of criminal legal aid is dealt with in Chapter 14.

The Phases of the Legal Aid Scheme

The parts of the scheme

13.2 In future, civil legal aid should, in our view, proceed in three phases which we describe below. These are the initial half-hour which should be provided free; work which the solicitor may do on his own authority, which in general should be limited to four hours; and work requiring the approval of a legal aid committee.

The initial half-hour

13.3 Since June 1977, a large number of firms of solicitors have provided an initial interview of half an hour for a fixed fee of £5. This arrangement, which is not covered by either the green form or the civil legal aid schemes, was introduced by the Law Society because social agencies, such as CABx, had found that some clients were reluctant to go to solicitors' offices when it was not possible to tell them in advance the maximum cost of an initial interview.

13.4 This scheme has proved valuable in persuading clients to consult solicitors and we regard its introduction as greatly to the credit of those many solicitors who thereby participate in providing a subsidised service. We consider that the cost of this service should no longer be borne by the profession and recommend that it should become the first element in the civil legal aid scheme. It should be used by the solicitor to examine the case, explain the scope of the legal aid scheme and make a preliminary assesement of means as set out in paragraph 13.16.

13.5 Although the introduction of a fixed fee for an initial interview has undoubtedly been of value, it is nevertheless open to the criticism that it does not wholly overcome the fears of those who are, or might be, eligible for legal aid, in particular their fear of a means test. Accordingly we recommend that this initial half-hour's interview be available to any applicant who seeks advice from a solicitor who undertakes legal aid work. It should be provided irrespective of the applicant's means and without charge, provided that the subject in question is one for which assistance may properly be provided under the legal aid scheme. This service should, therefore, be paid for out of the legal aid fund.

13.6 There are two objections to the arrangements we propose. The first is that many people are able to afford half an hour's advice and the state should not subsidise them. While we recognise the truth of this, we nevertheless believe that unless the initial period of advice is known to be free in all cases, those who have most need of the services of a solicitor may still be deterred from approaching him. The second objection is that the scheme may be abused by vexatious litigants and other persons who, having been advised that a case is bad or not worth pursuing, seek to go from solicitor to solicitor in hope of discovering one who will give them more encouraging advice. The number of vexatious litigants is not high and there is no evidence that the present arrangements are abused in the way suggested. To reduce the risk of abuse, however, we consider that a solicitor approached by a client seeking free advice under the half-hour scheme should ask the client whether he has previously obtained free advice on the matter. If so, the solicitor should charge the client for the interview. The cost of the scheme is uncertain and estimates vary widely. It cannot be predicted with any certainty whether or not it will be used for inessential purposes or largely by those who can afford to pay for advice. We recommend, therefore, that a carefully monitored pilot scheme be set up without delay to enable accurate assessments to be made.

The four-hour scheme

13.7 We propose that the second phase of the civil legal aid scheme should be the advice and assistance (but not, as a general rule, representation) which the solicitor may provide on his own authority and in respect of which he both assesses and collects the contributions (see paragraphs 13.16 – 13.17 below). This element should be broadly similar to the present green form scheme subject to a number of variations.

13.8 The amount of advice and assistance that a solicitor may provide on his own authority under the green form scheme before he must obtain permission from the legal aid area office is defined in terms of a money sum (see paragraph 11.5). We think that this is inappropriate in an age of inflation. We recommend, therefore, that the amount of work that a solicitor may do on his own authority should be defined in terms of a number of hours of work. The limits now imposed on the fees which may be charged are £45 for matrimonial work where it is intended to file a petition for divorce and £25 in all other cases, representing at present about three hours of work in the first case and about two hours in the second. Applications for leave to incur additional expenditure in 1977/78 were

135

made in about nine per cent of cases. Taking this into account, and with a view to providing a sufficient time to enable most cases to be dealt with without an extension, we regard four hours' work as appropriate in addition to the initial half-hour referred to in paragraph 13.5. If a solicitor wishes to provide more than four hours' advice and assistance, he should be allowed to do so only on the authority of the legal aid area committee.

13.9 The four-hour period should be kept under review. If it proves too long or too short, either in general or for specific classes of work, appropriate changes should be made. The Lord Chancellor under recent legislation has power to prescribe matters or proceedings in respect of which the solicitor may, on his own authority, (a) undertake more than £25 worth of work for the client; or (b) represent the client in proceedings before a court or tribunal, without reference to the legal aid committee as described in paragraph 13.8. Similar provisions should apply to the scheme we propose.

Representation
13.10 The third part of the civil legal aid scheme should cover representation in proceedings. This part should be on the same lines as at present in that authority would have to be obtained from the appropriate legal aid committee. Some variations in procedure however would in our view be advantageous, as we explain later in this chapter.

Assessment and Contributions

The present position
13.11 As we explained in Chapter 11, under the green form scheme the client's means are assessed and any contribution payable is calculated by the solicitor on the basis of information supplied by the client. The solicitor himself collects the contribution from the client in whatever way is agreed between them. Under the civil legal aid scheme, the solicitor forwards the client's application to the local legal aid office, whence it is sent to the Supplementary Benefits Commission (SBC) which gathers and verifies information about the applicant's means and calculates the maximum contribution that is payable. From April 1979, as a result of the regulations then brought into force this procedure has been simplified. If the application is approved and the applicant decides to proceed, the contribution is collected by the Law Society. Generally speaking, that part of the contribution derived from capital is collected in advance in the form of a lump sum; that part derived from income is collected in monthly instalments as the case proceeds.

Weakness of the present system of assessment
13.12 The system which we have described above has been developed in its present form because it has been considered necessary, since the start of the scheme, to ensure that assessments of eligibility and of the contributions payable are made with the greatest possible accuracy. The assessment of eligibility and of the level of contributions under the green form scheme have been left in the

hands of individual solicitors because the cost to public funds of each case under this scheme is small; a more complex system of assessment would be neither practical nor cost-effective. The more detailed method of assessment, tailored to fit the circumstances of each applicant is, however, considered necessary for cases under the civil legal aid scheme, where the cost to public funds of each case is likely to be substantially greater.

13.13   This dual system is open to criticism. Although there is force in the argument that every case should be assessed as accurately as possible, especially if the levels of eligibility and rates of contribution are such that a small variation in the assessment may have a disproportionate impact on the ability of the applicant to proceed with his case, the present system of assessment under the civil legal aid scheme is complex and time-consuming. The cost of the assessments carried out by the Supplementary Benefits Commission during 1977/78 amounted to some £3.3 million. As can be seen from Table 5.1, this cost was barely covered by the amount collected in contributions under the civil legal aid scheme which amounted to some £3,650,000. Under the regulations recently introduced the cost may be lower, but the simpler the requirements of assessment, the stronger the case for avoiding the expense of a reference to the SBC.

13.14   Another aspect of the present system which is open to criticism is that a client who has received assistance under the green form scheme and has undergone a test of his means subsequently has to submit to a further test in applying for civil legal aid. As we showed in paragraph 11.7 in 1977/78, some 26 per cent of clients who obtained legal advice and assistance under the green form scheme subsequently applied for civil legal aid in respect of the same problem. However short the case and however low the contribution, if any, a complete reassessment of means was nevertheless required in every case.

The proposed new system of assessment
13.15   The SBC and its predecessor, the National Assistance Board, have formed an important part of the legal aid administration for over twenty five years and tribute is due to the service they have provided. Their knowledge and expertise was necessary when the financial conditions of legal aid were complex and in some cases required detailed investigation. In April 1979, at the time when the levels of eligibility for civil legal aid were raised, the opportunity was taken to simplify the calculation of disposable income. We consider that in these circumstances it should not be necessary to call on the services of the SBC and that in future the responsibility for assessing income and capital should be transferred to the Law Society.

13.16   We envisage that the procedure to be adopted will be as follows. We propose that, in every case, an initial assessment of means should be carried out by the solicitor on the basis of information supplied by the client. The solicitor will seek information from the client about his capital and income. In a large number of cases it will be found that the applicant's means are clearly below the

137

limits of capital and income and no further assessment will therefore be necessary. If it appears that the client is, or might be, liable to pay contributions it will be necessary for the solicitor to make a detailed assessment on the basis of the client's disposable income and of his capital resources. He should be paid for doing this (see paragraph 13.68).

13.17   If the services provided for the client are restricted to those which the solicitor may undertake on his own authority, as defined in paragraph 13.8, the assessment which he performs will be final and he will collect the contribution from his client in a single sum or on whatever basis may be agreed between them. We envisage that a solicitor will need to request guidance or assistance from the legal aid committee only in cases of doubt or difficulty when the means of an applicant are not easy to quantify; this is most likely to occur with the self-employed. In such cases he should ask the legal aid area committee for advice. Should the solicitor provide more than four hours' advice and assistance on the authority of the legal aid area committee, he will still assess and collect the client's contribution.

13.18   When services are provided on the authority of a legal aid committee for representation in proceedings (these being the services that are likely to be of greater cost to public funds), the solicitor should continue to make the assessment which will be subject to checking and verification by the Legal Aid Department of the Law Society. The Department should also undertake any special investigation or other work which may be needed in difficult cases. In all such cases, the Law Society should also be responsible for collecting the contribution from the client in the form of a lump sum or in instalments or a combination of both, as appropriate.

13.19   We believe that this procedure will reduce both the time spent and the cost of assessing contributions. Simple ready reckoner tables should be provided to facilitate the work of solicitors.

Aggregation of resources of minors and spouses
13.20   Regulations made under the Legal Aid Act 1974, provide that, when legal aid is applied for on behalf of a minor who is not above school leaving age, his eligibility and contribution shall be determined not on the basis of his own means but on the basis of the aggregated means of the minor and his parents or guardians. The effect of this rule is, therefore, that no minor may obtain legal aid unless his parents or guardians, who are themselves not necessarily parties to the case in question, are themselves eligible. The result of this may be that a minor's interests may be allowed to go by default if the parents or guardians are unable or unwilling to bear the risk and cost of litigation. We think it undesirable that the rights of minors should be capable of being harmed in this way and we recommend, therefore, that the aggregation rule relating to minors should be abolished.

138

13.21   The regulations under the Legal Aid Act 1974 also provide that the eligibility and liability to pay contributions of an applicant for legal aid shall be calculated on the basis of the aggregated means of the applicant and his or her spouse, unless the spouses have contrary interests in the matter for which legal aid is being sought, or are separated and living apart. When limits of eligibility and dependants' allowances were low, this rule excluded from eligibility many families, often poor families, in which both parents worked, and it contributed therefore to the sharp decline in the number of families eligible for legal aid, which we discussed in paragraphs 12.5–12.6. This difficulty has, to some extent, been reduced by the improvements made in April 1979 but we believe that it can only fully be overcome by the abolition of the aggregation rule. The rule as to aggregation of the incomes of husband and wife operates for many different purposes, such as taxation and social security, with which our terms of reference are not concerned. Even so, we consider that the benefits to be obtained from relaxation of the rule in relation to civil legal aid are considerable and we recommend, therefore, that the incomes of husband and wife should not be aggregated in assessing legal aid contributions, unless the need to apply this rule consistently in this and other fields constitutes a compelling reason of social policy to the contrary.

Scope of the contribution

13.22   We recommended earlier that the level of contributions and the procedure for assessing them should be the same whether services are provided by a solicitor on his own authority or on that of a legal aid committee. It follows that, if the legal services provided under both headings are concerned with a single problem, they should be covered by a single assessment of contribution. Thus, if a client receives advice and assistance on a particular matter and subsequently engages in litigation on the same matter, he should be liable to pay a contribution once only. It sometimes happens that a client who has obtained advice and assistance on a matrimonial problem discontinues the matter for a period in order to seek a reconciliation but subsequently, on the failure of the attempted reconciliation, seeks further advice. In such cases, for the purpose of computing the contribution payable, the further assistance, provided that it is sought in reasonable time, should be regarded as a continuation of the previous advice and assistance. Should a client, however, obtain legal services on two different and unrelated matters he should be liable to pay a separate contribution in respect of each of them.

The Administration of Legal Aid

The merits of the case

13.23   We have already referred in paragraph 11.9 to the procedure under the civil legal aid scheme whereby each application is considered on its merits before a certificate is granted. Litigation involves two or more parties. A person should not be allowed, with support from public funds, to involve others in litigation without good reason. Moreover, the commitment to litigation is open-ended. It cannot be predicted for certain at the outset whether a case will go to appeal or what the final cost will be. It is therefore appropriate that any person who wishes to engage in private litigation in any civil matter, at public expense, should be required to show that he has reasonable grounds for doing so. Examination of the case may show that he is best advised not to pursue it, but to abandon or settle it. Any applicant, whether plaintiff or defendant, should be required to justify an application for legal aid in order to avoid maintaining with public funds a case which is without foundation.

The tests to be applied
13.24   An applicant for civil legal aid is required to show that he has reasonable grounds for taking, defending or being a party to proceedings. In addition, he may be refused legal aid if it appears unreasonable that he should receive it in the particular circumstances of the case. Under the first part of this test an applicant has to show that he has a good case in law and in fact. In our view, this test should be retained unchanged.

13.25   The second part of the test is concerned with the merits of the case generally and the extent to which there would be real advantage in pursuing it. This involves wider considerations going beyond the legal merits. The time honoured method used by legal aid committees in applying this test is, as the Law Society have told us in evidence, to ask:—

> What advice would be given to the applicant if he were a private client with means which were not over-abundant but were adequate to meet the probable costs of the case without involving him in hardship?

This test is not appropriate to a case in which legal aid is needed to relieve the financial plight of the applicant, for example to obtain benefit under welfare legislation or maintenance from a spouse. In such cases, the Notes for Guidance issued by the Council of the Law Society say:—

> . . . it is unrealistic to consider what decision a properly advised client of adequate means would make, and attention has to be directed to the value of the benefit sought for that particular applicant, bearing in mind the chances of success and the cost of achieving it.

13.26   The matter was considered in 1956 by the Select Committee on Estimates of the House of Commons which took the view that it is wrong to adopt the actions of the man of adequate but not over-abundant means as the test of whether legal aid should be granted. We agree with the Select Committee and, while we believe that it is important that legal aid committees should continue to apply strict criteria in sifting the applications for legal aid which come before them, we think that they should take into account any factors peculiar to the applicant or his case which might justify the grant of legal aid. For the reasons given by the Select Committee, the factors to be considered should include such matters as injury to an applicant's reputation, status, civil rights or personal dignity; in such cases, we think that a certificate will often be justified though the sums of money involved may be small. We agree with the change in the criteria which enables legal aid to be granted where a case is of such a nature that success by an applicant would benefit a large number of other people in similar situations. This might include claims by consumers and social security or employment cases of potentially wide application though involving relatively small claims. Where a benefit is conferred in this way on an identifiable group, it may be appropriate to recover a contribution, under the arrangement proposed in paragraphs 12.62–12.63.

The handling of legal aid applications

13.27 There are two tiers of administration responsible for legal aid in any given area, each with its committees: these are the area committees and, under them, the local committees to whom applications for legal aid are made. Although made to a legal aid local committee, by no means all applications go before a committee as such. Since 6th April 1979, local secretaries have delegated powers in all cases to grant, but not to refuse, applications for legal aid without referring them to a certifying committee. Accordingly, in such cases the papers go before a committee only when its secretary is uncertain whether legal aid should be granted or considers that it should be refused. This is, in our view, a sensible arrangement.

13.28 Where an appeal is lodged against a decision by a local committee it is determined by the area committee. A hearing takes place at which the applicant has a right to appear on his own behalf or to be represented by a solicitor or any other person he chooses. We think that the present system whereby an initial decision not to grant legal aid, or to grant it for a limited purpose only, is subject to appeal is sound and should be retained but there is room for some rationalisation of present arrangements.

13.29 The Law Society is already taking steps to regroup local committees and their staffs into the same premises as area committees. We agree with this policy, since local offices do not in practice provide a local service. They are not often visited by members of the public and solicitors deal with them by post and by telephone. We suggest that these changes should make it possible to merge the area and local committees and, in effect, abolish the local committees. The power to grant legal aid on the basis set out in paragraph 13.28 would thus be assumed by the secretary of the area committee. Where in particular cases he was not minded to do so the matter would go to a panel of the area committee. For the purpose of an appeal the panel's decision should be subject to review by another panel of the area committee.

13.30 In order to ensure the continued participation of practitioners in the work of area committees, it may be undesirable appreciably to reduce the existing number of legal aid areas. We understand, however, that it is the policy of the Law Society to bring the boundaries of legal aid areas into line with the reorganised local government boundaries. This accords with our proposals in Chapter 6 for the establishment of regional committees to coordinate legal services.

The membership of legal aid committees

13.31 Local and area committees consist of solicitors and barristers. Some 3,000 solicitors and 600 members of the Bar sit on these committees. Local committee members are normally called on three or four times a year. Area committee members are called on up to twelve times a year. Preparation for a meeting can take up to five hours, and the meeting itself up to three hours, to which must be added travelling time. Members receive an *honorarium* of £11 for each meeting they attend. A number of us have visited area committee meetings and have been impressed by the high standard of service which is provided. We consider it essential to the proper administration of civil legal aid that members of the legal profession should continue to provide this important service which is carried out in a thorough and painstaking manner, often outside normal working hours.

13.32 We have considered whether laymen should sit on the committee panels which grant or refuse legal aid. The Legal Aid Advisory Committee, while advocating the participation of laymen in the administration of the legal aid scheme at both national and regional levels, considered that such a development should not interfere with the principle that a decision whether legal aid should be granted should be taken by a committee composed of practising lawyers, being both professionally skilled and independent. We agree with this opinion.

Emergency certificates for representation

13.33 In urgent cases application may be made to the Law Society for an emergency grant of legal aid. We are satisfied that in cases where the facts themselves constitute an emergency, for example where a child is about to be removed from the country, the procedure is in general working satisfactorily, but difficulties may arise if during a public holiday it is not possible to get in touch with the appropriate officials.

13.34 In those cases where it has proved impossible to obtain an emergency certificate because the officials or committee members could not be contacted at short notice and in which it can be shown that a genuine emergency existed, we think that an application made after the event should, in proper circumstances, be approved retrospectively by the Legal Aid Committee of the Law Society. The number of cases in respect of which retrospective certificates might properly be granted is likely to be small and they should not be issued in cases where there has been a failure to obtain legal aid for any other reason, such as oversight by the solicitor.

Delays in granting certificates

13.35 We have examined the time taken to grant civil legal aid certificates and the reasons for the delays that occur. The following were the main factors which determined the length of time taken to issue a legal aid certificate.

(a) *Time taken by the Supplementary Benefits Commission*
The present system requires the Commission to conduct a detailed assessment including in some cases, unless the applicant is in receipt of supplementary benefit, personal interviews.

(b) *Delays resulting from incomplete applications*
In some cases an applicant's solicitor failed, or was unable without delay, to produce information or documents which were required before the application could be dealt with.

(c) *Delays between meetings of legal aid committees*
Although local and area secretaries have delegated powers to deal with cases, there are still some cases which have to go before a committee.

(d) *Delays between the offer of legal aid and the issue of a certificate*
When legal aid is offered subject to a contribution the applicant is given an opportunity to decide whether or not to accept the offer. The time taken in 1976 by such applicants varied, on average, from 16 days at the Hull local office to 40 days at the Manchester local office.

13.36   In civil cases analysed in a survey during 1976, the average time taken to issue a legal aid certificate was 49 days, 28 days of which were taken up by the SBC's determination of eligibility and liability to pay the contributions. In cases where the applicant was adjudged liable to pay a contribution, it took an average of 69 days to issue the legal aid certificate, of which 36 days were required by the SBC. The figure of 69 days is distorted by a small but significant proportion (some 12 per cent) of applications which took more than 3 months to process. The average time taken in these cases was 122 days: in the remaining 88 per cent it was 38 days.

13.37   There is a difference, as between the local committees, in the time taken to handle legal aid applications. For example, in 1976 it varied, for all cases, between an average of 34 days in Hull, 67 days in Plymouth and 79 days in London West. The percentage of cases taking more than 84 days to handle was 4.3 per cent in Hull, 24.4 per cent in Plymouth and 38 per cent in London West. The London committees handle a larger number of complex and weighty matters than do others; there are also regional variations in the tempo at which administrative, business and legal life is conducted. Nevertheless we believe it should be possible to achieve greater uniformity, as well as an overall reduction in the time taken to handle applications. We recommend that the Law Society includes details of the time taken to handle such applications in its annual report to the Lord Chancellor.

13.38   These delays should be considerably reduced as a result of our proposals in this and the previous chapter, in particular our recommendation that the procedure whereby contributions are assessed should be streamlined and transferred from the SBC to the individual solicitor and the Law Society. In addition the transfer of the functions of local committees to area committees will eliminate one layer of administrative work and, in many instances, will enable time and money to be saved.

The conduct of cases under legal aid

13.39   While a legal aid certificate is in force, the assisted person's solicitor conducts the proceedings in the same way as in any other case, subject to certain controls which are intended to protect the public purse. Thus a solicitor must obtain the authority of the area committee for any steps requiring significant extra expense, such as instructing leading counsel. In some cases a legal aid committee may impose an additional control by granting a legal aid certificate limited to a certain purpose, such as obtaining counsel's opinion, in which case fresh authority is needed before taking further steps in the proceedings. If the assisted person requires his case to be conducted in an unreasonable manner, leading to unjustified expense, his solicitor or counsel must make a report to the area committee who may discharge the certificate.

13.40   These requirements should encourage a good standard of legal work. From the point of time when legal aid is applied for, solicitors have to provide detailed information in support and this means that care has to be exercised in preparing a case before the application is made. Where a certificate is issued on a limited basis, for example limited to obtaining counsel's opinion, a solicitor is again required to ensure that his case is sound before he can take any further steps. Solicitors can be required to report to the area committee on the progress of a case and its cost to date and, where delay occurs in the conduct of a case, a report is commonly called for.

13.41   All these requirements are, we consider, in the public interest, not only in ensuring that public funds are properly administered but also in protecting the interests of assisted persons.

The cost of administration

13.42   In Table 5.1 we set out the cost of the green form, civil and criminal legal aid schemes in 1977/78. This shows that the Law Society's administrative costs amounted to some £7.3 million and those of the SBC to some £3.3 million. Out of these totals, £6.9 million of the costs incurred by the Law Society and nearly all the costs incurred by the SBC can be attributed to the green form and civil legal aid schemes.

13.43   In its 26th annual report, the Lord Chancellor's Legal Aid Advisory Committee commented on the cost of administering the schemes as follows.

> The scheme is economically administered, but the proportion of expenditure which goes on administration continues to be, as it always has been, relatively high. This is inherent in the structure of the scheme, with its complex rules as to eligibility, contribution, control of proceedings and protection of the Legal Aid Fund and of the rights of other parties.

13.44   The Law Society pointed out that no other organisation in England or Wales, whether financed privately or from funds allocated by Parliament, has a function comparable with that which the Society performs under the Legal Aid Act 1974 and that it is not possible to compare the Society's administrative costs with those of any other body.

13.45   The Law Society also pointed out that the Legal Aid Act 1974 is designed not only to enable anyone who qualifies financially to obtain legal aid, once it is established that he has a reasonable case, but also to prevent the waste of public funds and unfairness to opponents by use of the power given to the Law Society to bring an assisted person's legal aid to an end before his case has been pursued to a conclusion, if it becomes apparent that he will fail.

13.46   The cost of administering the green form and civil legal aid schemes reflects their complexity and we believe that the Law Society has discharged a difficult function with success. As we have indicated previously, we believe that our recommendations will lead to an overall reduction in the cost of administering the schemes. The part attributable to the Law Society will, however, increase when, as proposed in paragraphs 13.15 and 13.18, the SBC ceases to handle applications and the Society becomes responsible for scrutinising the assessments carried out by individual solicitors.

13.47   We think it likely that the Law Society will find that, in order fully to perform its duties in connection with the administration of legal aid it will need further internal statistical support. We consider that the cost of employing a statistician for this purpose should be met out of public funds.

The role of the Lord Chancellor
13.48   It follows from the Lord Chancellor's responsibility to answer to Parliament for civil legal aid that he should be in a position to ensure good long-term management and financial planning in this field of public expenditure. The Lord Chancellor should therefore possess the following powers.

(a)   He should have access to all information held by the Law Society relating to legal aid, but not, save in exceptional cases, the identities of individual assisted persons. This includes information on finance, caseloads, remuneration and administrative methods.

(b)   He should have the power, which we would not expect him to have to use with any frequency, to issue directives to the Law Society on matters relating to the administration of legal aid. Such directives should be published.

13.49   These powers already exist in relation to certain aspects of civil legal aid. We consider that they should be of general application.

13.50 The Law Society has consistently kept the Lord Chancellor informed and has regularly drawn his attention to possible changes in legislation and procedure which would reduce the cost of administering the scheme or otherwise improve its efficiency, both through its formal annual reports on the scheme and through regular informal contact with the Lord Chancellor's Department. We believe that the suggestions for improvement put forward by the Law Society have been an important element in the success of a system whereby the Lord Chancellor is accountable to Parliament for a scheme whose administration is devolved to a professional body. We regard these informal contacts as a valuable part of the administration of the legal aid scheme and are confident that the Law Society will continue to promote improvements in the legal aid scheme as conscientiously as hitherto.

Informing the public
13.51 We have received a considerable volume of evidence that members of the public are not always adequately informed about the availability of legal aid and of their right to obtain advice and representation. In Chapter 27 we examine this problem and suggest various remedies. One of our recommendations in paragraph 27.8 is that every person who is involved as a party in proceedings should as a routine be advised at the outset about the availability and conditions of legal aid.

Costs, Remuneration and Scope

Matters relating to costs
13.52 One of the distinctive features of the legal system in England and Wales is the principle that the losing party in a civil case is normally expected to pay the costs of the successful party. The following paragraphs are concerned with the present system in which this principle operates, so far as it affects legally aided litigants and those engaged in litigation against them.

13.53 In paragraph 37.32 we endorse the general principle just described but recommend that costs should be awarded on a more generous basis. This recommendation, namely that costs should be awarded on a common fund basis instead of on a party and party basis as hitherto, has influenced many of the proposals in the following paragraphs and should be borne in mind when considering them.

The unsuccessful litigant
13.54 When a legally-aided litigant loses his case, he is liable first to pay his own costs up to the limit of his contribution; the balance of his own costs, if any, is met from the legal aid fund. He is protected against any further payment in respect of his own costs by the fact that his solicitor and counsel may not accept payment other than from the legal aid fund. In addition to paying his own costs, the unsuccessful litigant may be ordered by the court to pay some or all of the

costs of his successful opponent, but such an order may not be made unless in all the circumstances, including his means, it is reasonable for him to be expected to make such a payment.

13.55 We indicated in Chapter 12 that the amount of the contribution for which every user of legal services should be liable is the amount which his means make it reasonable for him to pay without incurring an undue financial burden. It follows that this contribution should cover all payments which he is required to make. Accordingly, if costs are awarded against an assisted person, any balance of his contribution remaining after payment of his own costs should be applied in reduction of the costs ordered against him, but no further sum should be required of him.

The successful litigant

13.56 Even when the successful party in litigation obtains an order from the court entitling him to recover his costs from his unsuccessful opponent, the opponent may be unable to pay. The successful party will then have to meet some or all of his costs out of his own resources or from any damages or other money recovered in the proceedings. If, in such cases, the contribution paid by a successful assisted litigant is less than the amount of his own costs the balance becomes a first charge on any property which is recovered or preserved in the proceedings; this is known as the "statutory charge".

13.57 Although certain forms of property recovered or preserved are exempted from the charge, notably payments of maintenance or money or property not exceeding a value of £2,500 transferred as a result of a court order in divorce proceedings, the charge is often a cause of disappointment and hardship to a litigant. The provision can have a harsh effect in personal injury cases, swallowing up a large part of what a litigant has won, and on occasions, as a result of some matrimonial cases, it has been levied on the disputed matrimonial home.

13.58 There are a variety of reasons why a successful litigant will often fail to recover his full costs from his opponent. These vary according to whether either or both parties are assisted out of the legal aid fund and whether it is the plaintiff or the defendant who is the successful party. The following table shows, in respect of each possible combination of assisted and unassisted plaintiffs and defendants, how the costs of the successful party are met in practice if they are not recovered from his unsuccessful opponent. In this table 'plaintiff' and 'defendant' refer to the litigant's status in the court of first instance.

147

TABLE 13.1

Payment of costs

Serial	Winner	Loser	By whom winner's costs paid
1	Assisted	Assisted	By the loser, on the party and party basis, up to an amount considered reasonable by the court given his means. The balance, on the common fund basis, is found by the winner out of his contribution and the statutory charge.
2	Assisted	Unassisted	By the loser, on the party and party basis, to the limit of his means. The balance, on the common fund basis, is paid by the winner out of his contribution and the statutory charge.
3	Unassisted plaintiff	Assisted defendant	By the loser, on the party and party basis, up to an amount considered reasonable by the court given his means. The balance of the costs incurred are paid by the winner out of his own resources or damages recovered.
4	Unassisted defendant	Assisted plaintiff	By the loser, on the party and party basis, up to an amount considered reasonable by the court given his means. The balance of the costs incurred are paid by the winner out of his own resources unless the court makes an order against the legal aid fund on the ground of hardship.

The successful assisted litigant

13.59 In the case of a successful assisted litigant, the fund may receive in costs a larger sum than is paid out of it. This arises because costs are recovered on the party and party basis, usually between 5 and 10 per cent less than if assessed on the common fund basis (see paragraph 37.31). The assisted person's solicitor is entitled to recover his charges out of the fund on the common fund basis, but in the High Court and Court of Appeal this is subject to a deduction of ten per cent. Where this applies, therefore, a balance remains in the fund. This will no longer be the case under our recommendations in paragraph 37.32, that the costs payable by the unsuccessful party should henceforward be calculated on the common fund basis and, in paragraph 13.66 that the 10 per cent deduction be abolished.

A successful litigant against an assisted opponent

13.60 A successful litigant, whether assisted or unassisted, may also fail to obtain much or all of his costs from his unsuccessful opponent if the latter is legally-aided (Table 13.1, serials 1, 3 and 4). As we said in paragraph 13.54 above, the unsuccessful assisted litigant may be ordered by the court to pay some or all of the successful party's costs only if this is reasonable given his means. It follows that if the sum ordered to be paid is less than the successful party's costs the latter has to find the difference.

13.61 Since 1964, there has been provision for an unassisted defendant in the court of first instance (Table 13.1, serial 4) who is successful against an assisted plaintiff to have his costs paid out of the legal aid fund. The court may make such an order in relation to a case at first instance only if the successful unassisted defendant would otherwise suffer severe financial hardship. The Court of Appeal in *Hanning* v. *Maitland* (No. 2) [1970] 1 Q.B. 580, held that the expression "severe financial hardship" should not be construed so as to exclude from benefit "people of modest income or modest capital who would find it hard to bear their own costs".

Payment of costs by the successful party

13.62 If the recommendation made above is implemented, the number of cases in which the successful litigant is required to contribute towards the costs of his case will be greatly reduced. There will, however, remain some instances in which the successful litigant will not recover his full costs: we have in mind cases where the unsuccessful party is not legally-aided and is unable to afford to pay his opponent's costs or where a settlement is reached whereby each party pays his own costs. In such cases, the unassisted successful litigant will have to bear part or all of his costs out of his own resources. The assisted successful litigant will have to pay any costs not borne by the opponent out of his contribution and under the statutory charge, on the basis set out in paragraph 13.56.

The statutory charge

13.63 We have considered whether, in such cases, the statutory charge should be abolished and the amount that a legally-aided litigant should be required to pay towards his own costs should be restricted to the amount of his contribution. We have decided that abolition of the charge would be undesirable because it acts as a sanction against an assisted person who requires his legal advisers to conduct his case unreasonably. It would also remove the incentive for assisted litigants and their advisers to seek an order for costs on behalf of the legal aid fund or to make a proper provision for costs in out of court settlements. This would put the amount of costs recovered by the fund at risk.

13.64 Although we do not propose the abolition of the statutory charge we believe that it should be calculated in a different way. We recommend that any sums recovered in proceedings should be aggregated with the capital resources of the assisted person as assessed. If this total exceeds the maximum disposable capital allowance, the excess should be subject to the charge. Furthermore the value of the principal dwelling house should always be excluded not only from disposable capital but also from the amount subject to the statutory charge even if it is included among the assets recovered or retained. Under this proposal, regard is paid to the actual means of legally-aided litigants without giving them an undue advantage over those who pay for their litigation. It will, however, only prove of significant help provided that the contribution-free limit for capital is increased to the level we recommended in paragraph 12.43. Given this increase, the effect of the proposal is set out in the following table.

TABLE 13.2

The operation of the statutory charge

Assumptions		
Assisted person's capital as originally assessed:		£8,000
Free capital allowance as recommended in this report:		£10,000
Sum recovered: Case A		£1,000
Case B		£4,000

Computation	Case A	Case B
Original capital assessment	£8,000	£8,000
Sum recovered	£1,000	£4,000
Total	£9,000	£12,000
Deduct free capital allowance	£10,000	£10,000
Amount subject to statutory charge	nil	£2,000

Remuneration

13.65 One of the effects of our recommendations in Chapters 12-14 is that an increasing proportion of the income of solicitors and barristers will be paid from the legal aid fund. The fees payable will be determined by the rules which set out the amounts that may be charged for particular forms of legally-aided work and by the process of taxation.

13.66 In Chapter 37, we deal generally with the remuneration of both branches of the profession and discuss the means by which the procedures set out above and levels of remuneration should be kept under review. We emphasise here that the rates of remuneration for all work done under either the civil or criminal legal aid schemes should be fixed at a reasonable level and kept up-to-date. This is no more than fair to those who offer such services and is an essential pre-requisite in overcoming the shortage of solicitors, which we discuss in Chapter 5, who are willing and able to provide services under the legal aid scheme. For this reason, we regard the deduction of ten per cent from the fees of barristers and solicitors in legally-aided cases before the High Court and Court of Appeal as unreasonable and we recommend that this should cease.

13.67 A minor point which has been brought to our notice is that a solicitor claiming a fee from the legal aid fund under the green form scheme has to break down his claim between time spent writing letters, telephoning and on other purposes. We think that such a division is unnecessary, especially in the light of our recommendation in paragraph 13.8 that the second phase of the civil legal aid scheme should be defined in terms of four hours' work. If all solicitors keep time records as we recommend in Chapter 37, the permitted period can be closely identified.

13.68　In recording the time spent on work done under the legal aid scheme, solicitors should be entitled to include time spent assessing the client's means and collecting his contribution. As the changes we have recommended in this and the previous chapter are introduced, we think it may be appropriate to review all the present forms and procedures involved in the administration of the scheme, with a view to removing all requirements that are no longer necessary.

The scope of the legal aid scheme

13.69　This matter was considered in detail by the Legal Aid Advisory Committee in its twenty fifth annual report, and in the recommendations of its Working Party on Legal Aid Legislation which was annexed to it. We have found the views of the Advisory Committee a helpful guide.

13.70　We agree with the Advisory Committee that legal aid should be made available for the following proceedings:—

(a) defamation;

(b) relator actions for defendants;

(c) contested election petitions;

(d) all those civil proceedings in magistrates' courts, other than licensing proceedings, to which it does not extend.

(e) proceedings in the Court of Protection which cannot be dealt with by the Court's Personal Application Branch.

13.71　In addition we recommend that legal aid should also be made available in coroners' proceedings in respect of which the Advisory Committee made no recommendation.

13.72　Legal aid is not at present available for proceedings before the Judicial Committee of the Privy Council. The Advisory Committee considers that it should be extended to appeals by individuals to the Judicial Committee from decisions of professional bodies in disciplinary matters. We agree.

Conclusions and Recommendations

Paragraphs

Initial half-hour	R13.1	Half an hour's legal advice and assistance from solicitors who undertake legal aid work should be available to everyone, irrespective of means, free of charge. The introducduction of this proposal should be preceded by a carefully monitored pilot scheme.	13.5–13.6
Four-hour scheme	R13.2	A solicitor should be able to provide legal advice and assistance for a further four hours on his own authority.	13.7–13.8
Authority of the legal aid committee	R13.3	A solicitor providing representation should be required to obtain the prior permission of the legal aid area committee.	13.10
Assessment and collection of contributions	R13.4	The assessment of means and of contributions should no longer be carried out by the Supplementary Benefits Commission.	13.15
	R13.5	The initial assessment of contribution should in all cases be made by the solicitor.	13.16
	R13.6	When providing legal services under his own authority, the solicitor should collect the client's contribution.	13.17
	R13.7	When a legal aid committee authorises representation in proceedings it should scrutinise the assessment of means and collect the contribution.	13.18
Aggregation	R13.8	The rule under which the resources of parents or guardians are aggregated with those of a minor should be abolished.	13.20

Paragraphs

R13.9   The aggregation of the resources of   13.21
spouses should, if possible, be discontinued.

Merits of the cases   R13.10   The criteria for the granting of aid by   13.26
the legal aid committee should be revised as set out in the text.

Handling of applications   R13.11   The functions of local committees   13.29
should be transferred to legal aid area committees.

R13.12   The geographical boundaries of   13.30
legal aid areas should be brought into line with local government boundaries.

Retrospective authority   R13.13   Retrospective authority for work   13.34
done should be given only in the circumstances set out in the text.

Delays   R13.14   Delays in granting legal aid applica-   13.37–13.38
tions should be reduced in future. The Law Society should give details of the time taken to handle applications in its annual report.

Statistical support   R13.15   The Law Society's Legal Aid Depart-   13.47
ment should be provided with the services of a statistician at public expense.

Overall responsibility   R13.16   The Lord Chancellor should have   13.48
access to all information relating to the administration of legal aid and should have power to issue directives to the Law Society.

Costs   R13.17   The liability of an unsuccessful   13.55
legally-aided litigant to pay costs should be limited to the amount of his maximum contribution.

153

CHAPTER 14

Criminal Legal Aid

Eligibility for Criminal Legal Aid

Introduction

14.1 Criminal legal aid is granted either by the court hearing the case in respect of which assistance is granted, or by the court committing the case for trial. The criteria applied by the courts in determining whether criminal legal aid should be granted, and whether a contribution should be required, differ from those governing eligibility and liability to contributions under the civil scheme. In this chapter we consider to what extent criminal legal aid should be available in respect of each kind of proceeding for which it might be sought, the circumstances under which contributions should be payable and any changes that will be needed in the administration of the scheme.

The present position

14.2 Before granting legal aid, the court must apply two sets of criteria designed to assess the applicant's need for assistance in the light of his means and of the seriousness of the charge which he faces. On financial grounds, anyone whose available funds do not exceed £75 if single or £120 if married, or who is on supplementary benefit, is eligible. Anyone else, however large his means, is eligible provided that it appears to the court that his means are such that he requires assistance in meeting the costs which he might incur.

14.3 Provided that the applicant is eligible on the grounds of means, the court must grant legal aid to defendants in all cases of murder and in all cases where the provision appeals on a point of law from the Court of Appeal (Criminal Division) to the House of Lords. In all other cases, the trial court or the appellate court has power to grant legal aid where it appears desirable to do so in the interests of justice. If there is doubt whether a legal aid order should be made, this doubt must be resolved in favour of the applicant.

The Widgery criteria

14.4 The criteria used for determining whether it is in the interests of justice for legal aid to be granted are those recommended by the Departmental Committee on Legal Aid in Criminal Proceedings, the Widgery Committee, which reported in 1966 (Cmnd. 2934). The Committee recommended that in the higher courts it should be the general practice, subject to financial eligibility currently at the level described above, to grant legal aid to those committed for trial or sentence. The Committee considered, however, that there should be a

155

discretion to refuse legal aid on grounds other than means "in those rare cases where, for exceptional reasons, the court is of the opinion that it is not desirable in the interests of justice to grant it".

14.5 The following table demonstrates that, following these recommendations, all but a small minority of defendants tried in the Crown Court have received legal aid.

TABLE 14.1

Legal representation in the Crown Court, 1977

Type of proceedings	Number of persons			
	Total	Represented under a legal aid order	Privately represented	Not represented
Trial on indictment	79,214	76,053	2,681	480
Proceedings relating to sentence ..	16,715	16,260	192	263
Appearance to be 'dealt with'	826	710	22	94
Appeal against magistrates' courts decisions:				
conviction only or conviction and sentence	6,667	3,727	1,405	1,535
sentence only..	8,140	5,387	1,415	1,338

Source: Criminal Statistics for England and Wales, 1977, Table 24(c) (Cmnd. 7289).

14.6 So far as concerns cases in the magistrates' courts, the Widgery Committee recommended that the main factors, apart from means, which might entitle an applicant to legal aid, were the following:—

(a) that the charge was a grave one in the sense that the accused was in real jeopardy of losing his liberty or livelihood or suffering serious damage to his reputation;

(b) that the charge raised a substantial question of law;

(c) that the accused was unable to follow the proceedings and state his own case because of his inadequate knowledge of English, mental illness or other mental or physical disability;

(d) that the nature of the defence involved the tracing and interviewing of witnesses or expert cross-examination of a witness for the prosecution;

(e) that legal representation was desirable in the interest of someone other than the accused as, for example, in the case of sexual offences against young children in which it was undesirable that the accused should cross-examine the witness in person.

156

Criticisms of the criteria

14.7 We have received compelling evidence, from various sources, that these non-statutory criteria, in so far as they relate to proceedings before magistrates' courts, are not working well. They are said to be both complex and imprecise and are open to a wide range of interpretations in cases of the same type. There have been continuing complaints about variations, as between magistrates' courts, in the frequency with which applications are refused. These variations are illustrated by the table below, which relates to refusals of legal aid by magistrates' courts in Inner London.

TABLE 14.2

Refusal of legal aid for summary proceedings, as a percentage of applications: Inner London magistrates' courts, 1977

Court	%
Highbury Corner	42
South Western	17
Woolwich	16
Horseferry Road	15
Tower Bridge	15
Old Street	14
Marlborough Street	13
Thames	12
Bow Street	10
Camberwell Green	9
Greenwich	8
West London	8
Inner London Juvenile	6
Marylebone	5
Wells Street	5
Clerkenwell	4
Hampstead	3

Source: Criminal Statistics for England and Wales, 1977, Table 21 (Cmnd. 7289).

General principles

14.8 In Chapter 12, we recommended a substantial extension of civil legal aid so that it might be available, subject to a contribution where appropriate, to any individual who had reasonable grounds for pursuing a case before the courts. The defendant to a criminal charge brought by or in the name of the state has a stronger claim to support. He has no choice as to whether his case proceeds, the outcome will affect his standing in the eyes of society and, in many cases, he may lose his liberty. In the adversarial system which prevails in the courts in this country, representation is needed on both sides. A wrong verdict is strongly against the public interest. In these circumstances the state should ensure that all those who would be seriously affected by a finding of guilt are able to obtain the representation they need. We set out below the criteria which we consider should be applied.

Proposed criteria

14.9 In our view, there should be a statutory right to legal aid in all criminal cases apart from those relating to offences that are triable only by magistrates. In other words, legal aid should be available as of right for proceedings in the Crown Court (other than appeals from the magistrates' court in respect of offences triable summarily only); for all committal proceedings; for proceedings which are triable either by magistrates or before a jury (that is, those defined as "triable either way" in the Criminal Law Act 1977) irrespective of whether they are heard in a magistrates' court or the Crown Court; and also for any proceedings in which the defendant is refused bail and is remanded in custody.

14.10 In cases relating to offences that are triable only by magistrates, legal aid should be granted as a matter of statutory right, unless the court is satisfied both:—

(a) that there is no likelihood:—
    (i) that a custodial sentence, a deportation order or, in the case of a juvenile offender, a care order will be imposed; or
    (ii) that there will be substantial damage to the livelihood of the defendant or his reputation;
and

(b) that adequate presentation of the defendant's case, including a possible plea in mitigation, does not require representation by means of legal aid.

It may be helpful to illustrate criterion (b) with two examples. First, if a defendant by age, infirmity or for any other reason is unable to represent himself, legal aid should be granted. Secondly, if, in a motoring case, a defendant has access to legal services provided by a motoring association, any form of group scheme, or insurers, legal aid should not be granted.

14.11 The effect of this recommendation will be that, although the courts will retain the discretion whether or not to grant legal aid in cases which are triable by magistrates only, the emphasis will now be reversed so that it will be necessary for a court to grant legal aid unless it finds grounds for refusing it while hitherto it has been necessary to find grounds for granting it. If a magistrates' court decides to refuse legal aid to an applicant it should give its reasons.

Availability of legal aid for appeals

14.12 Appeals against conviction or sentence in the Crown Court lie to the Court of Appeal (Criminal Division). An appeal can be brought as of right only on a point of law; these constitute a small minority of appeals. In other cases, based on fact or mixed fact and law, the leave of the Court of Appeal has to be obtained. This may be granted by a single judge or, if leave is refused by him, by the full court. Argument will be heard by the full court, but only when the appellant is represented, either under legal aid or at his own expense. After conviction or sentence, following committal, in the Crown Court, a legal aid order continues in force to enable advice to be given where there appear to be reasonable grounds for appeal and to prepare an application for leave to appeal or to give notice of appeal.

14.13 A barrister whose client is convicted is under a professional duty to see him personally after the trial or to ensure that his solicitor does so. At present there is no formal requirement to advise the client on a possible appeal although it is expected that the prospects of an appeal will be discussed. The *Guide to the Professional Conduct of Solicitors* issued by the Council of the Law Society states that, if a solicitor considers that there are grounds for an appeal, he should so advise the client; there is, however, no duty to advise the client if there are no grounds for an appeal. Enquiries made, on our behalf, of a number of convicted persons on their entry into prison, showed that a proportion believed that they had received no advice about an appeal. It was not possible to validate their statements and these may or may not have been accurate. We think it likely that, in practice, a discussion immediately after a trial, though desirable on humanitarian grounds, may not be the best means of conveying advice about an appeal. In a number of cases the client may be too confused or shocked by the sentence to take in what is said to him. We therefore recommend that solicitors and barristers should be subject to the same rules on the lines set out below and that the legal aid order for trial should cover the work required to be done.

14.14 A convicted defendant in the magistrates' court who receives a non-custodial sentence or a custodial sentence of less than three months' duration should be seen after the proceedings by his solicitor or barrister. He should be given oral advice on the prospects of an appeal when such advice is sought, when his legal advisers consider that there is a reasonable prospect of a successful appeal or when the sentence, though less severe than three months' imprisonment, will have serious consequences on his employment or reputation. A defendant sentenced to three months' imprisonment or more in the magistrates' court or sentenced in any case in the Crown Court should not only be seen by his barrister or solicitor after the hearing but should also in due course be advised in writing of the prospects of success in an appeal. We consider the most suitable procedure would be for the barrister, if retained, to send written advice to the solicitor, who should send it on to the client with a covering letter containing his own views. In a very large number of cases it will be possible to give reasoned advice in short form. There is no objection to this, provided the client is left in no doubt of his position. In cases where an immediate written opinion cannot be given the client should be informed by letter that he will be fully advised in due course.

14.15 The legal aid order in the court of trial enables advice to be given on the prospects of an appeal, but does not extend to representation on appeal or any work beyond the preparation of the application for leave to appeal. Further legal aid, that is to say legal aid to present argument on the question of leave to appeal, may be granted by the Court of Appeal. When leave has been granted, legal aid will normally also be granted for the appeal itself but it will be limited to the services of counsel only, unless a solicitor is considered to be needed, for example for the purpose of collecting fresh evidence.

Proposed improvements

14.16 The present arrangements covering the preparation and lodging of an appeal or an application for leave are not, in our view, entirely satisfactory. Even when counsel advises against an appeal there are some cases where convicted persons proceed to lodge their own applications. We think it desirable, even when an appeal appears to counsel to have little merit, that the convicted person should have legal assistance in preparing his appeal or application. We therefore recommend that legal aid in criminal cases should continue up to the point at which an appeal or application for leave is lodged, whether or not counsel has advised against an appeal.

14.17 For the reason given in paragraph 14.15, legal aid for appeals is normally limited to counsel only. We consider that this arrangement requires to be modified. An assisted person may find it disconcerting if the solicitor who acted for him at his trial is no longer available to him and is replaced, for the purpose of retaining counsel, by a court official whom he never sees. We consider therefore that the solicitor who acted for the defendant at his trial should, if the defendant wishes, see him in order to ensure that there is no additional material which the defendant wishes to be put to counsel as part of his instructions. The legal aid order made for the purposes of the trial should continue in force for this purpose. Further legal aid to enable a solicitor as well as a barrister to be instructed to attend court for the purpose of arguing the appeal should not be available unless it is necessary to obtain further material for the purpose of instructing counsel or, unless the case is one of complexity, the advocate instructed in the appeal is not the advocate who represented the defendant at the trial and it is desirable for the solicitor to attend to assist counsel.

Applications for bail

14.18 Any person who is in custody, charged with an offence, may apply for bail; that is, release from custody upon certain conditions. When a person is charged he may be granted bail by the police; if not, he may apply for bail on appearing before magistrates within 24 hours of being taken into custody or as soon as practicable thereafter. If bail is then refused and the defendant is remanded in custody, he will appear before the magistrates at regular intervals until his case is heard. At each appearance an application for bail may be made. If the defendant is committed to the Crown Court he may make an application for bail to the Crown Court judge. If a magistrates' court or the Crown Court refuses bail at any stage before conviction or while an appeal is pending, the defendant may apply for bail to a judge of the High Court. There are two ways of applying. The first involves an oral application, by a barrister or a solicitor, to a High Court judge. The application is supported by affidavit and a summons must be served on the prosecutor at least 24 hours before the day of hearing.

160

The second method involves giving notice in writing to the judge in chambers in the High Court that the defendant desires to apply for bail, and requests that the Official Solicitor shall act for him in the application. Forms are provided in prisons for the purpose of making an application in this way. The Official Solicitor, if his services are granted, lays before the High Court judge the defendant's written application for bail and the prosecutor's observations. The judge usually decides the case on the papers, though in some cases he may ask for more information or for oral argument on the issues.

14.19   Under present arrangements a grant of legal aid covers an application for bail to the magistrates' court or the Crown Court, as the case may be. The defendant may also be given assistance in making a written application to the High Court judge, using the services of the Official Solicitor. Criminal legal aid is not available for an oral application by a barrister or solicitor to a High Court judge. Civil legal aid is available for this purpose, but it has been granted on only a few occasions.

14.20   The statistics relating to 1976 show that 40 per cent of those on whose behalf an oral application was made to a High Court judge were successful in obtaining bail. Of those who applied in writing through the Official Solicitor 13 per cent were successful. The difference may be accounted for in part by the fact that those making oral applications would have had to pay to do so, and would have been less likely to proceed had they been advised that there was no prospect of success. By contrast, those making written applications had nothing to lose by proceeding. Allowing for this, the figures nevertheless suggest that there was some advantage in making an application orally rather than in writing. Since these statistics were collected, the Bail Act 1976 has come into force and magistrates are now required to record their reasons for refusing bail. This will make it easier for a judge considering a written application to decide whether the magistrates' decision was sound. Even so, there is likely to be some advantage in making an oral application to a judge.

14.21   When a case reaches the Crown Court, an oral application for bail can be made to the judge of that court under the legal aid certificate granted in respect of the trial or appeal. We doubt the need for a further oral application to a High Court judge in this type of case and and think it reasonable that legal aid should be available only for the purpose of a written application. Different considerations apply to a defendant who is remanded in custody by magistrates pending his reappearance before them and who, if refused bail, has at present no entitlement to legal aid for the purpose of making an oral application to a judge. It has been proposed by the Law Society that, where a defendant is remanded in custody by a magistrates' court, his solicitor should be able to make a single oral application to a Crown Court judge in chambers, recovering the fee from criminal legal aid funds. Legal aid for a second application to the Crown Court judge should be allowed only in the event of a material change in circumstances. This arrangement, combined with the present assistance of the

Official Solicitor in making a written application to the High Court, should provide an adequate safeguard against unreasonable refusals of bail by magistrates. We recommend that this procedure should be adopted as an interim measure, and that the system as a whole should be reviewed when the effects of the Bail Act 1976 can be fully assessed.

Care proceedings

14.22   The Legal Aid Act 1974 empowers the courts to grant legal aid not only to a child or young person who is the subject of criminal proceedings but also to one who is the subject of care proceedings under section 1 of the Children and Young Persons Act 1969. Although care proceedings are civil, not criminal, matters, they are covered by the criminal legal aid scheme and are dealt with, therefore, in this chapter.

14.23   Section 64 of the Children Act 1975 empowers the courts to appoint a guardian *ad litem* in any case involving the making, variation or discharge of a care or supervision order under the Children and Young Persons Act 1969. Guardians *ad litem* in this type of case are persons such as local authority children's officers or probation officers appointed by the courts to protect the interests of children in proceedings when these do not coincide with those of their parents. The cost of this service is borne by the authority or organisation providing the guardian. Section 65 of the Children Act 1975 provides that, when a court has appointed a guardian *ad litem* to safeguard the rights of a child under the 1969 Act, it may also grant legal aid to the child's parents to enable them to take part in the proceedings. For want of resources, section 64 has been implemented only in respect of proceedings arising from unopposed applications for the discharge of a care or supervision order made in or arising from care proceedings.

14.24   The effect of this is that, in all other cases, no legal aid, and thus no separate legal representation save at their own expense, is available to parents whose child is the subject of the care proceedings. In *R* v. *Welwyn Justices, ex parte S* (reported in The Times newspaper, 30th November 1978) the Court of Appeal reluctantly held this to be the present position and called for the provisions of section 64 of the Children Act 1975 to be implemented.

Extension of legal aid

14.25   We have received evidence from a number of witnesses that to deny legal aid to parents in care proceedings involving their children is unjust. If a care order is made, custody of the child is transferred from the parents to another. For most parents, no event could be more serious. Moreover, a care order may inflict a lasting stigma on the parents. We consider, therefore, that the parents of a child involved in care proceedings should have legal aid to enable them to be represented separately from the child.

162

14.26   The principle to be followed is that a child in care proceedings and its parents should be separately represented, with legal aid if necessary, unless it is clear that there is no conflict of interest between the parties. The child should be represented either by a guardian *ad litem*, when section 64 of the Children Act 1975 is brought into force, or by means of legal aid as recommended in paragraph 14.25. In either case, if there is any risk of a conflict of interest, the parents should have legal aid for the purpose of separate representation.

Financial Considerations

Contributions

14.27   In England and Wales (but not in Northern Ireland or Scotland) the court of trial may require a defendant who is legally-aided to pay such a contribution in respect of the costs incurred on his behalf as appears reasonable to the court, having regard to the defendant's resources and financial commitments. The contribution may be required as a lump sum after the case has been disposed of, or an initial deposit may be required at the time the legal aid order is made.

14.28   The report of the Widgery Committee in 1966, on whose recommendations the present system is based, predicted a level of contributions totalling £400,000 a year in respect of trials on indictment and committals for sentence, from which, after allowing for costs of assessment and collection and bad debts, the benefit to public funds was expected to be not less than £350,000 a year. The Committee appears to have based its figures on the financial year 1963/64 in which year expenditure on legal aid for trials on indictment and committals for sentence amounted to just under £1,200,000. The expectation was therefore that contributions would meet about a quarter of the cost. It can be seen from Table 5.1 that, by 1977/78, total expenditure on criminal legal aid in the higher courts had grown to some £23.6 million. Contributions received in respect of proceedings in these courts in 1977/78 totalled £457,000. They constituted no more than one fiftieth of the cost of criminal legal aid in the higher courts. In the magistrates' courts, for the same period, contributions received amounted to £877,000, or two fiftieths of the total expenditure of £21 million on criminal legal aid.

Drawbacks of the present system

14.29   In order to assess eligibility and contributions, the courts must impose a complex and costly means test. During 1977, the average sum ordered to be paid in each case by way of contribution was £23 in the magistrates' courts and £83 in the Crown Court. As indicated in the preceding paragraph, the total sum collected in contributions in all criminal proceedings in 1977/78 amounted to £1.33 million. The costs of assessment and collection are heavy and are referred to in paragraph 14.37. The effect of ordering contributions at the end of a case and then seeking to collect them, often by instalments, is not satisfactory. Contributions out of income can normally only be ordered against those who receive a non-custodial sentence or are acquitted. When a case has been concluded a convicted person has no incentive to contribute towards the cost of his representation; it is those who are acquitted who are usually best placed to pay a contribution.

A new system of contributions

14.30 We do not regard the present system of levying contributions as satisfactory. In principle, we do not consider it right that a contribution should be required from anyone who is found not guilty. Furthermore, there are strong practical grounds for abolishing contributions, given that the cost of collection and assessment may in many cases swallow up a large part of the contribution. At the same time, those who are convicted of a serious offence and are in a position to meet, or to contribute to, their own costs, should be required to do so.

14.31 For these reasons we cannot see that any useful purpose is served by retaining contribution orders in the magistrates' courts. We consider, however, that they should be retained in the Crown Court. The procedure we recommend is that, when a defendant has been convicted in the Crown Court, the judge should have a discretionary power to order him to pay a contribution towards the cost of his defence. This power should be available also to judges of the appellate courts hearing appeals from the Crown Court against conviction or sentence. Although contribution orders would not be made in the magistrates' courts, judges in the higher courts should be able to order contributions in respect of committal proceedings.

14.32 In the exercise of this discretion, we recommend that the judge should have regard to:—
(a) the means of the accused; and
(b) the extent, if any, to which the accused was responsible for unreasonable expenditure being incurred in his defence.

14.33 Reasons should be given for any order to contribute to costs, and there should be a right of appeal. The courts would thus not be expected to enquire into the means of all defendants as at present, but only into the means of those on whom a judge proposed to impose a contribution order.

Advice and assistance

14.34 From the time a defendant is charged the provisions for criminal legal aid come into operation. Before that time advice may be required for two purposes: first, a person may need advice because he believes he may be at risk of facing a criminal charge; secondly, he may need advice when being questioned by the police. In both cases we consider that advice should be given, as at present, under the same arrangements as are proposed for legal advice and assistance in civil matters. Criminal legal aid is not appropriate, because at that stage there is no court to award it and the applicant may not be charged with a criminal offence. If legal advice is obtained in this way while the person is being questioned by the police, (see paragraphs 9.11 – 9.12) no contribution should be required.

This proposal is consistent with the recommendations made in paragraphs 14.30 – 14.33.

Administrative arrangements

14.35 The effect of these recommendations will be to simplify the task of the courts in administering legal aid in criminal cases. It will be necessary, for contribution purposes, to make an assessment of the financial eligibility of an applicant only in a limited number of cases. In cases other than those of a summary nature legal aid will be granted automatically. In summary cases the justices' clerk will consider the application and authorise legal aid unless the case falls outside the criteria in paragraph 14.10; if he considers that legal aid should not be granted the matter should be referred to the bench.

14.36 Some witnesses have put it to us that there should be an appeal from a refusal of legal aid in the magistrates' courts. Since, if the criteria in paragraph 14.10 are properly applied, it is only in cases of lesser importance that there will be a question whether or not legal aid should be granted, we see no need for such an appeal.

Financial effects of the proposals for contributions

14.37 At present a little over £1 million is collected in contributions. Against this must be reckoned the cost of assessing and collecting them. The cost so incurred in the magistrates' courts is not recorded; it has been estimated to amount to ten per cent of the amount collected but we have no means of verifying this figure. Further costs in administration and in making assessments are incurred by the Crown Court and the Supplementary Benefits Commission. If the costs of administration are set against the contributions received, the net loss of revenue will be appreciably less than £1 million. As against this, the courts will be able to make expeditious decisions, inconsistencies will be avoided and the arrangements can be put on an uncomplicated and efficient administrative basis.

Conclusions and Recommendations

Paragraphs

Criminal legal aid R14.1 Defendants should have a right to   14.9
legal aid in all criminal cases except
those which are triable only by magistrates.

R14.2 In cases triable only by magistrates,   14.10
legal aid should be granted unless the
court decides to the contrary on the
basis of the criteria set out in the text.

Appeals   R14.3   A person convicted of an offence   14.14
                        should be seen after the hearing by
                        his barrister or solicitor; in the
                        circumstances described in the text
                        he should be advised orally or in
                        writing on his prospects of success
                        in an appeal.

                R14.4   Legal aid in the Crown Court should   14.16
                        continue up to the point at which an
                        appeal, or application for leave to
                        appeal, is lodged.

                R14.5   The arrangements for retaining a   14.17
                        solicitor to attend an appeal should
                        be confined to those stated in the
                        text.

Applications   R14.6   Legal aid for appeals against the   14.21
for bail   refusal of bail should be available
                        on the basis set out in the text.

Care proceedings   R14.7   In care proceedings, unless there is   14.26
                        no conflict of interest, the parents
                        should have legal aid for representa-
                        tion separately from the child.

Contributions   R14.8   Contributions in respect of criminal   14.30–14.31
                        legal aid in the magistrates' courts
                        should no longer be required.

                R14.9   In the Crown Court and appellate   14.31
                        courts, convicted offenders should be
                        required to pay contributions at the
                        discretion of the judge.

Advice and   R14.10   Legal advice and assistance under the   14.34
assistance   civil scheme should continue to be
                        available to a person who is at risk
                        of facing a criminal charge and no
                        contribution should be required
                        from a person who is being ques-
                        tioned by the police.

166

CHAPTER 15

Tribunals

The Present Position

Introduction

15.1 In Chapter 2 we referred to the increasing number of tribunals with judicial, quasi-judicial and administrative functions. The majority of these tribunals come within the purview of the Council on Tribunals. Table 2.2 gives the number of cases disposed of during 1978 by nine major tribunals. The total number of cases heard by tribunals in 1978 was six times the number of contested civil cases that were disposed of at trial before the High Court and county courts. The number of hearing days in tribunals has in recent years exceeded the total number of hearing days before judges in the High Court and county courts, including days in chambers.

Representation before tribunals

15.2 Clients are entitled to be represented by solicitors or barristers before all tribunals except the committees that hear complaints against National Health Service practitioners, from whose hearings, by rules of procedure at present under review, paid advocates are excluded by statute.

15.3 The rights of audience of lay advocates and other representatives vary from tribunal to tribunal. Applicants before many tribunals, including Rent Tribunals, Industrial Tribunals, Mental Health Review Tribunals and Supplementary Benefit Appeal Tribunals, are entitled to be represented by a person or persons of their choice, whether a lawyer or not. Representation by a non-lawyer before certain tribunals, such as the Common Commissioners, the Lands Tribunal and the Performing Rights Tribunal, is permitted only at the discretion of the tribunal.

Financial assistance for proceedings before tribunals

15.4 The Legal Aid and Advice Act 1949 empowered the Lord Chancellor, subject to Parliamentary approval, to extend legal aid to any tribunal. In 1957, the Franks Committee on Administrative Tribunals and Enquiries recommended in principle that there should be such an extension. In 1968 the Legal Aid Advisory Committee recommended that legal aid should be extended to the Lands Tribunal, but not to other tribunals. At the same time it called for research, in the light of which it might re-examine its findings.

15.5 The Advisory Committee reconsidered the matter in 1974 and recommended that legal aid should be extended to all statutory tribunals within the supervision of the Council on Tribunals in which legal representation was permitted, and to the Patents Appeal Tribunal. It also recommended that financial support should be given to existing non-legal agencies which provided assistance and representation, without charge, before tribunals. In its annual report for 1974/75, the Council on Tribunals expressed general support for the recommendation that legal aid should be extended to all statutory tribunals within its purview in which legal representation was permitted and also drew attention to the need for financial assistance for non-legal advice and representation. Other bodies and individuals with experience of tribunals have, at various times, made similar recommendations.

15.6 The only tribunals to which legal aid has so far been extended are the Lands Tribunal (to which it was extended in 1970), the Commons Commissioners (1972) and the Employment Appeal Tribunal (1976).

The Need for Improvements

Evidence
15.7 Two main themes can be distinguished in the evidence that was put before us. The first of these, expressed by various organisations concerned with the work of tribunals, concerned the need to expand the use of lay representatives before tribunals. The second theme which had widespread support among many witnesses with first-hand experience of tribunals, was the need to extend legal aid to some or all tribunals.

15.8 A number of witnesses suggested that the need for legal aid was greatest before Industrial Tribunals. These tribunals handle a complex body of recent statutory law which requires advice of a technical nature and a high standard of representation. A large proportion both of applicants and respondents are already legally represented before such tribunals. A survey conducted during October 1977 showed that 49 per cent of respondents and 33 per cent of applicants were represented by lawyers. Many other applicants were represented by their trade union or by other organisations of the kind described in paragraphs 15.15–15.17 below.

The need for advice, assistance and representation
15.9 It has been recognised in recent years that it is important for anyone appearing before a tribunal to have the benefit of advice before the case is heard. Research by Professor Kathleen Bell into proceedings before Supplementary Benefit Appeal Tribunals and National Insurance Local Tribunals emphasised the desirability and value of appellants before these and other tribunals having access to advice and representation, advice before the hearing being of particular value. It is also important that appellants should

attend the hearing. Statistics relating to Supplementary Benefit Appeal Tribunals in 1976, provided by the Department of Health and Social Security, show that the relationship between presence and/or representation at a hearing and a favourable decision was as follows.

TABLE 15.1

Success rate before supplementary benefit appeal tribunals, 1976

Appellants	Number of appellants	% of all appellants	Number of favourable decisions	% success rate
Present and represented	9,887	18	3,715	38
Present and unrepresented	15,607	28	4,177	27
Absent and represented	2,067	4	705	34
Absent and unrepresented	27,564	50	1,708	6
Total	55,125	100	10,305	19

Source: Department of Health and Social Security.

15.10 Although the extent and nature of representation at Supplementary Benefit Appeal Tribunals is not necessarily typical of all tribunals, these figures indicate that success is related to representation and that, even in the absence of representation, attendance may have an influence on the outcome.

Suggested Changes

Future policy
15.11 The present position is, in several respects, unsatisfactory. Representation by a lawyer is available only to those able to pay for it, unless the lawyer provides his services free of charge; the availability and quality of lay representation varies; and through nervousness or unfamiliarity with the procedure applicants often find it difficult to present their cases in person. In addition, proceedings before tribunals have become increasingly complex. As pointed out in paragraph 15.10, an applicant who is present or who is represented is more likely to be successful than one who is absent and unrepresented. It follows that it is desirable that every applicant before any tribunal should either be able adequately to present his case in person or to obtain representation. To achieve this it will be necessary to overcome each of the weaknesses mentioned above. For this purpose, three separate but linked policies will be needed. These are the simplification of tribunal procedures, the development of lay advice and representation and the extension of legal aid to tribunals. We discuss each of these in turn in the paragraphs following.

Procedure

15.12   We have received evidence that the procedures of certain tribunals have become "legalistic". This is attributed partly to the increasing complexity of cases handled by tribunals and the relevant legislation and partly to the influence of lawyers and court room techniques. The main factor, however, is the nature of the legislation on which the work of the tribunals is based. We doubt whether great simplification of the procedure of tribunals will be possible unless the relevant law is first made less complex. Subject to this, the procedures of tribunals, including for this purpose the Immigration Appeals Adjudicators, should be reviewed in order to ensure that applicants in person are able to conduct their own cases whenever possible, bearing in mind the proposals for procedural changes included in Part VI. In this context we draw attention to the research conducted by Professor Kathleen Bell (see paragraph 15.9 above) among whose findings was that appellants preferred a form of hearing in which they could participate rather than a formal hearing modelled on the procedure of a court.

15.13   We recommend that such a review should be undertaken, under the general oversight of the Lord Chancellor, by the Council on Tribunals in association with the government departments concerned and other interested parties. We consider it essential that this review should be carried out at an early date since it will provide the context within which other reforms should take effect.

Extension of lay assistance

15.14   A variety of agencies provide lay representation before tribunals. For example the trade unions represent their members before National Insurance Local Tribunals, Medical Appeal Tribunals, Industrial Tribunals and, in some cases, before Supplementary Benefit Appeal Tribunals.

15.15   Projects associated with the CAB service, established in the last three years in Birmingham, Leeds, Newcastle, Sheffield and Wolverhampton, provide representation before Supplementary Benefit Appeal Tribunals and National Insurance Local Tribunals. They also undertake some work before Industrial Tribunals. Advice and representation is provided partly by volunteers and partly by paid staff.

15.16   The Free Representation Unit, consisting mainly of young barristers and bar students, provides a free advocacy service before tribunals in London. The Royal British Legion undertakes representation before the Pensions Appeal Tribunals. The Child Poverty Action Group specialises in social security cases.

15.17   A special organisation has been established to assist those who wish to appeal against a decision by the immigration authorities, namely the United

Kingdom Immigration Advisory Service (UKIAS). In 1975/76 this service handled over 36,000 enquiries, the majority being dealt with by giving advice only. Some 5,000 cases dealt with during the year involved appeals. UKIAS has 35 staff at senior levels, including immigration counsellors. Of these, 14 are members of the legal profession or law graduates. This is a unique counselling and advocacy service, dealing with one field of tribunal work and manned by a full-time salaried staff.

15.18 The foregoing list of agencies that provide tribunal services is by no means comprehensive. Many others provide similar services on a local basis. The evidence that has been submitted to us indicates that there are wide variations in both the scope and quality of the advice and representation provided by lay agencies. In the light of the evidence submitted to us, we make the following observations in order to assist in the formulation of future policies towards such agencies.

Support for lay agencies
15.19 Agencies which provide lay advice and representation before tribunals, in particular those which we have mentioned above, have devoted much time and effort to the subject and have acquired considerable expertise. They provide a sound and useful service and we do not think it necessary or desirable to establish a new national organisation to provide lay representation before all tribunals. It would be preferable to encourage existing agencies to develop or expand where necessary the specialist services that they now provide.

15.20 If agencies which provide advice and representation before tribunals are to give an adequate service, they should have enough money to provide training for staff, an up-to-date information service and proper administrative support. In some cases they may need solicitors on their staff, or available on a consultancy basis, to give advice in individual cases and to provide assistance and support to the lay advisers.

15.21 Lay organisations which provide advice and representation before tribunals do not all have the financial resources needed to develop in the way proposed in paragraph 15.20. So that the standard of service required may be maintained, we recommend that public funds should be made available to approved agencies to assist in the training of tribunal representatives. Funds for this purpose should be granted only to those organisations which provide services to members of the public at large and do not confine them to a restricted class of subscribing members. It is to be expected that the Lord Chancellor would seek the advice of the Council on Tribunals, and the Council for Legal Services referred to in Chapter 6, before deciding to make funds available for this purpose from his Vote.

Informing the public

15.22 In Chapter 27 we recommend that every person who is involved as a party in proceedings before any court or tribunal should be advised at the outset, as a matter of course, about the availability and conditions of legal aid. We consider that the parties appearing before a tribunal should, in the same way, receive information about the lay agencies willing and able to provide advice and representation. The list of lay agencies available for this purpose should be drawn up after consultation with the Council on Tribunals and the Council for Legal Services.

Legal aid

15.23 One of the main purposes of giving jurisdiction to a tribunal rather than to the courts is to provide for informality, simplicity of procedure and accessibility. If this is achieved, self-representation by the applicant is often all that is needed, on occasion with the support of a trained representative from a lay agency. Both forms of representation should be encouraged and they should be effective in the majority of tribunal cases.

15.24 However, even when the procedure of a tribunal and the law with which it is concerned are not unduly complex, there are cases when a denial of legal aid for representation by a lawyer will put the applicant at a disadvantage. We have in mind, for example, cases before Supplementary Benefit Appeal Tribunals which involve allegations of cohabitation or dishonesty, and some of the claims before Industrial Tribunals which involve difficult problems of law and fact.

15.25 In the light of these considerations and of the volume of authoritative evidence put before us, we are satisfied that, before all tribunals, there are some cases in which legal representation is needed. In such cases legal aid should be available unless legal representation is specifically prohibited by statute. This also applies to such appeals against decisions by tribunals for which legal aid is not at present available. We set out in paragraphs 15.28–15.29 criteria that should be applied before granting legal aid.

The green form scheme

15.26 Under the green form scheme a solicitor may give legal advice and assistance to an eligible client who is an applicant before a tribunal, but may not at the time of writing represent him at the proceedings. The availability of such advice is of value to applicants who represent themselves in person, by helping them in the preparation of their cases. It has however proved inadequate in other cases when applicants have suffered from lack of support at the hearing. In paragraph 13.8, we recommend that a solicitor should be able to provide up to four hours' legal advice and assistance on his own authority under the legal aid scheme. This recommendation will enable applicants who wish to represent themselves before a tribunal to be better prepared, but will not allow the solicitor to provide the representation.

The Legal Aid Act 1979 empowers the Lord Chancellor to designate proceedings in which solicitors may provide representation under the green form scheme. We recommend that the Council on Tribunals together with the Council for Legal Services should consider at regular intervals whether, and if so which, proceedings before tribunals should be designated by the Lord Chancellor and should offer advice accordingly.

Eligibility for legal aid

15.27 If representation by a solicitor under the legal aid scheme is desired, the solicitor will, as in cases involving representation before the courts, have to seek authority to proceed. The decision whether or not to grant legal aid should, we consider, be exercised by or on behalf of the Law Society's legal aid area committees. The power to authorise representation could be delegated to the secretaries of such committees who would, as in other cases, refer the matter to the committee only if they were not disposed to grant the application or had doubts about whether it should be granted. The Law Society told us that there would be no difficulty in providing the necessary administrative arrangements.

15.28 In considering an application for legal aid, the legal aid committee or its secretary, as appropriate, should be satisfied that the applicant's case fulfils two criteria. The first of these would be the traditional test, applied to all applications for legal aid, that the applicant has reasonable grounds for bringing or contesting the case. In tribunal cases, a further test should be applied, namely, whether the applicant has reasonable grounds for employing a legal representative. The Council on Tribunals, the President of the Industrial Tribunals and the Law Society have each suggested detailed criteria on which this test might be based. We recommend the adoption of criteria based upon those proposed by the Council on Tribunals in its evidence to us, as follows.

> When a person applies for legal aid in connection with any proceedings in a tribunal, he shall not be given legal aid unless he shows that in the particular circumstances of his case he reasonably requires the services of a lawyer, and the certifying committee shall in this respect have regard to the suitability and availability of any other forms of assistance . . . A small claim (e.g. for a social security benefit) may well be greatly exceeded by the cost of furnishing legal aid to pursue it but, relative to the claimant's resources, it could be of the greatest importance to him. It is, for example, questionable whether an application for legal aid in pursuing a claim to employment benefit of (say) £15 before a National Insurance Local Tribunal, which depended on a valid and arguable point, should be turned down on the ground that it would cost £60 or more to press it with adequate legal representation.

> The following list (not exhaustive) covers the principal instances in which legal representation might be considered appropriate:—
> (i) Where a significant point of law arises.
> (ii) Where evidence is likely to be so complex or specialised that the average layman could reasonably wish for expert help in assembling and evaluating the evidence and in its testing or interpretation.

173

(iii) Where a test case arises.

(iv) Where deprivation of liberty or the ability of an individual to follow his occupation is at stake.

15.29   The instances proposed by the Council on Tribunals are not exhaustive and should, we think, be amplified to make it clear that legal representation should also be available under the following circumstances:—

(a) when the amount at stake, although low, is significant in relation to the financial circumstances of the applicant; or

(b) when suitable lay representation is not available; or

(c) when the special circumstances of the individual make legal representation desirable or when hardship might follow if it was withheld.

Conclusions and recommendations

Paragraphs

Procedures	R15.1	The procedures of all the main tribunals need to be reviewed; this should be undertaken by the Council on Tribunals under the general oversight of the Lord Chancellor.	15.12–15.13
Lay advice and representation	R15.2	Advice and representation by lay agencies for applicants before tribunals should be encouraged.	15.19
	R15.3	Agencies wishing to provide advice and representation before tribunals should have adequate resources for the purpose.	15.20
	R15.4	Public funds should be made available to assist in the training of staff of approved lay agencies.	15.21
Informing the public	R15.5	A person appearing before a tribunal should be informed at the outset of the availability of legal aid and of lay agencies providing advice and representation.	15.22

Paragraphs

Legal aid R15.6 In some tribunal cases (whatever the 15.25
tribunal) legal representation is neces-
sary and should be available unless
representation is prohibited by
statute.

R15.7 The criteria to be applied for the 15.28–
purpose of granting legal aid in tri- 15.29
bunals are stated in the text.

CHAPTER 16

Alternatives and Supplements to Legal Aid

Introduction

16.1   A variety of methods of paying for legal services are used in different parts of the world. In a number of countries experiments are in progress on methods of providing and paying for legal services for those of moderate means as well as for the poor. We received helpful information from those engaged in this work. Some of the systems in use elsewhere, such as pre-paid legal services schemes of various kinds, have not been attempted in this country and seem unlikely to become established here. A number of proposals were, however, made to us in evidence concerning various means, other than by the provision of legal aid, for providing legal services, in particular litigation. We deal below with four of these proposals, for contingency fees, a contingency legal aid fund, legal costs insurance and a suitors' fund.

Contingency fees

16.2   The expression 'contingency fee' indicates an arrangement by which a lawyer agrees to act for a client on the basis that, if damages are recovered, the lawyer will receive an agreed proportion of them, while if the case is lost he will receive nothing. While it no longer constitutes an offence or civil wrong to make an arrangement of this kind (technically known as champerty) we understand that a contract based on it would be unenforceable in this country as being contrary to public policy and it is forbidden by professional rules of conduct.

16.3   A few witnesses have advocated the introduction of contingency fees on one or more of the following grounds.

(a)   Such fees would enable plaintiffs, who would not otherwise be able to afford litigation, to take their claims to court.

(b)   Lawyers accepting cases on a contingency basis would have a stake in winning them and would therefore be more committed and more diligent in their preparation and presentation.

(c)   Contingency fees would benefit lawyers by simplifying the administrative procedures by which they were paid and by increasing their earnings.

16.4   The overwhelming weight of the evidence that we have received is opposed to the introduction of contingency fees. It was pointed out that arrangements of this kind encourage lawyers to concentrate only on strong cases and on cases which, while without real merits, have a high nuisance value which makes them worth pursuing. The fact that the lawyer has a direct personal interest in the outcome of the case may lead to undesirable practices including the construction of evidence, the improper coaching of witnesses, the use of professionally partisan expert witnesses (especially medical witnesses), improper examination and cross-examination, groundless legal arguments designed to lead the courts into error and competitive touting. A client may lose by this arrangement in two ways: a proportion—often substantial—of any damages recovered goes to the lawyer; and as the lawyer pays all the costs of the case in return for this proportion of the damages, he is exposed to strong temptation to settle the claim before incurring the heavy expense of preparing for trial and of trial itself, although it may not be in his client's interests to do so. Alternatively, the client, having nothing to lose, may insist that a hopeless or irresponsible claim be pursued to litigation in the hope that some profit will result.

16.5 We consider that these criticisms have force. It should also be recognised that the contingency fee system has become established in jurisdictions where parties to litigation bear their own costs, regardless of the outcome of the case. In this country it is the rule that the loser pays both parties' costs. Thus, if contingency fees were to be allowed here, it would either be necessary for the plaintiff to risk having to bear the defendant's costs, while escaping his own, or for his lawyer to undertake that in the event of failure he would not only forgo his own fee but would also pay the costs of the successful defendant. To guard against this, he would wish for a contingent fee amounting to a large proportion of the damages, giving an excessively high reward if the claim succeeded.

16.6 We believe that a system of this type would not work well in this country and would give rise to serious dissatisfaction. It would benefit only a limited class of litigants and would reward some lawyers disproportionately. We are satisfied that this type of arrangement should continue to be prohibited.

A Contingency Legal Aid Fund

16.7 The scheme which has been proposed to us by Justice as a Contingency Legal Aid Fund (CLAF) is intended to retain the advantages of a contingency fee system, whilst avoiding some of the main disadvantages. It is proposed that a fund be set up under the control of a small number of independent administrators. Initially, finance would have to be provided by the Government, though the intention of the proposal is that the fund should in time become self-supporting. Its purpose would be to provide certain financial guarantees to plaintiffs of moderate means who would otherwise be unable to afford to bring their cases before the courts.

16.8 The arrangement made with prospective plaintiffs would be that in the event of success the plaintiff would contribute to the fund a proportion of the damages awarded to him, his legal costs being paid, in accordance with the

177

usual practice, by the losing side. If the plaintiff lost his case, the fund would guarantee to pay his costs and those of the successful defendant. The cost of administering the scheme would be met by charging a registration fee to all applicants, and a reserve of money for the payment of costs in unsuccessful cases would be built up from the fund's share of damages of successful assisted plaintiffs. For this reason, it is suggested that assistance from the fund should be available only to plaintiffs who, in the event of success, would be likely to obtain a money judgment exceeding £500. It is also proposed that any plaintiff save a large corporation should be eligible for assistance, provided he could show that his claim had a reasonable prospect of success.

16.9 This proposal would avoid some of the disadvantages inherent in a contingency fee system. The lawyer conducting a case supported by the fund would have no personal interest in the amount of damages awarded but would receive his normal fee whether the case was won or lost. This factor, combined with the need to show that there were reasonable grounds for bringing the case, would prevent the encouragement of vexatious and unnecessary litigation.

16.10 We were told in evidence that it was hoped that the scheme could eventually be widened to include defendants, but that nothing had so far been formulated. It was acknowledged to be a disadvantage of the scheme that it would support only plaintiffs who were claiming relatively large sums of money. There are many kinds of case, in particular matrimonial cases, which form a substantial proportion of the litigation before the courts, for which the fund would provide no assistance.

16.11 There is a danger that plaintiffs with good prospects of success would decline to use the scheme but those with a poor or doubtful case would seek to do so. The financial viability of the scheme would thereby be put in jeopardy. Moreover it would be a hazard of a scheme of this kind that those who administered it would be under constant pressure to give assistance in cases where the plaintiff attracted strong sympathy but where the prospects of success were not great. There would be public disappointment if it failed to give assistance to what were regarded as deserving cases. This fact, combined with the possibility that plaintiffs with strong cases would be disinclined to apply to the fund, would operate as a constant risk to its solvency. If deficiencies occurred and were met out of public funds, there would be a drain of resources which might otherwise be used to support the provision of other important services.

16.12 We believe, furthermore, that it would be wrong to expect successful clients to subsidise those who were unsuccessful. We are particularly concerned about this because, under a proportional contribution system, those clients who had suffered most and were awarded the greatest damages would be expected to contribute most to the fund. This in turn might also lead to an increase in the amount of damages awarded to litigants assisted by the fund. For these reasons, and for the reason given in paragraph 16.22, we consider that an arrangement of this type should not be adopted.

Legal cost insurance

16.13 Legal cost insurance is available in a number of countries. In West Germany, for example, where legal aid is not available, such insurance has operated on a large scale for many years. Until recently, it was virtually unknown in Britain, but in the last few years some insurance companies have begun offering legal cost insurance to individuals as well as to companies, in addition to the more traditional insurance cover for personal injury and damage to property.

16.14 A form of group cover of a different character is also available, either directly or indirectly, by virtue of membership of various organisations. Thus the Medical Defence Union pays the legal costs of member doctors who are sued for negligence and both trade unions and motoring organisations pay the legal costs of their members who are involved in certain forms of litigation.

16.15 If our recommendations as regards civil legal aid are adopted, the scope of the assistance available to individuals will be widened Nevertheless, there will always be those who are either ineligible for legal aid or might be liable to substantial contributions, who may wish to insure against these risks. Insurance may also prove helpful to companies, trade unions, small businesses and other bodies to provide cover for their members or their staff. Individuals or organisations in such circumstances are best placed to decide what insurance cover they consider appropriate. We do not recommend support for such arrangements out of public funds.

A suitors' fund

16.16 It has been suggested to us that a suitors' fund should be established to compensate litigants who incur exceptional costs through no fault of their own. It is proposed that the fund would reimburse the extra costs incurred as a result of any of the following circumstances: —

(a) the reversal of a decision of a lower court on appeal;

(b) the illness or death of the trial judge;

(c) the need to determine an unsettled point of law of public importance.

16.17 A litigant who receives legal aid would benefit from a suitors' fund only if relieved of the need to pay part of his contribution. It is intended, however, that contributions should be fixed at a level which impose no undue financial burden on the litigant, without regard to the length or complexity of his case. The main benefit of such an arrangement would therefore be felt by litigants, such as corporate bodies, who are not entitled to legal aid.

16.18 We are not satisfied that financial assistance should be available for cases in which the decision of a lower court is reversed on appeal. The risk that a decision may be overturned on appeal is inherent in all litigation and should be taken into account by all who embark on it.

16.19 Where additional expense arises because a judge becomes ill or dies different considerations prevail. While the conduct of a case is subject to the control of a litigant and its complexity and the risk of an appeal can be assessed, an event such as the illness or death of a judge cannot be predicted. It is possible to obtain insurance against such an event and this is sometimes done in heavy cases. It is not, however, always easy to obtain such insurance and it is not the practice to do so in cases of ordinary length. In such cases, however, the costs of a second hearing caused by the illness or death of the first trial judge might well be disproportionate to the amount involved. We have therefore reached the conclusion that there is a good case for paying out of public funds the amount of the costs thrown away as a result of the illness or death of a judge in the course of a trial.

16.20 So far as concerns paragraph 16.16 (c), we think it appropriate that the resolution of points of law of public importance, which benefits the community as a whole, should be financed out of the public purse. In 1953 the Evershed Committee on Supreme Court Practice and Procedure (Cmnd. 8878) recommended that public funds should be made available for litigating points of law of exceptional public interest either at first instance or on appeal. We support this and recommend that public funds should provide finance for this purpose also. This would supplement the existing legal aid system by repaying to the litigant his legal aid contribution.

16.21 The Evershed Committee recommended that it should be the task of the Attorney General to determine whether a case involved a point of law of public importance for which financial support should be provided. While endorsing this view, we consider that it should, additionally, be open to the judge to determine eligibility for support out of public funds, either at first instance or on appeal, with a right of appeal against a refusal to order such a payment. Our reason for proposing this variation of the Evershed Committee's recommendation is that it is not always possible to determine at the outset of a case whether a point of law of public importance arises and we think that the court should be empowered to determine eligibility at any stage of the proceedings.

Conclusions on alternative systems

16.22 Save for the proposals discussed under the heading of a suitors' fund, none of the alternatives or supplements to legal aid which we have discussed above is satisfactory in all respects and some have serious defects, in particular the contingency fee system. They all suffer from the general disadvantage that they are palliatives; they were designed, not unreasonably, to offer support in a limited number of cases at a time when the legal aid arrangements were inadequate. The changes made in April 1979 show that it is not unreasonable to look for substantial improvements in the provision made out of public funds rather than to promote alternatives which are intended to be self-financing. We advocate the continued development of the legal aid scheme on the lines recommended in this report. We do not consider it would be in the public interest to recommend the adoption of alternatives and supplements which, at best, could be no more than half-measures and, at worst, would serve to prevent or delay the improvements in the present scheme which we have recommended.

Grants and loans to private practitioners
16.23   It will be necessary in the coming years to encourage the provision of legal services in areas where there is at present scarcity of solicitors. One means of providing such services is by opening citizens' law centres, as recommended in Chapter 8. A second method, which we consider should also be adopted, is to encourage private solicitors to open practices in such areas.

16.24   Our recommendations concerning proper remuneration for legal aid work should enable solicitors working in deprived areas and concentrating on this class of work to do so more profitably than at present. They should be assisted in obtaining business by the recommended relaxations in the present restrictions on advertising (see Chapter 27). The Law Society should offer encouragement and advice where necessary.

16.25   The provision by the state of a guaranteed income for practitioners in deprived areas would do little to stimulate a vigorous development of practices and could give rise to justifiable objections by solicitors in neighbouring areas. It would, moreover, be difficult to fix the income of individual solicitors' firms which would probably be necessary under such an arrangement.

16.26   We have, however, received evidence that, although loans for the purpose of establishing a new office can usually be raised from banks or other lending agencies, there is considerable difficulty in meeting interest payments and making repayments of capital during the early years. We consider that practical support for solicitors establishing themselves in such areas should take the form of interest-free loans from public funds, deferring repayment of capital in the early years.

16.27 If such loans were made they should be subject to the following conditions.

(a) The loans should be available for the establishment of solicitors' offices, whether by new or existing firms, in areas of need defined for the purpose. These areas should be determined by the Lord Chancellor in consultation with the regional committees we recommend in paragraph 6.32.

(b) Solicitors to whom loans are made should establish that they have experience in the type of legal work which is needed in the area.

(c) Loans should be repayable with interest if recipients move their practices within a prescribed period.

16.28 For the purpose of financing these arrangements we propose that the Law Society should be responsible for monitoring the suitability of each application, for ensuring that the conditions set out in paragraph 16.27 are complied with and for making interest-free loans to the firms of solicitors concerned on suitable terms as to repayment. In order to provide the funds for this purpose the Lord Chancellor's Department should make corresponding loans to the Law Society but limited at any one time to a maximum of (say) £500,000 in total. The Law Society should be responsible for collecting the repayments of the loans from the solicitors on the due dates and repaying the loan from the Lord Chancellor's Department *pro tanto*. The Law Society should be entitled to charge the individual firms of solicitors an annual commission to reimburse the costs of administration.

16.29 We would expect the incidence of bad debts suffered by the Law Society to be small because failure to repay would involve the bankruptcy of the solicitors concerned who would thereby be prevented from continuing to practise. Occasionally, however, it might be appropriate for part or all of a loan to be cancelled for special reasons and, if approved by the Lord Chancellor's Department, a corresponding amount of the loan to the Law Society from the Department would be cancelled. The Law Society should be required to make an annual report to the Lord Chancellor on the operation of this scheme.

Conclusions and Recommendations

Paragraphs

Contingency fees R16.1 The system of remunerating lawyers 16.6
by contingency fees should not be
permitted.

Contingency Legal R16.2 A Contingency Legal Aid Fund 16.12
Aid Fund should not be introduced.

Legal cost R16.3 Legal cost insurance on a voluntary 16.15
insurance basis may prove a useful supplement
to legal aid in some cases.

Suitors' fund R16.4 Payment should be made from public
funds:—

  (a) to reimburse costs thrown away 16.19
      by the illness or death of a judge;
      and

  (b) to pay the costs incurred in 16.20
      determining a point of law of
      public importance.

Grants and Loans R16.5 A scheme for interest-free loans to 16.26–16.29
encourage private practitioners to
move to areas of need should be
introduced.

PART III

The work of lawyers

CHAPTER 17

Fusion

The Present Position

Introduction
17.1 The legal profession is organised in two separate branches each with its own governing body, rules of conduct and discipline, conditions of practice and system of education and training. Each branch has its own functions, maintained by the rules that solicitors may not appear as advocates in the superior courts, and that barristers may not normally accept instructions directly from lay clients. In this chapter we consider the advantages and disadvantages of the present arrangements as compared with a fused profession in which there would be no distinction between barristers and solicitors.

The functions of solicitors and barristers
17.2 The main function of a solicitor is to give general advice on legal matters and to conduct the day-to-day legal business of the lay client. As might be expected from the fact that solicitors take instructions directly from the public, their offices are widely spread throughout the country. Although, as we mentioned in Chapter 4, their distribution is uneven, a potential client in a town of any size may expect to find one or more solicitors' firms within easy travelling distance.

17.3 In April 1979, the total number of solicitors' firms in England and Wales was 6,667 and the total number of partners in these firms was 20,193. In the following table, we show in columns 1 and 2 the distribution of firms of different sizes and in columns 3 and 4 the distribution of partners as between the different sizes of firm.

TABLE 17.1

Size of solicitors' firms in England & Wales, 1979

	Firms		Partners	
	Number	%	Number	%
Sole practitioners	2,285	34·3	2,285	11·3
2 partners	1,608	24·1	3,216	15·9
3—4 partners	1,575	23·6	5,306	26·3
5—9 partners	942	14·1	5,864	29·0
10 or more partners	257	3·9	3,522	17·4
Total	6,667	100·0	20,193	100·0[1]

[1] Because of rounding, the sum of this column is not exactly 100 per cent.
Source: London Insurance Brokers Ltd.

17.4 A barrister is retained by a solicitor from time to time to perform a specific task: to draft a document, settle a pleading, advise in writing or in conference or to represent a client in court. He is not in regular contact with his client, nor does he normally communicate with others on a client's behalf. As we show in Table 33.2, barristers' chambers in England and Wales are concentrated in London and in a number of provincial cities. They have become more widely spread in recent years, but the extent of their distribution in no way resembles that of solicitors' offices. The number of barristers practising outside London has increased in recent years but the proportionate increase is only slightly larger than the increase in the size of the Bar as a whole. The report of the Royal Commission on Assizes and Quarter Sessions (Cmnd. 4153) recorded in appendix 12 the number of barristers practising in London and outside. In 1953, 451 barristers out of 1,907 practised wholly or largely outside London; in 1968, 606 out of 2,379. In 1st January 1979, there were 4,363 barristers practising in 303 sets of chambers, 3,080 of whom were in 199 sets of chambers in central London and the remaining 1,283 were in 104 sets in 28 provincial centres.

17.5 There is some overlap in the work of solicitors and barristers: both give legal advice and both act as advocates. Only barristers have a right of audience in all courts. Solicitors have full rights of audience in the magistrates' and county courts, where, as can be seen in Table 2.1, most criminal and civil cases are dealt with, and have limited rights of audience in the Crown Court. Solicitors frequently instruct barristers to appear for their clients in courts in which they have rights of audience, either because this is more convenient or because the barrister has the necessary experience or knowledge of a certain branch of the law.

17.6 It is therefore an over-simplification to say merely that solicitors are general practitioners and barristers are specialists, or that advocacy is the business of barristers but not of solicitors. Some solicitors specialise in particular branches of the law, or act frequently as advocates; most barristers, however, regard advocacy as their main function, are trained for this purpose and, as we say in paragraph 17.38, can fairly claim to be specialists in advocacy; many specialise also in specific and limited branches of the law. The distinction between the two branches may be regarded partly as that between general and specialist practice and partly as a matter of function, the solicitor acting in particular cases (and sometimes generally) on a continuing basis for the client, the barrister being retained only when circumstances require it, usually to provide specialist advice or advocacy.

17.7 The different functions of the two branches of the profession determine the way in which their offices and chambers are organised. A firm of solicitors must be so organised as to handle efficiently, on a continuing basis, its clients' files, records and money, employing as fee-earners for this purpose solicitors, legal executives and other staff. By contrast the administration of a set of barristers' chambers is mainly concerned with keeping the barristers' working diaries, watching court lists, communicating with listing officers and arranging the billing and collection of fees. A barrister offers his services on a personal basis, employing no other fee-earning staff. Solicitors' firms in general employ larger staffs than barristers' chambers and incur higher overheads. Out of his gross fees, a solicitor principal will pay 65 per cent – 70 per cent towards running his office and the other overheads of practice, whereas a barrister will pay approximately 33 per cent.

Court procedures

17.8   Unlike the majority of systems of law in Europe, English law is neither codified nor inquisitorial. It is based on precedent and adversarial procedures. Issues of fact and law which arise in a lawsuit are determined at one and the same time, in the course of a single continuous trial, almost entirely by oral evidence and argument. The paper work done in the preliminary stages is directed to establishing the issues to be resolved at trial. There are some exceptions to the practice of taking evidence in oral form, but it is an invariable rule that argument on the law and on the conclusions to be drawn from evidence may not be submitted in writing.

17.9   In many countries, judges employ a legal staff or work in teams for the purpose of legal research and have a career structure of their own. The whole of the argument in a case may be submitted in writing before the hearing, which is often very short. In our jurisdiction, judges have no professional staff to assist them and legal argument is presented orally. Since the judge in most cases delivers judgment either immediately the evidence and argument are concluded or very shortly thereafter, he relies on the advocates who appear before him to bring out the facts of the case, to test the evidence and argue the law fully, referring to all relevant authorities, whether they advance their clients' cases or not.

17.10   The quality of advocacy is important in a system of this description. Lord Justice Roskill told us in evidence: —

> No-one without judicial experience can perhaps fully appreciate how much a judge relies upon the advocates before him in arriving at what he believes to be the correct decision. Bad advocacy may lead to the right points being missed, the right questions not being asked, and therefore the right answer not being given by the judge.

17.11   Some might argue that our entire system of justice should be changed so that it resembled the other systems we have mentioned. As Part VI shows, we received many suggestions for improvements, but there have been few proposals for so fundamental a change. Our task, in any event, was to examine the organisation of the profession on the basis of our present legal system and the present rules of court procedure. In this system the quality of advocacy remains an essential component of the quality of justice.

17.12 Even if our system were modified so that less was done by means of the spoken word, it would not follow that the quality of advocacy would cease to have importance. In the United States judges of the superior courts have, in their law clerks, professional assistants of high quality. A great deal of legal argument is committed to paper, in the form of briefs. In those circumstances it might be thought that the standard of advocacy would be a matter of less concern. The contrary is the case. The Honourable Warren Burger, Chief Justice of the United States of America, told us in oral evidence of his concern for the standards of advocacy in his jurisdiction, and of the difficulties which arose from advocacy of poor quality. He said:—

> My observation from sitting in trial of cases in the *nisi prius* court* was that something less than half of the lawyers who appeared there were minimally qualified to perform their function . . . over a long period of time I undertook to take soundings in state courts and in federal courts throughout the country, and the most pessimistic view was that only 25 per cent of the lawyers appearing in our courts were really qualified to represent their clients properly and to move the case along adequately. Some judges placed it as high as 75 per cent. Somewhere near the mid-way mark is probably correct, and it will vary to some extent from place to place.

The Chief Justice remarked that cases were dealt with in British courts more quickly than in American, and went on:—

> From time to time I have been asked how I account for this. It is not easy to account for it but an over-simplification perhaps is that in your courts generally you have three experts who have all been trained in the same tradition and in the same pattern. The judge almost by definition has been one of the leading members of the Bar, and the two advocates appearing before him are trained in the same way the judge was trained. This is not so on our side . . . the trial of a case resembles in a way a three-legged stool. If any one of the legs is very much shorter than the other you have not got a very good stool. If any one of them is weaker than the other the stool might collapse if weight is put on it. In our system, unfortunately, too often all three of the legs of the stool are not as competent as they should be . . . Even if you have a very experienced judge and he has two mediocre, badly-trained or untrained advocates before him he has difficulty.

The attitude of the profession

17.13 Members of both branches would find some advantages in a fused profession. Firms of solicitors, particularly the larger, could expect to gain, materially and in prestige, by having as partners barristers who were the acknowledged leaders in various fields. Barristers, particularly those in the lower and middle ranges of income, might earn in a solicitors' firm as much as or more than they could at the Bar, with the additional advantages of greater security and provision for retirement. The start of professional practice would be easier in a fused profession than it now is at the Bar. In spite of these advantages, the weight of evidence from both branches of the profession is opposed to fusion. We comment on this point in greater detail in paragraph 17.28.

---

*Court of first instance.

Criticisms of the Two-Branch Profession

The main criticisms

17.14   Of the many witnesses who submitted evidence on the structure of the profession, a small minority advocated fusion. These witnesses put forward three main criticisms of the two-branch profession, that it was inefficient, harmed the confidence of clients and was more expensive. It was argued that these defects could be cured by the creation of a fused profession.

Efficiency

17.15   The efficiency of the two-branch profession was criticised on the grounds that the structure caused failures in communication and was a source of delay. Failures in communication were said to arise because the professional relationship between barrister and solicitor was distant and formal, because the written instructions sent to counsel were in some cases inadequate and late in arriving and because barristers were reluctant to complain about inadequate instructions for fear of offending a solicitor client. There was also said to be poor service when a brief was returned by a barrister at a late stage, because the barrister to whom it was reallocated had insufficient time to make himself familiar with the case and with the client. In Chapter 22 we examine these criticisms in detail and propose various remedies. The question with which we are concerned in this chapter is whether fusion of the two branches of the profession would, in itself, improve the situation.

17.16   Problems of communication would not arise if the advocate in a case personally undertook the necessary preparatory work. We doubt whether, even in a fused profession, this could be done as a matter of regular practice, except in minor cases. If a partner in a firm of solicitors did all the work now sent to a barrister, he would face practical difficulties in dealing with both preparatory work and advocacy, even if he thought it desirable to do so. A solicitor who specialises in advocacy told us that he did not himself interview witnesses or prepare a case for trial. He found it best to deal with his cases at the same stage, and in the same way, as a barrister. If a small firm had no partner to do the work, it would have to retain another firm as agents to undertake advocacy on behalf of its clients. In any circumstances where an advocate did not undertake the preparatory work, communication would not necessarily be any better than at present. The main reason why essential material is omitted from a brief is that the case has been inefficiently prepared, and this is as likely to occur in one system as in another.

Delay

17.17   One of the main criticisms of the operation of the law is that it is too slow and unnecessarily long drawn out. The existence of the two-branch profession is regarded by some as a major source of delay. The group of barristers working in the Wellington Street Chambers put it this way.

The system inevitably produces delays which are often inordinate. Every busy practitioner will put off non-urgent work until time becomes available, and often until he is chased. When two busy lawyers have to set aside time, the delay is doubled.

We think it an exaggeration to say that periods of delay are necessarily doubled under the present system, but it is clearly correct that, if cases must wait first for a solicitor's and then for a barrister's attention, there will be an increase in the total time taken to complete the work. It is, however, possible only to speculate on the improvement to be expected in a fused profession. As we show in Chapter 22, the causes of delay are many and complex. It has not been established that fusion is necessary, or would be sufficient, to overcome them.

17.18   It was suggested that clients received more efficient and quicker service in foreign countries in which unified professions operate. The majority of the witnesses who submitted evidence on this point however held the opposite view. This is illustrated by the evidence of Mr. A. F. Bessemer Clark, a former barrister and manager of a shipowners' insurance association, undertaking worldwide legal business, who said:—

> I have not found that countries operating a fused profession provide a more efficient service than that available in London. On the contrary, my experience has been that because of the greater emphasis on specialisation both in the science of advocacy and in individual fields of law, we are better served in London.

In relation to the speed of legal work, he said:—

> Lawyers are always blamed for being too slow. The English system perhaps accentuates this, in that unlike, for example, the United States, there is only one real bite at the cherry. The trial is the focal point. In the United States, the evidence of fact comes out separately from the trial, often almost at once, through depositions. In France, the court will appoint surveyors who will report on the facts. In Germany, the judge will pick off the issues one by one. In England, law and facts are all decided at one time and, not unnaturally, particularly in a big case, there is a long delay between incident and final judgment. However it is not my experience that English claims remain open longer than those for other countries. On the contrary, the experience of the solicitors and the detached advice of counsel tends to lead to early settlements . . . I do not believe that fusion would tend to speed up our legal services. On the contrary, it would tend to reduce the number of experienced advocates available and, hence, in my view, increase the delays.

Return of briefs
17.19   Many of the present criticisms of the quality of service provided by the profession relate to the return of briefs. It was argued that, in a fused profession, the function of representation would be spread among a larger number of practitioners, reducing the risk of clashes of engagements. Against this, it was pointed out that the working lives of most barristers were organised for the conduct of advocacy and that there had been built up a system of

communication solely concerned with the listing of cases and appearance in court. Moreover, it is more difficult for a solicitor than for a barrister to keep his working diary clear in court hours. All solicitors are familiar with the necessity of arranging meetings for internal purposes or in order to accommodate clients. They must also undertake a large amount of correspondence and routine office work. While solicitor-advocates might be able to establish a tradition of keeping clear of other engagements at any time when they might be required to appear in court, it would be more difficult to do so in a fused profession, particularly for experienced and sought-after advocates, than in the barristers' branch of a two-branch profession. Our conclusion is that, in a fused profession, the number of additional advocates is unlikely to be so great as to lead to an appreciable reduction in the problem of clashes of engagements, and that these would be less easy to cope with than at present, because of the loss of some of the advantage of quick and informal communication between barristers and their clerks which is possible under present centralised arrangements.

Confidence of the client

17.20 Some of those who advocated fusion argued that the present divided profession reduced the client's confidence in the quality of the service received. The barristers working in the Wellington Street Chambers said:—

> A considerable degree of mutual confidence is required, if the client is to communicate and the lawyer is to understand. The sooner and more fully the trial advocate is brought into the case, the better will be the advocacy. The divided profession is an obstacle, often fatal, to this relationship. The client must first express his or her problem to a solicitor, and may in doing so come to trust and have confidence in the solicitor, only to learn that the advocate in court will be someone else. Thereafter at best, the client will be taken to see counsel, and start a second time to establish a relationship of understanding and confidence.

The Legal Action Group said:—

> We think that the "detachment" which the Bar claim as an advantage of separateness is rarely so. What the barrister calls detachment the client may well view as ignorance of his case and circumstances. It matters not that the client may be wrong, and that the barrister in fact knows quite as much as the court needs to know: if clients are left with the feeling that the legal profession does not bother on their behalf, then public confidence in the legal system suffers.

These witnesses stated that it is common practice, particularly in criminal cases, for the client not to meet his counsel until the day of the hearing.

17.21 There was also criticism of the situation arising when a brief is returned, so that a client, who may have established a good relationship with the barrister intended to represent him, encounters a total stranger on the day of the hearing. In these circumstances, as the organisation Justice remarked:—

> Nothing is more calculated to shake the lay client's confidence in the legal system than to be told at the last minute that X cannot take the case and it will have to be done by Y, who has not previously been involved and indeed may belong to a different set of chambers.

We agree with this view and make recommendations in paragraphs 22.38-22.42 on this point. As we said in paragraph 17.19, however, we doubt whether fusion would solve this particular problem since there is no reason to suppose that advocates in a fused profession would be more successful than barristers under present arrangements in avoiding clashes of engagements and consequent withdrawals.

17.22   It was argued against the view that barristers are too remote from their clients that it is a benefit to clients to have a detached second opinion, and that if they are properly informed about the arrangements by which they are to be advised and represented, and if those arrangements are properly carried out, the divided profession offers a superior service. Mr. B. J. Brooke-Smith, a director of a firm of marine insurers, who are frequently involved in litigation in many parts of the world, expressed this view.

> The detachment from both the pressures of the potential litigant and the documentary spadework which barristers enjoy quite definitely produces advice of a judicial quality markedly absent from most opinions given by lawyers in Europe or the USA. This does not mean that an English barrister will not advise a client with full enthusiasm on the various alternative courses open to him if he wants to pursue them, but certainly for our insurance purposes we find invaluable the element of warning (which English barristers would never fail to give) whether or not any particular course of action is likely to prevail at law.

In its evidence the Council of HM Circuit Judges quoted one of its number as saying:—

> . . . for some eight years . . . I was a solicitor-advocate appearing almost daily in the magistrates' courts and taking many criminal cases. I often took my own statements, always interviewed the client and generally the witnesses, if any. In these circumstances it was very difficult to preserve the correct balance between one's duty to one's client and one's duty to the Court. The relationship with the client was too close and when I subsequently practised in the criminal courts as a member of the Bar the situation was quite different and the presence of the solicitor or his clerk acted as a buffer so that I could take a more detached view of the case possibly to the benefit of the client and certainly to the benefit of the Court.

17.23   The contrasting arguments set out in the previous paragraphs may both have some justification, but in relation to different classes of case. In the larger civil actions, in particular in commercial proceedings and in serious criminal cases, there are clear advantages in bringing in a specialist advocate and in most such cases we believe that the client benefits from such representation. In the smaller cases, and in particular in minor criminal cases, in which solicitors already have rights of audience, a client with no previous knowledge of the law may find it disconcerting that it is necessary to instruct counsel and that his own solicitor, in whom he has confided, does not handle the case alone from start to finish. For the reasons already given, we are not persuaded that fusion of the two branches of the legal profession would, in itself, overcome this problem.

Cost of legal services

17.24 Those who submitted evidence in favour of fusion argued that, by reducing the number of lawyers involved in a case, legal work would, in general, be done more cheaply in a fused profession. As Professor Zander put it, "there would be only one taximeter instead of two or three". Against this, the Senate argued that it was a fallacy to suppose that a two-branch profession led to two people doing the work of one and said that any double-manning could and should be eliminated under the present system. It concluded, "there may be a few residual instances of unavoidable duplication of effort which would be offset many times over by the cost-effectiveness of separation". This point was also made in the evidence of the London Criminal Courts Solicitors' Association.

> We have no doubt that in a fused profession the costs of legal services would escalate enormously, the range of choice available would decline and the degree of specialisation possible in the present system would also decline . . . The result of fusion would be a general decline in the service offered to the clients at a considerably increased cost.

17.25 The taxing masters of the Supreme Court at our request made comparative estimates of the costs of a sample of cases, on the basis of a fused and of a two-branch profession. They found they could do this only if they made a number of assumptions about the conduct of litigation in a fused profession which, they warned us, were speculative, and about which both the Senate and Law Society expressed strong reservations. In the light of the views expressed, we consider that no firm conclusion could be drawn from this exercise.

17.26 It has been argued that, even if the fees actually incurred are somewhat higher than they would be under a fused system, the present system is more cost effective. For example, it has been suggested that the effect of the intervention of a barrister is often to promote negotiations for a settlement, on which he can advise more objectively that a solicitor who has identified himself with the client and the client's wish to pursue the proceedings. It is impossible to quantify any saving which arises in this way. We are satisfied however that the independent view which is brought to bear by counsel can have the effect of limiting the issues or bringing about a settlement. Other things being equal, this may represent an important saving in time and cost to the client.

195

Arguments against Fusion

Purpose of the present restrictions

17.27   The two-branch profession is maintained by the rules which restrict the rights of audience of solicitors and access to barristers by lay clients. These rules have, in each case, a direct and an indirect object. The direct object of the rule governing rights of audience is to ensure, so far as possible, that advocacy in matters of substance is performed only by practitioners who specialise in it, and who have the time and the facilities to do so. The direct object of the rule which prevents access save through a solicitor by the client to the barrister is to ensure that barristers are free from hour-to-hour distractions and that specialist matters with which they deal are presented to them by a lawyer who has already identified the issues and sifted out the relevant facts, rather than by the lay client himself who can only present his problem as a whole. The object is not to put the barrister at a distance from his client, but to ensure, so far as possible, that his specialist skills are efficiently used, that he is ensured, so far as possible, the time necessary to concentrate on them and —this is put forward very much as a secondary objective—that he remains sufficiently detached from his client to be able to give him advice which is wholly objective. The indirect object of both these rules is to prevent the fusion and blurring of the two categories of practitioner, by ensuring that the solicitor does not undertake work for which a barrister is required and by ensuring that the barrister is not diverted to functions outside his specialty functions which can be better performed by the solicitor.

The weight of evidence

17.28   A number of large undertakings, in both the private and public sectors, gave evidence in support of the present system. Amongst lawyers who gave evidence, there was a clear weight of opinion against fusion. With the exception of the Legal Action Group and the United Lawyers' Association, all the professional bodies who submitted evidence to us on this topic were against fusion in principle. They included not only the Senate and the Law Society, but also the British Legal Association, the West Country Young Solicitors' Group, a number of local law societies, the London Criminal Courts Solicitors' Association, the Institute of Legal Executives, the Society of Labour Lawyers, the UK Association of European Law and a number of others. The current of opinion amongst the judges was emphatic and equally one-way. They favoured the present system, and submitted evidence to this effect in groups and singly.

Quality of service

17.29   The reason given by nearly all the witnesses, including the judges, for their opposition to fusion was that it would lead to a serious fall in the quality of advocacy and hence also, because of the nature of court proceedings, in the quality of judicial decisions. They argued that this would damage not merely the interests of individual litigants, but the administration of justice itself. In the following paragraphs we set out these arguments in more detail.

Access to advocates

17.30   It will be observed from Table 17.1 that, in April 1979, 58.4 per cent of all firms of solicitors had one or two partners and that a further 23.6 per cent had three or four partners. As we show in paragraph 17.38 below, the partners in these firms do not and cannot be expected to have between them all the experience or knowledge necessary to deal with every one of the wide range of problems brought to them by their clients. When court or tribunal work is involved they cannot always absent themselves from their offices for most of the working day, sometimes for many days on end, to represent their clients. It is therefore important that solicitors, especially those in small firms, should have ready access to barristers who can provide services which they cannot themselves provide. Any solicitor may retain a barrister to advise on a particular point of law or to represent his client in court or in a tribunal, sometimes for weeks on end. If necessary, he can obtain for any client the highest skills which the Bar can offer. It is therefore possible to select a barrister of standing and expertise equivalent to that of the barrister retained by the other party.

17.31   If the two branches of the profession were fused, it is likely that the larger firms of solicitors would seek to consolidate their position by inviting the leading barristers to join them as partners. This would enable these firms to provide most services likely to be required by their clients. Medium-sized firms of solicitors might wish to take one or more barristers into partnership to provide some, at least, of the services which they could not provide for their clients without them. To take one barrister only into a partnership would in practice be unlikely to be effective for this purpose. For example, if a firm absorbed a barrister who was skilled in criminal law and advocacy it would need another barrister if it wished to provide a comprehensive service in, for example, chancery work. It is unlikely that many such firms could provide enough work to keep one or more barristers employed solely as advocates unless they were able to obtain instructions on a regular basis from smaller firms of solicitors. In the event, many firms would not be able to recruit barristers because there would be too few to go round. This difficulty would be exacerbated if a large number of barristers decided to set up their own firms which they are not at present permitted to do.

17.32   The likely consequences of the situation that we have described are set out in the evidence of a barrister with knowledge of practice both in this country and in California who said:—

> Once the ability to instruct counsel is removed, by fusion, the tendency will be for lawyers to set themselves up as law firms providing a comprehensive service with 'trial lawyers' salaried by the firm. This will lead to bigger firms with bigger premises and the one man firm practising in the poorer areas will have to join the big firm in the richer area. My experience of law firms in California is that none have their offices in the poorer areas; in these parts the only lawyers available are young enthusiasts who set up legal 'co-operatives' and are more concerned

with righting political and economic injustices than doing day to day case work. I believe that the 'local' solicitor makes an important contribution to the present system in the United Kingdom and that his existence would be imperilled by fusion.

The Doncaster and District Law Society, in common with a number of other local law societies, mentioned the benefit of a divided profession to its members' clients.

> For the public . . . the existence of a divided profession is an advantage in that it makes available to everyone, in however remote an area geographically, or however complicated his legal problem, the best advice the Bar has to offer.

17.33   As the law becomes more complex and as the need for specialisation increases, solicitors' firms are likely to continue to increase in size by mergers and amalgamations and by natural growth. Up to a certain point, size has advantages both for the firm and for the clients. It is possible to specialise to a greater extent and thereby to offer the client a higher degree of technical expertise in certain classes of work. For these and other reasons the level of earnings in large firms is higher than in small ones and the provision for pensions is better. If, however, the pattern of the profession were to move too far towards a small number of large firms, as we believe would tend to happen in a fused profession, the effect would be to diminish the number of firms available to the public and thus to limit competition and freedom of choice, especially in smaller towns and rural areas. Such a development would clearly be against the public interest.

17.34   This assessment of the results of fusion is shared by many members of the legal profession as the following extracts from the evidence show. The Bristol Young Solicitors' Group said:—

> Complete and formal fusion with solicitors and barristers practising in partnership is not recommended by us. Services to people living in less populated areas of the country are already being eroded and formal fusion would hasten the decline of the many small firms of lawyers practising in such areas. The best barristers would, in our view, tend to disappear into the larger firms of solicitors in the conurbations thus giving rise to unmet needs in the case of smaller firms and their clients.

The Gloucestershire and Wiltshire Incorporated Law Society put the point in this way.

> It would be impossible for country solicitors in particular, and indeed the larger firms in the cities, to give the service to their clients which they give at the moment had they not the freedom to call on the specialist Bar where and when needed.

The Doncaster and District Law Society made the observation:—

> The most important argument against fusion lies in the long term disadvantage to the public. If there is fusion as it is generally understood, barristers would be free

to join solicitors' firms as partners or as retained counsel. They would naturally be attracted to those larger firms of solicitors especially in High Court centres, who could offer them the best terms of employment. The reserve of experience at the door now open for every solicitor to tap would be drained off into the large city practices.

17.35 In a fused profession, a partner in a small firm or a sole practitioner, one of whose clients required the services of an advocate, would either have to refer the client to another firm or undertake the advocacy himself, whether or not he was able satisfactorily to do so. If the case were referred to another firm to act as agents for advocacy alone, the criticisms of the present system, such as the cost of employing two lawyers and the need for one to brief the other, would apply. The cost could be expected to be higher, because, as we pointed out in paragraph 17.7, a solicitor's overhead expenses are appreciably higher than a barrister's. Moreover, it would be more difficult to obtain the services of a suitable advocate from amongst those employed in firms of solicitors, because their dispersal would complicate the process of selection and because the chosen advocate might prefer, quite properly, to give priority to the existing clients of his own firm. This could lead to the undesirable situation that, because only those litigants who retained the services of a large firm with advocacy partners would be assured of an advocacy service of the highest standard, there would be greater disparity that at present in the standards of advocacy on either side in cases coming before the courts.

17.36 Even if it were desirable to do so, a solicitor might be reluctant to refer a client to another firm because of the risk that he would permanently lose the client. A solicitor who himself favoured fusion told us, in answer to the point, that in a fused profession a firm which was not large enough to employ its own specialists would have to refer clients to larger firms: —

> . . . that is one of the arguments against my whole ethos, because it sounds the warning knell, if not the death knell, of the small firm of provincial solicitors. I can see the argument that the small firm would send the client with the difficult case to the large specialist firm. The practical result of that in certain cases will be that they will lose the client for ever. That has happened.

Decline in standards

17.37 The main argument put forward against fusion of the two branches of the profession, as already stated in paragraph 17.29, is that it would lead to a decline in the overall standard of performance by diluting the specialist knowledge and experience of the Bar.

17.38 In Chapter 27 we explain why no lawyer can reasonably be expected to be competent to deal with every matter brought before him. There is a growing need for lawyers to specialise. Specialisation involves not only an adequate theoretical and practical training, but also regular practice in the speciality. Because of the nature of their training and because they concentrate on it, many barristers may fairly claim to be described as specialists in advocacy.

199

17.39   We have already mentioned as a likely result of fusion that the amount of advocacy undertaken by non-specialist advocates would increase. The effect of a separate Bar is that most barristers are continuously engaged in advocacy and in work closely related to it. They regularly pit themselves in public against other practitioners, usually of equal calibre, sometimes acknowledged masters in their field. These factors enable them to keep up-to-date with case law and practice and the trend of judicial thought and developments in professional opinion, and also to develop and maintain their skill and experience.

17.40   We received evidence that if an advocate does not appear regularly before the courts, the standard of his work will fall. Lord Justice Roskill cited the following example : —

> I have known of one firm of solicitors who wished to specialise in a particular field having sought to secure the services as a partner of a barrister specialising in that field. They were disappointed in the result because that former barrister's skills began to diminish in quality once only a limited source of supply of work—the clients of that particular firm—was available to him.

We find this argument convincing and consider that it accurately reflects one likely outcome of fusion.

Selection of judges

17.41   Nearly all the judges are recruited from among the senior members of the Bar, although it has recently become possible for a solicitor, who has served as a recorder for three years, to be appointed a circuit judge and nine solicitors have been so appointed. The Lord Chancellor's Department stressed to us that it is necesssary for the Lord Chancellor to have the fullest possible information about candidates for appointment to judicial office. This is available under the present system because the number of practising barristers is not great, because their talents are well known in the profession and are often on public display and because the Lord Chancellor and his senior advisers are likely to have personal knowledge of the most senior members of the Bar. Fusion would increase the numbers available for consideration but might increase the possibility of making an unsuitable choice.

The effect of present trends

17.42   Because of the growing trend towards specialisation and the need at all levels for effective advocacy, we think it likely that, if the profession were fused, there would be a demand for the kind of service which is now provided by the Bar. This is visualised by those who support fusion, one of whom, Mr. A. Huxley, said in evidence:—

> . . . in my submission there must be, even if one has fusion, a rump of the Bar. Call it what you will, there will be some kind of lump advocacy labour, in other words, a pool on which one can draw for a particular case. That has to exist even under a fused system.

17.43 This view is supported by experience in other jurisdictions, in particular New Zealand and Australia. When the legal profession began to operate in these countries the distances which practitioners had to travel were often considerable, communications were bad and slow and the countries were sparsely inhabited. In these conditions no separate Bars were established. In more recent times specialist Bars have developed in order to meet an increasing demand for specialisation in the practice of the law. The results are said to have been beneficial. The Chief Justice of Australia, in oral evidence, made the following comment.

> *Q.* Chief Justice, you said that some of the States which were originally fused had become divided and that you had seen this happen. As a consequence of the division do you think that the quality of the advocacy has improved?
>
> *A.* Yes it has. That I can say. I have watched these Bars grow in my time as a practising man but even more so since I have been in this office, which I have now held for 13 years.

17.44 In New Zealand a number of lawyers practise as barristers, although the profession is not formally divided. The former Chief Justice, the late Sir Richard Wild, expressed the view in oral evidence that formal division, on the British pattern, was unlikely. Whilst agreeing that the system worked well in New Zealand, his colleague Sir Robin Cooke, a judge of the New Zealand Court of Appeal, who was the first lawyer in his country to practise as a barrister from the start of his professional career, said:—

> I am one of those who does subscribe to this concept of a separate Bar and I make no secret of the fact that I think it is one of the great British achievements to have evolved such a system or institution. One would be somewhat dismayed to find that in the country of its birth it was either abolished or radically altered. I think that the idea of an independent body of men and women, specialists and skilled in their type of legal service, and not mere paid agents for the clients but recognising that they owe some responsibility to the courts and having the confidence of the courts, and the standard of ethics and professional skill that tends to go with that, is an extremely valuable concept, and long may that continue.

Summary

17.45 In the light of all the considerations set out above we have reached the following conclusions. We consider it likely that in a fused profession there would be an unacceptable reduction in the number and spread of the smaller firms of solicitors and an increase in the proportion of large city firms. This would accentuate the present uneven distribution of solicitors and reduce the choice and availability of legal services. We are satisfied that in the future there will be a greater need for specialisation. Fusion would disperse the specialist service which is now provided by the Bar and we consider that this would operate against the public interest. In a large firm with an advocate partner there would be readier communication than is usual between solicitor and barrister; but this advantage would not be realised in a fused profession to the extent that it proved necessary for the smaller firm to refer its clients to larger firms for an advocacy service.

17.46 In terms of cost, it is difficult to make accurate estimates, because they depend heavily on assumptions. On balance, we believe that in small cases there might be some saving, but that in the larger cases this would not be so and the expense might be greater. With regard to the administration of justice, the weight of evidence is strongly to the effect that a two-branch profession is more likely than a fused one to ensure the high quality of advocacy which is indispensable, so long as our system remains in its present form, to secure the proper quality of justice. These considerations lead us to the unanimous conclusion that it is in the public interest for the legal profession to be organised, as at present, in two branches.

Conclusion

Paragraphs

| **Structure of the legal profession** | R17.1 | The legal profession should continue to be organised in two branches, barristers and solicitors. | 17.45–17.46 |

CHAPTER 18

Rights of Audience

Introductory

Existing rights of audience

18.1   A right of audience entitles a person to address a court of law or tribunal, on his own behalf or on behalf of another, otherwise than as a witness. In England, Wales and to a lesser extent in Northern Ireland restrictions are placed on rights of audience in all courts of law and in some tribunals. In this chapter we deal with the questions whether the present restrictions in England and Wales are in the public interest and whether they should be removed, extended or modified.

18.2   The present arrangements as to rights of audience are set out in detail in annex 18.1 to this chapter, and are summarised in the following paragraphs.

18.3   In all courts and tribunals a party who is not represented by a lawyer has a right of audience on his own behalf. He is known in the courts as a "litigant in person". Except for the litigant in person, a layman—which, for this purpose, means a person who is not a practising member of the legal profession—has no absolute right of audience in any court, but at the discretion of the court may be allowed audience in the county courts and magistrates' courts.

18.4   The rights of audience of practising members of the legal profession vary according to the branch of the profession to which the practitioner belongs. A barrister in private practice has a right of audience before all courts. A solicitor with a practising certificate has a right of audience in the magistrates' courts and county courts, a limited right of audience in the Crown Court and save in a few cases and when the court is sitting privately in chambers, no right of audience in the High Court, the Court of Appeal or the House of Lords.

Proposed changes

18.5   Proposals made to us for change fell under two heads, relating to rights of audience for laymen and to the present differences in the rights of audience of barristers and solicitors. As to laymen, the proposals ranged from the total abolition of all restrictions on rights of audience to the imposition of additional restrictions to prevent laymen, in tribunals as well as courts, appearing on behalf of others. With regard to barristers and solicitors, the proposals ranged from giving solicitors an equal right of audience in all courts or substantially extending their right of audience in the Crown Court, to making modifications to enable solicitors to appear in certain uncontested matters in the High Court and Crown Court.

General considerations

18.6 As a general rule, restrictive practices must be shown to be in the public interest. If, in any given case, it is established that restrictions are desirable in the public interest, some dividing line must be drawn beyond which they operate. This cannot be done to suit every individual case: instances will arise in which another line, more or less restrictive, would be more suitable.

18.7 The arguments we have considered are related to the nature of our legal system. We have pointed out in Chapter 17 that, if there are any changes in the system, in particular in the direction of a system based on codified law rather than precedent, the importance of advocacy as an integral part of the administration of justice may be reduced. We have dealt with the following issues on the assumption that the present system will remain.

Rights of Audience: Laymen

The litigant in person

18.8 We have received evidence from the judges that a person who is a party to proceedings in the superior courts is ill-advised to conduct his case on his own behalf. In the great majority of cases a litigant in person lacks the necessary knowledge to present his case properly and this adds appreciably to the difficulties of the court in ensuring that his case is properly brought out and that justice is done. But it is a long-established right in our law that a person is entitled to speak on his own behalf in any court. It has not been suggested that this right should be removed, although it may lead to undesirable results in some cases. We do not recommend any change in the present arrangement nor in the related rules concerning the right of a litigant to dismiss his legal representatives in the course of proceedings and thereafter to represent himself.

Lay advocates

18.9 It has been suggested in evidence submitted to us that no restriction should be imposed on rights of audience in any court. The Trades Union Congress proposed in its written evidence that laymen should have a general right of audience on this basis, though in oral evidence its representatives confined their argument to union officials who, they said, should have a right of audience in the lower courts on behalf of their members in cases in which their experience of industrial work and practice and of matters relating to employment gave them special expertise.

18.10   It has been argued, in favour of a complete abandonment of restrictions on rights of audience, that public dependence on professional services should be reduced and that, therefore, formal rules maintaining such dependence should be abrogated, that the courts should be made less legalistic and that litigants should have an unrestricted choice of advocate, lay or professional, in particular in cases where they cannot obtain or cannot afford the services of a lawyer.

18.11   We think it desirable that all citizens should have some understanding of the law and its operation and of the procedure of the courts. We support simplification of law and procedure for the purpose of enabling a layman to handle his own case if it is reasonably straightforward. But court proceedings, particularly in the higher courts, inevitably call for special skill and expertise. Moreover they represent for the individual involved a crisis in his affairs which may affect the rest of his life if, for instance, he is convicted of a serious offence. Elsewhere in this report we recommend increased financial support for the provision of legal services, including representation in court. We propose improvements in professional training, disciplinary procedures and arrangements for handling complaints and in the quality of service in general. Our purpose is to make skilled assistance available at need. We are all dependent on the knowledge and skills of others, for legal advice and representation as for other forms of service. In our view it would be inconsistent to propose increased effort and expenditure on a skilled legal service and at the same time propose that, when the protection it confers is most needed, it may be discarded.

Lay representation in the superior courts

18.12   In the interest of protecting litigants from ill-formed or inefficient representation, and to avoid increasing the difficulties of the courts in ensuring that justice prevails, we are satisfied that laymen should have no rights of audience, save as litigants in person, in the superior courts, that is, in the Crown Court, the High Court, the Court of Appeal and the House of Lords. We do not consider that an exception can be made in favour of a lay advocate merely because he is unpaid. Such an arrangement does not meet the objections expressed above. The same applies to close relatives of the litigant, though it is always possible for a relative or friend to sit beside a litigant in person to give him advice and support: see annex 18.1 paragraph 2.

Lay representation in the lower courts

18.13   In the lower courts, there are many cases in which the issues of fact are simple and the law is certain. Accordingly, both county courts and magistrates' courts have a statutory discretion to confer a right of audience on any person, lawyer or layman. We have received no criticism of the way in which this discretion is exercised in the magistrates' courts. It has, however, been said that certain county courts are unduly restrictive in their attitude to lay representation in general, and that particular difficulties arise in the case of registered companies. We deal with these two categories of complaint below.

Lay representation in the county court

18.14 The jurisdiction of the county court covers a wide field. It may deal at one extreme with claims in contract or tort amounting to £2,000 and with land and property of a rateable value up to £1,000. The jurisdiction of the county court overlaps that of the High Court because cases may, in certain circumstances, be transferred to the county court from the superior court. Some cases in the county courts involve complex issues of law and fact, for the proper resolution of which there is as great a need of skilled legal representation on either side as in the High Court. At the other extreme are claims of up to £200, in dealing with which the court has power to proceed by way of informal arbitration. A small case, like any other, may involve complex issues, but, in a county court arbitration, it is the practice for the arbitrator to intervene in the presentation and discussion of a case so as to assist the parties. In view of this, and of the amount at stake, legal representation is discouraged in arbitrations of this type by making no award of costs to the successful party.

18.15 It is clearly necessary in these circumstances that the county courts should maintain a flexible attitude in exercising their discretion concerning the right of audience of laymen. It appears from the evidence submitted to us that there are some courts in which too restrictive an attitude is taken. We can best illustrate this by means of an example taken from evidence given to the Commission.

18.16 The British Actors' Equity Association, on behalf of its members, claims money due in respect of fees for professional engagements. Although it is frequently necessary to obtain judgment in the county court in order to secure payment, the sums claimed are usually too small to justify the cost of employing a solicitor to pursue a claim. In these circumstances, it is the practice for the officials of the union to prepare the necessary court papers and appear on behalf of members at hearings. In many cases it is not practicable for a member to appear on his own behalf because of professional commitments elsewhere in the country. We have been told that there are some county courts in which the union is not permitted to represent its members in this way, even in cases where the member could not attend court without losing a valuable professional engagement and where the amount involved is too small to justify the employment of a solicitor. We think it unreasonable that a responsible layman, authorised by an association of this kind, should be refused a right of audience in such a case.

Representation of companies

18.17 Registered companies, and other corporations recognised as such by the law, are legal, not natural, persons and for the purposes of their day-to-day business are represented by their directors and officers. For the purpose of legal proceedings, a company is represented by a solicitor and, if necessary, a barrister. In the lower courts, however, it is possible for a company to be represented at the court's discretion by any person associated with it, usually a director or officer.

18.18 We received complaints from a number of witnesses that, in some county courts, companies were unreasonably required to be represented by a solicitor, even where a case involved no difficult issues of law and fact (and might even be uncontested) and the amount at stake did not justify the cost of retaining a solicitor. We accept that the complexity and cost are not the only relevant criteria. It may be necessary, for example, to require legal representation to ensure that a claim is not handled oppressively or improperly. But, in general, we consider that a director or officer of a company, who is able to produce evidence of proper authorisation for the purpose, should be entitled to represent the company where the amount of the claim does not justify the employment of a solicitor and where there are no complex issues of law and fact or other reasons for requiring legal representation.

The need for consistency
18.19 An unsatisfactory aspect of the present situation is the lack of consistency in the application of discretion as between one court and the other. The exercise of this discretion is judicial in character, and is not, therefore, subject to administrative directions in any given case. This being so, we consider that the best means of securing greater consistency would be to include in the relevant rules of court certain guidelines for the operation of the discretion.

Guidelines
18.20 In the guidelines we consider that the court should be required to have regard, amongst other factors, to the amount at stake in relation to the likely cost of representation, the complexity of the issues of fact and law, the nature of the claim and the risk that it would not be properly handled in the absence of legal representation. Where there are classes of case in which procedural safeguards are of importance, it may be necessary, on the principles stated in paragraph 18.11, to provide that legal representation shall as a rule be required. The guidelines should apply to lay representation in general, not only to representation of a company by a director or officer; and it should be provided that where an application for lay representation is refused, reasons should be given.

Representation before tribunals
18.21 We received two criticisms of the present arrangements for rights of audience before tribunals. The first was that, although legal representation is permitted before all tribunals except the committees that hear complaints

against National Health Service practitioners, the majority of applicants before tribunals are unable to afford legal representation and legal aid is not available to them. We have made recommendations in Chapter 15 to remove this defect. The second criticism was more fundamental. It was argued that legal representation alone should be permitted in any court or tribunal. This was associated, in the evidence submitted to us, with the proposal that the county courts should take over all the present functions of tribunals. This proposal ignores, or seeks to change, the policy established over the past half-century that there is a class of work best dealt with in specialist tribunals. It is the intention in most tribunals that the lay applicant or claimant should be able to represent himself. We think it right, in the public interest, to propose an extension of legal aid to tribunals to enable the legal profession to make its services available where they will be useful. But it is not realistic to propose that the legal profession, with its present or potential numbers and training, can be expected to assume, to the exclusion of laymen, functions of advocacy in tribunals of all kinds, even if it were desirable in practice that they should do so. We do not accept this proposal.

Rights of Audience: Lawyers

Scope of section
18.22   We deal in Chapters 20 and 31 with the rights of audience of employed lawyers and of unadmitted staff in solicitors' firms. We are concerned in the following section solely with the rights of audience of barristers and solicitors in private practice.

Proposals for change
18.23   In addition to a number of minor variations on the present arrangements, the major changes proposed to us are for: —

(a)   a general extension of the right of audience of solicitors to all courts;

(b)   specific extensions of the right of audience of solicitors, in particular in certain classes of case in the Crown Court.

18.24   The general considerations arising here are the same as those arising from the issue of fusion discussed in Chapter 17, namely whether it is in the public interest to change the present arrangements and if so, to what extent. The particular considerations are also the same: so far as concerns the individual client, the efficiency and quality of the service available, its cost and the client's confidence in it; and from the viewpoint of the public as a whole, the maintenance of the quality of justice and its effective administration.

18.25   The most convenient way of dealing with this topic is to take first proposition (b) in paragraph 18.23, that solicitors should have an extended right of audience, in particular in the Crown Court. This involves the same questions of principle as proposition (a).

Solicitors' right of audience in the Crown Court

18.26   The Law Society proposed that solicitors should have an extended right of audience in the Crown Court. In order to explain what was proposed it is necessary to describe the way in which the business of the Crown Court is organised. For the purposes of the distribution of criminal business in the Crown Court, cases coming before the court are divided into four classes. Classes 1 and 2 comprise capital offences and others of the greatest gravity; classes 3 and 4 comprise the remaining indictable offences, of varying degrees of gravity. The purpose of this classification is to enable cases to be assigned for hearing by the appropriate judge. Class 1 cases can be dealt with only by a High Court judge; class 2 cases are normally dealt with by a High Court judge; class 3 cases may be dealt with by a High Court judge, but are usually assigned to a circuit judge or recorder; class 4 cases are as a rule dealt with by a circuit judge or recorder.

18.27   The Law Society proposed that solicitors should have a right of audience in all cases listed for trial by a circuit judge, deputy circuit judge or recorder. It agreed that solicitors should not have a right of audience in civil cases before a High Court judge in open court nor before a High Court judge in the Crown Court. It pointed out that, in civil cases, solicitors at present have a right of audience in the county courts in which cases are heard by circuit judges, and that a solicitor who has served as a recorder may now be appointed a circuit judge.

18.28   Any system of allocating work amongst advocates which depends on the status of the judge who is to try the case is in our view impracticable. It may not be known, for example, until a late stage which judge is to hear the case. The court, in order to expedite business, may reassign a case to a different judge shortly before the hearing. We think that this practical difficulty rules out the Law Society's proposal in its present form. We have nonetheless considered it on the basis that solicitors should have rights of audience in the Crown Court in all cases falling within classes 3 and 4 which are, as a general rule, heard by a circuit judge, as well as in all appeals and committals for sentence from the magistrates' courts.

18.29   For the purpose of weighing the effect of this proposal, it is necessary to consider the volume of business in the Crown Court in the various classes of case. The number of cases heard in 1978 is set out in the following table.

TABLE 18.1

Cases disposed of in the Crown Court, 1978

Committals for trial		
Class 1	381	
Class 2	711	
Class 3	5,261	
Class 4	44,275	73,520
Appeals	16,195	(92%)
Committals for Sentence	13,050	
Total	79,873	

Source: Lord Chancellor's Department.

Note: About 95 per cent of all criminal cases are dealt with in the magistrates' courts. Such cases are generally much shorter than those dealt with in the Crown Court.

18.30 The following table shows the average hearing times of the cases disposed of in 1978 which went to a full hearing.

TABLE 18.2

Average hearing times by class of case:

Crown Court, 1978

	Number	Average time (hours)	Total (hours)	As % of total
Committals for trial[1]				
Cases involving (Class 1) ..	202	19·57	3,954	1·7
a plea of (Class 2) ..	320	13·56	4,340	1·9
not guilty: (Class 3) ..	2,148	14·04	30,158	13·3
(Class 4) ..	19,206	7·66	147,082	65·1
Guilty pleas:	28,750	0·68	19,492	8·6
Appeals[2]	13,806	0·97	13,426	5·9
Committals for sentence:[3]	15,708	0·49	7,623	3·4
Total	80,140	2·82	226,075	100·0

[1]Excluding cases which were disposed of without a hearing, which are, however, included in Table 18.1.
[2]Excluding abandoned appeals, which are included in Table 18.1.
[3]Including cases 'brought back' and deferred sentences, which are excluded from Table 18.1.
Source: Lord Chancellor's Department.

18.31   Table 18.1 shows that over 95 per cent of the cases disposed of in the Crown Court could, in the proposal under consideration, be dealt with by solicitors. Table 18.2 shows that the same would be true of the caseload measured by time.

18.32   For the purpose of providing evidence on this issue the Law Society sounded out opinion amongst the local law societies. Enquiries of this character do not give a precise indication of the state of opinion within the profession. Some local societies canvassed opinion amongst all their members, some only amongst committee members. The result, however, was as follows. Out of a total of 121 local law societies, 108 replied: 33 sought a greatly extended right of audience, 15 sought some limited extension and 60 wished for no additional right of audience.

18.33   Amongst barristers, a minority favoured an extended right of audience for solicitors; but the Senate, speaking for the profession as a whole, was against the proposal. Strong opposition to it was expressed by the Criminal Law Bar Association and the Young Barristers' Committee of the Senate. The judiciary as a whole was against an extension of solicitors' right of audience. The presiding judges of the six circuits, the High Court judges and the Council of Her Majesty's Circuit Judges all gave firm and unanimous evidence on this point.

18.34   The Crown Court handles less than 5 per cent of criminal cases. The effect of extending solicitors' right of audience to 95 per cent of Crown Court cases would therefore be to enable them to appear in nearly all criminal cases, omitting only the most grave.

18.35   For the purposes of considering the immediate effect on the interests of the client and of the public of such an extension, it is necessary to identify the nature of the work involved, and the special skills, knowledge or experience necessary for the competent performance of it.

18.36   None of the cases falling within the jurisdiction of the Crown Court is trivial in character. Class 3 cases include all robberies, including armed robbery, all cases of wounding and causing grievous bodily harm with intent, all affrays and all frauds including conspiracy to defraud. Class 4 cases include forgery, obtaining goods and services by deception, all offences of causing bodily harm and many of criminal damage. Many of the offences include issues of substantial difficulty, and may attract sentences of many years' imprisonment. All cases tried at first instance in the Crown Court are heard by a judge and a jury. The Crown Court is now the only court operating in our jurisdiction in which jury trials are a regular occurrence.

211

18.37 As a general rule, advocacy in the higher courts, in particular jury advocacy, calls for particular skills which can be maintained only by constant practice. Whereas the skills and knowledge involved in addressing a magistrate, a county court judge and a High Court judge have much in common (although a greater knowledge of law may be necessary in addressing a High Court judge, and the issues will be more important), the skills involved in addressing a jury are unlike those involved in any other form of professional advocacy. They are more akin to the skills involved in public speaking and even those with natural talent and proper training need constant practice if they are to improve those skills. The other qualities which are called for in the Crown Court, more so than in a county court or a magistrates' court, are a detailed knowledge of the laws of evidence and skill and experience in cross- examination, sometimes prolonged, which is one of the most difficult of the advocate's arts to perfect. Finally, where the outcome may have very grave consequences for the defendant, it is necessary for his advocate to be able to combine the proper balance between identification and detachment, and to be accustomed to working in an environment in which emotions run high. It is significant that the London Criminal Courts Solicitors' Association regards the element of objectivity which a barrister is able to bring to a case as of value in presenting a case to the judge and jury.

18.38 Many solicitors make competent advocates in magistrates' courts and county courts and some are very good. Some could achieve the same standard in the Crown Court if they could so arrange their professional lives as to enable them to concentrate on the work there. We have remarked that the majority of firms are not organised so as to enable one or more partners to concentrate only on advocacy and, even were they able to do so, the ready availability of the solicitor to his other clients might well be jeopardised. Given the present structure and distribution of the solicitors' branch of the profession (see Table 17.1), we do not think it realistic to suppose that more than a relatively small number of firms could organise themselves in this way. In short, we think it unlikely that many solicitors, except in large firms, would be able under present conditions to have the constant practice in Crown Court advocacy which competence and progressive improvement require. If changes in the profession took place which enabled this difficulty to be avoided, other undesirable consequences would follow, as we have found in Chapter 17. We therefore believe that if rights of audience were exercised by solicitors generally in the Crown Court, the quality of service would decline.

18.39 The question of costs is important but, for the reasons which are given in Chapter 17, we do not think that the changes proposed by the Law Society, taking one case with another, would be likely to effect any significant economies.

18.40 The present arrangements ensure a system of objective selection which the proposed arrangements would lack. At present, to judge from the data obtained by our Users' Survey, a client goes to a solicitor, usually by way of personal recommendation, without any informed knowledge of his capacity for handling the class of work required. The number of firms available in a given area and likely to be known to a potential client is limited and the area of choice is not wide. However, when it is necessary to instruct a barrister, it is the responsibility of the solicitor to advise his client which of the barristers practising in the relevant field is fitted to take the case in question. The qualities required are more likely to be found by this method than any other. Accordingly, we consider that, under the present arrangements, the range of informed choice is wider and selection of a suitable advocate more likely.

18.41   The conclusion just stated would not be correct if sufficient barristers were not available to do the work required. In this respect the position has changed in recent years. The Royal Commission on Assizes and Quarter Sessions, in its report published in 1969 (Cmnd. 4153), found that there was a shortage of barristers to deal with criminal work in certain areas. It ascribed this, in part, to a general shortage of barristers and in part to the awkward distribution of court business. Following this report, the Bar undertook a recruiting campaign and the administration of the criminal courts was re-organised. Since 1968, the number of barristers working in the provinces and the number of provincial chambers has doubled. Across the country as a whole, there is now a surplus rather than a shortage of barristers.

18.42   Under the Courts Act 1971, the Lord Chancellor has power by regulation to enable solicitors to appear in the Crown Court in specific areas. When the legislation came into effect, the Lord Chancellor designated five areas for this purpose, in which solicitors had traditionally exercised a right of audience at quarter sessions. Since then, no request for an extension of the right of audience in any other area has been received by the Lord Chancellor's Department from the Law Society, from any local law society or from any organisation connected with the legal profession. If it should occur that there were too few barristers of sufficient experience and ability to deal with the work arising in any area, no doubt a right of audience for solicitors would be sought. But at present, even in areas where solicitors now have a full right of audience, the number of occasions on which this right is exercised is negligible.

18.43   In one significant respect the present arrangements serve what many regard, we think rightly, as an important public purpose, by ensuring that in the Crown Court the case for the prosecution is put by an advocate who is independent both of the police and of the prosecuting authority. The Law Society accepted the desirability of the present arrangement and said that the right of audience in the Crown Court should not be extended to solicitors employed by the county prosecuting solicitors' departments, ". . . unless there is a statutory separation of the office of the prosecuting solicitor from the police authority". There is, for instance, such a separation between the office of the Director of Public Prosecutions and the police. It is for the Royal Commission on Criminal Procedure to make recommendations on this point.

18.44 Whatever the outcome, we think that the effect of the present arrangement on prosecution work should not be disturbed. It provides in every case an advocate from the available range of privately practising barristers who is seen by the court, the accused and the public at large to be independent of the police and the prosecuting authority; one who, by the nature of his training and daily practice, is more likely to be able to bring the essential qualities of detachment and balance to bear on the problem in individual cases. These are considerations which we regard as crucial not only to the actual conduct of a jury trial but also to the proper administration of justice in general, including the institution or continuance of criminal proceedings, the acceptance of proposed pleas of guilty and the proper handling of evidential problems.

18.45 There is one other consideration to which we should refer. In some magistrates' courts there is already appearing a separation between "prosecuting solicitors" drawn from prosecuting departments either locally (county prosecuting solicitors) or nationally (the Customs and Excise or the Inland Revenue and "defending solicitors" drawn from private firms of solicitors. In many cases there is little, if any, interchange between the two groups. If encouraged, this trend would lead to the loss of the substantial advantages to be gained by practitioners with experience in both types of work, and to the identification of certain lawyers as being invariably on the side of, or invariably in opposition to, the authorities. Experience outside the United Kingdom suggests that this would be a retrograde step to take, and would not contribute to demonstrably just and fair results.

18.46 It has been pointed out in paragraph 18.27 above that the circuit judge before whom a right of audience is sought sits in both the Crown Court and the county courts. It was argued that, as solicitors have a right of audience before the circuit judge in the county courts, they should not be denied a right of audience before him in the Crown Court. Secondly, it was argued that because a solicitor after a period as a recorder may be appointed a circuit judge, solicitor-advocates should have a right of audience before a circuit judge.

18.47 As to the first point, we see a clear distinction between the work of the county courts and that of the Crown Court. The county courts have a limited jurisdiction and deal with minor civil cases. The same is not true of the Crown Court. All indictable criminal offences falling within the original jurisdiction of the Crown Court involve a jury trial and many may attract severe sentences.

18.48 We do not regard the second argument, which turns on the fact that a solicitor may become a circuit judge, as of any weight. A solicitor may well be fitted for judicial office, and it would be wasteful if there were no means by which he could achieve it. It does not follow that all solicitors should be regarded as qualified to practise advocacy in courts in which former solicitors may sit as judges.

18.49 Defining rights of audience by reference to a certain level of court produces arbitrary results. Cases of difficulty can arise in the lower courts, while straightforward cases may be dealt with in the superior courts. But it is common ground that advocacy in the higher courts is, in general, more demanding than elsewhere. The fact that a dividing line is arbitrary does not imply that it should be entirely removed.

18.50 It was suggested to us that if solicitors were not to have a full right of audience in the Crown Court, they should be entitled to appear in a case in which a brief is returned so late that it is not possible adequately to instruct another barrister. One purpose of this proposal is to discourage the late return of briefs, but it could also be argued that a better service to the client would result. The late return of briefs is in any event an unsatisfactory practice, and we think it better to avoid it by more direct means. We deal with this point in Chapter 22. This apart, it would be difficult in practice to establish at what point it would be appropriate for the solicitor to keep the case, rather than to seek another barrister free to undertake it. The solicitor concerned might not be capable of attaining the standard of advocacy required in the case; at the same time, if his client wished him to do so, he might feel impelled to deal with it himself, when it would be more in the client's interest to obtain, even at a late stage, the services of an experienced advocate capable of preparing the case quickly. We consider that, if there is not enough time for an experienced advocate to prepare a case, the only solution which protects the interests of the client is an adjournment. A solicitor should not find himself under pressure to take over the conduct of a case in court precisely when it is most difficult to do so.

18.51 The foregoing analysis leads us to the view that the Law Society's proposals should not be supported. We have also considered a further question, namely, whether an extension of solicitors' right of audience in the Crown Court would be likely to damage the Bar in such a way as to jeopardise its future existence as a separate branch of the profession. The Senate and members of the Bar are emphatic that this result would follow and have drawn our attention to the following matters.

18.52 Tables 18.1 and 18.2 show that the proposed extension of rights of audience would enable solicitors to deal with 95 per cent of the work in the Crown Court, whether assessed by case load or by working time. The surveys of remuneration (Volume II sections 16 and 18) show that the barristers' branch of the profession depends heavily on earnings from criminal work. The total gross receipts of the solicitors' branch in all classes of business in 1975/76 were calculated to be about £633 million; of this £141 million was in respect of contentious business, which comprises both criminal and civil litigation. The total fee income of the Bar in 1976/77 amounted to approximately £48 million, of which not less than 25 per cent was estimated to relate to work in the Crown Court. It appears to be correct that an extension of solicitors' work in the Crown Court would have a serious and disproportionate impact on the income and capacity of barristers to continue in practice. This is borne out by Table 18.3 which shows the dependence of barristers on criminal work for their livelihood. It will be seen that, at the junior end of the Bar, barristers are heavily dependent on this source of income which represents about 50 per cent of the total. It will also be observed from Chapter 36 that the incomes of young barristers are already low by comparison with other occupations.

TABLE 18.3

Sources of barristers' fees, 1976/77

Seniority of barristers	Proportion of 1976/77 gross fees on criminal work provided from public funds		
	Total	Criminal[1] Public Funds	Criminal[2] Legal Aid
	%	%	%
QCs			
appointed before 1974	21	7	14
appointed in or after 1974	29	14	15
Juniors			
called over 15 years	31	18	13
called 9 – 15 years	36	19	17
called 4 – 8 years	46	19	27
called 3 years or less	52	15	37

[1]'Criminal Public Funds' indicates fees paid for prosecution work.
[2]'Criminal Legal Aid' indicates fees paid for criminal defence work.
Source: Consultants' report on the survey of income at the Bar, 1976/77 (Volume II section 18).

18.53 It is possible that if their right of audience was extended, solicitors would, in general, make as little use of it as they do in those Crown Court centres in which, at present, they have a full right of audience (see paragraph 18.42 above). No certain predictions can be made because of the number of assumptions involved. There are, however, factors which would attract firms of solicitors to aim at building up more substantial advocacy practices. First, it is natural to extend business wherever possible, especially in well-established lines such as advocacy. Secondly, subject to whatever changes in fee structure may be made, there is at present a tendency to reward advocacy more highly than work done out of court. Thirdly, advocacy in the Crown Court receives wider publicity than advocacy in magistrates' courts; successful advocacy in the Crown Court would be both a proper and effective means of building up a firm's reputation. Finally, the volume of work available would enable firms who built up substantial advocacy departments to attract recruits of high calibre with a vocation for that class of work.

18.54 There is evidence that it would be contrary to the public interest if substantial advocacy practices in the Crown Court were built up in any one area by a limited number of solicitors' firms, who thereby established a near-monopoly of criminal business. We have evidence that in some provincial areas a limited number of firms have tended to monopolise criminal work in the magistrates' courts. It is said to be one of the advantages of a duty solicitor scheme that, fairly organised, it can help to reverse this tendency. If the firms concerned were in a position to offer a complete service of representation, including advocacy in the Crown Court, their ability to build up and maintain a monopoly position in this class of work would be strengthened. This would be a step towards a system which, as we said in paragraph 18.45, we do not favour, in which all criminal work becomes concentrated in relatively few firms and public offices, each consistently representing only one side, either defence or prosecution.

Practical issues
18.55 The merits of granting rights of audience to solicitors have been argued in this chapter from the point of view of principle but there are in addition important practical issues. Solicitors are not short of work and many of them complain that they are already overstretched. If the solicitors' branch of the profession is to provide for the needs of the public, it will have a substantial programme of work before it to meet deficiencies in many aspects of social welfare work (see Chapter 4); heavier burdens will fall upon it if duty solicitors are established in all magistrates' courts and prisons (see Chapter 9); the arrangements proposed for a free initial half-hour will further enlarge the scope of its day-to-day work (see Chapter 13); much will have to be done in the educational field (see Chapter 39). These and other changes will provide a substantial programme of future work over a period of years. The suggested extension of solicitors' right of audience would involve considerable changes in the profession over the same period and would distract it from the need of the public for forms of service other than advocacy which, within the present structure, solicitors could and should undertake. By contrast the Bar, particularly the junior Bar, which is already equipped to provide the needs of the public in the Crown Court, has surplus capacity. There seems to us little sense in making a change which would put additional burdens on the solicitors' branch, which is already overloaded, and at the same time would erode the position of the Bar, in particular its junior members.

18.56 For the reasons given above we have reached the conclusion that the solicitors' right of audience should not be generally extended in the Crown Court. We see no reason, however, to disturb the present arrangement by which a solicitor for the defence has a right of audience in the Crown Court in an appeal or committal for sentence from a magistrates' court, if his firm represented the defendant in the court below. We have considered as a separate issue whether solicitors should have a right of audience to deal with pleas in mitigation on behalf of a defendant who has pleaded guilty.

Pleas in mitigation

18.57 The main argument in favour of permitting solicitors to undertake pleas in mitigation following a plea of guilty in the Crown Court is that they regularly undertake such work in the magistrates' courts and have, therefore, the necessary skills and experience. In support of this argument it is pointed out that a plea in mitigation can be distinguished from other types of advocacy before the Crown Court in that it is addressed solely to the judge and not to the jury. It is said to be comparable with an appearance before a judge in chambers, in respect of which solicitors already enjoy a right of audience. It is also said that it is a positive advantage if the advocate making the plea in mitigation has direct personal knowledge of the client and has himself gathered the information and interviewed those providing the material on which the plea is to be based. For these reasons it is argued that the clients' solicitor will be able to present a more personal and more committed, and thus a more effective, plea.

18.58 The main argument against permitting solicitors to undertake pleas in mitigation in the Crown Court is based on the fact that a plea in the Crown Court relates to a serious offence attracting a penalty more severe than a plea in the magistrates' court. The plea is therefore said to be of greater importance to the defendant, to the public, and to the judge who normally has to determine the sentence on his own instead of (as with lay justices) as one of a bench. In this country it is not the practice for the prosecution to ask for a particular sentence, or to comment on the offence; nor can the prosecution appeal against sentence. When deciding upon a sentence, therefore, the judge is especially assisted by, and to some extent dependent upon, the skill and objectivity of the practitioner making the plea. It is argued that since the consequences of a sentence, particularly a custodial sentence, are likely to be serious, the convicted offender requires the highest possible standard of representation which can only be provided by a specialist advocate. If all solicitors were enabled to undertake this category of work the likely result would be a lowering of the necessary standards. An additional argument against permitting solictors to undertake pleas in mitigation following a plea of guilty arises from the fact that some 50 per cent of defendants tried in the Crown Court plead guilty to all charges. If solicitors were given rights of audience in all these cases in addition to committals for sentence and appeals where they already have rights of audience they would be able to appear in over 60 per cent of all Crown Court cases. If this were to occur the strength of the young criminal Bar, economically already weak, might be sapped and some local Bars might wither.

18.59 We have found the arguments on the issue of pleas in mitigation to be evenly balanced. A majority of us have reached the view that it would be preferable to make no change and we therefore recommend that solicitors should not be granted the right to make pleas in mitigation following a plea of guilty in the Crown Court.

A general extension

18.60   It will be clear from the fact that we do not favour an extension of the solicitors' right of audience in the Crown Court that we do not recommend a general extension in all courts. We need not repeat the detailed arguments. In general, as we have said in Chapter 17, we believe that the existence of a corps of specialist advisers and advocates serves the public interest. We emphasise in Chapter 27 a need for a greater degree of specialisation in performing adequately the work of the legal profession. We do not wish, therefore, to see the number of specialists and advocates reduced below what may reasonably be required, nor the quality of the service diluted.

Minor extensions of rights of audience

18.61   In its evidence to us the Law Society suggested a number of minor proceedings in the High Court and Crown Court which it considered could be handled by solicitors. As an example, it suggested that, in the High Court, solicitors should appear in unopposed applications for adjournments and other purposes, or to mention terms of settlement to the court. It would be inappropriate for a solicitor to make an application for an adjournment which is opposed and which may be refused, for in that event the case would have to proceed. But where proceedings are formal or unopposed, we consider they should be dealt with by the most economical means possible and that for this purpose a solicitor should have the appropriate right of audience—if, indeed, the matter cannot for any reason be dealt with by letter or telephone.

Conclusions and Recommendations

Paragraphs

Laymen	R18.1	Laymen, other than litigants in person, should not have rights of audience in the superior courts.	18.12
	R18.2	Guidelines should be issued to achieve greater consistency in the exercise of judicial discretion in county courts to allow laymen rights of audience in certain cases.	18.20
	R18.3	The rights of audience of laymen in tribunals should not be further restricted.	18.21

219

Paragraphs

Solicitors R18.4 Subject to the exercise of the Lord 18.42,
Chancellor's power to extend the 18.55 and
rights of audience of solicitors in 18.59
specific areas, there should be no
extension of such rights in Crown
Court business.

R18.5 There should be no general extension 18.60
of the rights of audience of solicitors.

R18.6 A solicitor should have a right of 18.61
audience to enable him to deal with
formal or unopposed matters in any
court.

ANNEX 18.1
The present position
(paragraph 18.2)

1. The present position is as follows.

(a) The litigant in person has a right of audience in all courts and tribunals.

(b) In the House of Lords barristers have rights of audience in all cases; a solicitor has right of audience in the House of Lords on an application for leave to appeal.

(c) In the Court of Appeal and High Court, barristers have rights of audience in all cases, and solicitors have rights of audience: —

    (i)   in the Court of Appeal, in applications to the single judge (Criminal Division) sitting in chambers;

    (ii)   in the High Court, in open court in respect of certain bankruptcy applications; and

    (iii)   in any proceedings in the High Court which are heard in chambers before a judge, official referee, master or registrar.

(d) In the Crown Court barristers have rights of audience in all cases; solicitors have rights of audience: —

    (i)   in appeals to the Crown Court from a magistrates' court, or on committal for sentence, if the solicitor or anyone in his firm appeared in the court below;

    (ii)   in civil proceedings in the Crown Court on appeal in similar circumstances;

    (iii)   in a limited number of court cases in remote areas where solicitors traditionally had full rights of audience at quarter sessions, which have been replaced by the Crown Court.

(e) In the county courts barristers and solicitors have a right of audience; laymen (that is persons not in practice as barristers or solicitors) may have a right of audience cn behalf of another person at the judge's discretion.

(f) In the magistrates' courts a number of persons by custom have a right of audience including barristers, solicitors, police officers, local government officials, civil servants employed by the Director of Public Prosecutions; certain others have a right of audience at the magistrates' discretion.

(g) In most tribunals, including the Employment Appeals Tribunal which ranks as a division of the High Court, there are no restrictions on rights of audience.

The "McKenzie man"

2. In the case of *McKenzie* v. *McKenzie* [1971] P.33, the Court of Appeal expressed approval of an arrangement by which a litigant in person had by him a lay friend or relative to "take notes, quietly make suggestions and give advice". This arrangement has been widely used in certain classes of case. On occasions, the McKenzie man has sought also to address the court, sometimes successfully; but in the case of *Mercy* v. *Persons Unknown* [1974] C.L.Y. 3003, the Court of Appeal made it clear that a McKenzie man should not be permitted to address the court. Nor is it permissible for a litigant to submit to the court a written brief setting out arguments on the law.

221

CHAPTER 19

Restrictions on Practice and Competition

Introduction

19.1 In some countries legal work of every kind is reserved to lawyers. In this country, there is no general restriction. Specific activities, few in number but important, are reserved to lawyers. They include handling cases in court, with which we dealt in Chapter 18, and conveyancing, dealt with in Chapter 21. In this chapter we deal with certain other functions reserved in this way and with restrictions operating within the profession.

Barristers

Restrictions on direct access to counsel

19.2 A barrister may accept professional work (whether for a fee or not) only if instructed by a solicitor, except where he has instructions from:—

(a) a patent agent in respect of non-contentious matters relating to patents, trade marks and designs or in respect of hearings before certain tribunals;

(b) a parliamentary agent, in respect of draft bills or amendments to bills;

(c) a clerk to a local authority in respect of non-contentious business or to appear at a local inquiry;

(d) the Chief Land Registrar, to advise on titles;

(e) the Secretary of the Church Assembly to draft Church Assembly Measures, amendments thereto or rules thereunder;

(f) a lay client, in order to examine for libel and contempt material which is to be published;

(g) a foreign lawyer, if no United Kingdom litigation or arbitration has been instituted and the instructions do not involve work in the United Kingdom of a character which is customarily associated with solicitors;

(h) a lay client who is not resident in the United Kingdom, in respect of a matter "essentially arising outside the United Kingdom";

(j) a prisoner in the dock in the Crown Court.

History of the restrictions

19.3 Until well into the nineteenth century, it was permissible for a barrister to appear in court without an instructing solicitor. By the middle of that century, this freedom had all but gone, to the resentment of some sections of the Bar who objected to the power of solicitors to deny business to those barristers who were not "kinsman or friend". In 1888, the Attorney General of the day stated that a barrister should not act or advise in contentious business without the intervention of a solicitor, who was needed to establish the facts of the matter, but that a solicitor was not normally necessary in non-contentious business. This statement was superseded in 1955 when the then Attorney General said that, save for the exceptions listed above, it was improper for a barrister to do non-contentious legal work without instructions from a solicitor.

Proposed changes

19.4   We received evidence in favour of maintaining the present restrictions, of abolishing them altogether and of adding to the exceptions listed in paragraph 19.2.

19.5   Abolition of the present rule was advocated both on the general ground that all restrictions of this character should, if possible, be removed and on the particular ground that the change would save money and reduce delays in all but the most substantial cases. Against this it was argued that the rule should be maintained because it enabled the barrister to concentrate on those functions in which he best served the client. The Senate, representing the Bar, argued that barristers were not at present equipped to deal with the routine office work necessary if they were to deal directly with their clients. To do this would require substantial changes in the basis on which barristers operate, in the organisation of their chambers and in the system of discipline and regulation of the Bar—in relation, for example, to the handling of clients' money.

19.6   As we showed in Chapter 17, we have reached the conclusion that it is in the public interest to maintain a two-branch profession. The main features of this arrangement are the exclusive rights of audience of barristers in the higher courts, discussed in Chapter 18, and the restriction whereby clients must normally approach a barrister through a solicitor. As we said in those chapters, we do not think that it would be possible to maintain an effective two-branch profession if barristers received clients directly and, in order to compete effectively with solicitors, had to run offices organised in the same way and subject to the same disciplines. The advantages of the present arrangements would be lost. We are not, therefore, satisfied that the public interest would be served by permitting direct access to counsel in all cases.

Modification of the restrictions

19.7   A number of witnesses proposed that the existing restrictions should be relaxed so as to enable members of professions in general to have access to a barrister without the intervention of a solicitor. The dividing line between occupations which are professions and those which are not is not well defined and membership of a profession does not thereby imply possession of the ability or knowledge required to prepare instructions for counsel, or to deal with associated work, in the way in which a solicitor is trained. We therefore see no merit in an extension in favour of the professions generally. An alternative proposal is that a number of specific professions should have direct access to counsel. We deal below with these proposals, except that relating to employed barristers which we discuss in Chapter 20.

Patent agents

19.8 Under the existing rules a registered patent agent may instruct a barrister directly in non-contentious matters concerning patents and registered designs and in litigation in the Patent Office or before the Patent Appeals Tribunal. However, a barrister who appears in the Court of Appeal on an appeal from that tribunal must be instructed by a solicitor. The Chartered Institute of Patent Agents, which represents the majority of registered patent agents, said that the intervention of a solicitor at this stage is "quite unnecessary and merely causes expense without giving any advantage either to the litigants or the court" and suggested that this requirement should no longer apply. The Institute did not suggest that patent agents should be entitled to instruct a barrister directly in other patent disputes in the High Court.

19.9 We dealt in Chapter 18 with the general question whether an unqualified person should be entitled to appear in court on behalf of another. In this respect, we do not think it would be right to describe a patent agent as "unqualified". Patent agents have long briefed counsel in cases in the Patents Office and before the Patent Appeals Tribunal, without the intervention of a solicitor. They may do so because they have studied the law relating to patents and are better qualified to practise in this area of the law than many solicitors. A patent agent can do the preparatory work for an appeal to the Court of Appeal and is fully aware of the responsibilities involved. We regard patent agents as a proper exception to the general rule and recommend that a registered patent agent should be entitled to instruct counsel direct in an appeal from the Patent Appeals Tribunal.

Notaries public

19.10 The main functions of notaries public are to draw up and authenticate documents for use in evidence in foreign courts and to prepare commercial agreements and documents connected with shipping and international trade. Many also offer a legal translation service. Notaries are of two kinds, provincial notaries, nearly all of whom are practising solicitors, and London or scrivener notaries, who are under the jurisdiction of the Society of Notaries Public of London and are not normally solicitors. London notaries provide a specialist notarial service and give advice on foreign law and procedure. Unlike provincial notaries, they are required to pass examinations, set by the

Scriveners' Company, which include papers in English commercial and property law, notarial practice, the law of a foreign jurisdiction and two foreign languages but not papers in tort or criminal law. These examinations are said to be comparable in standard to those taken by solicitors. There are, at present, about 25 London notaries.

19.11 A London notary who requires counsel's opinion in the course of his work may approach him only through a solicitor. The Society of Notaries Public of London pointed out that notaries were likely to have greater knowledge and expertise in their special field than solicitors and were better fitted to instruct counsel to advise in such matters. It therefore requested that London notaries should have direct access to counsel in non-contentious cases. As a London notary is qualified in his branch of the law and provides for his client a legal service similar to that provided by solicitors, we consider that this request is reasonable. We doubt whether a solicitor could add anything to the work of a London notary in non-contentious matters. Accordingly, we see no necessity to instruct a solicitor in such cases.

Chartered accountants

19.12 The Consultative Committee of Accountancy Bodies told us that an accountant who requires the advice of tax counsel is often in a better position to instruct him than a solicitor and that, in such circumstances, it would be more efficient if the accountant were allowed direct access to the barrister. No doubt there are occasions when an accountant could put a case to a barrister as competently as a solicitor. The same may be true, in occasional cases, of doctors, architects and engineers. But if there is to be a line, it must be drawn somewhere. All patent agents and London notaries by virtue of their specialist knowledge of the relevant field of law can be expected to instruct counsel adequately in their own areas of practice. The same is not true of accountants, not all of whom have the necessary training and experience. In cases involving accountants and members of other professions, therefore, it is desirable that there should be a general rule that a solicitor should prepare the case for counsel. Accordingly, we consider there should be no modification of present arrangements in cases involving professions other than London notaries and patent agents.

Solicitors

Introduction

19.13 The following paragraphs are concerned with work reserved to solicitors. As we said in paragraph 19.1, the functions reserved are few in number, but important. The effect of the restrictions is that most legal work is done by solicitors. Legal advice is given for a fee by others, such as patent agents, notaries or accountants, but only in specialised fields. Legal advice over a wide area of law is given by voluntary organisations, such as the CABx, and a number of organisations offer a conveyancing service; but solicitors are the only practitioners in every department of the law to whom the general public has access.

Litigation

19.14 Under section 20 of the Solicitors Act 1974 it is an offence for any unqualified person to:—

(a) act as a solicitor, or as such issue any writ or process, or commence, prosecute or defend any action, suit or other proceeding, in his own name or in the name of any other person, in any court of civil or criminal jurisdiction; or

(b) act as a solicitor in any cause or matter, civil or criminal, to be heard or determined before any justice or justices or any commissioners of Her Majesty's revenue.

Section 22 (1) (b) of the Act makes it an offence for any unqualified person, for reward, to "draw or prepare any . . . instrument relating to . . . any legal proceedings." In this context, "instrument" means any formal document. It would therefore be an offence for an unqualified person for or in expectation of a fee or reward, to settle a writ, statement of claim, defence or any other document of a similar character on behalf of another person.

19.15 This restriction is reflected in the rules of court. These provide for a solicitor to conduct litigation on behalf of another person and for a litigant to act in person, but do not allow a person other than a solicitor to act for a litigant.

19.16 We received a number of proposals for relaxing this rule. Some witnesses favoured allowing anyone to conduct litigation on behalf of another person, whether or not for fee or reward. We discussed this point in Chapter 18. Others proposed that special classes of persons, for example, claims assessors and debt collectors, should be permitted to conduct litigation for fee or reward on behalf of another.

19.17 As regards rights of audience, the dominant principle for consideration is the proper administration of justice. As has been said elsewhere in this report, this is a function not of the court alone but of a combination of the court and qualified practitioners. In the course of civil proceedings, heavy reliance is placed on the knowledge and integrity of the practitioner acting, as a solicitor does, as an officer of the court. For example, it is for the solicitor to draw up lists of documents and to specify, from his knowledge of the facts and of the law, which are available for inspection and which are privileged from production. He must also decide which documents are relevant and which are not; this can involve difficult and technical questions relating to the issues pleaded in the actions. It is his responsibility to disclose relevant documents though it may be against his client's interests to do so. A person who was not subject to the same direct duty to the court and to professional disciplines could not be expected to exercise responsibilities of this sort, and the courts as now constituted have no means of exercising direct supervision over work of this character.

19.18 Accordingly, we do not recommend any relaxation of the present restrictions on the right to conduct litigation in courts of law in favour of those without legal qualifications, or any special group, whether or not acting for fee or reward.

Probate

19.19 Probate business is concerned with the admission of wills to probate or, in the absence of a will, with obtaining letters of administration. It can be either contentious or non-contentious. Approximately one-quarter of the applications made in 1977 for grants of probate or letters of administration were made by applicants in person.

19.20 If a case is contentious, it is covered by section 20 of the Solicitors Act 1974 and the arguments and conclusions in paragraphs 19.14–19.18 above apply. The overwhelming majority of probate matters are not contentious. In such cases section 23 of the Act applies. Under this section it is an offence if any unqualified person, for or in expectation of reward : —

(a) takes instructions for a grant of probate or of letters of administration; or

(b) draws or prepares any papers on which to found or replace such a grant.

The effect of this provision is that solicitors alone may for reward apply on behalf of others for a grant of probate or letters of administration and may take instructions for this purpose.

19.21 It is common practice for a testator to nominate a trust corporation as executor of his will. The expression "trust corporation" includes the Public Trustee, a corporation appointed by the court in any particular case to be a trustee and a corporation entitled, under rules made under the Public Trustee Act 1906, to act as a custodian trustee. A corporation is so entitled if it is incorporated in the United Kingdom or in any other member state of the EEC, is authorised by its constitution to undertake trust business in England and Wales and has an issued capital of £250,000 of which not less than £100,000 has been paid up in cash. Examples of trust corporations, the Public Trustee apart, are banks and insurance companies.

19.22 A trust corporation is, like any other executor, entitled to administer the estate in respect of which it has been appointed. However, as it receives a fee for being executor and is not a "qualified person" for the purposes of section 23 of the Solicitors Act 1974, it cannot prepare the executor's affidavit which is the document on which the grant of probate is founded. Moreover, a trust corporation, being a body corporate, cannot, like an individual executor, apply for probate as that application is a court proceeding. It must therefore act through a solicitor.

19.23   It was put to us in evidence by the Association of Corporate Trustees and the Committee of London Clearing Banks that trust corporations should be permitted to apply for grants of representation without intervention of a solicitor. The Association said that all necessary preparatory work in done by the trust corporation concerned and the solicitor's functions are, in this respect, largely formal.

19.24   The Law Society opposed any relaxation of the present restrictions. It said that difficult questions of law could arise during the administration of an estate. This does not seem to us a strong point, because in the interests of their clients and also to protect themselves from charges of breach of trust or negligence trust corporations are punctilious in seeking legal advice when the need arises. The Law Society also said that a trust corporation was not under the same duty as a solicitor to the client and to the court and that the fees charged by trust corporations were not subject to any control and might, at the date of death, be quite different from those in force when the testator made his will. Trust corporations, however, have for a long period been allowed to administer estates for reward. We have not found in the evidence put before us any grounds for a general change in this respect. However, as we explain in paragraph 19.27, we consider that some control should be exercised over charges.

19.25   We think it reasonable that a trust corporation, approved for the purpose by the Bank of England, should be permitted, in non-contentious cases, to apply for probate of a will in which it is named as executor, without the intervention of a solicitor. Implementation of this recommendation will require amendment to section 23 of the Solicitors Act 1974 and the grant of a right of audience to the proper officer of a corporation sufficient to enable it to perform this function. We emphasise that our recommendations are confined to non-contentious cases and there should be a requirement that, if a probate case becomes contentious, the trust corporation must cease to have a right of audience and be required to appear by a solicitor.

Wills

19.26   There is at present no restriction on the preparation of wills, whether for reward or not, by an unqualified person on behalf of another. The Law Society proposed to us that solicitors alone should be allowed to prepare wills for reward. It pointed out the importance of accurate wording and sound legal knowledge in drafting a will. We accept that the home-made will is a frequent source of trouble. We consider, nevertheless, that it would be impracticable and unacceptable to ban preparation of a will by a testator himself, whether or not he is advised, without payment, by a friend. Having regard to the circumstances in which many wills are drafted, there would be serious objections to imposing a total ban on their preparation by unqualified persons. Preparation for reward is another matter; but there is no evidence that there is a class of persons, other than solicitors, who hold themselves out to draft wills for reward. We do not recommend legislation to prevent a practice which is not known to occur.

19.27 At present a trust corporation or any other person or organisation may draft a will in which it is nominated as executor with power to charge for its services. Except when a solicitor is so authorised, there is no check on the reasonableness of the charges made, which, as we pointed out in paragraph 19.24, may be quite different from those prevailing when the will was signed. This is particularly important because the testator, who authorised the charge, will not be alive when the charges are made. We consider therefore that there should be the same safeguards as would apply if a solicitor handled the administration. In short, an interested party should have the right to require the charges to be taxed by the court in the same way as solicitors' charges may be taxed at present. In cases where a bank, or a member of a banking group, acts as executor those safeguards should cover not only acceptance, administration and annual charges but also any associated bank charges and other financial advantages arising in the course of the administration.

19.28 In our discussions on this topic, we considered whether a central registry of wills should be established. It is possible voluntarily to deposit a will in the Principal Probate Registry or at a district registry. The question whether all wills should be deposited is outside our terms of reference. We suggest that solicitors should advise their clients of the advantages of depositing a will, and that information about the procedure should be given on the printed will forms sold to the public.

Other restrictions on unqualified persons

19.29 Section 22 of the Solicitors Act 1974 contains certain restrictions relating to documents prepared in connection with registered land. These are dealt with in Chapter 21. Sub-section 1 (b) of section 22 provides that it is an offence for an unqualified person, for or in expectation of reward, to draw or prepare "any other instrument relating to real or personal estate, or any legal proceedings". Certain "instruments" are excepted from these provisions; they are:—

(a) a will or other testamentary disposition;

(b) an agreement not under seal;

(c) a letter or power of attorney; and

(d) a transfer of stock containing no trust or limitation thereof.

19.30 Two points were drawn to our attention in the evidence we received concerning these provisions. First, the Society of Pension Consultants said that pension consultants are prevented, by these provisions, from preparing the formal documents required to set up or vary occupational pension schemes because they are documents under seal relating to personal property. While it would be more convenient for them not to have to consult a solicitor when such documents are required and while some expense might be saved, these provisions do not prevent pension consultants from carrying on their business. We do not consider that a convincing case has been made out in favour of a relaxation of the existing rules.

19.31 The Law Society argued that the restrictions should be strengthened. We have already dealt, in paragraphs 19.26–19.27 above, with the preparation of wills. The Law Society proposed that the preparation for reward of powers of attorney should be restricted to solicitors. At present no such restriction exists. The Society said that if a solicitor were instructed he would be on the alert for signs of possible exploitation of the donor by the attorney and he could urge the donor to make other arrangements if he thought the attorney unsuitable. We received no evidence suggesting that there are abuses in this field. Accordingly, we see no need to recommend any change in these provisions.

Conclusions and Recommendations

Paragraphs

Access to counsel   R19.1   Registered patent agents and London notaries should be permitted access to barristers as described in the text; save for those exceptions no change should be made to the existing rules.   19.7–19.12

Work of solicitors   R19.2   An unqualified person should not be permitted to act as a solicitor and as such to conduct litigation.   19.18

   R19.3   Trust corporations should be permitted, in non-contentious cases, to apply for grants of probate without retaining a solicitor for the purpose.   19.25

   R19.4   It is unnecessary to impose a restriction on the drafting of wills for reward.   19.26

The effect of professional rules

20.4   A solicitor in employment may, in compliance with the Law Society's Practice Rules, work in the same way as a solicitor in private practice, save that he is retained by one client rather than many. Barristers are not in the same position. In the Bar's rules of conduct it is laid down that a practising barrister, except in specified circumstances, may receive instructions only from a solicitor; under the cab-rank rule, he may not, provided he is offered an appropriate fee, refuse a brief in the area of law in which he practises; he must work from practising chambers; he must charge fees and may not work for a salary. An employed barrister cannot comply with these rules. His work, therefore, differs in form and content from that of a barrister in private practice. The majority of the problems with which we deal below arise in this connection.

General considerations

20.5   In some countries, practising lawyers are permitted to work as such only in private practice. A lawyer who enters employment ceases to be a member of the profession for as long as he retains his salaried post. We consider that such a rule should not be adopted in place of the present well-established arrangement in this country by which lawyers may work as salaried employees. It is in the public interest that those who are employed in a legal capacity in the national or local government service and in business should be subject to the same discipline, rules of conduct and professional standards of integrity and independence as lawyers in private practice.

20.6   In Chapter 17 we concluded that it is in the public interest to maintain a two-branch profession. Each branch needs its own form of training in order to perform its particular functions. All solicitors, whether intending to enter private practice or not, are to be required to undergo practical training before the final examination and to serve two years in articles thereafter before qualifying. A barrister is required to take a full-time vocational course leading to the final examination and to have a year's pupillage after the examination if he intends to enter private practice (see Chapter 38).

20.7   The organisation and rules of conduct of the two branches of the profession reflect their different functions. Rules affecting barristers are concerned with the duties of an advocate and consultant. Rules affecting solicitors are concerned with such matters as communications with the public and the protection of clients and their money. In respect of functions such as handling clients' money, no barrister, in his training or practice, has the opportunity to acquire knowledge and experience of a kind indispensable to a practising solicitor.

20.8   However much financial assistance is given to beginners at the Bar, a number of those who qualify will find that they prefer to enter employment rather than private practice. If, as we propose in paragraphs 33.45-33.46 and paragraph 39.7, school leavers and graduates are given better information about prospects at the Bar, the proportion of those who give up practice for want of work may not be as great as in the past. There will, however, continue to be each year a number of barristers who wish to take up legal posts in salaried employment. It would be a waste of their talents and knowledge if they were unnecessarily put at a disadvantage in competing for these posts.

The nature of legal work in employment
20.9 The nature of work open to employed lawyers varies widely. Much of it can be handled by members of either branch of the profession. There are a few posts, mostly in the public service, open only to barristers. There are many posts, in all forms of employment, whose occupants are expected to do all the work of a practising solicitor.

20.10 The numbers recruited to the government legal service from the two branches are about the same. Barristers are required to be fully qualified to practise as such, having done a year's pupillage, and preference is given to those with longer experience in practice. Lawyers employed in certain departments, from whichever branch of the profession they come, have statutory authority to act as solicitors.

20.11 A local authority usually requires its senior legal officer to act as its solicitor. Difficulties may arise if he does not have a solicitor's practising certificate. Solicitors in local government greatly outnumber barristers and constitute the largest group of solicitors outside private practice. Barristers in local government are not required to have completed a pupillage.

20.12 In commerce, finance and industry, the position varies from one employer to another. In general, anyone who employs a lawyer otherwise than in a large and specialised legal department will wish him to deal with as wide a range of work as possible to avoid unnecessary recourse to outside solicitors. In these circumstances the employed lawyer is called on to perform the day-to-day office work similar to that of a practising solicitor. Requirements as to the qualifications demanded of barristers vary widely.

20.13 Finally, there is one group of employed lawyers whose work is of a special character. We refer to those working in law centres. Law centres have been treated as a special case and special provisions have been made for those who work in them; they are not therefore dealt with in this chapter, but are treated separately in Chapter 8.

Employed Solicitors

General
20.14 Recent decisions of the courts have established that the employed

234

solicitor and his client are in the same legal position, as regards their rights, duties and privileges, as the solicitor in private practice and his client: (see paragraph 3.22). We received no evidence criticising this principle; a number of matters of detail, important to those directly involved, were however drawn to our attention.

Working for fellow employees

20.15 Some employers wish to offer their staff, as a fringe benefit, the services of their employed lawyers, free of charge. It is difficult to do this under the present rules of practice, in particular the rule by which a solicitor is prevented from advertising or touting or permitting anyone else to do so on his behalf. Moreover, an employed lawyer would face a conflict of professional duties if his services were retained by a fellow employee whose interests differed from those of the employer.

20.16 The Law Society recently modified its rules to make it easier for an employed solicitor to act for fellow employees who are required, for the purpose of their employment, to move house. Provided that there is no conflict of interest and that the employer makes provision to pay the fee of any outside solicitor whom the employee might instead choose to retain, it is permissible for the employer to offer the services of a solicitor employed in the company to carry out the conveyancing required without charge, although to do so would normally contravene the rule against advertising and touting for business. We welcome the modification of this rule, but we consider that it could go further. In Chapter 27 we propose modifications of the rule restricting advertising which, in certain circumstances, would make it easier for employed solicitors and their employers to draw attention to the services they can offer to fellow employees. We can see no objection in principle to allowing employed solicitors to give free legal advice to colleagues, on the same basis as they may now provide a conveyancing service, on matters which are not related to their employment and which do not involve the employer. We do not consider it objectionable that fellow employees should be informed that this service is available.

Spare-time practice

20.17 An employed solicitor who works only for his employer must, if he takes out a practising certificate, contribute to the compensation fund, but is not required to take out indemnity insurance. An employed solicitor must, however, conform with the rules as to compulsory indemnity insurance if he undertakes professional work other than for his employer. We have received evidence from an employed solicitor, who, in his free time, undertakes conveyancing work for friends and relatives, amounting only to a handful of cases in a year. He faces difficulties as a result of the requirements for indemnity insurance. When conveyancing is done as a modest sideline, the premium can be as great as the yearly total of fees earned. We sympathise with the difficulties of employed solicitors who wish to undertake spare-time work of this type. However, we do not recommend modifications in their favour of the requirements for indemnity insurance because these would be difficult to supervise and might be open to abuse. Whether or not reduced premiums can be negotiated for specific cases, however, is a commercial question which should be resolved by the profession and its underwriters.

Legal advice to local authorities

20.18 The profession takes the view that a solicitor working for a local authority should treat the authority itself as his client and, if he is not the chief officer, should not receive instructions from, or tender advice through, an official of the organisation who is not himself a solicitor. The same rule does not appear to apply to solicitors employed in other fields. In the government service, legal advisers do not insist on giving advice only to the responsible minister. In private practice, solicitors or barristers retained on behalf of a large corporation communicate with its executives and do not insist on communicating only with the board. We believe the reasons for the present attitude of the profession may be historical. Until fairly recently, it was traditional for a local authority to employ a solicitor (sometimes a barrister) as its chief officer. Since the re-organisation of local government in 1974, however, the trend has been for authorities to employ chief executives who are not lawyers. It is natural that, in legal matters, a solicitor employed by a local authority should prefer to retain the direct relationship which was once traditional with the members of the council rather than to take instructions and give advice through a layman in a senior position.

20.19 In our view the profession will have to accept that, in this respect, times have changed. In most cases it would be unnecesarily obstructive for a lawyer employed in a local authority to insist on giving advice only to the council. This is an area in which we hope it will not prove necessary to lay down strict rules. It is essentially a matter of sensible working arrangments to be made between the senior officers of local authorities. Important questions of principle may arise upon which, if there is a difference of opinion between officials, a lawyer may properly insist on communicating his advice directly to the council. We are not convinced that it is necessary, for the proper performance of his professional duties, that he should insist on this on every occasion.

The right of audience of employed solicitors

20.20 An employed solicitor who holds a practising certificate enjoys the same right of audience, on behalf of his employer, as a solicitor in private practice on behalf of his client. In Chapter 18 we deal with the question whether the right of audience of solicitors should be extended. Our conclusions in that chapter apply equally to employed solicitors and those in private practice.

Employed Barristers

General

20.21 Employed barristers wish their prospects at work to be as good as those enjoyed by solicitors. They do not seek to perform the same duties as practising barristers, such as representing their employers in the higher courts. They do not, in general, wish to transfer to the solicitors' branch of the profession or to carry out the full range of professional activities of employed solicitors with practising certificates. However, in order to have the same opportunities as solicitors for appointment and advancement, employed barristers wish to be able to carry out, for their employers, certain functions which are at present reserved to solicitors, in particular conveyancing and advocacy in the lower courts. We discuss these proposals in the following paragraphs.

The right of audience of employed barristers

20.22 The organisations representing employed barristers argued, in support of extended functions for their members, that, while there is a clear distinction between barristers and solicitors in private practice who offer their services to the public at large, the same distinction does not apply in the case of employed lawyers, who may be regarded as having only one client. The point was put in this way during the oral evidence of the Senate.

> There is one view, and it is not an official Senate view, but it is a view, I know, held by some people, including myself, that there are three branches of the profession, there is the practising barrister, the practising solicitor, and the employed lawyer, and that really different considerations apply to each of those three groups . . . there is no functional reason why there should be any difference between the employed solicitor on the one hand and the employed barrister on the other, they are together members of one group, the group being employed lawyers.

The evidence of the Law Society's Commerce and Industry Group is in similar terms.

> There is little practical distinction between a solicitor and a barrister after each of them has spent some years in a company legal department, apart from the technical distinctions imposed by reason of rules of conduct already referred to.

20.23 The Law Society disagreed with these views. It cited the following passage from the *Guide to the Professional Conduct of Solicitors.*

> A solicitor who is employed whole-time by a non-legal employer is in law in the same position as any other practising solicitor and is, therefore, bound to comply with the Solicitors' Accounts Rules, the Accountant's Report Rules, where he holds or receives clients' money as defined in the Rules, and the Solicitors' Practice Rules and to observe the standards of conduct applicable to all solicitors.

It argued that a person who wished to practise as a solicitor should become a solicitor.

20.24   In our view, the extent and nature of the work which an employed barrister should be permitted to undertake should be decided on a pragmatic basis. We do not accept the argument that an employed lawyer should be regarded as belonging to a third branch of the profession nor do we agree that an employed lawyer may undertake work appropriate to a solicitor only if formerly qualified as such. We consider that an overlap between the work of barristers and solicitors in employment is acceptable provided that the interests of the administration of justice and of the public are preserved.

Conveyancing by employed barristers

20.25   Barristers, as well as solicitors and notaries, are permitted by statute to act as conveyancers. There is a paper on conveyancing in the Bar final examination, but it is not compulsory. In the course of his vocational training and in his year of pupillage (if he serves a term in pupillage), a barrister will have no instruction in the day-to-day work of conveyancing, nor any practical experience of it. There are no regulations governing the handling of clients' money by barristers. They have no client accounts and are not subject to audit under professional rules on the pattern of the Solicitors' Accounts Rules. There is no compensation fund to provide for cases of dishonesty and indemnity insurance is not at present compulsory. Chambers are not equipped to deal with the day-to-day office work required in a conveyancing practice. In short, in conveyancing transactions, a barrister cannot offer a service, except as a consultant, of the same standard or level of security as a solicitor.

20.26   In 1955, the Bar Council laid down a general rule that, with the exception of barristers then in local government service, barristers should no longer undertake conveyancing work, except in a consultative capacity on the instructions of a solicitor or when retained by the Land Registry to scrutinise titles. We consider this ruling was in the public interest so far as it relates to barristers in private practice because a barrister is not trained or set up to maintain a general conveyancing practice.

20.27   The question remains whether it is proper for a barrister in employment who is not subject to all the limitations mentioned above to act in a conveyancing transaction in which his employer is a party. We consider that he should be permitted to do so provided that the education and training he has received in this discipline is equivalent to that of a solicitor and provided that members of the public doing business with his employer have the same protection as they would if the conveyancing were undertaken by an employed solicitor.

20.28   In order to have the same level of education and training as a solicitor, a barrister would have to take the conveyancing paper in the Bar final examination, receive training in the subject during the vocational course, and have direct working experience of practical conveyancing, possibly in employment, but in any event under professional supervision, in the same way as an articled clerk. Provision must be made for protection against dishonesty either by setting up a compensation fund or by requiring that the employer takes out a fidelity bond. As in the case of employed solicitors, insurance cover need not be compulsory and, if there is no client account, accountants' reports need not be submitted. It is for the Senate to make the appropriate arrangements.

20.29 In the course of conveyancing work, the exchange of undertakings between solicitors is important. Employed solicitors as well as those in private practice are professionally bound by the undertakings they give, whether personal or on behalf of the employer. The Professional Purposes Committee of the Law Society has made a number of decisions relating to undertakings and their interpretation and a body of case law on this subject has been built up. An employed barrister, dealing with conveyancing, would have to be subject to the same code of professional conduct in relation to the exchange of undertakings as an employed solicitor. The Senate would have to be prepared to enforce the present code against an employed barrister in the same way as the Law Society does against an employed solicitor.

20.30 We consider that the requirements set out above are necessary, in the public interest, if employed barristers are to undertake conveyancing work. Barristers who are entitled to undertake such work should be identified accordingly in the Bar List.

20.31 We accept that it may not be possible for a barrister to satisfy these requirements in all cases. Where this occurs, there is always the alternative, in many ways more suitable, of transferring to the solicitors' branch of the profession.

Direct access to counsel
20.32 At present a barrister in employment, in the absence of any statutory authority, may not send instructions to a barrister in private practice on behalf of his employer. Instructions to counsel must be sent through a solicitor, either in the same employment or in an outside firm.

20.33 Although it is the experience of those working in the government service that barristers may adequately instruct counsel in all classes of business, the opinion expressed in oral evidence by the Bar Association for Commerce, Finance and Industry (BACFI) was that it was best, in general, to leave the preparation of contentious work to solicitors. Employed barristers do however seek the right to consult counsel in non-contentious matters; that is to say, where advice only is required and litigation is not in prospect.

20.34 We indicated in Chapter 19 that we consider there should, in certain circumstances, be direct access to counsel by patent agents, on the basis that it should not be necessary to approach counsel through a solicitor when the solicitor has only formal functions to perform. Applying this principle in the case of employed barristers, we agree with the view expressed by BACFI that, although the instruction of counsel for the purpose of litigation should be reserved to solicitors, there is no reason why employed barristers should not obtain advice directly from counsel in non-contentious matters.

Rights of audience

20.35 If an employed solicitor has a practising certificate, he may, as of right, appear as an advocate in the magistrates' courts and county courts. An employed barrister may be allowed a right of audience in the magistrates' courts and in the county courts in his capacity as an officer of a company or as the representative of a local authority, but only at the discretion of the court. Except in cases governed by statute, an employed barrister cannot claim a right of audience in any court by virtue only of his professional qualification.

20.36 The present rule affecting employed barristers is based on the same principle as is held to justify the existence of separate branches of the profession and the restriction of rights of audience in the higher courts to barristers alone. This is that the proper administration of justice under our system depends on the independence of the advocate from external influences and, subject only to his duty to the court, on his undivided loyalty to the client. In its evidence on the quality of service provided by barristers, the Senate laid stress on the importance of working from professional chambers in which advice on professional problems is always available and where there is a tradition of conduct and service, and strong pressure to maintain freedom from external influences in the interest of serving the client. In this connection it must be remembered that some employed barristers have qualified without having undertaken a year's pupillage and have no practical experience of the Bar or the work of barristers in private practice.

20.37 The representatives of BACFI agreed in oral evidence that an in022 dependent Bar was indispensable but distinguished between the different grades of court. It had always been their case that, in the higher courts, it was necessary to have a two-branch profession and representation only by barristers in private practice; in magistrates' courts and county courts, however, the position is said to be different in that, if an employed solicitor had a practising certificate, he would enjoy the same right of audience as a solicitor in private practice. BACFI argued that an employed barrister should have a similar right of audience.

20.38 If a lawyer, whether in employment or in private practice, has a right of audience in a certain court, it may at present be exercised on behalf of any litigant by whom he is retained. The Senate said in evidence that it would be inappropriate for employed barristers to have rights of audience in all courts since they do not practise from chambers and are not equipped for this task. In May 1978, however, the Bar Council decided in principle that employed barristers who had completed pupillage should be entitled to appear for their employer in all courts in which solicitors had a right of audience. A group of barristers employed by the Confederation of British Industry said in evidence to us: —

> We believe that UK accession to the European Communities will have an effect on the freedom of employed barristers to take cases unconnected with the work of their employer. We understand that in practice German lawyers who are employed on a salaried basis are free to undertake cases independently of their employers' work. We make no judgment on whether this is desirable or not. We merely remark that the rules of professional conduct in this country prevent non-practising barristers from undertaking such work. It is for consideration by the Royal Commission whether, subject to the agreement of their employer, non-practising barristers in the United Kingdom should be permitted to do so in future, at least as regards common market law.

20.39 Representatives of employed barristers agreed in oral evidence that an alternative solution, so far as they were concerned, would be to take the right of audience away from employed solicitors. This may be a logical solution but it is impracticable. The right of audience of employed solicitors is too deep-rooted to be removed. The question is whether, because such a right exists, employed barristers should also have a right of audience.

20.40 It is in the public interest that the Senate preserve strict discipline and high standards in advocacy. For this purpose, it is desirable to maintain the methods of control, formal and informal, which exist at present. Developments which led to widespread advocacy by employed lawyers in cases of substance would be contrary to the public interest. In Chapter 18 we recommend that county courts should permit the authorised officer of a company to appear on its behalf provided the case can adequately be dealt with by this means. If this approach is adopted, an employed barrister would be able to appear in appropriate cases; there should be no rule of professional conduct against his doing so. Bearing these factors in mind, we do not consider that an employed barrister should have a right of audience by virtue alone of his qualification.

Conclusions and Recommendations

Paragraphs

Employed   R20.1   Subject to certain conditions em- 20.16
solicitors   ployed solicitors should be permitted to deal with conveyances on behalf of, and to give free legal advice to, fellow employees.

241

CHAPTER 21

Conveyancing

The Nature of Conveyancing

Introductory

21.1 Conveyancing is a subject on which we received a large volume of evidence from both laymen and lawyers in this country and abroad. Included in this evidence were numerous suggestions for the improvement and simplification of conveyancing law and procedure which we consider in the annex to this chapter and which we brought to the notice of the Law Commission. These will require careful consideration by the Law Society and others but their implementation is not dependent upon that of the other recommendations in this chapter. In this chapter we deal with the question whether non-solicitors should be permitted to undertake conveyancing for gain and whether changes should be made in the system of conveyancing charges.

Definition

21.2 The expression "conveyance" means a deed or other document by which the ownership of property is transferred. In transactions affecting land, a deed which transfers the ownership of unregistered land is called a "conveyance" and the document which transfers registered land is called a "transfer". They both fulfil the same function. The meaning of the expression "conveyancing" is not limited to the preparation of the documents just described, but covers the enquiries made and other documents drafted in connection with the sale and purchase of land and interests in land. We describe this procedure in detail in paragraphs 21.12–21.20 below.

21.3 Although it is now customary to think of conveyancing as lawyers' work, it was in earlier centuries frequently undertaken by laymen. In the sixteenth and seventeenth centuries a large proportion of conveyancing work was gradually taken over by attorneys and, in the City of London, by scriveners. By the Stamp Act 1804 the drawing and preparation for gain of conveyances and deeds relating to property, real and personal, was confined to "serjeants at law, barristers, solicitors, attorneys, notaries, proctors, agents or procurators having obtained regular certificates and special pleaders, draftsmen in equity and conveyancers being members of one of the Inns of Court". After the Stamp Act 1804 conveyancing was not only done by solicitors but also by a number of other qualified persons, in particular barristers and conveyancers certified by one of the Inns of Court. By the end of the nineteenth century, the present position had been reached in which solicitors handled all the day-to-day work of conveyancing. Barristers are now retained only as consultants and by the Land Registry to examine titles on first registration.

The present restrictions

21.4   The present restrictions are set out in section 22 of the Solicitors Act 1974, as follows:—

> (1) ... any qualified person who directly or indirectly:—
> (a) draws or prepares any instrument of transfer or charge for the purposes of the Land Registration Act 1925, or makes any application or lodges any document for registration under that Act at the registry; or
> ((b) draws or prepares any other instrument relating to real or personal estate, or any legal proceeding,
>
> shall, unless he proves that the act was not done for or in expectation of any fee, gain or reward, be guilty of an offence and liable on summary conviction to a fine not exceeding £50.

The Act provides that for the purpose of sub-section (1) (b), "instrument" does not include (*inter alia*) an agreement not under seal. Consequently the ordinary contract for the sale of land, which is not a document under seal, is not within the restrictions.

Improvements in title

21.5   A major weakness of the conveyancing system before the middle of the nineteenth century was that title to property (that is, the evidence of ownership of it) was often unclear and difficult to prove. The usual reason was that inadequate records had been kept of changes in ownership or of rights, such as rights of way, which might affect the owner's enjoyment of his property. The unskilled conveyancer was often blamed. William West in *Symboleography* (1590) and the author of *Sheppard's Touchstone of Common Assurances* (1642) both complained of the inefficiency of lay conveyancers. At a later stage scriveners' work became so unsatisfactory that eventually they were compelled to swear to draw "no deed touching inheritance nor other deed of great charge save with the good advice and confirmation of counsel". Oliver Cromwell advocated a universal register of titles to combat the "ungodly jumble" of the land law. The Real Property Commission said in 1830:—

> ... of the real property of England a very considerable proportion is in one of these two predicaments: either the want of security against the existence of a latent deed renders actually unsafe a title which is yet marketable or the want of means of procuring the formal requisites of title renders unmarketable a title which is substantially safe.

244

Since then there has been a steady improvement and the position is now very different. Although certain features of modern conveyancing practice, for example the inadequacy of some plans, may be criticised, it is rare to encounter a modern title with a serious and previously undetected defect or to find that the documentary evidence of title is inadequate.

Land registration

21.6 A system of compulsory registration of titles was introduced by statute in 1897. It first operated in the former county of London between 1898 and 1902. By February 1978 the area of compulsory registration, which had grown spasmodically through the present century, comprised Greater London, the whole of 12 counties including the six metropolitan counties and 110 other districts in England and Wales, with a population of 36.5 million: that is, 74.2 per cent of the population. The Chief Land Registrar expressed the hope to us that the whole of England and Wales would be subject to compulsory registration by about 1985. Not all property in an area designated for compulsory registration is immediately put on the register. Registration must take place under the compulsory provisions when property changes hands on a sale or when a lease is granted for a term of not less than 40 years or is assigned when there are not less than 40 years to run. Registration may also be requested at any time in a compulsory area. Outside the designated areas of compulsory registration, a limited class of transactions may be registered voluntarily; these include building estates of 20 or more units, sold to owner-occupiers.

21.7 The object of the land registration system is both to maintain a record of the ownership of land in a simple form and also to guarantee the owner's security of title. The register of each owner's title is divided into three parts:—

(a) The property register identifies the site of the property by description and by reference to a plan based on the Ordnance Survey, specifies whether the title is freehold or leasehold and contains a note of rights enjoyed with the land.

(b) The proprietorship register specifies the class of title, the name and address of the owner and any restrictions on his dealing with the property.

(c) The charges register contains particulars of registered mortgages and other financial burdens on the property and gives notice of third party rights and interests to which the property is subject.

The information contained in the register, combined with the guarantee of title and the use of short printed documents, simplifies the process of transferring or dealing in registered land.

245

21.8 The number of cases of registration and the number of transactions in registered land in recent years are shown in the following table.

TABLE 21.1

Output of Registration of Title Department, HM Land Registry, 1973–78

Year ending 31st March	New titles brought on to the register (first registration)	Transfers, charges and other dealings with registered land (number of transactions)	Office copies, official searches and other preliminary services (number of services provided)
1973	217,050	1,552,511	1,815,991
1974	189,715	1,558,956	1,591,148
1975	186,102	1,293,557	1,501,153
1976	264,776	1,684,610	1,662,992
1977	311,234	1,806,893	1,588,274
1978	364,275	1,979,522	1,844,357
1979	417,080	2,265,282	2,026,615

Source: HM Land Registry.

21.9 The following table shows the steady growth in the estimated proportion of transactions in registered land in the years 1976–1979.

TABLE 21.2

Estimated proportions of transactions in registered and unregistered land, 1976–79

Year ending 31st March	Approximate population: England and Wales, in millions.	Approximate population in areas of compulsory registration		Transactions in registered and unregistered land, expressed as percentages of all transactions in England and Wales.[1]		
		number in millions	percentage of total population	registered titles %	first registrations %	unregistered titles %
1976	49·26	31·7	64·4	47·5	21·0	31·5
1977	49·26	33·9	68·7	50·5	21·5	28·0
1978	49·26	36·5	74·2	55·0	23·4	21·6
1979	49·26	36·5	74·2	55·0	25·0	20·0

[1] The percentage figures for transactions involving registered titles and first registrations are based on the actual numbers of such transactions; but the percentages are estimates because the number of transactions involving unregistered titles is, of necessity, an estimate.

Source: HM Land Registry.

Home ownership and mortgages

21.10 A great increase has taken place in recent years in home ownership and in transactions in land. At the end of the first world war about 10 per of the housing stock was owner-occupied; according to the National Dwelling and Housing Survey 1978 sponsored by the Department of the Environment, 53 per cent of the housing stock in that year was owner-occupied. In the month of November 1977, there were 109,000 transactions in residential property to the approximate value of £1,286 million, and 16,000 transactions in non-residential (including agricultural) property, to the value of £296 million. In the years 1971–78 the number of new mortgages issued by building societies in the United Kingdom were as follows.

TABLE 21.3
Number of new mortgages, 1971–78

Year							Number of new mortgages
1971	..	..	..	..	..	..	653,000
1972	..	..	..	..	..	..	681,000
1973	..	..	..	..	..	..	545,000
1974	..	..	..	..	..	..	433,000
1975	..	..	..	..	..	..	651,000
1976	..	..	..	..	..	..	715,000
1977	..	..	..	..	..	..	738,000
1978	..	..	..	..	..	..	804,000

Sources: "Housing Policy: A Consultative Document", Cmnd. 6851, June 1977, Table 14. Building Societies Association.

As we show in Table 35 of the appendix to our consultants' report on the Law Society's remuneration survey (see Volume II section 16) the estimated gross fees earned by solicitors' firms for conveyancing in 1975/76 was £299.7 million.

Improvements in land law

21.11 Efforts to improve and simplify the law relating to the holding and transfer of land culminated in the Law of Property Act 1925 and related legislation. Despite such improvements, land law is still complex. It may give rise to problems the solution of which requires considerable skill and experience. Since 1925 efforts to simplify property law have been offset by the growing importance and intricacy of other branches of the law with a bearing on the ownership and use of land, notably the law relating to landlord and tenant, planning, taxation and the matrimonial home. The standard textbook, *Emmett on Title,* contains references to 400 statutes and some 4,700 decided cases. Thus, although the modern purchaser of property may in general be assured of a sound title, he has to be alert to factors which may affect his present or future enjoyment of the property or his own and his dependants' financial interests.

The process of conveyancing

21.12   There is nothing to prevent a vendor and purchaser from entering into a binding contract for the transfer of land without advice or any preliminary investigation. In practice, as a matter of ordinary prudence and common sense, the parties usually take advice and the transaction proceeds in a number of stages. The two main stages are: —

(a)   the contract, by which the parties bind themselves to complete the transaction, at which time the purchaser pays a deposit, usually of 10 per cent of the purchase price; and

(b)   completion, when a formal deed, recording the sale and conveyance of the land, is handed with the existing documents of title by the vendor to the purchaser in exchange for the balance of the purchase price.

Before and after these two stages there are a number of intermediate steps and matters dealt with by the parties and their advisers.

21.13   A preliminary stage in the sale of a dwelling house takes place when vendor and purchaser agree in principle on the sale and the price. Such an agreement is normally expressly or by implication made "subject to contract", and, if so, is not legally binding. The next step is for the purchaser to make enquiries, as a preliminary to the formal written contract. At this stage, as a general rule, each party instructs a solicitor.

21.14   It is the duty of the purchaser's solicitor, before contract, to make enquiries about the property which are addressed to both the vendor and the local authority and, when appropriate, other authorities or bodies such as the Registrar of Commons and the National Coal Board. In some cases, the solicitor also assists in arranging a mortgage. It is often necessary for both the purchaser's and the vendor's solicitors to arrange for their clients to sell or buy another property and there may be a long chain of such transactions. The purchaser's enquiries are usually made in a standard form with additional enquiries relating to the particular property added by the purchaser's solicitor. They ask about disputes, the ownership of boundary walls, hedges or fences, the existence of main services, of public and private rights of way, drainage and other easements affecting the property, fixtures and fittings to be included in the sale and other matters. Enquiries of the local authority, again as a rule in standard form, concern planning matters, compulsory purchase orders and matters arising in connection with the Community Land Act 1976 which affect the property, the ownership of roads serving the property, the connection of the property to main services and similar matters. Surveyors may be retained to examine the structural condition of the house on behalf of the prospective purchaser and to advise the proposed mortgagee on its value as a security.

249

21.15 Sometimes because of exclusions or limitations in the contract, some investigation of title takes place at this stage. It is at this point that the solicitor should discuss with his client all the matters which the client should consider carefully before deciding to enter into a binding contract, for example the means of financing the transaction, the type of mortgage required, the necessity for mortgage protection, the names in which the property will be taken, matters relating to capital gains and capital transfer tax and the date required for completion. In general the solicitor will discuss whether the client is satisfied with the survey, has taken account of any proposed development in the neighbourhood and, in general, whether the property suits his requirements.

Contract

21.16 During the period of preliminary enquiries the vendor or his solicitor drafts a contract for the sale of the property. For this purpose it is necessary for the vendor or his solicitor to scrutinise the title deeds or, in the case of a registered title, an official copy of the register, to ensure that the vendor has a sound title and can make good his bargain, and that all adverse interests affecting the property, such as leases, rights of way or restrictive covenants, are specified in the contract. If the property is subject to a mortgage the documents of title will be in the possession of the mortgagee or the mortgagee's solicitor. It is sometimes necessary to examine title deeds in the office of the mortgagee or his solicitor, but it is common practice to release them into the custody of the vendor's solicitor, on his undertaking to hold them on behalf of the mortgagee until the mortgage is discharged. A solicitor's undertaking is a promise or statement of fact on which anyone affected by it is entitled to rely. As we explain in paragraph 21.25 solicitors' undertakings play an important part in facilitating and expediting conveyancing transactions.

Exchange of contracts

21.17 When the preliminary enquiries are completed, the necessary financial arrangements made and the draft contract agreed, the purchaser and vendor sign separate copies of the contract which are exchanged by their solicitors. The vendor and purchaser are then legally commited to complete the transaction.

Title

21.18 After contract, it is necessary for the vendor to satisfy the purchaser that he has a good title to the property and that it is subject only to the adverse interests specified in the contract. If the title is registered, the purchaser's solicitor, who will have been supplied with office copies of the entries in the register before exchange of contracts, is given authority to inspect the register. If the property is unregistered, the vendor's solicitor supplies an abstract of the title of the property, showing the dealings affecting it over at least the past fifteen years. If the entries or the abstract disclose apparent defects in the title (for example, the absence of evidence of the death of a joint tenant or an undischarged mortgage) the purchaser is entitled to make enquiries, called "requisitions". When the requisitions have been answered to his satisfaction, the purchaser's solicitor checks the abstract against the title documents. When satisfied that the title is in order, and that no adverse interest affects the property other than those specified in the contract, the purchaser's solicitor sends the vendor's solicitor a draft conveyance, or in the case of registered property a draft form of transfer, for approval.

Completion

21.19 When approved, the draft conveyance or transfer is engrossed (that is, a fair copy is typed on durable paper). The purchaser's solicitor makes such final searches as may be appropriate in the central Land Charges Registry, the Companies' Registry, the Land Registry and the local authority register to ensure that the property remains clear of undisclosed mortgages and other adverse interests. Completion follows. On the agreed date the purchaser and, if there is a mortgage, his mortgagee, through their solicitors, produce bankers' drafts for the total value of the purchase price less any deposit already paid. In exchange, the vendor's solicitor hands over the deeds (including the new deed of conveyance or the transfer from vendor to purchaser) and the keys of the property. If the vendor had a mortgage, his solicitor gives an undertaking to the purchaser's solicitor to discharge it. The purchaser's solicitor then prepares a statement giving information about the transaction required by the Finance Act 1931 for the purpose of the Inland Revenue and sends the conveyance or transfer to the Stamp Office for recording and, in appropriate cases, the payment of stamp duty. If the land is registered the purchaser's solicitor will then send the documents, certified where necessary, accompanied by a form of application duly completed and the fee, to the Land Registry for registration.

21.20 The following chart sets out the main steps in a straightforward domestic conveyance of the kind described above. More extensive details of various forms of transaction, also in chart form, may be found in the evidence of the Law Society. All steps of the kind we have described above are generally, and in our view properly, regarded as part of the normal service to be provided in a conveyancing transaction.

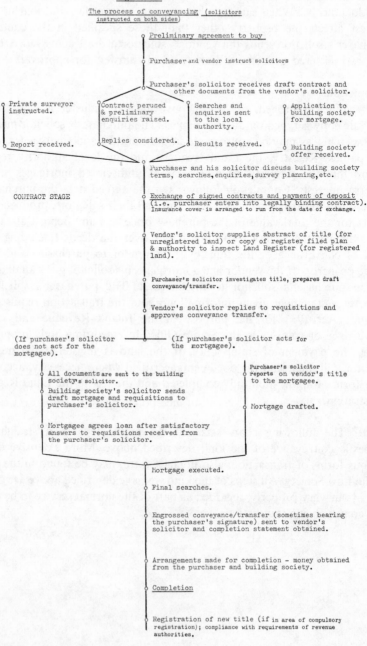

Figure 21.1

The process of conveyancing (solicitors
instructed on both sides)

Preliminary agreement to buy

Purchaser and vendor instruct solicitors

Purchaser's solicitor receives draft contract and
other documents from the vendor's solicitor.

| Private surveyor instructed. | Contract perused & preliminary enquiries raised. | Searches and enquiries sent to the local authority. | Application to building society for mortgage. |
| Report received. | Replies considered. | Results received. | Building society offer received. |

Purchaser and his solicitor discuss building society
terms, searches, enquiries, survey planning, etc.

CONTRACT STAGE — Exchange of signed contracts and payment of deposit
(i.e. purchaser enters into legally binding contract).
Insurance cover is arranged to run from the date of exchange.

Vendor's solicitor supplies abstract of title (for
unregistered land) or copy of register filed plan
& authority to inspect Land Register (for registered
land).

Purchaser's solicitor investigates title, prepares draft
conveyance/transfer.

Vendor's solicitor replies to requisitions and
approves conveyance transfer.

(If purchaser's solicitor does not act for the mortgagee).   (If purchaser's solicitor acts for the mortgagee).

All documents are sent to the building
society's solicitor.
Building society's solicitor sends
draft mortgage and requisitions to
purchaser's solicitor.

Purchaser's solicitor
reports on vendor's title
to the mortgagee.

Mortgage drafted.

Mortgagee agrees loan after satisfactory
answers to requisitions received from
the purchaser's solicitor.

Mortgage executed.

Final searches.

Engrossed conveyance/transfer (sometimes bearing
the purchaser's signature) sent to vendor's
solicitor and completion statement obtained.

Arrangements made for completion - money obtained
from the purchaser and building society.

Completion

Registration of new title (if in area of compulsory
registration); compliance with requirements of revenue
authorities.

252

Protection for the Client

The need for protection

21.21   In most domestic conveyances the parties are engaging in the most expensive transaction of their lives, in which large sums, usually borrowed from a building society or a local authority, and their personal savings are at stake. It is, therefore, of the utmost importance to those involved that the process proceeds without mishap. The purchaser must be confident not merely that he obtains a good title to the property but that there are no restrictions or problems of which he is left unaware. The vendor must be assured that he and his mortgagee will receive the money handed over by the purchaser during the course of the transaction. At the same time, as financial resources are often stretched to the limit, the cost of the whole undertaking must be kept down as far as possible. It follows that it is essential that, in his relationship with a conveyancer, the client should be protected from: —

(a)   dishonesty or carelessness with money;

(b)   ignorance and incompetence; and

(c)   a level of charges higher than is fair and reasonable.

The present position

21.22   In Chapter 23 we set out in detail the protection available to the clients of solicitors, in particular the protection afforded against dishonesty by the rules governing the holding of clients' money and by the existence of the compensation fund out of which clients who have suffered loss by reason of misuse of funds by a solicitor or his staff are reimbursed. We consider too the protection afforded against negligence by the requirement that every solicitor shall be covered by an insurance policy against claims for negligence.

21.23   The level of protection is increased by other traditions and rules of the solicitors' profession, for instance the rules mentioned in Chapter 25 which make it professionally improper for a solicitor to take advantage of a client, to purchase property from a client who is not independently advised or to obtain any personal benefit in a transaction in which he is acting as a solicitor without disclosing this fact to the client. Breach of these rules attracts disciplinary sanctions imposed by the Law Society. There is also the protection conferred by the standards of education and training, including vocational training, which must be attained before anyone is entitled to practise as a solicitor, details of which are set out in Chapter 38.

21.24   In order to provide the necessary high level of protection against dishonesty, carelessness with money, ignorance or incompetence, rules and obligations of the kind described in paragraphs 21.22–21.23 are necessary. It follows that the public interest requires not only that any person who undertakes conveyancing for gain must be required to conform to these or equivalent standards and obligations, but also that there shall be effective means of ensuring that, if he fails to do so, his client shall not suffer.

Undertakings

21.25 By virtue of long-standing tradition, solicitors are able to exchange undertakings amongst themselves, with building societies and others and accept them on behalf of clients knowing that they will be honoured. The Law Society insists that a personal undertaking given by a solicitor be honoured. Disregard of a ruling of the Council in any case or other failure to implement an undertaking personally binding on a solicitor may result in proceedings being instituted by the Law Society against him before the Solicitors Disciplinary Tribunal. In the last resort a personal undertaking can be enforced by the court, which has direct powers of control over solicitors as officers of the court. Such undertakings are an important means of avoiding difficulties or delay in conveyancing transactions; it is possible, for example, to receive purchase money on an undertaking to discharge a mortgage, or to hold papers on an undertaking to return them on request. Purchasers are often allowed to move into the property on a solicitor's undertaking to complete the transactions and banks frequently advance money for deposits or bridging finance on solicitors' undertakings. The difficulties, chiefly in terms of additional delays, which would arise if undertakings could not be exchanged would not be insuperable but an alternative arrangement would be bound to be more cumbersome.

Effectiveness of the present system

21.26 The level of satisfaction with solicitors' services is generally high, but there are certain matters which regularly attract complaint. We discuss these in more detail in Chapter 22. We identify as the main weakness of the present system of conveyancing that it does not provide an effective method of promoting competition between conveyancers and ensuring that the level of charges paid by the client for conveyancing are, and are seen to be, fair and reasonable.

The Right to Undertake Conveyancing

Alternative proposals

21.27 Two rival proposals for change in the present restrictions on conveyancing by non-lawyers were put before us. One proposal was that the present restrictions should be removed or relaxed; the other was that they should be clarified and extended by introducing a requirement that no person should enter into a contract relating to a conveyancing transaction without previously having obtained legal advice. The object of the first proposal was to promote and widen competition in the provision of conveyancing services and thus to reduce charges; that of the second was to remove a possible gap which might appear in the protection conferred by the present arrangements if a person chose to proceed without legal advice.

"Do-it-yourself" conveyancing

21.28 Books explaining how the layman may deal with his own conveyancing transactions enjoy a ready sale. It is not known how many of those who buy such books put what they have read into practice. We are aware, however, that in a small proportion of transactions the vendor or purchaser acts on his own account. The argument was advanced that it is illogical to allow an individual to carry out his own conveyancing transaction, with assistance if he so desires from an unpaid friend or agent, and at the same time to insist that the public needs protection against a paid agent. For a number of reasons we reject this argument. The individual who acts for himself cannot embezzle his own money and rarely, if ever, entrusts his money in a conveyancing transaction to an unpaid friend. The individual acting without professional assistance may harm himself, but is not in a position similarly to harm anyone who is legally represented. Such an individual is, in practice, likely to benefit from the protection afforded by solicitors acting for mortgagees and for other parties to the transaction, in whose interest it is to ensure that the transaction proceeds efficiently. We have no evidence that do-it-yourself conveyancing, to the extent that it is practised at present, gives rise to unacceptable difficulties.

21.29 Different considerations may, however, arise where an individual, with experience of property dealing, buys or sells in the course of business, since, through his superior knowledge, he may induce another person to enter into a contract (or to give him an option) on terms which are disadvantageous to that other party. We believe that the inexperienced party should if possible be offered some protection and that this problem should be considered by the Law Commission. We comment on this point further in paragraph 16 of annex 21.1.

Competition and the level of fees

21.30 A monopoly or restrictive practice should be regarded as against the public interest unless shown to serve it. In the ordinary sense there is no monopoly of conveyancing work, because over 6,500 firms of solicitors may do it in competition. It may more accurately be described as a closed shop, because only those with certain qualifications may do it for gain. The technical description is unimportant, provided the public are given a service of necessary quality at a competitive cost. Before 1973 there was virtually no competition. The scale of charges operated to prevent undercutting. We had evidence that, for a period after the abolition of scale charges, solicitors were in general unwilling to give estimates of charges and some refused to do so if they suspected a potential client was shopping around. It appears that more recently this attitude has been changing. Enquirers can now more readily obtain estimates of cost and thus compare prices; in many cases, they may find that a wide range of prices is offered. The Consumers' Association in a recent survey (see paragraph 21.80) found that the fees for buying a £15,000 house varied from £130 to £240, for a £20,000 house from £140 to £260 and for a house around £30,000, from £200 to £400. Charges for selling a house varied equally widely between lower limits.

Abolition of all restrictions

21.31   Some witnesses argued that anyone who so wished should be entitled to act as a conveyancer, on the grounds that any person who could not provide an adequate service would go out of business. This view had few supporters. The majority of the witnesses who were opposed to the extent of the present restrictions accepted that the public needed some protection from incompetence and dishonesty. Their view was summed up by Mr. Ken Weetch MP, recently the sponsor of a private member's bill to set up a system of licensed conveyancers subject to certain restrictions. He was convinced that the present restrictions should be abolished and that conveyancers other than solicitors should be entitled to practise, but was, nevertheless, conscious of the difficulties and dangers. In his oral evidence, he told us that a licensing system would not be sufficient without some test of competence and that controls had to be laid down. On the question of the effect of a free-for-all, he said : —

> If you are asking me, if the monopoly is broken—putting the word "monopoly" in inverted commas—what sort of shape the industry is going to take, it is my personal view that unless you take a very critical look at it, you are going to get all sorts of sharks in this field of service. You are going to get all sorts of undesirable people moving in, and I think the public will be at risk. There is no question about that. What we have to decide is the degree of control and levels of competence we are going to lay down, and I do not pretend anything other than this is a very difficult question on which I certainly have not made up my own mind.

Mr. Weetch went on to say that the building society movement, which had the confidence of the public and a wide distribution of offices, was well placed to offer a package service including conveyancing and had the necessary facilities and standards to do it well and economically.

21.32   We are unanimous that a free-for-all in conveyancing would not be in the public interest, and are reinforced in this view by the information we have received about the practice in many parts of the United States where there is no limitation on the right of any person to undertake conveyancing. The results are not encouraging; in 1972 a report to the United States Congress by the Secretary of the Department of Housing and Urban Development and the Administrator of the Veterans' Administration contained the following passages.

> In most cases, competition in the conveyancing industry is directed toward other

participants in the industry, and not toward the home-buying public. Lenders compete to get business from realtors or escrow companies. Title companies compete to get business from attorneys, brokers, or lenders, and so on . . . the competition that exists in this industry, therefore, is not based on price, because the ultimate consumer has a small voice in that decision. Although this industry is very competitive in many areas, the competitive forces that do exist manifest themselves in an elaborate system of referral fees, kickbacks, rebates, commissions and the like. These practices are widely employed and have replaced effective price competition. These referrals or kickbacks paid by or to lawyers, lenders, title insurance companies, real estate brokers and others result in unnecessarily high costs . . .

21.33 The American Bar Association in 1976 approved a report which contained the following passage.

In some sections of this country all parties are represented by lawyers from the beginning and the system works well. In England, in modern times, this has been the universal practice and this system provides greater service at less cost than in America.

We have concluded that the total abolition of restraints on conveyancing for gain would be against the public interest.

A limited class of conveyancers

21.34 It was argued that it would not be necessary to require conveyancers to obtain formal qualifications provided that they were restricted to undertaking domestic conveyancing and were subject to certain constraints. This was based on the premise that domestic conveyances involved no difficult questions of law and presented only administrative problems; in support of this, it was pointed out that a certain proportion of domestic conveyances presented no serious legal difficulties and could properly be delegated to subordinate staff, subject to the general supervision of a solicitor who bears the ultimate responsibility. A number of witnesses expressed the belief that nearly all conveyancing work in solicitors' offices is done by non-solicitors, working unsupervised. This is not supported by the information we obtained in our survey of conveyancing work and charges (Volume II section 6). This showed that of the total time spent on conveyancing work in the firms surveyed, 70 per cent was that of qualified solicitors, 30 per cent of other fee-earners. In 17 per cent of cases, the time recorded was that of other fee-earners alone. In general, the evidence of those advocating abolition of the present restrictions tended to underestimate the number and frequency of difficulties which may be encountered unexpectedly in any conveyancing transaction, domestic or otherwise, and which require the advice and skills of a qualified practitioner. Among the difficulties we have in mind are those arising from planning and revenue law, the Matrimonial Homes Act 1967, the making of wills and purchases by two or more persons. Problems of great complexity can arise when charities, limited companies, religious bodies and unincorporated associations appear in the abstract of title. It was argued that a licensed conveyancer in doubt or difficulty could seek the advice of a solicitor or barrister. Such a precaution would, however, be effective only if a problem were seen to require expert advice and the advice was taken and we consider that there would be insufficient protection in any such arrangement.

21.35 It was suggested that one could define certain types of domestic conveyancing unlikely to attract difficulties, which could be undertaken by persons with no formal qualifications. Registered conveyancing is usually given as an example. This argument does no more than repeat the argument in the preceding paragraph in a more restricted application. We are satisfied by all the evidence given to us that any form of conveyancing, whether described as domestic, registered or in any other way, may give rise to difficulties apparent only to the expert. In any case which may be specified, ancillary problems may arise and strict control will be needed over the handling of clients' money.

21.36 We find support for our view in the evidence of various building societies who told us that they would not be willing to instruct conveyancers who were not as well qualified as solicitors in appropriate branches of law and practice nor subject to the same safeguards in respect of handling clients' money. Indeed, the largest building society in the United Kingdom, the Halifax Building Society, stated that it would insist that the title to any property offered as a prospective security should be examined by a solicitor. The Committee of London Clearing Bankers, the members of which conduct a large volume of mortgage business, expressed the same view in its evidence.

> In so far as the banks require title to be investigated on their own behalf (whether in respect of registered or unregistered land) they would invariably instruct a solicitor for that purpose. They would not be willing to pass out work of this nature to a third person who is not a qualified solicitor.

In the same vein, the Chief Land Registrar stressed the importance of the work of solicitors in transactions subject to first registration and the reliance which he places on the certificate as to title which they give when applying for registration. If restrictions were modified the pace of registration would be reduced and the cost increased because more legally-qualified professional staff would have to be employed by the Land Registry.

Relaxation of the present restrictions
21.37 Having concluded that the present restrictions on conveyancing should not be wholly abandoned, it is next necessary to consider whether they can be relaxed in such a way that non-solicitor conveyancers are made subject to rules and obligations equivalent to those governing solicitors; then to consider whether in such circumstances conveyancers could provide an effective service more cheaply than solicitors.

Licensed conveyancers
21.38 One method of achieving a certain measure of control over non-solicitor conveyancers would be to require them to be licensed by a government department or agency, such as the Office of Fair Trading, to perform certain functions. This procedure could provide for financial supervision, audit of books, regula-

tions for handling clients' money, indemnity insurance and fidelity bonds. Proof that all such conditions were being met could be made a requirement for issuing an annual or periodic licence. The cost of setting up adequate surveillance of these matters would, however, be appreciable and initially would have to be met out of public funds, because licence fees could not be expected to cover more than a part of the outlay involved until the number of licensed conveyancers was large.

21.39 A system of this kind would provide no protection against the misappropriation of clients' money or other dishonesty by the conveyancer himself. A person cannot take out insurance against his own dishonesty. If the public were to be adequately protected against this risk, it would be necessary to establish some form of compensation fund. Under a system of licensing this would have to be backed by public money and administered by the responsible department or agency. Even if this were done, it would still provide no protection against incompetence or unconscionable conduct falling short of dishonesty.

21.40 These difficulties could be overcome if conveyancers had an organisation, not only to maintain a compensation fund and to impose and enforce rules of conduct, but also to establish appropriate educational standards and, if necessary, set its own examinations. Such a body would need to have the characteristics, not of a licensing body but of a full-scale supervisory body appropriate to an independent profession.

A professional governing body for conveyancers

21.41 There are various ways in which a governing body for conveyancers could be set up. It would, for example, be possible for non-solicitor conveyancers to be placed under the supervision and discipline of the Law Society; an existing body, such as the Institute of Legal Executives, could be empowered to authorise its members to perform this work; or a wholly new body could be set up to supervise non-solicitor conveyancers.

21.42 It could be suggested that the Law Society undertake the supervision of conveyancers, as it maintains comprehensive and well-established rules and procedures for protecting the public and determines and supervises courses of education and training. While no doubt the Law Society could devise and enforce appropriate rules and standards for non-solicitor conveyancers, we consider that it would be neither reasonable nor practicable to expect it to do so. The job of the Society is to promote high standards of probity and competence among solicitors and many of the recommendations in this report are directed to helping it achieve this end. It would not be reasonable to expect it at the same time to assume responsibility for a class of practitioner less well qualified than solicitors who were competing against solicitors in providing a service to the public. Even if this were feasible, those seeking to set up in

259

competition with solicitors, without themselves becoming solicitors, could not be expected to display towards the Law Society the loyalty and trust which is necessary if a professional body is to work effectively.

21.43 If an existing institution were to be developed so as to provide a new conveyancing service independently of the Law Society, a possible candidate would be the Institute of Legal Executives. This is because the Institute is the only body, apart from the Law Society and the Senate, to offer a formal qualification in conveyancing. We think it likely that, if non-solicitor conveyancing became an established occupation, many practitioners would come from the ranks of the legal executives.

21.44 We do not, however, consider that it would be appropriate for the Institute of Legal Executives to become the supervisory body for non-solicitor conveyancers. The Institute and most of the legal executives who submitted evidence to us did not advocate such a course. They considered that the unity of legal practice should be maintained, and that the work of conveyancing should continue to be the sole responsibility of solicitors. We doubt, in any case, whether the Institute, membership of which is voluntary, would have the necessary resources and organisation to act as a supervisory body, especially during the transitional period when non-solicitor conveyancers would be few in number but the whole apparatus of control would be required. At the very least, compulsory membership would be necessary for conveyancers and considerable financial support from public funds would be required. The most serious objection is that an arrangement of this kind would cause the Institute to break up. It would be composed of two different types of member: those working on their own account as conveyancers, and those employed in the traditional way by solicitors. They would have different attitudes, different interests and probably different qualifications. It could be only a question of time before the Institute divided.

21.45 There are precedents for creating a totally new supervisory body. A recent example is the Farriers Registration Council, set up under the Farriers (Registration) Act 1975. The first difficulty in the present case in that the existing conveyancers who are not lawyers are few in number. There is an insufficient base for any professional structure and there would have to be a lengthy transitional period. As we said in the previous paragraph, the supervisory body would, at the outset, have no resources and these would take time to build up. These problems are not insuperable, but the difficulties and possible cost to public funds arising in the early years would be substantial.

Quality of service
21.46 Assuming that an appropriate and effective means of regulating non-solicitor conveyancers could be devised, it must also be considered whether such conveyancers could, as claimed by their proponents, provide services on

any significant scale more cheaply or more efficiently than is done by solicitors. Three factors, namely the number of conveyancers coming forward, the terms on which they were enabled to practise, and the arrangements for financing transactions and for the legal representation of mortgagees, would have to be taken into account. The important result from the point of view of the public is the impact of any new arrangements on the total cost of the transaction.

Numbers of non-solicitor conveyancers

21.47   The number of new conveyancers likely to be available is a matter of speculation. Anyone who was able to qualify as a solicitor would probably choose to do so rather than to qualify as a conveyancer alone, in order to have the opportunity of a wider practice. If, as we think would be the case, most conveyancers were drawn from the ranks of the legal executives or of those who now become legal executives, the maximum number able to take up conveyancing, on present showing, would be slightly under 100 per year. This was the average annual number of passes in the Institute of Legal Executives' Conveyancing II paper (which is said to be equivalent to the conveyancing paper in the Solicitors' Final Examination) in the eleven years from 1966 to 1977. This figure assumes that all those passing this paper would be equally successful in attempting a wider range of papers and would set up in practice. Apart from those who now work in conveyancing organisations, very few people who submitted evidence to us said that they wished to work as conveyancers. From the considerations we have mentioned and the evidence submitted there is at present no indication that a new profession would be large in numbers or likely to provide widespread competition.

Charges by non-solicitor conveyancers

21.48   It was argued that the charges likely to be made by non-solicitor conveyancers would be appreciably lower than solicitors' charges, so as to provide the prospective client with a choice which would promote effective price competition. The conveyancing organisations which gave evidence to us argued that their fees were lower than those of solicitors and would continue to be so. By contrast, the Institute of Legal Executives said in its evidence that, if permitted to offer the service, a legal executive would expect to charge the same as a solicitor.

21.49   When we began our enquiries there appeared to be about four organisations and five or six individuals who provided conveyancing services to the public and were not qualified solicitors with practising certificates. Some of these conveyancing organisations allowed us to examine their accounts. These indicated that their profit margins were in some instances inadequate for normal commercial purposes and in one case very heavy losses were being incurred. Their financial stability was a matter of concern. In one instance, the accounts showed manifest defects in presentation and the firm was in an unstable financial position as its current liabilities exceeded its current assets;

it had at that time no insurance arrangements to protect its clients against negligence or loss of money. A professional body, responsible for supervising the affairs of its members, would be bound to take action in such a case. One conveyancing organisation went into liquidation shortly after we began our work and another became insolvent during the course of it.

21.50 The evidence put before us made it clear that the conveyancing organisations have been able to charge less than solicitors because they do not provide the same type of service, their overheads are lower and they do not subscribe to a professional organisation or to a compensation fund, or, in some cases, hold indemnity insurance cover. It would be difficult for them to maintain their present level of fees if their overhead expenses were the same as those of a solicitor. The more stringent the requirements which are necessarily imposed on a profession for the protection of the public in observing professional and ethical standards, training students, taking out indemnity insurance, making contributions to a compensation fund and maintaining a proper accounting system for the control of clients' money, the greater the overheads of practice and the cost of running an office. Moreover, if the profession is not large, the overhead cost to practitioners of maintaining the governing body will be high. For these reasons, non-solicitor conveyancers who were subjected to a proper system of financial and professional control would not, in our view, be able to keep charges at the present level of the existing conveyancing organisations.

Service provided by non-solicitor conveyancers
21.51 We received little formal evidence concerning complaints by clients of the existing conveyancing organisations and some expressions of satisfaction. Nevertheless, the impression that we gained from our own investigations of these organisations is that they provide both a narrower and less effective service than do solicitors. Many of them operate on a small scale and provide little more than a postal service and, in such cases, are unable to provide prospective vendors or purchasers with independent oral advice which they may require about the merits and financing of the proposed transaction. Lack of formal qualifications was a clear disadvantage. We encountered one conveyancer with inadequate knowledge of the law of agency and the law of real property and who did not know what had to be done if a power of attorney was encountered in the course of examining title or on completion. Another was ignorant of the law of trusts and did not appreciate the need for care when, as frequently happens, two or more persons contribute to the purchase price of a property. A number of conveyancing organisations submitted evidence to us containing claims as to the quality of service which they provide; we were not satisfied that these could be substantiated. Representatives from the National House Owners Society/House Owners' Co-operative Limited gave written and oral evidence but declined to allow us to make the oral evidence public.

21.52 We are satisfied that the claim by the existing conveyancing organisations that they are capable of providing a service both better and cheaper than that provided by solicitors is without foundation. Many of them, like the layman who undertakes his own conveyancing, benefit from the safeguards provided by solicitors acting for the other party or the mortgagee. Furthermore, we have no evidence which would lead us to the view that, if non-solicitor conveyancers were subject to strict requirements as to qualifications and rules of conduct, the standard of their service would surpass, or even equal, that of solicitors.

Conveyancing by building societies and other organisations

21.53 It was suggested to us that conveyancing could be done well and economically by organisations connected with transactions in land, such as building societies and builders' firms or by local authorities. We, therefore, wrote to a number of the leading building societies and larger construction firms and followed up our letters by personal visits to discuss in detail the possibility of their offering a conveyancing service. Among the building societies, only one expressed an interest in providing such a service. The others did not wish to extend their existing functions as institutional lenders by offering a service to borrowers similar to that of a solicitor to his clients.

21.54 None of the construction firms wished to offer such a service. A typical view was put by George Wimpey & Co. Ltd., which pointed out that the actual legal work was only part of the service provided by solicitors.

> . . . the personal contact, the advice explanation and guidance are probably the most important part of the service provided and undoubtedly the most appreciated by clients . . . the only way this service could in some measure be achieved would be by setting up sections of the Legal Department throughout the region . . . alternatively, there could be itinerant legal representatives visiting estates. In either case, the whole situation would be constantly fluid because estates are developed and completed and other estates are not always started up within the same locality . . . the cost involved could not be less and might have to be more than would be charged by a private practitioner so as to try to meet the cost of, either establishing an office in an area or having a visiting legal representative . . .

21.55 The advantage claimed for this proposal is that it would generate competition with private practice. The main objection is that the public might not obtain from building societies and builders the independent advice in particular in relation to financial matters which solicitors now offer. The business of a building society is to lend and of a builder to sell what he has built. No doubt most building societies and builders would endeavour to give unbiased advice and to provide an adequate and safe service. Nevertheless, a lawyer employed by the organisation to handle this service would face possible conflicts of interest between the society or builder and mortgagor or purchaser. We consider, therefore, that even if it were possible to devise a suitable system for licensing and supervising conveyancing by building societies and builders that was not cumbersome and expensive such a development would not be in the public interest.

21.56   Many local authorities would have the staff and facilities to provide a conveyancing service. Whether a local authority should extend its activities into conveyancing is a question of policy which can be determined only by the government and by each local authority. In years to come more use of computer-based information systems, at present in early infancy, may greatly develop the role of national and local authorities. It does not, however, follow from improvements in information systems available to such authorities that they should take over the function of giving private advice. We have no evidence to suggest that under present conditions a local authority service would be any quicker, cheaper or more efficient than the service now provided by solicitors in private practice.

21.57   Other professions associated with land transactions do not compete with solicitors for conveyancing work. These professions, like the Law Society, follow the principle that neither vendor nor purchaser should be committed to a conveyancing transaction until he has obtained independent legal advice. This principle, with which we are in agreement, is supported by the Royal Institution of Chartered Surveyors, the Chartered Land Agents' Society, the Chartered Auctioneers' and Estate Agents' Institute and the Incorporated Society of Auctioneers and Land Property Agents. To avoid situations in which a purchaser might commit himself without obtaining advice, their members do not undertake conveyancing work, but advise clients to consult their own solicitors.

Notaries public
21.58   The notary was in origin an ecclesiastical official, and appointments to the office in England are still made by the Archbishop of Canterbury. In Wales they are made by the Permanent Secretary of the Lord Chancellor's Department. There are two classes of notary: the London notary must be a member of the Scriveners' Company, which conducts examinations for candidates for admission; his business is largely concerned with international trading transactions and the preparation of documents relating to them. The provincial notary has certain formal procedural functions in relation to verifying and attesting documents. In all but a few cases, the provincial notary is a practising solicitor.

21.59   For historical reasons, notaries are within the class of practitioners to which conveyancing is restricted. London notaries are qualified by examination in conveyancing and are frequently required to prepare documents relating to title to property. Provincial notaries, who are not also solicitors are, however, required to have no formal qualifications in the subject, and belong to no professional organisation charged with the duty of maintaining the necessary level of protection for the public. We received evidence from one provincial notary who happens not to be a solicitor but who, by virtue of his appointment as a notary, carries on a conveyancing practice. We intend no discourtesy to this practitioner in recommending that, although no notary should be deprived of his existing right to practise, no newly-appointed provincial notary who is not also a qualified solicitor should be permitted to undertake conveyancing.

Summary

21.60   It is convenient at this stage to summarise our views.

(a) The main purpose of removing or relaxing the present restrictions on conveyancing would be to reduce charges by widening competition.

(b) Steps to simplify the land law and the progress of registration have been offset by the increasing need for advice on matters ancillary to a conveyance, such as planning, taxation and matrimonial law.

(c) It is agreed by all but a few witnesses that the public should be protected in conveyancing transactions from incompetence, dishonesty and unfair dealing.

(d) Subject to some improvements proposed in Chapters 22, 23 and 25, an adequate level of competence and probity is maintained by the solicitors' profession. This should be maintained in any alternative system.

(e) A free-for-all, in which any person may offer conveyancing services without restriction, is unacceptable for the reasons given above.

(f) A licensing system would be unable to provide the level of positive control required, particularly in respect of standards of competence and ethical conduct.

(g) There is, in general, no interest among organisations connected with land transactions, such as builders and institutional lenders, in providing a conveyancing service and we are not satisfied that it would be in the public interest that they should do so.

(h) In order to secure the necessary standards of competence and probity, it would be necessary to set up a new profession of non-solicitor conveyancers, subject to requirements similar to those affecting solicitors in respect of qualifying examinations and conditions of practice.

(j) Conveyancers working under the same conditions as solicitors would have equivalent overhead expenses. The effect of setting up a new profession to operate in a single field would be to dilute the service available but without creating conditions in which competition was likely to be effective in holding down charges. To achieve this purpose, therefore, some other means must be found.

Changes in the present restrictions

Contracts

21.61 The present restrictions, set out in paragraph 21.4 above, prevent an unqualified person from drawing up a conveyance or document of transfer but do not prevent such a person from drawing up the binding contract which is exchanged by the two parties. We consider that this is an anomaly which should be rectified because the client needs the same degree of protection in respect of the contract as he does in respect of the document by which the transaction is completed. Some would go so far as to say that the need for protection is even greater at this stage. We recommend that the Solicitors Act 1974 should be amended to prohibit an unqualified person not merely from drawing up for gain the final document but also from preparing a contract for the sale or other disposition of land or any interest in land.

Prosecution and penalty

21.62 At present the responsibility for initiating prosecutions for breaches of section 22 of the Solicitors Act 1974 rests on the Law Society. This is unsatisfactory for two reasons. First, if the law is to be enforced as a matter of public policy in order to protect the citizen, prosecutions should be the responsibility of the appropriate public authority. Secondly, we believe that the Law Society should not be required to exercise a function of this kind in circumstances in which it is bound to appear merely to be protecting the financial interests of its members. The Law Society is, we understand, anxious to give up this function. We consider that arrangements should be made for the police or the appropriate government department to assume responsibility for prosecutions of this character.

21.63 The maximum penalty that may be imposed on anyone convicted of a contravention of section 22 of the Solicitors Act 1974 is a fine of £50. This sum has long ceased to bear any relation to the amount that may be earned by contravening the Act and should, we think, be substantially increased. We have noted that the maximum penalty for acting as an architect while unregistered was increased, under the Criminal Law Act 1977, to £500. Similar maxima were enacted for unlawfully acting as a nurse, a midwife or an optician. We consider that a similar maximum would be appropriate in respect of offences under section 22 of the Solicitors Act 1974.

Acting for two or more parties

21.64 By rule 2 of the Solicitors' Practice Rules 1936–1972, introduced in 1972 shortly before scale charges were abolished, a solicitor may not act for vendor and purchaser or lessor and lessee, save in certain circumstances specified in the rule. This differs from the general rule, under which a solicitor may act for two clients in non-contentious business unless a conflict of interest arises. Until rule 2 was made, it was regarded as permissible for a solicitor to act for both vendor and purchaser in accordance with the general rule. In 1971 the National Board for Prices and Incomes found that there was a saving of some two weeks in time and some 26 per cent in cost when the same solicitor acted for both parties. Having struck their bargain, the parties to a conveyancing transaction are not antagonists, though their interests are not the same. The vendor wishes to bind the purchaser by contract as soon as possible and to secure completion and payment without delay. The purchaser needs time not only to investigate the title to the property and other matters, but also to find the purchase price, which often involves the sale of an existing property. Difficulties may arise over the agreed completion date and other matters, involving clashes of interest. In spite of the additional expense, we believe therefore that separate representation is desirable in some cases. However, in many domestic conveyances and conveyances between local authorities, when the vendor and purchaser have agreed, subject to contract, on a sale at a specified price, it may well be found that there is little risk of a conflict arising. In such circumstances a solicitor might, in our view, with propriety act for both parties unless and until a conflict arises. We recommend, therefore, that the Law Society should allow the normal rules as to acting for two clients to operate in these cases. When a solicitor acts for both parties the fees should be reduced and the standard charge should be amended appropriately. We set out the procedure for doing this in paragraph 21.98 below.

One solicitor for borrower and lender
21.65 The evidence suggested that, while the parties to a transaction may well have opposing interests, the purchaser's mortgagee is unlikely to have interests conflicting with those of the purchaser and both have an identical interest in securing a good title. The fee for acting for both mortgagee and borrower should be appreciably lower than the aggregate of the fees for acting for the two separately. We consider, therefore, that every effort should be made by both building societies, banks and other lenders and solicitors to ensure that solicitors are not appointed separately for mortgagee and borrower except in a case where a conflict of interest arises. Furthermore, use of standard documents by the Building Societies' Association could lead to savings in legal costs. We refer further to this point in the annex to this chapter.

Title insurance
21.66 Insurance against defects in title is well established in the United States of America as a substitute for, or supplement to, a detailed investigation of title and, in many areas, plays a leading part in property transactions. It is a recent arrival in this country. Within the last few years a subsidiary has been established here by an American company, the Chicago Title Insurance Company (CTI) to provide title insurance. At one stage, the company also undertook conveyancing, using notaries to draft the conveyances, and included title insurance as part of the package. It has, however, recently withdrawn from conveyancing and now offers title insurance as a supplement to the services

provided by solicitors. CTI submitted written evidence which was made public. Oral evidence was also given by its representatives but it has declined to allow this to be made public.

21.67 Title insurance provides financial compensation for defects in title, undisclosed encumbrances, undisclosed restrictions and adverse rights. In the United States of America it has proved its value in those states where conveyancing is open to unqualified conveyancers or where land registries, if they exist, contain uncertain or incomplete information. In addition it is helpful to an American mortgagee who, for example, operates in the East and knows nothing of the local laws or conveyancers dealing with property offered as security in the West. Title insurance does not cover defects in the contract by which the purchaser has become committed to a purchase but covers defects which do not appear on the face of the conveyance and which, at the date of completion, have not been disclosed and are not apparent. It is not regarded as the business of title insurance companies to advise a purchaser whether, or how and on what terms and after what investigation, it is prudent to enter into a binding contract.

21.68 A standard title insurance policy requires the purchaser to acknowledge the accuracy of a plan of the property. The policy also naturally and inevitably exempts the insurance company from liability for any matters which are apparent on inspection or which are known to the insured. A purchaser who did not employ a solicitor might well not appreciate the effect of the limitations in the policy on the liability of the insurance company in the light of the information available to the purchaser from the vendor, from the local and other authorities, and from an informed investigation of title. By its very nature, therefore, title insurance is, as described in CTI's latest brochure, "a supplement to and not a substitute for careful conveyancing practice".

21.69 The main claim advanced in favour of title insurance was that it would compensate the client who suffered loss through a defect in title or a contested title which did not result from negligence by his solicitor, as where a local authority or the vendor is given in accurate information. We do not, however, find the claims as to the merits of title insurance entirely convincing. Although there might have been a strong case for title insurance many years ago before the introduction of land registration, the improvement in land law and the restriction of conveyancing to qualified persons, described earlier in this chapter, we can see little need for it now.

21.70 It was also suggested that the safeguard of title insurance would enable conveyancing to be carried out by persons other than solicitors. The safeguard would be far from complete, because title insurance is not designed to provide cover against the dishonesty of a conveyancer in the way that the Law Society's compensation fund protects clients against dishonesty by solicitors and their staff. Even if title insurance were to provide adequate cover in such cases, we do not consider that it would be in the public interest for good titles unsupported by insurance to be replaced by unsound titles supported by insurance but which could be rectified only with cost and delay. In general, it is clearly more in the public interest to prevent defects in title and loss of property rights than to provide monetary compensation for them. We consider, therefore, that the availability of title insurance does not in any way weaken the case for retaining the present restrictions.

Conveyancing Charges

Introductory

21.71 The level of charges for conveyancing is the most widely criticised aspect of the present system. The theme of much of the evidence submitted on this point was that the abandonment of scale charges has not had the effect of promoting competition between solicitors in such a way as to have any real impact on the general level of charges and that only competition with non-solicitors would achieve this. As pointed out in paragraph 21.30 however, a range of prices may now be found to be offered by solicitors if, as happens with increasing frequency, clients shop around. We gave above our reasons for doubting whether a new system based on conveyancing by non-solicitors would have the result of increasing competition appreciably. There remains the question in what way the level of charges can be kept to a reasonable and competitive level.

Scale charges

21.72 Before January 1973 the statutory scales of fees set out in Table 21.4 were in force for most conveyancing work, and the provisions of rule 2 of the Solicitors' Practice Rules 1936 precluded solicitors from holding themselves out as being prepared to do the work for less except in one of the following circumstances.

(a) It was open to local law societies under rule 2 to permit solicitors to hold themselves out as being prepared to charge less than the scale in transactions affecting land in their area.

(b) It was open to the Law Society under rule 2 to give permission to individual firms of solicitors to hold themselves out as being prepared to charge less than the scale in particular circumstances.

(c) If a solicitor was of the opinion that the scale fee might be inadequate, he could elect to charge on a fair and reasonable basis provided the election was made before he accepted instructions from the client.

269

(d) Solicitors could charge less than the scale fee where they were of the opinion that the scale fee would, in the circumstances, be an excessive charge, provided that the solicitor did not hold himself out as prepared to charge less.

TABLE 21.4
Scale charges for conveyancing, January 1973

Purchase price or mortgage money not exceeding	Solicitor's fees for deducing or investigating title		Purchase price or mortgage money not exceeding	Solicitor's fees for deducing or investigating title	
	unregistered land	registered land		unregistered land	registered land
£	£	£	£	£	£
500	20·00	15·00	16,000	135·00	81·25
1,000	30·00	22·50	16,500	137·50	82·50
1,500	37·50	27·50	17,000	140·00	83·75
2,000	45·00	30·00	17,500	142·50	84·75
2,500	48·75	32·50	18,000	145·00	85·75
3,000	52·50	35·00	18,500	147·50	86·75
3,500	56·25	37·50	19,000	150·00	87·75
4,000	60·00	40·00	19,500	152·50	88·75
4,500	63·75	41·87½	20,000	155·00	89·75
5,000	67·50	43·75	20,500	157·50	90·75
5,500	71·25	45·62½	21,000	160·00	91·75
6,000	75·00	47·50	21,500	162·50	92·75
6,500	78·75	49·37½	22,000	165·00	93·75
7,000	82·50	51·25	22,500	167·50	94·75
7,500	86·25	53·12½	23,000	170·00	95·75
8,000	90·00	55·00	23,500	172·50	96·75
8,500	93·75	56·87½	24,000	175·00	97·75
9,000	97·50	58·75	24,500	177·50	98·75
9,500	101·25	60·62½	25,000	180·00	99·75
10,000	105·00	62·50	25,500	182·50	100·75
10,500	107·50	64·37½	26,000	185·00	101·75
11,000	110·00	66·25	26,500	187·50	102·75
11,500	112·50	68·12½	27,000	190·00	103·75
12,000	115·00	70·00	27,500	192·50	104·75
12,500	117·50	71·87½	28,000	195·00	105·75
13,000	120·00	73·75	28,500	197·50	106·75
13,500	122·50	75·00	29,000	200·00	107·75
14,000	125·00	76·25	29,500	202·50	108·75
14,500	127·50	77·50	30,000	205·00	109·75
15,000	130·00	78·75	(Above £30,000. Schedule II)		
15,500	132.50	80·00			

Sources: Solicitors' Remuneration Orders 1883-1970.
Solicitors' Remuneration (Registered Land) Orders, 1927-1970.

Surveys by the National Board for Prices and Incomes
21.73 The National Board for Prices and Incomes reported on the remuneration of solicitors in the years 1968, 1969 and 1971. The Board drew the conclusion that, although in the case of property of low value conveyancing was unremunerative, it was in general profitable. Its 1968 survey showed that conveyancing accounted for 55.6 per cent of solicitors' incomes and 40 per cent of their total expenses.

21.74 In 1971, the Board studied the time spent by each fee-earner in a sample of firms on every conveyance over a set period. It found that about 50 per cent of the conveyances took less than 12 weeks to complete and 6 per cent longer than six months. The average period between instructions and completion was 13 weeks in the case of properties up to £10,000, and slightly longer for those between £10,000 and £20,000. The time taken was said by solicitors to depend on the ease or difficulty of arranging finance and synchronising chains of sales and purchases. Recent surveys suggest similar average times. The Consumers' Association recent survey (see paragraph 21.80) found the average time from initial offer and acceptance to completion was four months. Our Users' Survey showed that 32 per cent of transactions took up to two months and 53 per cent between two and six months (see Table 22.12).

21.75 The Board noted a fairly consistent relationship between the value of property and the cost to the solicitor (on a time cost basis) of undertaking the work. The average cost of acting for a purchaser was found to show no significant variation between registered and unregistered property. However, the costs of a solicitor acting for the vendor were less than those of the purchaser's solicitor and the difference was more marked in the case of the transfer of registered land. About 20 per cent of conveyances were carried out by legal executives, working under minimum supervision.

21.76 The Board found that when the same solicitor acted for both parties the costs were on average 26 per cent less than the aggregate costs of separate representation and that those conveyances in the sample (11 per cent) in which one solicitor acted for both parties took about two weeks less on average than those where each party had his own solicitor.

21.77 In 1969 and 1971 the Board reported that the profitability of conveyancing, particularly of properties of higher value, remained high and that the balance of charges between different classes of work was not satisfactory. It recommended adjustments to the statutory scale.

Abolition of scale charges in 1973
21.78 Following the reports of the National Board for Prices and Incomes, there developed increasing dissatisfaction amongst both the public and the profession with the operation of the system of scale charges. In January 1973, on the initiative of the Lord Chancellor of the day, Lord Hailsham, scale charges were abandoned. In the absence of scale charges, the formal rule against undercutting ceased to operate but *A Guide to the Professional Conduct of Solicitors* says:—

> The Council are of the opinion that the public interest requires that solicitors should not use the giving of quotations or estimates of their fees as a means of attracting professional business since, whilst this might provide a cheaper service, it would almost certainly lead to a diminution in the quality of that service.

Existing basis of charge

21.79 The normal basis for conveyancing charges is now contained in the Solicitors' Remuneration Order 1972 which provides that the amount charged should be "such sum as may be fair and reasonable", taking into account such matters as the difficulty of the transaction and the number and complexity of the documents, the time, labour and skill needed to deal with it, the value of the property, whether it is registered, and other factors.

Consumers' Association surveys

21.80 The Consumers' Association has carried out a number of surveys of conveyancing transactions, details of which have appeared in its magazine *Which?* and the Association has kindly allowed us to extract information for our purposes from the surveys conducted in 1977 and 1979. The earlier report focused on the wide variations in solicitors' charges since the abolition of scale fees and hence the desirability of shopping around, and it concluded that an end to present restrictions on conveyancing by non-lawyers would further encourage competition and reduce charges. The 1979 report was concerned more generally with the high costs of moving home, of which the fees charged by solicitors are a part. Both reports illustrated, though they did not specifically draw attention to, the relative sizes of solicitors' and other charges. In 1977, the Association obtained estimates of charges from 100 solicitors, practising in London and Newcastle-upon-Tyne. These included both the solicitors' fees and other charges. Because the estimates were based on the sale and purchase of a £13,000 house, stamp duty (which is not charged on transactions of less than £15,000) was not included amongst the other charges. The solicitors' fees accounted for nearly half the total charges associated with a purchase and approaching one-third the charges associated with a sale, the remaining two-thirds being largely accounted for by the estate agent's commission which is not incurred in all cases. A further survey, based on questionnaires to 5,000 readers, was reported by the Association in May 1979. On this occasion the transaction selected as typical involved the sale of a £23,000 house and the purchase of a £28,000 house. The charges other than solicitors' fees included £420 stamp duty. The solicitors' charges accounted for slightly more than one-quarter of the total cost, assuming as before that estate agent's commission was payable on the sale: see Tables 21.5 and 21.6. The addition of removal costs (£108) and charges for abortive transactions brought the average total cost to £1,756, or $7\frac{1}{2}$ per cent of the value of the house sold.

TABLE 21.5

Average estimated charges for the purchase and sale of a £13,000 house with registered title and a £9,000 mortgage, 1977

Description of work	Charges		Proportion of total costs	
	solicitors	others	solicitors	others
	£	£	%	%
Purchase				
Solicitor's fee..	127·50	—	39	—
Fee for mortgage	32·50	—	10	—
Building society valuation fee ..	—	27·00	—	8
Survey	—	77·50	—	24
Land Registry fee	—	32·50	—	10
Local authority search fee	—	5·25	—	2
VAT	—	21·16	—	7
Total cost £323·41	160·00	163·41	49	51
Sale				
Solicitor's fee	125·00	—	30	—
Estate agent's commission	—	257·50	—	62
VAT	—	30·60	—	8
Total cost £413·10	125·00	288·10	30	70

Source: Consumer's Association

Note: In the above table the purchaser's solicitor's fees represent about 49 per cent of the total cost of the transaction; the fees of the vendor's solicitor, about 30 per cent of the total.

TABLE 21.6

Estimated average charges for the sale of a £23,000 house and the purchase of a £28,000 house, 1979

Description of work	Charges		Proportion of total costs	
	solicitors	other	solicitors	others
	£	£	%	%
Purchase (£28,000 house)				
Solicitor's fee (including work for building society)	245	—	28	—
Building society valuation fee ..	—	44	—	5
Survey	—	83	—	9
Land Registry fee	—	70	—	8
Stamp duty	—	420	—	47
VAT	—	31	—	3
Total cost £893	245	648	28	72
Sale (£23,000 house)				
Solicitor's fee	176	—	26	—
Estate agent's commission	—	463	—	67
VAT	—	51	—	7
Total cost £690	176	514	26	74

Source: Consumers' Association.

Note: In the above table the purchaser's solicitor's fees represent about 28 per cent of the total cost of the transaction including all ancillary costs; those of the vendor's solicitor, about 26 per cent of the total.

273

The Commission's enquiries

21.81 We investigated the remuneration and charges of solicitors, both in general and in respect of conveyancing. The results are shown in full in Volume II sections 6 and 16. In these surveys we found (as did the National Board for Prices and Incomes) that the majority of solicitors derive between 40 per cent and 60 per cent of their gross fee income from conveyancing. Our survey of conveyancing charges involved a sample of 2,000 firms throughout the country. Not all of them maintained time records in a form which enabled the time spent on conveyancing transactions to be given. For this reason estimated periods of time were given in three-quarters of the replies, actual time in one-quarter. In the following tables we show charges made for registered and unregistered transactions and those involving first registration, the average hours spent by all fee-earners, the amount of partners' time spent and that of other fee-earners.

TABLE 21.7

Average charge for transfers related to registration and price of property, 1978

	Average charge for transfer price of property					
Ranges of price (£'000)	0–5 £	5–10 £	10–15 £	15–20 £	20–30 £	Over 30 £
Sales						
Previously registered	77	103	127	153	190	304
Registered during transfer	71	112	140	165	212	333
Unregistered before and after transfer	77	114	140	164	210	342
All bills	74	110	134	159	200	322
Purchases						
Previously registered	76	100	121	153	187	296
Registered during transfer	74	115	139	168	213	310
Unregistered before and after transfer	78	110	137	166	211	328
All bills	76	108	131	160	199	309

Source: Charges for domestic conveyancing, Volume II section 6.

TABLE 21.8

Average hours spent by all fee-earners on conveyancing related to price of property: actual and estimated figures, 1978

| Price of property (£'000's) | Average hours of all fee-earners | | | |
| | sales | | purchasers | |
	actual	estimated	actual	estimated
Up to 5	5·5	6·0	5·6	4·6
5 – 10	5·7	5·2	6·7	5·8
10 – 15	6·1	5·8	7·1	6·3
15 – 20	6·3	6·6	7·7	6·7
20 – 30	6·9	7·0	8·2	7·4
More than 30	12·1	8·8	11·0	9·1
All bills	6·9	6·0	7·7	6·5
Number of bills..	925	3,007	1,036	3,048

Source: Charges for domestic conveyancing, Volume II section 6.

TABLE 21.9

Time spent on conveyancing, 1978

| Status of fee-earner | % of time | | | |
| | sales | | purchases | |
	actual	estimated	actual	estimated
Partners	55	58	53	56
Assistant solicitors	15	14	15	13
Trainee solicitors	4	3	6	3
Other fee-earners	26	26	25	27
Total	100	100	100	100
Number of bills..	925	3,007	1,036	3,048

Source: Charges for domestic conveyancing, Volume II section 6.

Conveyancing costs abroad

21.82 A number of witnesses suggested that we should compare the charges for conveyancing in England and Wales with those for a similar service in other jurisdictions. We therefore conducted a pilot study to see whether it would be possible to make valid comparisons. This is summarised in Volume II section 7. We would like to acknowledge the help we received from those we consulted and in particular the law firms in the United States of America who provided us with detailed and helpful information. We found that a wide and varying range of factors would have to be taken into account. For instance, some functions normally undertaken in this country by a lawyer are elsewhere performed by estate agents, title insurers, institutional mortgagees or by the state, in the person of a public servant or agency. The amounts

275

levied on land transactions for revenue purposes vary widely as do procedures and legal requirements. In such circumstances direct comparisons would be misleading.

Summary of evidence on charges

21.83 Comparison of the tables of charges set out above shows that the fees for a registered conveyance of a £13,000 house were much the same in 1977 (Consumers' Association, Table 21.5) and 1978 (Commission's survey, Table 21.7). In both cases the charge was appreciably higher than that for a registered transaction under the pre-1973 scale fees, but close to the fees for an unregistered transaction. The charges for unregistered conveyancing appear to have risen relatively little: for houses between £20,000 and £30,000, between £155 and £205 in the 1972 scales, compared with about £210 in 1978.

21.84 It must be borne in mind, however, that even after the abolition of scale charges, fees have remained closely related to the value of the transaction. Since 1973 houses have greatly increased in value. In respect of a particular house, therefore, the cost of conveyancing would have been substantially more in 1978 than in 1973.

21.85 The tables also show that the difference between the costs of registered and unregistered conveyancing has been greatly reduced. In 1973, in the case of a £25,000 house, the fee in respect of registered land was 55.4 per cent of that in respect of unregistered land. In 1975, the fee in respect of registered land was 90.4 per cent of that in respect of unregistered land in a sale, 88.6 per cent in a purchase. The National Board for Prices and Incomes found that the difference in the cost of transactions in registered and unregistered land was not as great as the difference in scale fees. This partly explains the fact that charges in transactions in registered land have risen to nearly the same level as those in unregistered land. It is also the case, according to evidence we received from a number of sources, that the need to investigate title, long regarded as the main difference between registered and unregistered work, is no longer as significant a factor in the cost as ancillary matters such as planning, taxation, trusts and matrimonial law which affect many transactions.

21.86 There remains the question whether conveyancing charges are excessive. Our investigations suggest that they are not. Nevertheless, it is clear that charges for conveyancing are out of line with those for some other types of legal work. We received evidence from many firms of solicitors, often supported by production of their accounts, that they are dependent on conveyancing to secure an adequate overall return on their practices. We return below to the question how this imbalance should be removed.

21.87 It was also clear from our investigations that there is considerable uncertainty in the profession as to the proper level of charges for conveyancing. We were told that, after scale fees were abolished in 1973, many solicitors continued to rely on the old scale charges, adjusted, largely by guesswork, to allow for inflation. At that time the levels of salaries and overhead expenses were rising faster than property values. The effect was to inflate costs while restraining gross incomes arising from conveyancing. At the outset, therefore, there was no justification for reducing fees. Moreover, for lack of efficient time-costing systems, the great majority of firms were unable to calculate the expenses of conveyancing and other forms of work. We are satisfied that the profession needs some guidance, though not necessarily in the form of a mandatory scale of charges, as to the proper level of fees for registered and unregistered conveyancing.

21.88 One factor in the cost of land transactions is not clearly understood by the public. This is that a large part of the cost arises from disbursements over which a solicitor has no control, though he may be obliged to collect them in the course of the transactions. The Consumers' Association's 1977 survey (Table 21.5) showed that charges other than those of the solicitor made up more than half the cost of a sale and 70 per cent of the cost of a purchase. Recent increases in property values have caused many domestic transactions to be subject to stamp duty. The Consumers' Association's 1979 survey (Table 21.6) showed that stamp duty on a £28,000 house was £420 while the solicitor's average charge for a purchase was £245. Our own survey (Volume II section 6) shows that, in relation to a house above £20,000, stamp duty was higher than the solicitor's average charge and for a house above £30,000, more than twice as high. Charges of this type may be shown on a solicitor's bill as disbursements and included in the total charge. Misunderstanding easily arises. To avoid it, solicitors should be careful to explain fully both at the outset of the transaction and when the final bill is presented, what inescapable charges there are.

Present methods of control
21.89 A client dissatisfied with the charge made by a solicitor may apply to the Law Society for an assessment of a fair charge for the work done. Additionally he may apply to have the charge taxed by the court. Both these procedures have long been available to the public but in practice, for reasons discussed in Chapter 37, they are little used. There are no established arrangements by which a prospective client may obtain from a solicitor, before committing himself, a firm estimate of the total charges.

21.90 The difficulty arises in some conveyancing cases that the person who pays the costs is not entitled to apply to the Law Society for a remuneration certificate. Several witnesses complained to us that, when the costs of the mortgagee's solicitors are paid by the purchaser, he is not entitled to apply for a certificate because he is not the client of the solicitor concerned. In such cases the bill will only be reviewed if the solicitor himself submits the bill for taxation or the client agrees to its submission. We consider that this is unreasonable and that the person who pays the costs should always be entitled to apply for a remuneration certificate: (see paragraph 37.14).

21.91 A further matter of criticism in the evidence submitted to us was that solicitors acting for vendors deducted their charges from money received on behalf of their clients and that solicitors acting for purchasers added their charges to the amount required to be paid by their clients on completion and deducted it before paying over the amount due. Such deductions by the solicitor do not operate as a bar to an application for a remuneration certificate. Even so, we think it unsatisfactory that they should be made before the client has had an opportunity of considering the bill. We consider that a bill should be submitted before a deduction is made and this should be made the subject of a Professional Standard (as to Professional Standards in general, see Chapter 22).

Reintroduction of scale charges
21.92 A number of witnesses argued that one of the main causes of discontent is that the client is often uncertain until he receives the bill of the likely amount of the solicitor's charges. This problem would, it was argued, largely be resolved by the reintroduction of scale charges for conveyancing.

21.93 The argument against scale charges is that they inhibit competition: even when intended to operate only as a maximum, they readily become, in practice, the normal charges. Sometimes (as was the case with scale charges for conveyancing until 1973) there is a rule of professional conduct against undercutting. Even when such rules do not exist, the view is often held by practitioners that it is unprofessional to undercut scale fees, or to charge less than the prevailing rate. The suggestion which we make later in this report for a "standard" charge with appropriate safeguards will we think overcome this criticism.

21.94 The evidence which we received together with our own enquiries and discussions lead us to the clear conclusion that, above all, members of the public wish to know from the outset of a conveyancing transaction where they stand with regard to fees. This is particularly important in the case of domestic properties where the parties to the transaction often have little experience of the law or previous contact with solicitors. Certainty as to the fees payable is an important advantage in that it enables the client to calculate the total cost of the transaction from the outset. This is true not only of private clients. The Association of Metropolitan Authorities, the Association of District Secretaries and the Agricultural Mortgage Corporation all advocated a return to some form of scale fees. Despite the abolition of the statutory scales, the Law Society and the Building Societies' Association agreed to recommend a scale of charges for work on a standard mortgage contemporaneous with a purchase in which the solicitor acts both for the purchaser and the building society.

21.95 We recommend that the Fees Advisory Committee proposed in Chapter 37 should set a scale of "standard" charges which would provide adequate remuneration for the general run of domestic conveyancing transactions which are neither unusually easy or usually difficult. We consider that the basis of the standard charge should be the amount of time which can reasonably be expected to be occupied (whether by partners, salaried solicitors or other staff) in the course of the transaction and should have some regard to the size of the consideration, particularly in the case of larger transactions. We encountered firms operating efficiently on a time cost basis, which prepared their own scales of charges for domestic transactions in this way. It may be desirable to specify circumstances in which a lower charge would be appropriate, as when a solicitor acts for both parties or for a vendor who is selling a large building estate in small lots.

21.96 We leave open, for decision by the Fees Advisory Committee, the question whether it is appropriate to provide for a supplement to be paid in the case of unregistered land, or for cases of first registration. We do not think it would be possible to fix standard charges for conveyancing other than of domestic property, because the requirements of clients relating to commercial and industrial property vary widely.

21.97 In *Property and Reversionary Investment Corporation Ltd.* v. *Secretary of State for the Environment* [1975] 2 All E.R. 436, *Maltby* v. *D J Freeman & Co.* [1978] 2 All E.R. 913 and *Treasury Solicitor* v. *Regester* [1978] 2 All E.R. 1920, the court attempted to interpret the prescribed criteria for the ascertainment of "fair and reasonable remuneration". Those cases illustrated the impossibility of deriving any figure which can be logically explained by reference to any criteria except time and value. The Monopolies Commission found that in conveyancing transactions there is a relationship between time and value, and a similar relationship, based in part on estimated figures, appears in Table 21.8. If conveyancing charges were based wholly on value there would be greater simplicity, thereby avoiding the complications of the three cases to which we have referred, absolute certainty, which the public is entitled to expect, and no measure of injustice. So far as the solicitor is concerned it will not hurt him to take the rough with the smooth. Provided the charges are fixed by the Fees Advisory Committee both the profession and the public should be content. We would see no objection if standard charges were to be based on value or bands of value, for example houses between £20,000 and £30,000.

21.98 We set out in Chapter 37 proposed arrangements for charging fees. In relation to conveyancing, they would apply as follows. Solicitors should be

279

free to charge less than the standard charge fixed by the Fees Advisory Committee, and entitled to charge more, subject to the following conditions.

(a) When first approached, the solicitor should inform the client in writing:—

    (i) of the authorised "standard" charge, if it is a type of conveyance for which a standard charge has been fixed;

    (ii) of his own proposed charge and, if this is more than the standard charge, of the basis on which his charge is calculated;

    (iii) whether he reserves the right to increase his proposed charge, and, if so, what his and his client's rights are in relation to an alteration in the proposed charge—see (b) below;

    (iv) that the client is free to approach another solicitor if he wishes.

(b) When a solicitor has given a proposed charge to a client for a domestic conveyance he should be entitled to reduce it if appropriate. He should not however be entitled to increase the proposed charge unless:—

    (i) he has told the client in advance that he reserves the right to do so;

    (ii) he informs the client as soon as the ground for increasing the charge becomes apparent;

    (iii) he explains to the client on what basis an additional charge is proposed to be made;

    (iv) he either:—

        (a) obtains his client's consent; or

        (b) applies to an assessment committee (see paragraph 37.14) to whom the client is also entitled to make representations.

21.99 The procedure is in our view suitable for inclusion in a Professional Standard. The information required to be given under (a) above could well be included as a supplement to a pamphlet informing existing or prospective clients of the services provided by solicitors in various types of business, and describing the usual courses of certain transactions; we deal with informative material of this type in Chapter 27.

21.100 The main reason for advocating the creation of a new profession of conveyancers is to increase the level of competition. For the reasons given earlier in this chapter, we believe that to set up a new profession would not achieve this purpose. We consider that the best prospect of securing a service of good quality and reasonable cost lies in the measures we have proposed above, combined with our recommendations in Chapter 27 that solicitors should be able to advertise details of any fixed charges including charges based on an *ad valorem* scale, and that firms should give information to potential clients which would enable them to shop around.

The future

21.101   In paragraph 21.56 we touched on the possible impact of the devolopment of computer-based information retrieval systems. Such systems are at present in the early stages of development and their full potential has not been realised. In this country, in particular in legal applications, their use has developed very little for want of the necessary capital investment. Increased use of computer-based information retrieval systems could have a significant impact on future conveyancing services. More information could be retained in the Land Registry and material that is at present obtained by means of detailed enquiries to local authorities could, in a well-constructed retrieval system, be immediately available. We urge that all those involved, including government departments, local authorities, building societies and the profession itself should begin now to plan and invest in the development of computer-based systems for improving and expediting the flow of information which is needed in conveyancing transactions. We believe that future benefits will repay the costs involved.

Conclusions and Recommendations

Paragraphs

Restrictions on practice	R21.1	A person buying or selling a house should continue to be entitled to act for himself, whether or not assisted by an unpaid friend or agent.	21.28
	R21.2	Notaries public, other than London notaries, should no longer be permitted to undertake conveyancing for reward but existing rights to practise should remain unaffected.	21.59
	R21.3	The present restrictions on conveyancing for fee or reward should be maintained and reformulated as proposed in the text.	21.61
Prosecution and penalties	R21.4	Prosecutions should be undertaken not by the Law Society but by the police or the appropriate government department.	21.62

R21.5   The maximum penalty for contravening the statutory restrictions on conveyancing should be increased.   21.63

Acting for two or more parties   R21.6   When no conflict of interest arises and he is so authorised in writing, a solicitor should be permitted to act for both parties with an appropriate reduction in fee.   21.64

R21.7   Building societies and solicitors should ensure that mortgagees are not represented separately from vendors or purchasers unless there is conflict of interest.   21.65

Fees and charges   R21.8   A person who is required to pay the charges of another party to a conveyancing transaction should be entitled to apply for a remuneration certificate.   21.90

R21.9   A bill should be submitted and agreed before fees are deducted from money received on behalf of a client.   21.91

R21.10   A system of standard charges for conveyancing transactions should be introduced.   21.95

The future   R21.11   All concerned in conveyancing transactions should begin to plan the development of computer-based systems.   21.101

ANNEX 21.1

Improvements and Simplification

(paragraph 21.1)

Machinery

1. We consider that there is force in the submissions made to us that, so far as possible, land law and conveyancing should be simplified. The problem is not easy. The present law could be substantially simplified only by extinguishing a number of existing rights and preventing the creation of such rights in the future. This would involve substantially restricting the freedom of contract which exists at present. The social reforms of recent decades have considerably extended the property rights of occupiers other than proprietors, especially spouses and tenants. At the same time, the complexity of modern society has led to an extension of the obligations imposed on property owners and has increasingly placed restrictions on the use of land. The growth of planning law has resulted in local authority planning departments exercising functions which previously were the prerogative of the large landowner in restricting the development and use of land.

2. We consider that land law and conveyancing require continuous scrutiny by lawyers and laymen. There are always extant a number of useful but uncoordinated suggestions designed to make conveyancing cheaper, safer, more expeditious and more comprehensible. We suggest that the Law Commission, which has already received a number of such suggestions, is a suitable body to consider the reform of conveyancing law and procedure and that for this purpose it should be empowered to appoint a Conveyancing Standing Committee which should comprise not only practising and academic lawyers but also representatives of the building societies, estate agents, consumer organisations, developers and others. The task of the Conveyancing Committee would be to examine in the first place the suggestions for reform which have already been made to the Law Commission and to this Commission and which require consideration by a body which has more time and more expertise than we have been able to employ. We consider briefly below some of the suggestions which could usefully be considered by a Conveyancing Committee of the Law Commission.

Simplification of the law

Restrictive covenants

3. Many thousands of words of restrictive covenants clutter the titles of house property and bedevil modern conveyancing. In many cases these covenants are difficult to construe and there is doubt as to whether they are enforceable or whether anyone has power to release them. The restrictions imposed by such covenants constitute separate obligations to which a purchaser must have regard in addition to his general duty to comply with planning legislation. It is doubtful whether estate schemes, in particular, are necessary under modern planning law. The time may have come to make past and present restrictive covenants unenforceable except as between the parties to the original agreement, and perhaps excepting also restrictions necessary to secure privacy provided they are in a suitable standard form authorised by statute and not capable of variation.

Tiers of leases

4. In parts of Lancashire in particular there are tiers of leases comprising one or more houses. At one and the same time there may exist leases for 999 years, for 999 years less 10 days, for 990 years, for 990 years less 10 days, for 99 years, for 99 years less 10 days and so on until eventually at the bottom of the ladder there is an actual tenant in occupation. As single houses are sold off there are informal apportionments, not binding on the landlord, of the rents and covenants. All this is an unnecessary complication of the normal conveyancing process. The compulsory enfranchisement by statute of all the leases except for the actual occupation tenancy would be a cure.

283

Matrimonial homes charges

5. The right of a deserted spouse to remain in occupation of the matrimonial home may now be registered. Many are not registered, others are registered as blackmailing devices which the vendor must pay to remove. Others are difficult to remove because the spouse has disappeared. It has been estimated that about 83 per cent of all matrimonial homes in England and Wales are currently being taken by husband and wife in their joint names. The necessity for the registration of the rights of a deserted spouse with all its consequent difficulties and uncertainty would be removed if the law prescribed that a matrimonial home must be taken, or be deemed to have been taken, in the names of the spouses jointly, and a presumption was introduced that it was beneficially owned by the spouses jointly, as was recommended by the Law Commission in its First Report on Family Property (Law Com. No. 52, 1973).

Third party rights

6. Different types of third party rights, such as easements, restrictive covenants and positive covenants, are governed by different rules of law. To some extent this is due to their different natures, but the rules could be assimilated and the law thereby simplified. The Law Commission has published a working paper (No. 36) proposing certain reforms in this area of the law. These reforms, together with a standardisation and simplification of the common forms of third party rights, would lessen the complication of conveyancing.

Simplification of records

Land registration

7. We have no doubt that it is in the public interest that the registration of title in the Land Registry should proceed as quickly as possible. It would not be in the public interest for the Land Registry to be overwhelmed by new work, and in our view the pace of registration should be dictated by the Land Registry, which is well alive to the importance of extending land registration as quickly as possible. In the past the pace of extending land registration has been slowed by shortage of staff. This may have been due originally to the desire to limit the number of civil servants. However, the Land Registry is now self-financing, and the limiting factor is, probably, the need to train staff properly. We consider that all necessary assistance should be given to the Land Registry, including support if necessary from public funds, to enable it to maintain and improve the pace of registration.

8. We have noted the success of the computerisation of the Land Registry's Land Charges Department and that trials are being conducted at a district land registry with a view to computerising the work of the Registration of Title Department. We are convinced that this is the right way forward and that it should be pursued with all speed.

Local authority searches and enquiries

9. One cause of delay in conveyancing is the interval which elapses between making searches and enquiries from the local authority and receiving the results and answers. For a variety of reasons the interval varies greatly from one local authority to another. We think that the Conveyancing Committee could usefully investigate the possibility of standardising a system for all local authorities. In addition there may well be scope for organising information on a regional basis not tied to the existing local authorities. Finally at some future date it might be possible to include in one computer-based service the information now held by the Land Registry and the information held by local authorities. In any event we consider that the Conveyancing Committee could usefully consult the Land Registry and the local authorities and consider the simplification and coordination of the similar tasks which they both undertake.

Simplification of procedure

Boundaries

10. Whether a title is registered or unregistered, one of the most fruitful sources of dispute and litigation relates to boundaries. Many conveyances have no plans. Some

have plans which are too small. Some plans lack measurements. Some plans have measurements but do not reveal the point from which the measurement has been taken. Many plans depict the size, shape and extent of the property wrongly. It seems to us that the Conveyancing Committee in conjunction with the Law Society and with surveyors' associations could prescribe the manner in which property included in a conveyance should be described and it should be the professional duty of surveyors and solicitors to see that the correct procedure is followed and that adequate plans and measurements are prepared, which, without departing from the principle that only general boundaries are depicted, would eliminate many of the boundary problems which from time to time arise.

Pre-contract procedure

11. We consider also that an agreed procedure, which it should be the duty of the legal profession to observe, would reduce the frustration now felt by both vendor and purchaser before contracts are exchanged. For example an estate agent should refuse to offer property for sale unless he is authorised at the same time to write to the vendor's solicitor and instruct the vendor's solicitor to prepare a contract. The vendor's solicitor should forthwith prepare a contract and should annex thereto the abstract. He should at the same time warn any mortgagee that the mortgage may shortly be redeemed. It has been suggested that the vendor's solicitor should make local enquiries and searches and annex the information to the draft contract. We think that this proposal has some merit and some objections which the Conveyancing Committee should consider. Similarly an estate agent should not forward an offer to purchase property unless the purchaser satisfies the estate agent that his income will be sufficient to attract a sufficient building society loan provided that the property furnishes adequate security. Other suggestions, such as conditional contracts, have been put forward to reduce the time which elapses before contracts are exchanged. The Law Commission considered many of these suggestions in its Report entitled "Subject to Contract Agreements" (Law Commission No. 65 of January 1975). In general we agree with its conclusions. We think however that the question of the standardisation of surveys and the elimination of dual surveys, one for the building society and one for the purchaser, should be further considered. One suggestion is that standard questions to be answered by a surveyor should be agreed and should be in two parts, the first part which need only be answered if the survey is to be provided for a mortgagee, and the second part which should provide additional information if the surveyor is instructed to make a survey on behalf of the purchaser as well. We understand that the Director General of Fair Trading is discussing proposals on these lines with the Building Societies' Association.

Simplification of documents

Restrictive covenants

12. We have already suggested that if restrictive covenants are to remain they ought to be in a standard form which will eliminate all or most of the problems of construction which arise when every vendor and every vendor's solicitor is free to invent his own form of restriction. We believe, however, that the use of restrictive covenants should be curtailed by statute and reliance placed in the main on planning uses as controlled by planning legislation.

Leases

13. We consider that efforts should also be made to standardise the provisions of a lease, particularly of residential property. At the moment a lease, whether of residential property or commercial property, may be around 40 or 50 pages and will contain provisions which are similar to, but not identical with, the provisions of other leases. Every landlord, landlord's solicitor, and landlord's counsel is free to prepare his own lease. Modifications may be introduced according to the success of the efforts of the tenant, his solicitor, or his counsel. In the result there are thousands of leases similar but not identical. If any problem arises the particular wording of each lease must be studied, argued about, construed by the parties who may not be the original landlords or the

original tenants, submitted to solicitors and counsel who probably had nothing to do with the original draft and finally if necessary construed by the court. Of course every lawyer prefers his own draft and may not take kindly to a statutory form of lease. We doubt however whether the need for flexibility requires liberty to invent a new form for each transaction. It is true that experience with the Leases Act 1845 showed that legislation of this sort goes quickly out of date. However, we hope that some means of standardising the provisions of leases will be found, and are encouraged by the fact that the Law Commission has this matter under consideration.

Mortgages
14. We think that mortgages also are ripe for standardisation. There are two forms of mortgage, one by demise and one by way of charge. We can find no logical reason to have two forms rather than one. In addition every mortgage contains provisions which can run to 20 or 30 pages all to the same purpose but all slightly different. The desire of the individual draftsman to keep his own wording sustains unnecessary diversity. Every building society, although performing precisely the same function as every other building society, insists at present on having forms of mortgage which are similar to, but not identical with, the forms of every other building society. We think that professional pride must give way to simplification. In the case of residential property in particular there is no reason why a statute should not lay down short and simple provisions applying in all transactions so that the forms of mortgage may be reduced to a minimum and difficult questions of construction eliminated.

Other documents
15. This principle could with advantage be applied to other parts of the transaction. We consider therefore that the Conveyancing Committee should explore with the interested parties whether and to what extent standardisation could be extended to other documents including the contract and the final conveyance or transfer.

Protection against unfair bargains

16. Cases arise from time to time in which a person with experience of property dealing induces a less experienced person to enter into a contract for the sale of land, or the grant of an option, on terms which are disadvantageous to the latter. In the absence of misrepresentation or undue influence, the law at present rarely affords relief in such a case. For the reasons explained in paragraph 21.28, we do not think it would be right to make contracts for the sale of land unenforceable if prepared by the parties without the intervention of a solicitor. If protection is thought to be desirable, one possibility would be to provide for a cooling-off period (as under the Consumer Credit Act 1974) in any case in which one party to a contract carries on the business of dealing in land, or negotiating as agent for others dealing in land, and the contract is not approved by a solicitor acting for the other party before it is signed. A possible alternative would be to extend section 22 of the Solicitors Act 1974 so as to make it an offence for a person carrying on such a business to prepare a contract or option agreement on his own behalf (and not only if he does so for reward, an essential element of the offence created by section 22). A somewhat similar provision is in force in South Australia under section 61(2) of the Land and Business Agents Act 1973, though it applies only where the dealer is acting in a capacity other than that of purchaser or mortgagee. The same section also makes it an offence for a person carrying on such a business to receive a fee from a legal practitioner for referring any business involving the preparation of instruments to him, or to procure the execution of any document by which a person requests or authorises the preparation by any person specifically named or generally described of any instrument. While the evidence which we have received does not suggest that practices of this kind exist in this country to anything like the extent indicated in the report to the United States Congress which we quoted in paragraph 21.32, we think that the Law Commission might usefully consider whether there is a need for further protection in this area.

CHAPTER 22

Quality of Service

Introduction

Background

22.1   In recent years the legal profession has been criticised in the press and in Parliament. The main themes of this criticism are, first, that the profession takes advantage of its privileged position, in particular in litigation and conveyancing, to charge fees higher than are justified by the work done, secondly, that standards of knowledge and competence in certain classes of work fall short of the level that clients are entitled to expect and, thirdly, that the profession provides an inadequate service to clients who are not well-to-do. We consider the extent of services in Part II and the remuneration of lawyers in Chapter 36; in this chapter, we take up the question of the extent to which the criticisms of the quality of service provided by the legal profession are justified.

22.2   The nature of the service provided by both branches of the legal profession is greatly influenced by rules relating to court procedures. These are outside our terms of reference, but in Part VI of this report we summarise evidence containing suggestions for improving the arrangements for court business and reducing cost and delay. We propose in Part VI that the responsible authorities should examine these proposals with a view to making changes where they would lead to improvement. Many of the proposals which we make in this report on matters which are within our terms of reference will be of limited value without such a treatment of the matters included in Part VI.

22.3   There are no simple tests of the quality of legal services. The requirements cannot be specified in the same way as those relating to products and some other types of service. The satisfaction of the user, though a proper subject of enquiry, is not always a reliable test, for it may be affected by the outcome of a case as much as by the lawyer's performance. The standard of any piece of legal work is largely a matter of opinion.

22.4   In spite of these difficulties, it is possible to make an assessment of the quality of legal services in various ways. We have taken evidence from numerous users of legal services and from informed observers such as the citizens advice bureaux and the Lay Observer. The governing bodies and members

287

of the legal profession, while holding the view that in general their profession had not failed the public, told us frankly of inadequacies and failings known to them. The judges offered their views on the standards of work achieved in the courts. Factual information was available from surveys of users' views and experiences and analysis of the duration of proceedings. We made comparisons with experience in other jurisdictions. We set out later in this chapter the conclusions which we have drawn from this evidence.

Principle

22.5 In order to provide a service for the public, a profession is given certain privileges. To justify them, it must accept the responsibility of ensuring as far as possible that its members' work is of a satisfactory standard, and that incompetence and slackness when brought to notice are not tolerated. This obligation rests both on individual practitioners and on the governing bodies.

Means of maintaining standards

22.6 In Chapter 25 we remark on the need for a practitioner to maintain a good reputation in order to attract work. This apart, all associations providing professional services have available to them the following means of securing the consistent performance of work of a satisfactory standard:—

(a) *Education and training for qualification*
This is the traditional means of securing that those who take up practice are fitted to do so. There is no effective alternative to formal qualification preceded by appropriate education and training, as a means of protecting the public from ignorance and lack of ability. In Chapter 39 we make a number of recommendations in this connection.

(b) *Post-qualification education and training*
Additional education and training after qualification is a formal requirement in some professions but is not at present required of lawyers. Nevertheless an increasing number of courses, attendance at which is voluntary, are now available to lawyers and these are usually well attended. Because of the deepening complexity of the law, the volume of legislation, and the need, if an adequate service to the public is to be provided, to become familiar with new disciplines and specialities, increasing facilities for post-qualification education and training will be required every year. We deal further with this point in Chapter 39.

(c) *Professional discipline*
All professions enforce, by internal discipline, rules of conduct applying only to their members. In the legal profession at present professional rules and disciplinary procedures tend to concentrate on misconduct rather than on the quality of professional work. We make recommenda-

288

tions concerning the discipline of both branches of the profession in Chapters 25 and 26.

(d) *The influence of the profession and its governing body*
The members of a well organised profession are attentive to standards of work, their own and others', and the governing body does all it can by exhortation and example to maintain the quality of its members' work. In Chapters 29 and 32 we make recommendations concerning the organisation of both branches of the profession which, in our view, will improve their standing and their ability to maintain a high quality of service.

(e) *Assistance to practitioners in difficulties*
A number of professions make arrangements to give assistance to a practitioner who runs into difficulties in order to protect him and his clients from harm. Among barristers, assistance of this kind is normally given as part of the routine of practising chambers. The Law Society runs a solicitors' assistance scheme and a number of local law societies coordinate assistance in times of emergency. We deal below with this problem so far as it affects sole practitioners.

(f) *Written standards*
In some professions, here and abroad, it is the practice to publish written standards for professional work. We make proposals in this connection later in this chapter.

The measures we have set out in sub-paragraphs (a) to (f) above are available to all professions. There are, however, a number of means of control which are peculiar to the legal profession. These are set out below.

(g) *Control by the courts*
Both branches of the legal profession are directly responsible to the courts for their part in the proper administration of justice. A judge supervises and controls the professional conduct of those who appear before him. An experienced judge can do much to promote high standards. We understand, however, that the courts today are less likely than they were twenty and more years ago to intervene when a case is being conducted in a second-rate way, for two reasons. The first is that the present generation of judges, when in practice at the Bar, suffered from frequent interventions from the bench in some courts, and have themselves resolved to behave differently. The second is that an intervention by the judge to reprove prolixity, repetition and inefficient handling of a case may give an impression of bias to the parties and to the jury, if there is one. In a jury case in particular it is acknowledged that it requires great skill on the part of the judge to intervene without giving an impression of bias.

289

(h) *Control of fees by certification and taxation*
The process of certification or taxation should prevent payment being authorised for work not reasonably required to be done. It should have the effect also of reducing costs where work properly required to be done was not done adequately or at all. In our recommendations in Chapter 37 we seek to preserve the effectiveness of this form of quality control, which we consider to be necessary in the public interest.

(j) *Control by legal aid authorities*
Civil legal aid authorities are under a duty to ensure that the public funds at their disposal are properly spent. They have the opportunity to review proceedings of any substance while they are in progress. Our recommendations concerning legal aid are intended to preserve supervision by the legal aid authorities. All those involved in the provision of legal aid should be alert to any failings in professional work paid for out of public funds.

(k) *Effect of a two-branch profession*
The work of any barrister is under the surveillance of his solicitor clients upon whom he depends for a future supply of work.

(l) *Council for Legal Services*
A Council for Legal Services on the lines proposed in Chapter 6, with its capacity for research, should have a considerable influence on the adequacy of legal work in general.

Present Quality of Service

Information available
22.7 We conducted a survey amongst a random sample of 16,000 members of the adult population in England and Wales, of whom over 2,000 had recently made use of legal services. One purpose of this survey was to provide balanced information upon which an assessment of the quality of service could be based. The findings, set out in full in Volume II section 8, show, amongst other things, the general level of satisfaction with legal services and the reasons for satisfaction and dissatisfaction. As shown in Table 22.1 in annex 22.1, those who had recently consulted a solicitor said that they were completely or fairly satisfied with 84 per cent of such consultations, somewhat or very dissatisfied with 13 per cent and expressed neither satisfaction nor dissatisfaction with 3 per cent. In Table 22.2 we give the breakdown of dissatisfaction between different classes of business. There was no significant variation in levels of satisfaction between different socio-economic groups.

22.8 The identities of all those who responded to the Users' Survey were treated as confidential and were not disclosed to us. When a solicitor was criticised, respondents were asked to agree that we should tell the solicitor concerned the nature of the criticism made, in order that we might hear his side of the case. Our consultants wrote therefore to every respondent who expressed dissatisfaction, asking permission to disclose to the Commission his name and address, which would otherwise have remained confidential, in order that our staff could find out the causes of dissatisfaction, and invite the solicitor concerned to comment on them.

22.9   Of the 224 users who expressed dissatisfaction with their solicitors in relation to 255 consultations, only 28 agreed that their names could be disclosed to us. Our staff wrote to all 28 of whom eight replied. A number of these replies suggested that the real cause of dissatisfaction was with the state of the law or its application rather than with the service provided by the solicitor. The number of cases on which we might have obtained the comments of the solicitor involved was so small a proportion of the total that no significance could have been attached to the results; we decided therefore not to proceed with this part of the exercise.

22.10   In response to our requests to the public to submit evidence, we received nearly 1,500 letters making complaints and relatively few expressing approval. This was to be expected. There would have been the same result if comments had been invited on any service available to the public. Those with a grievance come forward, the satisfied do not. Many of the complaints which we received related to events occurring many years previously; the total cannot, therefore, be related to any specific period. During a four week period in 1977 special records were kept by all citizens advice bureaux in the United Kingdom, who in that period received a total of 901 complaints about the provision of a legal service. The Law Society does not at present analyse all the complaints it receives, but a special investigation was made covering the period from November 1972 to May 1973, involving examination of 529 letters of complaint; some of these letters contained more than one head of complaint, and the total number of complaints considered was 712.

22.11   While recognising that our data are limited, we have made an analysis of the complaints we received and have made use of the analyses by the National Association of Citizens Advice Bureaux and the Law Society, for two reasons: first, because it is the first occasion on which such information has become available in a coherent form; secondly, because such analyses are helpful in showing up features of the service provided which call for attention.

22.12   In Tables 22.3 to 22.9 annexed to this chapter, we set out the stated grounds for satisfaction and dissatisfaction with the services of lawyers. These are derived from our own Users' Survey, from the complaints received by CABx and the Law Society, and from an analysis of the letters we received from members of the public. The main grounds for satisfaction are found to

291

be ease of manner and approachability, followed by efficiency and clarity of explanation. The main causes of complaint are inefficiency, incompetence or negligence, failure of communication, followed by delay and cost.

Complaints to the Law Society

22.13 The proportion of dissatisfied clients in the Users' Survey (13%) is appreciably higher than the proportion of clients who complain to the Law Society. A number of reasons for this may be advanced. Some people do not care to complain in any circumstances. Some may not regard the cause of complaint as sufficiently serious to justify pursuing it. Some limit themselves to complaining to the solicitor involved. Some have not been told that the Law Society will entertain complaints, or, if they have been told, have not understood the procedure. Only 17 per cent of those interviewed in the Users' Survey were aware that the Law Society investigated complaints. Others, who know what has to be done, may not think it worthwhile to address a complaint about a lawyer to other lawyers.

22.14 The Law Society emphasized in its evidence that not all the complaints received were found to be justified; the number of complaints from or on behalf of clients regarded as justified by the Society was constant at about 30 per cent. It does not, however, follow that the remaining complaints were of no substance. Some of them, no doubt, were incorrect or misconceived. A number, however, were rejected from consideration by the Society because they did not amount to professional misconduct or because they involved an allegation for which damages might be claimed in the civil courts. In Chapter 25 we indicate how we think that the Society should deal with complaints in future; we also suggest that all complaints received by the Society should be analysed according to the nature of business, the head of complaint and the action taken. The results of such analyses should be published.

Complaints against barristers

22.15 The number of practising barristers is small in comparison to the number of solicitors. There are correspondingly fewer complaints relating to the work of barristers. The Senate provided details of the numbers of complaints received in recent years. These are set out in Tables 22.10 and 22.11 in annex 22.1. The general opinion amongst judges and practising lawyers appears to be that standards fell in this branch of the profession in the nineteen sixties and early seventies, but that they are rising again.

Summary

22.16 To concentrate on complaints recorded gives a distorted picture. The evidence before us shows that year by year most legal work is transacted well and efficiently. Most clients are satisfied with the service they receive. The judiciary is in general able to rely on the quality of work performed in the courts. City institutions, including The Stock Exchange, the British Bankers' Association and the Committee on Invisible Exports told us that the legal services available in London are of a high standard; this attracts legal and other business from abroad which contributes to our invisible exports.

22.17   The foregoing summary puts the evidence concerning complaints into perspective; but these complaints show that, at the other end of the scale, some clients find that the services offered by both barristers and solicitors are slow and inefficient, that their standards of administration are not up-to-date or effective and that legal knowledge and expertise, particularly in topics such as social welfare law, are deficient. While the quality of the service provided by the legal profession is adequate for many purposes, there are a number of areas of practice where substantial improvements are needed.

Shortcomings and Remedies

Delay
22.18   Delay is a frequent cause of complaint against lawyers. Such complaints sometimes relate to failure to deal with a specific item of work in the time required, but as a rule they relate to the whole conduct of legal work, which is said to be slow-moving and long drawn-out.

Duration of legal work
22.19   In the Users' Survey, enquiries were made about the duration of particular types of business; we give details of the results, along with figures for the waiting times in the Crown Court and for the duration, both in total and stage by stage, of cases set down for hearing in the Queen's Bench Division in Tables 22.12 to 22.14 in the annex to this chapter. Among the findings of the Users' Survey were that half the cases involving making or altering wills were said to have been completed in less than a month, few lasted longer than two months. One in three conveyances took less than two months and half took between two and six months. The majority of personal injury cases were completed in a year; only a small proportion lasted longer than two years. Half the criminal cases were disposed of in two months or less, three-quarters in less than four months. In serious criminal cases, most of the time spent waiting for trial appears to have been due to the workload of the courts and of the police. We discuss this problem in paragraphs 22.32 to 22.38 below. Detailed information about the time taken to dispose of cases in the Queen's Bench Division in 1977 is to be found in Volume II section 10.

Causes of delay
22.20   It appears from the evidence we received that most non-contentious business is conducted with reasonable despatch. In this class of business delays

293

may occur which are beyond the control of the lawyer. In probate work, for example, the scheduling, valuation and subsequent realisation of assets may be a long drawn-out process; in a conveyance, it may take time for the purchaser to raise a mortgage, or sell his own property or for full answers to be obtained from local authority searches.

22.21 In contentious business, the causes of delay are more complex. One side or the other may have a vested interest in delay and if the conduct of proceedings is left to the parties, as is the case in civil proceedings in the High Court, many opportunities arise to slow them down. Even if there is the will to make progress, it may require considerable drive and determination in some proceedings to achieve the desired pace. Moreover, speed is not of itself a criterion of quality. A lawyer's duty is to secure enough time to develop and present a case in the way that is most advantageous to his client. But despite all these considerations, it is generally agreed, both within the legal profession and outside it, that legal proceedings of all kinds generally take longer than they should.

22.22 We have made some comparisons with the duration of litigation in other jurisdictions, the results of which are summarised in Volume II section 11. Direct comparisons are difficult to draw, because of the differences in legal systems and procedures, but there is no evidence that proceedings here take longer than abroad. In some areas, our procedure operates in a less cumbersome way than elsewhere. No easy means of reducing the duration of litigation emerged from our investigations.

Remedies for delay
22.23 If significant reductions are to be made in the duration of legal proceedings and in particular in the time taken to bring them to trial, a concerted effort is required from all involved, including the profession, the judiciary, court staff, the public service and insurance companies. It is not within our terms of reference to recommend specific measures in this connection. However, it is clear that no significant improvements can be looked for in civil cases unless there is a complete re-appraisal of the present organisation and procedures of the civil courts as proposed in Part VI. Improvements which would save time should also be made in the arrangements for granting civil legal aid, as recommended in Chapter 13.

22.24 It is acknowledged by the profession that some solicitors and barristers are dilatory in handling various classes of work. The courts could do much to prevent this in proceedings by enforcing time limits more strictly and refusing extensions unless there is good reason. The Senate and the Law Society both told us that the courts should show less leniency in this respect.

22.25 The analysis of the time taken to dispose of cases in the Queen's

Bench Division in 1977 (see Volume II section 10) shows that the average lapse of time between cause of action and trial was four years. Even allowing for the fact that on average 17 months elapse before a writ is issued, we regard this as profoundly unsatisfactory, especially as the average figure includes a substantial number of cases in which the time involved exceeded four years. Delay in the hearing of litigation also means delay in settlements. If actions do not come to trial for four years, those many actions which settle at the door of the court will not settle for four years. If an action must come on for trial in two years it will be settled within that period. The argument that speed will lead to more expense and to fewer settlements is, we think, unsound. Cases will settle as soon as professional advisers have enough information to decide the likely outcome of proceedings. There is no evidence that four years as opposed to two years is essential for this purpose.

22.26 In its recent report (Cmnd. 7476) following its inquiry into the question of delay, the Working Party on Personal Injury Litigation (the Cantley Committee) rejected proposals for sanctions and supervision by the court, save for the suggestion that the court should be empowered to intervene if it discovered that 18 months had elapsed after the issue of the writ without a case being set down for hearing. We do not think this goes far enough. There is need for a determined effort to evolve a simplified scheme for litigation which will contain sanctions for non-compliance. We consider that such measures should be considered by the body set up, as proposed in Part VI of this report, to review all civil procedures. Whatever changes are made to legal procedures and to reduce delays in litigation, we believe that a general improvement will also require pressure on the profession itself to ensure that its business is conducted with proper expedition. We consider that the public interest demands that such pressure should be exerted particularly on those members of the profession who are incompetent or take on too much work with insufficient skilled staff. We have no doubt that standards must be improved and that advice and exhortation alone will be inadequate for that purpose unless backed by sanctions.

22.27 Delay and procrastination in the conduct of cases in court arise from repetitive cross-examination, labouring points, good and bad, and general prolixity. The cure lies in good education and training, self-discipline, adequate research and careful preparation.

22.28 Students of each branch of the profession should be taught how to plan their practices so that work can be completed with proper despatch. Notes for guidance should be given to pupil masters and to principals of articled clerks to ensure that this topic receives adequate attention. The profession should make it clear that delay in the conduct of professional business is unacceptable and will, in serious cases, call for disciplinary sanctions.

Relations with clients

22.29 A frequent source of complaint arises from failure by a lawyer to establish a satisfactory relationship with his client and, in particular, to keep the client informed. Clients who are not kept in sufficiently close touch with the progress of their business are likely to feel that it is being handled in a dilatory or careless way. The point was well put by Mr Neville D. Vandyk, editor of the Solicitors' Journal.

> Over and over again when clients' complaints against solicitors are analysed, they are seen to amount to (often justified) bitterness that the clients have not been kept adequately informed of progress; the steps in the conveyancing, negotiating or litigation process, whichever applies, have not been explained in a comprehensible way. People fear the unknown. When they require a solicitor's help they are often worried and in an understandable state of nerves. Not keeping clients in the picture of what is happening (or not happening), and failure to explain any delays, is an indictment of what amounts to nothing more than thoughtlessness on the part of solicitors or their staff. If this cause for complaint is removed, other, perhaps imagined, grievances will not be built up on this justified foundation. Solicitors should thus give priority to seeing that there is nothing lacking in any routine arrangements laid down in their practices for ensuring that every client is at all times kept fully informed of what is involved in, and progress of, his or her particular matter.

22.30 This is borne out by the data from our survey set out in annex 22.1. Table 22.4 shows that an agreeable relationship with the solicitor was the most frequently stated cause of satisfaction. Table 22.3 shows that where complaints arose, it was often because the client felt (whether rightly or not) that his lawyer was taking an insufficiently active and personal interest in the case. Table 22.15 shows that if a client is given a clear idea of the amount of time a matter is likely to take and is kept in touch with progress, he is likely to end up amongst those completely satisfied with the service received; clients who ask for an estimate of time and do not receive it are more likely to be among the dissatisfied. A client who has received an estimate but is then not told why it is not being adhered to is also likely to be dissatisfied.

22.31 We consider that more should be done to emphasize the importance of gaining the client's confidence and establishing a sound professional relationship with him. This should be stressed at every stage of a lawyer's professional training. It may not be possible to learn how to do it entirely from books or theoretical teaching, but the basic principles can and should be taught to students. To establish good communications with another person is a professional skill which must be, and is, learnt by many others besides lawyers. We consider that there are, in addition, a number of practical measures which can be taken in all cases which will have the effect of keeping the client fully informed and of preventing the development of any sense of remoteness between the client and his advisers. We deal with these as subjects for written Professional Standards in paragraph 22.62 below.

Listing cases

22.32   We found in the course of our enquiries that discussion of problems arising from litigation, particularly in the criminal courts, frequently turned to the listing of cases. We have not been asked to offer recommendations concerning the way the courts organise their business, but it is necessary to say something about this topic for the better understanding of our recommendations on other points.

22.33   Every court is under pressure to utilise its time fully by dealing with cases throughout its sitting hours. In our system of uninterrupted oral hearings of uncertain length, an arrangement by which all cases were heard by appointment on fixed days would lead to considerable loss of court time. Such arrangements are rare, except in heavy cases. The establishment of additional courts and the appointment of more judges and court staff would reduce the delays but would involve considerable expenditure, especially if many cases were given fixed days for hearing.

22.34   Cases are usually listed for hearing in the order in which they will be taken. A warning that hearing is imminent may be given a week or less before trial, but whether or not a case is in the list for hearing on a given day usually cannot be known for certain until the day before. Even then, a case may not come on for hearing on the day it is listed if any of the cases ahead of it take longer than expected.

22.35   In these circumstances, it is not surprising if tension arises over the listing of cases. Those responsible must take account of a large number of factors other than the availability of counsel or solicitor-advocates. Regard must be had to such matters as the availability of a suitable judge, the likely length of the hearing, the availability of a court room and its staff, in a criminal case the readiness of the prosecution and defence and in all cases the availability of witnesses. Fair weight must be given to all these considerations. Listing officers face a difficult task requiring skill, sensitivity and experience.

22.36   There are repeated complaints from the Bar and from barristers' clerks that listing officers are not sympathetic to their problems and are reluctant to make changes in the list even when these would not be to the detriment of others. There is also said sometimes to be lack of communication between solicitors and listing officers. The position in the Crown Court was compared unfavourably by some witnesses with that which prevailed in the Assizes and Quarter Sessions courts which the Crown Court replaced. As a step towards improvement, a scheme designed, amongst other things, to improve listing arrangements was introduced at the Central Criminal Court in the latter part of 1977. The Criminal Bar Association told us that the scheme has been working smoothly but that no firm conclusions have yet been drawn from it.

22.37 We consider that the main source of difficulty lies not only in the factors listed in paragraphs 22.33—22.35 but also in the increasing pressure on the courts, and in particular the criminal courts. The length of time spent waiting for trial attracts critical comment, especially if the judges are not continuously occupied. It is not surprising in these circumstances if court time is treated as sacrosanct. If the recommendations we make in the following paragraphs are to have any effect, however, this principle will have to be modified; in some cases keeping the court continuously occupied will have to take second place to the reasonable requirements of the parties to the proceedings and their lawyers.

22.38 In order to keep a proper and consistent balance between the requirements of the courts and the interests of the parties it will be necessary for the judiciary, those responsible for the administration of the courts and the profession to agree on guidelines as to the circumstances in which the position of a case on the list for hearing should be changed to enable counsel originally instructed to appear at the trial. The fact that a case required one or more pre-trial conferences should be taken into account, for it is particularly important in such a case that the barrister with whom the client has conferred should represent him.

Briefs, conferences and court work

22.39 There has been criticism, which we consider is often justified, of the quality of briefs delivered to barristers, in particular in less serious criminal cases. This class of work is poorly remunerated, making it difficult in some instances for solicitors to spend the necessary time on the work. Some briefs are inadequately prepared. They do not all contain sufficient information and some contain little more than a formal instruction to appear. Some briefs are delivered late, sometimes on the day before the hearing or even on the hearing day itself.

22.40 There has also been justified criticism of the way barristers handle briefs. They are not always read promptly and even when delivered in good time, some receive detailed attention only a day or two before the hearing. Again, if there is a clash of engagements and a brief is returned, there may be insufficient time for adequate preparation or a pre-trial conference, if one is required. The barrister should study the brief early enough for there to be time for any additional preparatory work which he advises is necessary.

22.41 A brief that is not properly prepared or handled leads to inadequate presentation of the case in court. This is a source of complaint in particular by magistrates. The position deteriorates further if the barrister is accompanied in court not by a solicitor or experienced legal executive with knowledge of the case, but by a junior member of the solicitor's staff who has no experience of court work and knows neither the case nor the client. We have encountered and we deplore cases in which the barrister was attended by a person who was not even a member of the solicitor's staff, but was hired from an agency. In such circumstances, service to the client is bound to suffer. This practice is altogether unsatisfactory; it is not acceptable either to the Senate or the Law Society who invoke disciplinary proceedings if such cases are brought to their attention.

22.42 Though the faults we have described may exist in only a minority of cases, a sustained effort by both branches of the profession is required to secure uniform quality in the content and handling of briefs and the conduct of work in court. We consider that the first step should be to establish Professional Standards covering this class of work. We deal further with this in paragraph 22.63 below.

22.43 The profession should also settle acceptable standards for clients' conferences with barristers. The primary purposes of a conference are to enable a barrister to clarify his instructions by direct discussion with the lay client and to give advice more directly than is possible on paper. For either of these purposes, a conference at an early stage is desirable. A conference should also enable a barrister to establish a rapport with his client and give the client confidence that his case will be properly presented. This can be done, in some cases, shortly before the hearing. It would not be reasonable to require a conference to be held in every case a substantial time before the hearing. This would be both costly and time consuming, especially if it were necessary for the solicitor and barrister to visit their client in a distant remand prison. But a conference should be arranged if it is required for the proper presentation of the case, taking account not only of its gravity or complexity, but also of the circumstances of the accused, in particular young defendants and those standing trial for the first time.

22.44 As to attendance in court, we consider that the profession, the judiciary and those responsible for the administration of the courts should settle what is required in various categories of case. We question whether it is invariably necessary for a barrister to be accompanied by a solicitor. Some pleas in mitigation and some county court cases, for example, if properly prepared, may require no more than the attendance of an advocate in court. In such cases we consider a barrister should be permitted to appear without a solicitor. But where a solicitor's attendance is required, the solicitor should either attend himself, or send a member of his staff who is able to deal with any problems which are likely to arise. Fees for attendance in legally-aided cases should be at a level which enables this to be done when necessary.

22.45 In the magistrates' courts the legal aid fees for minor cases are for a solicitor only. Some solicitors do not themselves attend, but brief a barrister and pay him a proportion of the fee. This arrangement has been officially recognised to the extent that the barrister's share of the fee in such cases may be paid directly to him. Some of these cases fall in the category of those which the barrister may handle without being accompanied in court by a member of the solicitor's staff. In other cases, adequate attendance must be arranged. The level of fees allowed in cases where a barrister can appear unaccompanied should continue to be those appropriate for a solicitor alone.

Settlements at the door of the court

22.46 Many personal injury cases are settled at an early stage. If a case is not settled, the whole period of litigation is a worrying time for the plaintiff and we are not satisfied that lawyers always appreciate the ordeal that it can be. In particular we are concerned at the effect on the plaintiff under the present system when a personal injury action culminates in an offer of settlement at the door of the court. When this happens the litigant has to make within minutes a decision which may affect his or her whole life. We think it deplorable that pressure should be deliberately brought to bear on an inexperienced plaintiff by holding back an offer of settlement to the last moment. Even if not deliberately contrived, such situations should be avoided. It may help if, on the lines suggested in Part VI, there was a pre-trial review with the purpose among others of promoting a settlement. Under present circumstances, a plaintiff in such a case should be advised in writing, and if necessary also orally, at the time the case is set down, what, in the view of his solicitor and barrister, would be a reasonable figure for settlement, having regard to the probability of establishing liability and the value of the claim at full liability. He should be told of the possibility of an offer at the court's door and the likely offers canvassed and discussed so that an informed and considered decision can be taken at leisure before the hearing, to be applied if occasion arises. This duty, which we understand is accepted by many lawyers as the usual and proper practice, should be made the subject of a Professional Standard (see paragraph 22.62 below).

Returned briefs

22.47 Clashes of engagements occur in all occupations. On some emergency or unforeseen event, a client or patient may have to go from one practitioner to another. In the circumstances we describe in paragraph 22.34, barristers cannot avoid occasional clashes of engagements. When this occurs, one brief must be returned and sent to another barrister. In practice, it is normally transferred by the barrister's clerk, with the agreement of the solicitor, to another barrister usually in the same set of chambers. Although as is shown in Table 22.10 annexed to this chapter, few complaints have been made to the Senate on this score in recent years, we received adverse comment on the practice of returning briefs and we regard it as a serious matter.

22.48 The propriety of returning a brief and the time at which to do so depends on the nature of the case and the circumstances of the client. There are a number of minor criminal cases in which the client can be adequately represented without a conference before the day of trial and without lengthy preparation by the barrister. We can see no objection to transferring the brief in such a case shortly before trial provided there is sufficient time for preparation. The Senate told us of an arrangement which has been made between barristers and solicitors in Bristol, which might be adopted elsewhere. Solicitors (both prosecuting and defending) have drawn up a short list of barristers between whom briefs may be transferred without prior agreement of the solicitor. It has also been agreed that because of the number of locations at which the Crown Court sits in Bristol, briefs may be allocated in such a way that, as far as possible, a barrister is in only one court on one day. We see no objection to arrangements of this kind, provided that the papers are seen by a barrister at a suitably early stage and proper consideration is given to the need for a conference before the hearing day.

The internal administration of offices and chambers

22.49 We received evidence from both the profession and others that the internal administration of many offices, their physical nature and accessibility and the working methods used in them are unsatisfactory. We consider that this criticism is justified in some cases, and we propose remedies in the following paragraphs.

22.50 With regard to working methods, the British Legal Association told us that much more should be done to standardise solicitors' practising methods and equipment. Our own experience and observations support the view that in some barristers' chambers, solicitors' offices and law centres standards of organisation and administration are inadequate. It is said that a failure to reach adequate standards results from lack of resources. We believe, on the contrary, that it is false economy not to establish a good internal administration of professional work since it leads to an increase in profitability. A particular requirement is a good system of time recording; we deal with this in more detail in Chapter 37. In addition, as well as providing suitable surroundings in which to work, offices should have accommodation for receiving and interviewing clients, an efficient and up-to-date filing system with arrangements for bringing forward papers when action is required and for following up cases. Accounting procedures must be soundly planned, records kept up to date and bills despatched and followed up promptly. We set out in Chapter 34 the measures we believe to be necessary in barristers' chambers.

The role of the Law Society

22.51 It was, until recently, the view of the Law Society that it had no business to concern itself with the internal efficiency of solicitors' firms save for the purpose of investigating complaints or protecting clients' money. This attitude is changing. The Law Society is aware of the need for guidance on office administration and is providing a growing number of courses for solicitors. The Society also gives firms every encouragement to improve their own systems of time-keeping and has been instrumental in setting up a computer service for this purpose.

22.52 We welcome the part now being played by the Law Society and consider that the Society should press on vigorously with its programme of courses for qualified solicitors and the publication of articles on office administration and methods in professional journals. This subject should be treated fully in the education and practical training of articled clerks. In addition, the Law Society should issue guidelines to practitioners setting out the essentials of sound practice in all aspects of office administration and the conduct of professional business and should encourage solicitors who get into difficulties to seek prompt help from their local law society or from the advisory service provided by the Law Society. We return to this point in paragraph 22.70 below. As we say in Chapter 25, we consider that the Law Society should make use of its powers to inspect when, as a result of complaints lodged with it, there is occasion to suspect incompetence or inefficiency. Failings should be dealt with by giving advice and assistance or, where the circumstances warrant, by invoking disciplinary procedures.

Computers
22.53 Computers may be used in lawyers' offices, both for the purposes of accounting and administration, and as sources of information and a means of research. They are widely used for the first purpose, systems having been developed by the Law Society, a number of commercial concerns and by solicitors in private practice for their own purposes. Computerised information retrieval services have not been widely adopted in this country though their use is common in the United States and in some parts of continental Europe, notably Italy and France. In May 1979, however, it was announced that a company had been formed in this country to provide, on a commercial basis, computerised legal and tax information to the legal profession and other interested organisations. The Society for Computers and Law has recently produced a report recommending a computer-assisted legal information retrieval system for the United Kingdom. We welcome developments on these lines; we believe that services of this kind will have an essential part to play in the future in assisting the profession to maintain a high standard of service, in particular by keeping up to date with the law.

Inter-firm comparisons
22.54 In this country and overseas some professions arrange for inter-firm comparisons to be made. The results of the comparisons, in anonymous form, are circulated to the firms who voluntarily take part, for the purpose of measuring their own efficiency against others. It is usually convenient to set up an exercise of this kind on a regional basis. This procedure provides a useful means of maintaining efficiency and we recommend that the Law Society

should encourage its district organisation which we propose in Chapter 29 to promote such exercises.

Specialisation
22.55 In Chapter 27 we point out that the increasing complexity of the law can be expected to lead both barristers and solicitors to specialise more than at present. Firms of solicitors, if large enough, are increasingly organised in specialist departments. There is at present also a trend for firms to increase in size. If this is combined with a greater degree of specialisation, it is likely to lead to a higher quality of service to the client. This process will be encouraged if specialisation is formally recognised.

Responsibility for administration
22.56 While the Law Society may supply support and training, each firm is responsible for finding its own solutions to the problems we have mentioned, by reviewing its internal procedures, seeking advice where necessary from consultants and ensuring that it meets the necessary requirements. Every solicitors' office of any size should appoint a partner or a senior staff member to be responsible for internal administration and for setting up the necessary procedures and keeping them up to date.

Written Professional Standards
22.57 The law and the work of lawyers become more complex. The profession has grown rapidly in the last ten years. Public expectations become higher. It therefore becomes more difficult to maintain a uniformly high quality of service by traditional methods alone. We consider that both the public and the profession would find it helpful to have an authoritative indication of what good practice requires.

22.58 In these circumstances, we consider that the use of written Professional Standards within the legal profession is now desirable in the public interest. We therefore recommend that the Law Society and the Senate should each establish committees for the purpose of devising Professional Standards to be approved for publication by the governing bodies. Each committee should include members of the other branch.

22.59 The committees' first task will be to identify the topics upon which Standards are required, some of which are indicated below. The Standards would then have to be drafted and the drafts made public for consideration by the profession and a wide range of other interested parties including organisations representing the users of legal services. When comments have been received and assimilated, final drafts can be presented to the governing bodies for approval and publication. The task of devising Standards is long and difficult but the process of defining what is best practice is, in itself, valuable. The revision and updating of Standards at regular intervals is also a salutary process.

22.60   Standards should not be over-ambitious or unnecessary and should be applied with common sense. For example, a written Standard, as we suggest below, might call on a solicitor to give a client certain information at the first interview. If instructions are received in an emergency requiring immediate action, the required information should be given not at the outset, but at the first convenient opportunity thereafter. Subject to the need to interpret Standards reasonably, we consider that a serious or repeated failure to comply with them should be treated as a breach of professional discipline. This should be without prejudice to the rule that inefficiency (whether or not comprising proven breaches of Standards) may itself invoke disciplinary procedures.

22.61   It is not for us to write Professional Standards, but in the following paragraphs we give an indication of some of the topics they might cover, and of their content.

22.62   We said in paragraph 22.31 that certain practical measures should be taken to keep the client fully informed. They are as follows.

(a)   When first interviewed, the client should be given an explanation, in simple everyday language, of what the issues are and what is to be done about them. Similar explanations should be given when necessary at subsequent stages; for example, after conviction and sentence a defendant in criminal proceedings should be advised, for both humanitarian and practical reasons, about the prospects of an appeal.

(b)   The information given should include an explanation of the procedural steps to be followed in whatever business the client has in hand. For many classes of work, it should be possible to provide a written guide to what is involved. Guides could be prepared centrally under the aegis of the Law Society, which has already produced some. The solicitor should endeavour to ensure, by oral explanation, that the guide has been properly understood.

(c)   Fees and charges which have been and are likely to be incurred should be explained in detail, as recommended in Chapter 37.

(d)   When it is necessary to retain counsel, the client should be given information, in a form agreed by the Senate and the Law Society, about what is involved and the functions counsel will perform. We deal below in paragraph 22.63(c) - (e) with the desirability of conferences with counsel.

(e)   The client should be kept in touch by letter or telephone with the progress of events. Although unnecessary costs should not be incurred in this way, it should be borne in mind that inexperienced clients, or clients under pressure, are likely to need more frequent contacts of this sort.

(f) As we indicate in paragraph 23.17, a solicitor should, whenever appropriate, advise his client of the effect of the rules concerning clients' money and the interest thereon.

(g) In a personal injury case, the client should be advised in writing about the possibility of settlement, and preparations made to enable a decision to be taken in event of an offer at the door of the court.

22.63 In order to prevent an unsatisfactory service resulting from inadequacies in the preparation or handling of briefs we consider that Standards should be proposed on the lines indicated below.

(a) Briefs and instructions should contain all the available information which is required for the intended purpose, properly arranged.

(b) Briefs should be delivered in sufficient time before the hearing to enable them to be properly studied. The period will vary according to the nature of the proceedings.

(c) The solicitor, having discussed the matter with the client, should arrange a conference with the barrister if necessary.

(d) The barrister should read the brief as soon as possible after its delivery and should advise, in adequate time before the hearing, whether a conference before the hearing day is necessary and whether any further preparatory work is required. In criminal cases particular attention should be paid to the need for advice on the intended plea, to avoid changes of plea at the trial.

(e) If there has been no conference before the hearing day, arrangements must be made for a conference before the hearing to enable the barrister to establish a rapport with his client and to advise and receive instructions on the conduct of the case.

22.64 There are many other areas in which the use of written Standards would be beneficial. It is a matter for the profession, in the exercise of its duty to the public, to prepare written Professional Standards whenever experience shows them to be required.

Other Matters Requiring Attention

Sole practitioners
22.65 In many localities there is insufficient work for more than one or two small firms. If solicitors were not prepared to practise singly or in small partnerships the present spread of offices, already inadequate in some places, would be reduced. An important component of legal services can be provided by the solicitor willing to set up in practice on his own in a new area, and, starting in a small way, to build up his business to the point at which additional partners join his firm.

22.66   From the analysis of the size of solicitors' firms in paragraph 17.3 and Table 17.1, it will be seen that about one-third of solicitors' firms are run by sole practitioners. It has been suggested that the risk of losses arising, whether through negligence or through misappropriation of funds, is higher in the case of sole practitioners than in other firms. In fact, the figures published by the Law Society concerning the professional indemnity insurance scheme show that the claims records of sole practitioners are good. There is no reason to suppose that a client of a sole practitioner is exposed to any greater risk of professional negligence than a client of a firm with two or more partners. On the other hand, the number of claims on the compensation fund for misappropriation of money is proportionately higher in the case of sole practitioners than others. We were told that before the introduction of the professional indemnity insurance scheme this was in part accounted for by the fact that solicitors in partnership have less opportunity to misappropriate clients' money and in part accounted for by the fact that the larger firm is more likely to have the financial resources to meet its obligations without a claim on the fund. Since the introduction of the professional indemnity insurance scheme the fund has not been at risk at all in respect of individual dishonest partners except to the extent that the insurance cover might in a particular case be inadequate to cover the loss.

22.67   There was nothing in the evidence submitted to us to suggest that sole practitioners generally fail to carry on business in an efficient manner or to give a good and prompt service to clients. But there are circumstances which make it less easy for the sole practitioner than for a larger firm to maintain an adequate service.

22.68   A large firm enjoys certain material benefits in respect of premises, office equipment, conditions of service, profitability, pay and pensions. It can offer specialist services to clients. There appears at present to be a trend for firms to increase in size by amalgamation and merger. If this process is taken too far, or if solicitors find it too difficult to set up in sole practice, the result will be a gradual reduction in the spread of solicitors' firms, particularly in areas in which there is insufficient work for a large firm. It is in the public interest to have regard to the problems of sole practitioners and small firms and to alleviate them where possible.

22.69   Sole practitioners have no partners to whom work can be delegated in times of illness or in order to take a holiday. When the work of one client is given priority, other matters are kept waiting. No one of partner status is available in the office when the sole practitioner is at court. If attendance in court by a solicitor in sole practice is necessary for any lengthy period, the day-to-day work of the practice has to be done by working early and late. As we remarked in Chapter 17, this makes the services of the Bar particularly important to sole practitioners.

22.70 For the large number of solicitors who choose to continue in sole practice, practical assistance should be available as needed. Every sole practitioner is well advised to make arrangements with a neighbouring firm for assistance in emergencies. Sole practitioners should also be encouraged to make full use of the confidential advisory service provided by the Law Society so as to prevent work falling into arrears and the interest of clients being harmed.

Legal aid
22.71 Legal aid authorities have a duty to ensure that if work is paid for out of public funds, good value for money is given. They have an opportunity to do so in a civil case when considering reports and opinions from the lawyers conducting the case. In a criminal case, the court has a responsibility to draw attention to occasions when the provision of legal aid has been in any way abused.

Legal aid and prolixity
22.72 A number of judges, including the Lord Chief Justice, expressed the view to us that the increased availability of legal aid, in particular in criminal cases, has increased the length of trials, because counsel are more prolix, more willing to pursue bad points and more extravagant in the presentation of the case than formerly. Against this, it was said that before legal aid was available to the majority of defendants in criminal cases, the case for the defence often suffered by being put, for reasons of economy, in too abbreviated a form. There is in our view a measure of truth in the criticisms mentioned above. The lawyers involved, however, are not alone responsible for the increased length and complexity of criminal proceedings. There has been an increase in the number of offences, for example of fraud or corruption, where the facts are highly complicated. Such cases are more difficult to unravel and present in a coherent form to a court. There is an increasing tendency for the prosecution to bring before the court all defendants who have any association with the crime charged, and for indictments to contain an increasing number of counts. Much time is consumed when a large number of defendants are separately represented by the examination of witnesses on behalf of each in turn. It has been suggested that the number of counts should be no more than is essential to secure a fair trial and that, where a number of defendants are involved, there should be separate proceedings against the ringleaders and against those who are only marginally involved. These matters are outside our terms of reference, but we commend them for further consideration.

22.73 It has been proposed that the amount available from the legal aid fund for any criminal case should be subject to a maximum limit, so as to encourage lawyers to work as economically as possible, as in the days before legal aid was generally available in criminal matters. This would involve practical difficulties, because there would be no-one in a position to make the appropriate estimate, or vary it, if occasion required. The most serious objection to this proposal is that when the costs of a defence are paid out of private funds, lack of resources leads in some cases to inadequate representation. It would be inconsistent to recommend such a scheme for the purposes of economy while maintaining, as we do in Chapter 14, the principle that everyone charged with a serious offence should have adequate representation.

22.74 We doubt whether there are any quick or easy remedies for prolixity. To restore an efficient and economical style as the proper goal of every advocate will take time and effort. First, the governing bodies and senior members of the profession must make it clear, in the course of education and training and when giving guidance informally, that it is not creditable to take half a day in cross-examination or in an address to the court, when a few well-chosen questions, or a short but carefully prepared address, would achieve the desired result with greater impact.

22.75 The judiciary and taxing authorities also have a part to play. Accepting that there are difficulties involved, we consider that it is reasonable for a judge to intervene, or to speak to counsel privately, if time is unnecessarily taken up in examinations or addresses to the court. Taxing authorities should always be willing to give a fair return for careful preparation which leads to the minimum expenditure of time in court. As we show in Chapter 37, the way in which fees are assessed at present results in a barrister obtaining greater remuneration in respect of time spent in court than in respect of that spent in preparation. The result of this is often to penalise careful preparation and economical presentation of a case and to reward prolixity. We consider that the system of remuneration should have the opposite effect.

Conclusions and Recommendations

Paragraphs

General R22.1 A profession is responsible for en- 22.5
suring that the quality of its members' work is of a satisfactory standard.

    R22.2 In general, the legal profession pro- 22.17
vides an adequate standard of service, but there are shortcomings.

Delay R22.3 A sustained effort is required to re- 22.23
duce the length of all legal proceedings.

308

R22.4   A thorough re-appraisal of the organ-   22.23
         isation and procedures of the civil
         courts is needed to shorten the
         duration of civil litigation.

R22.5   The average time taken to dispose of   22.26–22.28
         cases in the Queen's Bench Division
         is not acceptable and should be the
         subject of specific inquiry.

Relations with   R22.6   All lawyers should be instructed in the   22.31
clients   importance of establishing a sound   and 22.62
                               professional relationship with the
                               client, and practical measures should
                               be laid down as Professional Stan-
                               dards.

Representation   R22.7   Guidelines for listing cases should be   22.38
                               agreed between the judiciary, the
                               courts administration and the pro-
                               fession.

R22.8   The procedure for handling briefs   22.39–22.42
         should be as stated in the text. Appro-   and 22.63
         priate Professional Standards should
         be issued to that effect.

R22.9   Both solicitor and barrister should   22.43
         consider and advise specifically   and 22.63
         whether a conference before the day
         of hearing is necessary for the proper
         presentation of a case.

R22.10   Guidelines are needed to define when   22.44
         a solicitor or a member of his staff   and 22.45
         should attend with a barrister in
         court.

R22.11   Measures should be taken as stated   22.46
         in the text to prevent parties being
         taken by surprise by offers of settle-
         ment at the door of the court.

Paragraphs

Administration R22.12 The Law Society should issue guide- 22.52
lines on methods of office admini-
stration.

R22.13 Proposals for legal information 22.53
retrieval services should be pressed
forward without delay.

R22.14 The use of inter-firm comparisons 22.54
should be encouraged.

R22.15 There will be an increasing need for 22.55
specialisation. Practising solicitors
should plan ahead for this purpose.

R22.16 Firms of any size should appoint a 22.56
partner or senior staff member to
supervise internal administration.

Professional R22.17 Written Professional Standards 22.58
Standards should be issued by both branches of and 22.59
the profession; failure to observe
them would involve disciplinary
proceedings.

Sole practitioners R22.18 Sole practitioners should make full 22.70
use of the support facilities available
to them.

Prolixity R22.19 Prolixity in court should be dis- 22.74
couraged by the judiciary, the taxing and 22.75
authorities and the profession.

ANNEX 22.1

TABLE 22.1

Degree of satisfaction with solicitors' services
(paragraph 22.7)

Degree of satisfaction							All consultations with solicitors in England & Wales
							%
Completely satisfied	..	..	..	..	..	..	67
Fairly satisfied	..	..	..	..	..	..	17
Neither satisfied nor dissatisfied	..	..	..	..	..		3
Somewhat dissatisfied	..	..	..	..	..	..	7
Very dissatisfied	..	..	..	..	..	..	6
Not stated	..	..	..	..	..	..	1
Total	..	..	..	..	..	..	100[2]
Number of consultations in sample		..	..	..	..	..	2,064

[1]Less than 0·5 per cent.

[2]Where figures have been rounded, the sum of constituent numbers may not be exactly equal to the total shown.

Source: Consultants' report on the survey of the use of legal services in England and Wales, Volume II section 7 Table 31.

TABLE 22.2

Dissatisfaction with legal services, by type of service
(paragraph 22.7)

Type of matter	Matters in which users were dissatisfied with lawyers' services		All matters in which lawyer was consulted	
	number	%	number	%
Civil litigation	41	16	258	13
Matrimonial ..	37	15	256	13
Conveyancing	65	25	639	32
Probate	32	13	217	11
Property	23	9	144	7
Crime	20	8	135	7
Miscellaneous	37	15	377	18
Total	255	100[1]	2,026[2]	100[1]

[1]Where figures have been rounded, the sum of constituent numbers may not be exactly equal to the totals shown.

[2]This number is lower than the total number of consultations given in Table 22.1 because some respondents consulted more than one solicitor on the same matter.

Source: Data obtained by the consultants; for further analysis see Volume II section 7.

311

TABLE 22.3

Reasons for dissatisfaction[1]
(paragraphs 22.12 and 22.28)

Reasons stated	number of occasions
Solicitor did not take an interest in it/did not do enough	75
Matter took too long/solicitor was too slow	75
Lack of communication/not kept informed of progress	38
Solicitor made mistakes/was forgetful	24
Solicitor gave bad advice/disagreed with the action he took	22
Complaints about solicitor's manner	20
Charged too much	20
Solicitor lacked specialist knowledge for case	8
Incurred unnecessary costs/outside costs too high	7
Solicitor was guilty of malpractice/unprofessional behaviour	3
Other answers	15
Not stated	4
Total	311[2]

[1]As stated by the respondents in Table 22.1 who expressed dissatisfaction.

[2]Dissatisfaction was expressed in respect of 255 matters out of a total of 2,064. The number of reasons given (sometimes more than one for each matter)amounted to 311.

Source: Data obtained by consultants; for further analysis see Volume II section 7.

TABLE 22.4

Features of solicitors' work which were particularly liked
(paragraphs 22.12 and 22.28)

Features cited	number of occasions
Solicitor was nice/friendly/easy to talk to	579
Solicitor was efficient/business like..	359
Solicitor explained things clearly	298
Solicitor handled things promptly/quickly	122
Solicitor was professionally expert	112
Solicitor was personal friend/acquaintance	36
Favourable comment on costs	32
Solicitor's manner was confident	28
Did what I asked/no problems/did a good job/other general favourable comments	79
Other answers	4
Total	1,649[1]

[1]The number of cases in respect of which a respondent mentioned a feature giving particular satisfaction was 1,188 out of a total of 2,064. The number of features mentioned was 1,649.

Source: Data obtained by consultants; for further analysis see Volume II section 7.

TABLE 22.5

Complaints received by the Commission, by nature of complaint
(paragraph 22.12)

Nature of complaint	Number
Inefficiency and negligence	446
Delay	420
Cost	407
Restrictions on legal aid	195
Difficulty in pursuing complaint against a solicitor	163
Complaints about a third party's solicitor	132
Conflict of interest	100
Complaints against barristers	68
Miscellaneous/not stated	298
Total number of complaints	2,229[1]

[1]The number of matters in which these complaints arose was 1,473.

Source: Analysis, by the staff of the Commission, of complaints received.

TABLE 22.6

Letters of complaint and complaints to NACAB by class of legal business
(paragraph 22.12)

Class of business	Distribution of legal business: Users' Survey	Classification of complaints:	
		Letters to Royal Commission	NACAB survey
	%	%	%
Civil litigation	13	29	13
Matrimonial	13	18	33
Conveyancing	32	17	22
Probate	11	12	8
Property	7	10	4
Crime	7	5	3
Miscellaneous	17	9	16
Total	100	100	100[1]
Number of matters	2,026	1,473	901

[1]Where figures have been rounded, the sum of constituent numbers may not be exactly equal to the total shown.

Sources: Data obtained by consultants; for further analysis see Volume II section 7.

Analysis, by the staff of the Commission, of complaints received.

Survey by the National Association of Citizens Advice Bureaux of complaints received by the bureaux.

313

TABLE 22.7

Nature of complaints in Users' Survey, Royal Commission correspondence and NACAB Survey
(paragraph 22.12)

Nature of complaint[1]	Users' Survey	Complaints received by Royal Commission	NACAB Survey
	%	%	%
Inefficiency, incompetence and negligence	42	20	44
Delay	24	19	17
Cost	9	18	22
Other causes	25	43	15
Total	100	100	100[2]
Number of reasons for complaint or dissatisfaction	311	2,229	1,245
Number of matters	255	1,473	901

[1]The cause of the complaint is shown in broad categories because the analysis into more specific categories was on a slightly different basis in each survey.

[2]Where figures have been rounded, the sum of the constituent numbers may not be exactly equal to the total shown.

Sources: Data obtained by consultants; for further analysis see Volume II section 7.

Analysis, by the staff of the Commission, of complaints received.

Survey by the National Association of Citizens Advice Bureaux of complaints received by bureaux.

TABLE 22.8

Complaints received by the Law Society, November 1972 – May 1973
(paragraph 22.12)

Complaints found not justified, or falling outside Society's powers	503	
Complaints found justified	209	
Cause of complaint:—		
Delay		140
Negligence..		20
Complaints about a third party solicitor		19
Conflict of interest		18
Costs		7
Failure to keep informed		5
Total complaints examined	712	

Source: Law Society.

TABLE 22.9

Total number of complaints received by the Law Society 1971-78
(paragraph 22.12)

Year	Complaints from solicitors	Complaints from laymen	Total	Number of solicitors with practising certificates[1]
1971	n/a	n/a	4,860	25,366
1972	n/a	n/a	5,270	26,327
1973	623	4,230	4,853	27,379
1974	626	4,116	4,742	28,741
1975	731	5,021	5,752	29,850
1976	827	5,007	5,834	31,250
1977	840	4,975	5,815	32,812
1978	909	5,006	5,915	33,864

[1]In the practice year ending in the calendar year indicated.
Source: Law Society.

TABLE 22.10

Complaints against barristers 1972-78
(paragraphs 22.15 and 22.44)

Nature of complaint	1972	1973	1974	1975	1976	1977	1978
Advertising, touting	8	5	2	10	7	5	6
Conflict of interest	3	1	1	4	3	1	1
Bad advice	2	4	10	4	7	9	6
Abuse of qualification	2	3	2	4	1	11	15
Acting without instructions ..	3	9	5	5	6	10	18
Acting contrary to instructions ..	3	2	2	5	2	8	1
Lack of courtesy	5	5	5	7	3	11	6
Unrelated to practice	6	4	14	8	9	11	11
Withholding information ..	7	10	6	8	8	—	1
Refusing to act	2	4	2	3	2	—	1
Inadequate representation ..	20	24	19	17	34	27	20
Undue influence	5	8	10	4	7	8	6
Conduct of proceedings	2	2	8	12	8	19	19
Fees	2	1	3	—	—	7	4
Late returns	4	5	1	3	3	—	3
Delay	—	6	4	4	5	4	6
Chambers practice	—	1	—	3	2	2	4
Absence	—	3	2	—	—	3	5
Total	74	97	96	101	107	136	133

Source: Senate.

TABLE 22.11

Sources of complaints against barristers
(paragraph 22.15)

Source of complaint	1972	1973	1974	1975	1976	1977	1978
Prisoners	21	26	21	18	20	31	23
Other lay clients	28	34	40	31	40	51	46
Courts	4	7	13	17	15	20	25
Solicitors	8	17	13	11	16	15	13
Barristers	4	6	3	9	5	10	19
Professional Conduct Committee	4	3	4	6	9	3	1
Law Society	—	2	2	3	1	2	2
Others	5	2	—	6	1	4	4
Total	74	97	96	101	107	136	133

Source: Senate.

316

TABLE 22.12

Duration of cases, Users' Survey[1]
(paragraph 22.19)

Class of business	Percentage of cases					Total[2]	
	Up to 2 months	over 2 months, up to 6 months	over 6 months, up to 1 year	over 1 year, up to 2 years	over 2 years	%	Number of matters
Buying or selling a house or a flat..	32	53	10	4	1	100	432
Making or altering a will	84	12	2	1	1	100	160
Dealing with estate of deceased person	26	41	23	6	4	100	96
Divorce and other family problems	24	23	27	15	11	100	93
Motoring and other offences	56	29	12	3	0	100	90
Personal injury compensation	19	27	32	17	5	100	41
Other matters/not stated	52	27	12	4	4	100	292
All classes of business	44	36	13	5	3	100	1,164

[1]The figures given relate to all cases in the Users' Survey in which action had been completed and the duration was stated.
[2]Where figures have been rounded, the sums of constituent numbers may not be exactly equal to the totals shown.
Source: Consultants' report on the survey of the use of legal services in England and Wales, Volume II section 7 Table 42.

TABLE 22.13

Waiting times in the Crown Court, 1978

(paragraph 22.19)

	Total defendants dealt with	Average waiting time in weeks	Waiting 8 weeks or more %	Waiting 20 weeks or more %
Committals for trial[1] Total ..	79,993	14.9	61	28
of which:				
Defendants pleading guilty..	46,971	11.51	48	16
Defendants pleading not guilty	28,338	20.41	81	44
and:				
Defendants on bail	60,091	16.1	65	30
Defendants in custody ..	15,219	9.8	42	10
Committals for sentence	14,105	5.1	10	1
Appeals	14,471	8.4	36	6

[1]This information is available in respect of only those defendants whose cases involved a court hearing. There were in addition 4,684 defendants for whom no plea was recorded because of death, being found unfit to plead or against whom a warrant of arrest was issued for failing to surrender to bail.

Source: Lord Chancellor's Department.

TABLE 22.14

Average duration of cases set down for hearing in the Queen's Bench Division, 1975–77[1]

(paragraph 22.19)

Months

		Cause of action to issue of writ	Issue of writ to setting down	Setting down to trial (or disposal)	Cause of action to trial (or disposal)
London					
	1975	17	17	11	45
	1976	16	18	11	45
	1977	17	18	14	49
Outside London					
	1975	17	16	9	42
	1976	17	18	9	44
	1977	17	17	9	43

[1]Further information on this subject may be found in Volume II section 10.

Source: Lord Chancellor's Department.

TABLE 22.15

Satisfaction with service related to estimate of duration
(paragraph 22.28)

Satisfaction with solicitor	All cases in which solicitor took action	Estimate of how long matter would take		
		given	not asked for	asked for but not given
	%	%	%	%
Completely satisfied	67	78	62	39
Fairly satisfied	17	14	19	27
Neither satisfied nor dissatisfied ..	3	2	5	4
Somewhat dissatisfied	6	4	7	16
Very dissatisfied	5	3	6	14
Not stated	1	0[2]	1	1
Total[1] %	100	100	100	100
Number in sample	1,849	848	762	176

[1]Where figures have been rounded, the sum of constituent numbers may not be exactly equal to the totals shown.

[2]Less than 0.5 per cent.

Source: Consultants' report on the survey of the use of legal services in England and Wales, Volume II section 7 Table 45.

CHAPTER 23

Protection of the Client: Solicitors

Introductory

23.1   In this chapter, we deal with the protection available to a client against suffering financial loss at the hands of his solicitor and the precautions taken to prevent such a loss. Loss may be suffered if a solicitor misuses money held by him on behalf of clients in connection with their affairs. It may occur if a solicitor is negligent. We deal with both these topics in the following sections. We also consider the solicitor's lien, which is the right of a solicitor to withhold papers from his client against payment of his charges.

Clients' Money

General

23.2   It is an integral part of the function of a solicitor to hold money on behalf of his clients under a variety of circumstances; principal among these is the holding of money received during conveyancing transactions and the administration of the estates of deceased persons. The sums so held by solicitors vary considerably, depending upon the nature of their practices, but the total amount held by solicitors at any one time is substantial. For instance, at the end of their accounting years which ended in 1976, solicitors held clients' money amounting to £760m (approximately £118,000 per firm). The length of time during which an individual sum is held varies with the nature of the transaction; in the case of many conveyancing transactions, the money is held for a short time, sometimes no more than two or three days.

The present regulations

23.3   Solicitors are in a position of great trust. It is essential to ensure that, if a solicitor abuses that trust, the client does not suffer and the profession does not lose the confidence of the public. To this end, rules made by the Law Society under the Solicitors Act 1974, with the approval of the Master of the Rolls, regulate the holding of clients' money.

23.4   The Solicitors' Accounts Rules 1975 and the Solicitors' Trust Accounts Rules 1975 specify various obligations and prohibitions which are binding on all solicitors holding clients' money. The main provisions of these rules may be summarised as follows:—

(a) a solicitor must, unless directed otherwise by a client, promptly pay into a client account all money received from any client, the only exception being receipts of fees or debts, or money that is immediately forwarded to a third party without being banked by the solicitor;

(b) a client account may contain only clients' money, trust money, such money of the solicitor as may be necessary to open or maintain the account and cheques or drafts which include clients' money or trust money;

(c) money may be withdrawn from a client account only for payment to or on behalf of the client concerned or on his authority;

(d) a solicitor must keep comprehensive written records of all his dealings with clients' money.

Monitoring

23.5 In order to ensure compliance with the Solicitors' Accounts Rules, section 34 of the Solicitors Act 1974 provides that every solicitor holding clients' money must furnish an accountant's report to the Law Society each year. The duties of the accountant and the form and content of his report are prescribed in the Accountant's Report Rules 1975. These rules require the accountant to make test examinations and to confirm that the account for each client is kept in a proper form. A complete audit is required if these procedures reveal a possible failure by the solicitor to comply with the rules.

23.6 The solicitors' Accounts Rules 1975 and the Solicitors' Trust Accounts Rules 1975 provide the Law Society with reserve powers enabling it to order the inspection of a solicitor's accounts at the request of a local law society, as the result of a complaint by a client, or on its own initiative, either because it suspects a breach of the rules or merely as a precaution.

The effectiveness of the rules

23.7 No rules can by themselves prevent the deliberate misuse of clients' money. The existing rules are therefore designed to ensure that the opportunities for such misuse are restricted and that any case that arises can easily be identified. They are backed up by the full range of disciplinary powers available to the Law Society. We are satisfied on the evidence submitted to us that these rules, which have evolved over many years, are sound and that they are being properly and responsibly applied by the Law Society.

The Law Society's compensation fund

23.8 Notwithstanding the precautions taken by the Law Society, there have been cases of solicitors using clients' money for their own purposes. In order to protect the public from such defalcations, the Law Society set up in 1942 a compensation fund. In the following table, details are set out of claims made upon the fund in each of the last eight years: —

TABLE 23.1

Compensation fund: claims made in each calendar year, 1971-78

Year	Number of claims	Number of solicitors involved	Amount claimed
			£
1971	147	11	496,444
1972	74	6	557,493
1973	102	12	848,362
1974	236	11	585,643
1975	296	20	1,135,080
1976	265	32	1,697,749
1977	99	16	889,184
1978	85	13	844,508

Source: Law Society.

23.9 The compensation fund is currently governed by section 36 of the Solicitors Act 1974 and the Solicitors' Compensation Fund Rules 1975. The main purpose of the fund is to replace, by means of discretionary grants, clients' money misappropriated by a solicitor acting in the course of his practice as a solicitor or misappropriated by a solicitor's employee, which cannot be recovered from any other source; in other words, it is administered as a "fund of last resort". Grants from the fund may also be made to persons suffering hardship as a result of the failure of a solicitor to account for money which he has received or to a solicitor suffering loss or hardship because of liabi'ities following misappropriations by a partner or employee.

Claims on the compensation fund

23.10 The Law Society informed us in evidence that in the 37 years since the establishment of the compensation fund, every claim which the Society has admitted, as being within section 36 of the Solicitors Act 1974 (or its equivalent in previous enactments), has been paid in full. A claim which does not fall within the scope of the compensation fund as defined in the Solicitors Act 1974 cannot be admitted. Examples of such claims are those where there is no, or insufficient, proof of loss or where there is no evidence of dishonesty. The Law Society pointed out that a claim otherwise falling within the scope of the fund might nonetheless not be admitted if, for example, there was evidence of criminal complicity between the claimant and the defaulting solicitor or the claim was in substance for monetary damages, in that it sought compensation for suffering or inconvenience rather than recovery of misused money. Additionally, a claim made by an institutional applicant, such as a bank or a building society, might occasionally be rejected in whole or in part on the ground either that the applicant had contributed substantially to the loss by want of ordinary prudence or that the loss was covered by the applicant's insurance.

23.11 In the following table details are set out of claims rejected in the years 1971-78 for any of the reasons given in the previous paragraph.

TABLE 23.2

Compensation fund: claims rejected in each calendar year, 1971-78

Year	Numbers of claims rejected	Aggregate amount of claims
		£
1971	11	47,782
1972	19	35,535
1973	5	78,558
1974	11	58,123
1975	8	32,241
1976	7	56,457
1977	4	31,734
1978	5	105,480

Source: Law Society.

If a claim is rejected, the rules require the Law Society to give reasons.

23.12 The constitution and operation of the compensation fund were reviewed during the progress through Parliament of the Solicitors Act 1974. It was suggested in the course of debate that the fund should become an indemnity fund on which applicants would have a legally enforceable claim. But those favouring the principle of a discretionary fund maintained that:—

(a) the rules as administered by the Law Society were sufficiently comprehensive to render it unnecessary for claimants to have legally enforceable rights;

(b) the Law Society was able to be more flexible in its consideration of individual cases and was able to demand less rigid standards of proof if it retained an element of discretion;

(c) a discretionary system was cheaper, easier and faster to operate and could reimburse the full costs incurred by a successful applicant in making a claim.

On balance, Parliament favoured the principle of an *ex gratia* compensation fund.

Sources of finance

23.13 The compensation fund is financed by an annual contribution imposed on all solicitors who take out practising certificates. Prior to the enactment of the Solicitors Act 1974, the maximum annual contribution was fixed by statute at £10. There is now no statutory maximum. The contribution is currently £30. The Law Society is also empowered from time to time to require all solicitors who hold or receive clients' money to pay a special levy of up to £50. Solicitors in their early years of practice are either relieved of both these payments or pay at a reduced rate. In addition the Law Society is empowered to borrow up to £100,000 at any one time for the purposes of the fund.

Financial viability

23.14   At an early stage in our work we made enquiries of the Law Society about the financial viability of the compensation fund. On 31st December 1976, the fund's assets stood at £947,253 whereas claims notified and outstanding totalled £2,242,880. This situation had arisen largely because delay in removing the statutory limit on the annual contribution payable by solicitors had prevented income from keeping pace with claims. During 1977, however, the position improved considerably. On 31st December 1977, the fund's assets stood at £1,026,321 whereas claims notified and outstanding totalled £1,475,747. By the end of 1978 the assets and claims outstanding were £1,070,495 and £1,434,353 respectively. These figures should be treated with caution since some claims may be outstanding for many years and may then be withdrawn or settled from other sources.

23.15   We think that the state of the fund at the end of 1978, viewed in the light of the Law Society's powers to maintain the solvency of the fund described in paragraph 23.13, provides effective protection for the public. We understand that it is the intention of the Law Society to build up a contingency reserve out of revenue as soon as circumstances permit.

Interest on clients' money

23.16   Until 1964, solicitors were considered to be entitled in law to retain at least some of the interest earned by clients' money. In 1964, however, the House of Lords ruled, in *Brown* v. *C.I.R.* [1964] 3 All E.R. 119, that a solicitor had to account to his client for all interest earned on his client account. This ruling was regarded as being impracticable as regards small sums deposited with solicitors for short periods; accordingly provision was made in the Solicitors Act 1965 for rules as to the payment of interest to clients. Similar provision was made in the Solicitors Act 1974. The present regulations governing the disposal of interest on clients' money are set out in the Solicitors' Accounts (Deposit Interest) Rules 1975 which, in brief, provide that interest ought "in fairness" to be paid to a client when the amount received by the solicitor exceeds £500 and is unlikely to have been disbursed within a period of two months of receipt. It is open to a solicitor and his client to make any other arrangement in writing which is satisfactory to both of them; in other cases interest which is not required to be paid to clients under the above rules may be retained by the solicitor. Such retained interest is subject to tax as investment income (including, in appropriate cases, the investment income surcharge) in the hands of the solicitor. Money received by a solicitor which is subject to a trust of which the solicitor is a trustee is excluded from the rules and all interest thereon is payable to the trust.

23.17   The rules provide a further protection for the client; if he is aggrieved at the failure of his solicitor to pay him interest on money held, he may require his solicitor to obtain from the Law Society a certificate indicating how much interest, if any, is payable. It is important, if this arrangement is to operate successfully, that solicitors, whenever appropriate, should advise clients of their rights in this respect. We recommended in paragraph 22.62(b) that this be made the subject of a Professional Standard.

Amounts retained by solicitors

23.18   As pointed out in paragraph 23.2, the total amount of clients' money held by solicitors at the end of their accounting years ending in 1976 was £760m. The total amount of interest earned in that year on clients' money is not known. Some of the money held for short periods would not have earned interest and some of the interest earned would have been paid to clients in accordance with the rules described in paragraph 23.16. The total interest retained by solicitors in their accounting years ending in 1976 amounted to £18,900,000 which was 2.76% of their total gross income for that period. It will be recalled that interest rates in 1976 were high, particularly in the last quarter.

Payment of interest to clients

23.19   A number of witnesses advocated that all the interest earned on clients' money, however small the amount, should be paid to the clients concerned. We do not think that this would be practicable for a number of reasons. Many of the sums received are either small in amount or held for short periods; not all the money received can be placed on deposit account because a working balance has to be retained on current account; as regards money held on deposit account, a period of notification before withdrawal is necessary; finally, interest rates are continually changing. Under these circumstances the cost of accounting for small amounts of interest would be uneconomic and would exceed the interest earned.

23.20   There are in addition certain offsets for outgoings and finance charges borne by solicitors which can, we think, fairly be taken into consideration. They are as follows.

(a)   The solicitor is responsible for the proper custody of the money, for the payment of his accountant's fees, for preparing the annual certificate and for his annual contribution to the compensation fund.

(b)   A solicitor in the ordinary course of business frequently has to make disbursements and pay other outgoings on behalf of his client before the client makes payment to him. Solicitors do not charge interest on money paid out in respect of such disbursements.

(c) Many clients are slow in paying solicitors' bills; the cost of financing these outstanding bills falls on the solicitor and can amount to a considerable figure.

If solicitors are deprived of this interest, the effect would probably be to increase solicitors' charges to the public in order to replace the source of revenue at present represented by retained interest.

The use of interest on clients' money for public purposes

23.21 It was suggested to us that the interest earned on clients' money should be used wholly or partly for public purposes such as an extension of legal aid, law centres, research, law reform, law libraries or vocational training. We do not agree with this proposal. Where the interest due to clients is large enough to be separately computed, we think it should be paid over, as is required under the present rules, to the clients to whom it belongs. As regards the interest retained by solicitors, we do not think a charge of this nature should be imposed upon solicitors alone unless it is applied in equal degree to all other professions and organisations which receive money on behalf of clients, such as bankers, accountants, estate agents, stockbrokers, travel agents, insurance brokers and others.

Summary

23.22 The arrangements under which solicitors receive and handle money on behalf of their clients and deal with the interest received thereon have evolved over a long period. We think they are satisfactory and do not recommend any changes.

Indemnity Insurance

The present scheme

23.23 The compensation fund referred to earlier is available only in respect of loss suffered as a result of dishonesty or failure to account for money received; it is not available in cases of loss caused by negligence. In respect of such loss the only remedy is a civil action for damages brought against the solicitor responsible. Until 1976 solicitors were not obliged to insure against civil liabilities incurred in the course of professional practice, though many did so. In 1975, by virtue of the powers contained in section 37 of the Solicitors Act 1974, the Law Society made the Solicitors' Indemnity Rules, under which, as from 1st September 1976, all solicitors who are principals in private practice are required to be insured against claims arising from professional negligence under the terms of a Master Policy taken out by the Law Society.

23.24 The Master Policy currently provides a minimum cover, in respect of each claim, of £50,000 in the case of a sole practitioner and £30,000 per partner in the case of a firm of two or more partners. Thus, for example, a firm of five partners is insured for £150,000 for each claim. On every claim there is an "excess" of £400 for each partner. In the example quoted above, a five partner firm would have to pay the first £2,000 of each claim. In Inner London, the premium payable for the insurance year 1978/79 in respect of this minimum cover is £888 in respect of each sole practioner or partner in a firm; elsewhere it is £658 for each sole practitioner or partner. Reduced rates are available for sole practitioners who are able to establish that they have a low level of fee income.

23.25　The scheme is one of indemnity insurance; that is to say, it covers not the client but the solicitor or his employee in respect of any civil liability resulting from his professional practice in this country. It does not cover loss arising from the assured's own dishonesty or fraud but does cover dishonesty or fraud by his partner. The policy provides cover up to the insured amount for all claims, however numerous these might be.

23.26　It is impossible, except by practical experience over a period of years, to determine the right level of indemnity insurance. The type of work, and accordingly the sums at risk, vary widely as between different firms of solicitors. Solicitors are advised by the Law Society to consider whether they should take out additional cover above the compulsory limits under the scheme. Many firms do so and insure voluntarily, with the insurers of the scheme or elsewhere, for sums in excess of the required minimum. The insurers of the scheme are also prepared to agree, on payment of an additional premium, to the removal or the reduction of the "excess" which is payable by the insured.

23.27　Recent years have seen the appearance of increasingly strict standards of liability and a substantial rise in the sums awarded in damages in respect of professional negligence. Liability has also, in recent years, been increasingly affected by statute law. We have no doubt that the Law Society is right to impose compulsory indemnity insurance on its members (save where it is appropriate to waive the rule), and that it is in the public interest to do so. As pointed out earlier, the amount of the minimum cover will require to be kept under review to determine whether it needs amendment from time to time.

Limitation of liability
23.28　The potential liabilities of solicitors and other professional persons to claims for negligence are now considerable and are continually rising in all countries. It should be appreciated that in some classes of commercial work in the legal profession, decisions are made on matters involving many millions of pounds. By way of illustration, we understand that in one case covered by the Law Society's Master Policy, the underwriters have a reserve of £840,000 and in another case, the potential liability of one small firm is

over 40 times the amount of its compulsory cover. It is clear that if claims as a whole continue to rise the cost of obtaining insurance cover will become very large. We have therefore considered whether some limit should be placed by statute on the amount which can be claimed in respect of professional negligence.

23.29 The view of the Law Society, which is endorsed by many individual solicitors, was set out in its evidence as follows.

> The question of possible limitation of professional liability is a matter of current debate because it is felt by some to be unreasonable that individual practitioners should be liable to the full extent of their personal resources for any professional liability incurred by them, their partners or employees as a result of negligence or any other breach of duty, irrespective of the degree of fault attaching to them or the amount of remuneration earned for the work in question. Against this the Council have taken the view that it is one of the marks of a fully developed profession that its members undertake to accept personal responsibility to those whom they serve, including full legal liability for loss caused by any failure.

Similar conclusions were reached by several professions who set up a joint working party in 1968, under the chairmanship of Sir Henry Benson, to consider the matter.

23.30 We respect the views of the Law Society on this matter which are consistent with a high standard of responsibility towards the client. Nevertheless, the developments to which we have alluded are now placing a great strain upon solicitors and upon members of other professions. Cases have been known in which partners have lost their personal assets as a result of a claim in excess of their insurance cover; yet, where the claim is large, the total personal assets of the partners will cover only a small proportion of it. We believe, therefore, that an enquiry should be set up without delay to review the issue of limited liability for claims of negligence. A limit might be fixed at an absolute sum for each claim or it might be related to a multiple of the fees charged for the work done. We have not attempted to conduct such an inquiry ourselves because we believe that it should encompass all the professions and not be restricted to solicitors who cannot for this purpose be considered in isolation.

The Solicitor's Lien
Definition

23.31 Lien is a right in common law which enables any creditor, who has rightfully come into possession of chattels belonging to his debtor, to retain them in order to enforce payment of the debt due to him by that debtor. This right is personal to the creditor and cannot be transferred by him to any other person. It is defensive only, in the sense that the unpaid creditor cannot be compelled by legal process to deliver up possession of the property. It is not, therefore, subject to any limitation of time imposed by statute on the right to pursue a claim. We have been unable to discover to what extent solicitors exercise their rights of lien; the Lay Observer commented, however, in his 1975/76 report that some solicitors waive their rights of lien as an act of courtesy.

Complaints about the exercise of lien

23.32   We understand, as a result of enquiries addressed to the Law Commission and the Consumers' Association, that there has been no dissatisfaction expressed with the operation of the law relating to lien in general, nor has there been pressure for change. We did, however, receive evidence criticising the manner in which solicitors have sometimes exercised their right of lien in cases where they were in dispute with their clients. Complaints about the exercise of lien arise in the circumstances described below.

(a)   Lien is sometimes exercised on completion of work when there is a dispute over the bill. Though the client has a right to submit his bill for a remuneration certificate or for taxation, the need to recover his papers for other purposes may induce the client to pay a disputed bill rather than exercise his right. If the proportion of the bill in dispute is relatively small, the client may prefer to pay rather than suffer delay in bringing the matter to a conclusion. The material damage is usually small, but the exercise of the lien is resented.

(b)   Lien is also exercised when a dissatisfied client changes his solicitor. He wishes to pursue his business but his second solicitor cannot do so without the papers, which the first solicitor retains until he has been paid for what the client regards as unsatisfactory work.

(c)   When the client wishes to sue his solicitor for negligence, a lien may be exercised in circumstances linked with either (a) or (b) above. The need to pay a bill for work regarded by the client as negligent can cause considerable resentment.

Safeguards for the client

23.33   There are already a number of safeguards designed to protect the client from the misuse of lien. When a solicitor declines to act further for a client, the client or his second solicitor may obtain an order from the court for delivery of papers, on an undertaking to hold them without prejudice to the first solicitor's lien and to return them on completion of the matter.

23.34   Where the client discharges his solicitor and this action is held to be justified, usually on account of delay, there is provision in the Solicitors Act 1974 for the Law Society to exercise powers to gain possession of documents and assets, notwithstanding the existence of lien. The Law Society exercises these powers sparingly and intervenes only if it has reason to believe that the lien is being improperly exercised.

23.35 There are also other limitations on the exercise of lien which are designed to protect the property of the client while it is held by the solicitor, and to protect the interests of third parties having a right of access to documents belonging to a client and held by his solicitor.

Changes in the law

23.36 As we indicated in paragraph 23.32, there has been no demand for changes in the general law relating to lien. We understand that the Law Commission intends, when it reviews the law of contract, to examine at least some aspects of the law of lien. We do not believe that there is any case for altering the law of lien so as to create a special code for solicitors alone. While we recognise that a solicitor is occasionally in the position where, by the exercise of lien, he can cause inconvenience to a client, we do not believe that solicitors, whose charges are subject to close control, should be placed in a more unfavourable position than other creditors. Accordingly, we believe that deficiencies in the present system should be remedied by modifying practice and not by introducing changes in the law which apply only to a particular group.

Modifications in practice

23.37 In cases in which, for any reason, a solicitor ceases to act for a client and the client engages a second solicitor, it should be regarded as normal practice for the first solicitor to release the papers against an undertaking by the second to hold them to the order of the first and to return them on demand. As an alternative, the papers could be surrendered to the second solicitor in return for an undertaking to pay the first solicitor's account at the end of the transaction. Arrangements such as these would preserve the lien while allowing the client's business to proceed. It would, we believe, strike a proper balance between the interests of the client and those of the solicitor. In cases of dispute, or when no second solicitor is instructed, we consider that the Law Society should exercise its power to obtain possession of documents and assets not only where a change of solicitor is considered justifiable, but also where the client would otherwise suffer, for example, if he were prevented from instituting or carrying on proceedings.

Conclusions and Recommendations

Paragraphs

Client's money	R23.1	The present rules governing the holding of clients' money by solicitors are sound and well administered.	23.7 and 23.22
	R23.2	The present compensation arrangements in the event of misuse of clients' money by solicitors are satisfactory.	23.15
Interest on clients' money	R23.3	The present arrangements for dealing with interest on clients' money are reasonable and should continue.	23.19 and 23.22

330

Paragraphs

Indemnity insurance R23.4 It is in the public interest that solicitors should be required to have indemnity insurance; the amount of cover required should be kept under review. 23.27

Limitation of Liability R23.5 An enquiry should be set up without delay into the desirability of a limit on the level of damages which may be awarded for negligence against professional persons. 23.30

Lien R23.6 The law on lien does not require amendment in respect of solicitors alone; the present safeguards for clients should, however, be strengthend as set out in the next. 23.36–23.37

CHAPTER 24

Protection of the Client: Barristers

Immunity from proceedings for negligence

24.1   If a professional person acts negligently so that a client suffers injury or loss, he will be liable in damages. An exception is made in the case of barristers acting as advocates. By a rule of law recently re-affirmed by the House of Lords*, a barrister is immune from proceedings for negligence in the conduct of a case in court and in certain preparatory stages. The immunity does not extend to any other work done by a barrister.

24.2   The rule, as stated by earlier authorities, suggested that a barrister's imunity from proceedings in negligence extended to all his work, and was based on the absence of a contract for services between the barrister and client. By contrast there was never any doubt that a solicitor was liable for negligence in dealing with his professional work. The recent decisions are based not on the absence of a contract but on grounds of public policy.

24.3   The present rule as laid down in the cases mentioned in paragraph 24.1 may be summarised in the following way. A barrister, like any other professional person, is under a duty to exercise reasonable care and skill in the work done for clients. He may be liable in negligence to a client who suffers damage as a result of a breach of the duty to take care. An exception is made, on the grounds of public policy, in respect of a barrister's conduct of a case in court. No action for negligence may be brought when the neglect complained of occurred during the trial of proceedings. This immunity extends also to work done in preparation for trial, provided that it was so intimately connected with the conduct of the case in court that it could fairly be said to be a preliminary decision affecting the way the case was to be conducted when it came to a hearing.

24.4   A number of reasons have been advanced in support of the immunity. It is pointed out that a barrister has a duty to the court, which may conflict with his duty to the client; that he must take his client as he finds him and runs the risk of acting for a litigious client likely to start vexatious or harassing proceedings if dissatisfied; that the action for negligence would require re-trial of the proceedings and might be used as a device to sidestep the regular machinery of appeals and re-open a civil or criminal case, perhaps after several years had passed; and that, in order to avoid the risk of misconceived claims, a barrister

---

Rondel v. Worsley [1969] 1 AC 191.
Saif Ali v. *Sydney Mitchell & Co.* [1978] 3 WLR 849.

might call all available witnesses and take every point however unnecessary, thus greatly extending the duration and cost of proceedings.

24.5 The barrister's immunity must be considered in the context of the immunities attaching to others involved in the administration of justice. The judge, witnesses and jurors in civil and criminal trials are all immune from liability for anything said in the course of the hearing. A witness may not be sued even for giving perjured evidence. This rule is not intended for the benefit of witnesses and others, but to protect the administration of justice. The policy of providing a remedy for a civil wrong takes second place, in this limited area, to the policy of protecting those involved from the risk of harassing actions and of confining dissatisfied litigants to the permitted methods of appeal. The barrister's immunity is based on the same principle.

24.6 It happens that we first considered this topic before the most recent decision of the House of Lords was made known. We considered that, on balance, it was in the public interest that there should be immunity in respect of an advocate's work in court and reached a provisional conclusion as to the proper extent of that immunity which was close to that which has now been laid down. Accordingly we have no recommendation to make in regard to the extent of immunity which would go beyond the law as now stated.

24.7 The House of Lords, in the two cases mentioned above, was concerned only with the position of barristers. It is clear from its decision that the immunity in no way depends on status. It is allowed to a barrister not because he is a barrister, but because he is performing a specific function. We think it incontestable that, if public policy requires a function to be protected, the protection should extend to all those who perform it. We consider therefore that the immunity should attach to any advocate in a court of law, whether barrister, solicitor or any other person who may have a right of audience on behalf of another.

Indemnity insurance: the present position
24.8 Although a barrister's immunity from proceedings for negligence has been confined in recent years to litigious work, the number of claims brought against barristers is small. So far as is known to the Senate, no court has yet held a barrister liable in damages for negligence either to his instructing solicitor or to the solicitor's lay client. Since 1971, 4 claims against barristers, to a total value of £35,000, are known to have been settled.

24.9 In spite of the infrequency of claims, the profession rightly regards claims for negligence as a serious risk; indemnity insurance has, therefore, been widespread for some years. We were told by the Senate that all barristers have been recommended by the Bar Council to insure against potentially actionable negligence, and professional indemnity brokers advise both the Bar Council and, either through distributed literature or in answer to particular requests individual barristers.

Extension of liability

24.10   The present insurance rates for indemnity insurance are low. We were informed that the maximum premium in respect of each individual barrister for indemnity cover of £50,000 in 1978 was £66; lower premiums were charged when one policy was taken out to cover all members of a set of chambers. These premiums are substantially less than those payable for each partner in a solicitors' firm (see paragraph 23.24). Whether or not the levels of premium rise will depend on claims experience, though we think some increase is likely. These considerations lead to the question whether insurance cover should be compulsory.

Compulsory cover

24.11   If insurance were a matter affecting barristers alone, the decision whether to take out insurance could be left to each practitioner to decide for himself. But the interests of claimants must also be considered. A barrister practises alone, without partners to share his liabilities. Except for books, he has no professional property or assets of any realisable value. Unless he has private means, he is unlikely, even after many years of practice, to have accumulated enough capital to satisfy a large claim. In these circumstances, unless he is insured, a client who has suffered loss by his negligence would be able to obtain judgment against him but would be unable to recover anything to satisfy it and might even be unable to recover the costs of the proceedings.

24.12   Having regard to this, and to the hardship likely to be faced by an uninsured barrister against whom even a small claim arises, we have reached the view that insurance on a voluntary basis is no longer appropriate. We recommend that all barristers should be required, as a condition of being in private practice, to have insurance cover against claims for professional negligence. We consider that the minimum cover should be £50,000. This is the minimum cover applicable to solicitors who are in practice in their own account. We consider that the cost of the premiums may properly be taken into account both when barristers' fees are fixed and when they are taxed.

24.13   Whether insurance should be arranged by a group scheme or some other method is a question for the Senate to resolve in the light of the most suitable commercial arrangements available and the best financial interests of practitioners. We understand that the Senate has set up a committee to review the question of compulsory indemnity insurance for barristers in the light of the ruling in the *Saif Ali* case.

Conclusions and Recommendations

Paragraphs

Immunity from suit	R24.1	No change is recommended in the present law relating to a barrister's immunity from suit.	24.6
	R24.2	Such immunity should extend to anyone acting as an advocate in a court of law.	24.7
Indemnity insurance	R24.3	All practising barristers should be required to have professional indemnity insurance cover against claims for negligence.	24.11
	R24.4	Minimum cover should be £50,000; this figure should be reviewed regularly.	24.12

CHAPTER 25

Discipline: Solicitors

Rules of conduct

Discipline in professions

25.1 Members of a profession are part of a private organisation, largely self-regulating, which provides a service to the public. For these reasons, the quality of service and the work and standards of a profession must be maintained at a high level. Accordingly, it is the tradition in all professions that the members serve their clients to the best of their ability and uphold the rules of conduct which have evolved over the years.

25.2 A professional person, like any person conducting a business, is subject to the discipline that his livelihood is dependent upon the quality of his work. If he carries on his practice with competence, his reputation spreads and he attracts work and clients. If he does not produce the quality of work and service which is expected, his reputation suffers and he soon begins to lose clients and fails to attract new ones. A single lapse can be very damaging and one serious mistake may lead to an irretrievable loss of reputation.

25.3 A further discipline which attaches to a person who offers services for a fee is that a single mistake can lead to bankruptcy. As we show in Chapter 30, professional people, and lawyers are no exception, do not normally conduct their business through limited liability companies. Insurance is usually taken out against claims for damages brought by clients, but if the cover is inadequate, the practitioner is liable for the excess to the full amount of both his professional and personal assets.

25.4 We draw attention to the disciplines to which all professional people are subject in the ordinary course of their work because they may not be fully appreciated by the public at large.

Solicitors' discipline

25.5 Apart from the disciplines which apply to professional people generally, solicitors are subject to a number of special restrictions and restraints. In particular, they are officers of the Supreme Court and subject to its jurisdiction. This is reflected in the provisions of sections 50 to 53 of the Solicitors Act 1974, under which the High Court and the Court of Appeal may exercise disciplinary jurisdiction over solicitors and hear applications relating to the conduct of solicitors.

Rules made by the Law Society

25.6   Solicitors are also required to comply with certain rules made by the Law Society, with the approval of the Master of the Rolls, under the Solicitors Act 1974. In this chapter, we deal with the Solicitors' Practice Rules 1936–1972 and the Solicitors' Practice Rules 1975. Other rules which relate to certain financial aspects of a solicitor's practice were discussed in detail in Chapter 23.

The Solicitors' Practice Rules

25.7   These rules lay down the basic principles of professional conduct which every solicitor is required to observe. Some of these rules are relevant to topics discussed elsewhere in this report and are dealt with in detail in the appropriate place. In the following brief summary of the rules, we give our comments or cross-refer to the relevant chapter where the subject is dealt with.

25.8   The rules provide that: —

> (a) A solicitor shall not attempt to gain business by inviting instructions, advertising or touting.

We think that a measure of informative advertising by individual solicitors or firms may be desirable in the public interest. We make recommendations on this topic in Chapter 27.

> (b) Subject to certain detailed exceptions, a firm shall not act for both parties in the transfer or lease of land.

We have made a recommendation on this topic in paragraph 21.64.

> (c) A solicitor shall not agree to share his professional fees except with another solicitor or a lawyer practising in another country.

Our comments on this rule are to be found in Chapters 30 and 31.

> (d) A solicitor shall not act in association with a claims assessor (that is one making, supporting or prosecuting accident claims), or handle a claim for a client introduced by a claims assessor acting as such.

This rule was introduced to prevent "ambulance chasing". This is less common than it once was but we recommend that this rule should remain in force.

> (e) A solicitor shall not act in a contentious matter for a contingency fee.

We endorse this rule for the reasons given in Chapter 16.

> (f) A solicitor shall not show on his nameplate or professional stationery the name of a person other than a solicitor with a current practising certificate except for: —
>> (i) former partners or predecessors;
>> (ii) the established name of the firm.

337

We do not think that, with the exception of those retained as consultants, the names of former partners or predecessors should appear on nameplates or stationery because it might be misleading to the public.

> (g) A solicitor shall ensure that his firm's offices are supervised in accordance with certain minimum standards. Each office shall be managed by a solicitor holding a practising certificate or a fellow of the Institute of Legal Executives of at least five years' standing. Each office must be attended daily by a solicitor who has held a practising certificate for at least three years. Certain exceptions are permitted in relation to staff who were in post when the rules were made.

We commented on this topic in Chapter 22.

25.9 It was put to us in evidence that the approval of these rules (including those dealt with in Chapter 23) should cease to be the responsibility of the Master of the Rolls and instead be that of a new committee consisting of the Master of the Rolls and representatives of bodies such as the National Consumer Council and the Monopolies Commission. The main argument in favour of this proposal is that a committee of this nature would help to ensure that the interests of consumer groups and others were represented.

25.10 The Master of the Rolls, in oral evidence, assured us that, in exercising his functions, he was concerned with the public interest and that although he had not previously done so, he would in future consult those able to offer relevant information or views. While we welcome this assurance, we consider that, in cases where a proposed practice rule concerns a matter which will affect the public interest, for instance rules concerning advertising, clients' money or fees, a copy of the proposed rules should be sent in draft to bodies, such as the National Consumer Council, with a direct interest in it. Such bodies, and also individuals, whether lawyers or laymen, should be free to make representations about the proposed rule to the Master of the Rolls which he should take into account when deciding whether or not the proposed rule should be approved.

Code of conduct

25.11 The practice rules deal with a restricted, but important, sphere of a solicitor's conduct. There also exists an extensive code of conduct described as *A Guide to the Professional Conduct of Solicitors* which the Society issues and, when necessary amends. This is sent to every solicitor on qualification; it is in regular use by practitioners and is a valuable means of maintaining a high standard of professional behaviour.

Complaints against Solicitors

Complaints to the Royal Commission

25.12 In the course of our enquiries, we received from members of the public and other sources a number of complaints about the work carried out by the legal profession, most of which related to the work of solicitors. Information about these complaints and an analysis of them appeared in Chapter 22.

Complaints to the Law Society

25.13 In order to help those who wish to make a complaint, the Law Society has published a pamphlet explaining how it handles complaints and the procedure which should be followed. A copy is sent to anyone who writes to the Law Society saying he wishes to make a complaint about a solicitor. This is to be commended, but the pamphlet has not always been updated as promptly as it should have been. This detracts from its usefulness and we suggest that the Law Society should arrange for regular revisions in future.

25.14 Before making recommendations for changes in the present procedure for dealing with complaints, we indicate below the nature of complaints which may be made to the Law Society. Complaints about solicitors fall into two categories.

25.15 The first category comprises complaints of "professional misconduct". In broad terms professional misconduct means conduct unbefitting a solicitor which includes, for example, moral turpitude, a criminal conviction for a serious offence, theft or misuse of money and similar defaults.

25.16 The second category comprises complaints of incompetence or inefficiency in the performance of professional work; this is sometimes loosely referred to as "professional negligence" but in the remainder of this chapter we use for this purpose the term "bad professional work". In some cases bad professional work may entitle the client to pursue a claim in the courts for damages.

25.17 When complaints of professional misconduct (paragraph 25.15) are brought to the attention of the Law Society, it investigates them and invokes disciplinary proceedings if the circumstances warrant such a course. Complaints of bad professional work are not further examined by the Law Society unless they are of so grave a character as to amount to professional misconduct. The Law Society's attitude to this is explained in the following two paragraphs taken from *A Guide to the Professional Conduct of Solicitors;* it will be seen from this passage that the question as to whether bad professional work amounts to professional misconduct is often difficult to determine.

> Professional negligence by a solicitor may in certain circumstances amount to unbefitting conduct rendering the solicitor liable to disciplinary proceedings, if the conduct is "dishonourable in his profession", or such as to be regarded as deplorable by his fellows in the profession.
>
> It is a question of fact whether the negligence is of such a character and so aggravated as to amount to unbefitting conduct. In this respect standards change

over the years and a higher standard of efficiency and attention to business is now expected of a solicitor than was the case in former years. On the other hand, a single act of negligence by itself, such as failure to issue a writ in time, would not normally involve disciplinary action, although civil proceedings might lie. Failure to disclose to the client, however, that something may have gone amiss and that he should obtain independent advice would amount to unbefitting conduct . . . There may, however, be cases in which the negligence is of such a degree as to amount to unbefitting conduct even though only committed on one occasion.

Statistics about complaints

25.18   In 1978, the Law Society received 5,006 complaints from laymen about solicitors. As had been the case in previous years, approximately 30 per cent of these complaints related to professional misconduct and were considered to warrant further investigation. The remaining 70 per cent, including complaints alleging bad professional work, were complaints which the Law Society did not regard as giving rise to an issue of misconduct and therefore did not consider appropriate for further investigation. The Law Society was unable to tell us how many of these rejected complaints concerned bad professional work nor indeed has it been its normal practice (apart from distinguishing between complaints made by solicitors and those made by others) to classify the complaints received either by nature or by subject matter. We therefore asked the Law Society to make an analysis over a recent period. This was carried out for the three months from the beginning of June to the end of August 1978 and we were informed that the result was as follows.

Total number of complaints received during the period	1,694
Complaints of professional misconduct found to be substantiated	157
Number not considered appropriate for action by the Law Society made up as follows: —	

Containing allegations of negligence	200	
Found to be unsubstantiated	1,294	
Frivolous complaints	43	1,537

The 1,537 complaints which the Law Society did not consider appropriate for censure represented 91 per cent of the total received. The 1,294 complaints that the Society found to be unsubstantiated included not only those which were rejected as not giving rise to an issue of professional misconduct but also those alleging professional misconduct which proved on investigation to be unfounded. The total also included a number of matters which it was not appropriate to investigate. These included the following.

Unjustified but apparently seeking or needing legal advice	86
Complaints not pursued	96
Simple requests for legal advice	30

25.19 We think that it would be advisable for the Law Society to make an analysis in future showing the nature of the complaints received and the action taken and to publish the results annually to its members. It would be helpful to solicitors to know the main areas of complaint so that, in appropriate cases, they can themselves take corrective action. An analysis of this nature would also be helpful to the Law Society in planning its educational and training programmes, in preparing notes for the guidance of solicitors and in laying down Professional Standards. It is relevant to observe that delay in dealing with clients' affairs is acknowledged by the Society as one of the predominant causes of complaint. We discussed this matter further in Chapter 22.

The Professional Purposes Department

25.20 When a complaint about a solicitor is made to the Law Society, it is dealt with initially by the Professional Purposes Department. The department decides whether the complaint is a matter involving professional misconduct by a solicitor. If so, it falls within the 30 per cent referred to in paragraph 25.18 and is dealt with in the way set out in paragraphs 25.31—25.33. As pointed out earlier, the Law Society does not concern itself with the remaining complaints except that, if it appears that the solicitor's performance of his work may have given rise to a possible claim in the courts, the complainant is advised to seek the advice of another solicitor about the possibility of bringing an action. If the complainant alleges both professional misconduct and bad professional work, he will be advised to pursue his claim for damages through the courts before disciplinary action is considered.

The policy for handling complaints

25.21 In the Law Society's response to our questions about advertising, the following statement appeared in a section headed "The Characteristics of a Profession".

> The Society considers it to be the essence of a profession that its rules should be self-imposed. The freedom to frame those rules has to be maintained because the profession itself bears the responsibility for maintaining the standards which the public interest requires.

Although that statement was made in the context of a particular question, it was clearly intended to be of a general character. We agree with the principle which it enunciates.

25.22 In a memorandum, supplemental to its oral evidence given on 2nd June 1978, the Law Society reaffirmed this principle in the following passage.

> It follows that the Society accepts, and has accepted for a great number of years,

responsibility not only for the maintenance of professional standards of behaviour but also for the maintenance of professional standards of competence and efficiency. Clearly, maintaining standards of behaviour, if only by disciplining those who stray from them, is a very much easier task than maintaining an acceptable standard of competence and efficiency throughout the profession. The responsibility does, however, exist.

25.23   In view of the fact, stated in paragraph 25.17, that claims are investigated fully only if they are regarded as matters involving professional misconduct, we are not satisfied that the above principle is always observed; in consequence, many complaints alleging bad professional work are not investigated. There were 200 allegations of negligence among the complaints listed in paragraph 25.18 which were not considered appropriate for action by the Law Society. Moreover, when complaints were made of the type indicated in paragraph 25.20, involving both professional misconduct and a possible claim in the courts, the Law Society in oral evidence said that the element of professional misconduct was seldom investigated.

25.24   We consider that a clear statement of policy by the Law Society is necessary, indicating that unless they are clearly misconceived or frivolous all complaints will be fully investigated and, if appropriate, disciplinary proceedings will ensue. The statement should indicate that this procedure will be followed as regards not only allegations of professional misconduct but also allegations of bad professional work irrespective of whether or not the act complained of may entitle the client to pursue a claim in the courts. We indicate in paragraphs 25.36—25.42 the way in which we recommend the process of investigation and discipline should operate.

25.25   The statement of policy which we recommend will raise a number of administrative problems which the Law Society will need to consider. It will be necessary to define the criteria by which bad professional work should be judged. We think that the test should be the quality of work and service which could reasonably be expected of members of the profession in good standing in the normal conduct of their business. If the Law Society publishes in the future a series of Professional Standards on the lines recommended in Chapter 22, a failure to comply with those Standards will be relevant to this question.

25.26   We have no wish to see the profession walk in fear of unreasonable or draconian measures. Our intention is not to threaten solicitors but to ensure that the Law Society takes action on bad professional work when it occurs. It follows that a solicitor should not be inhibited from giving advice because of the risk of disciplinary proceedings. Provided that his decision or his opinion is based on the research and enquiries which would be normal in the circumstances, he should not be impugned if his judgment proves to be wrong; no one can guarantee always to be right and clients need advice which is unequivocal.

25.27　We do not overlook the fact that bad professional work may entitle the complainant to an award of damages in an action brought against a solicitor. In recommending that bad professional work might expose a practitioner to the risk of disciplinary proceedings, we are not in any way seeking to supplant the function of the court to award damages. As in cases such as a road traffic accident, which may lead to both criminal and civil proceedings, there are two separate issues involved. The action for damages is intended to restore the plaintiff to the position he would have enjoyed had the solicitor not been negligent. Disciplinary procedures are invoked to avoid, as far as possible, a repetition of such failings, not only by the solicitor concerned, but by other solicitors in practice.

25.28　The Law Society's representatives in oral evidence mentioned two difficulties which they thought might arise if disciplinary procedures were taken in cases of bad professional work which involved a claim in the courts. First, they said that the Society's proceedings might be inhibited by the court proceedings. While we accept that disciplinary proceedings might sometimes have to be stayed while an action in court was in progress, the fact that a claim has been or could be made should not operate to block the disciplinary process.

25.29　The Law Society's other concern related to the compulsory indemnity insurance policy which is entered into on behalf of all solicitors (Chapter 23) and to the additional indemnity insurance policies which are taken out on their own account by many firms of solicitors. The policies contain clauses stating how a claim is to be dealt with from the time when it is first intimated. The Law Society considers that disclosures or admissions made in disciplinary proceedings might, on the basis of the clauses at present included in the policies, entitle the underwriters to disclaim liability. We appreciate that this might give rise to difficulty, but we do not think that clauses should be included in indemnity policies which effectively prevent the Society from exercising against its members the disciplinary measures which are necessary to maintain the competence and efficiency of the profession. In any event the passage quoted from the *Guide* in paragraph 25.17 suggests that there have, in the past, been cases involving both professional misconduct and claims against solicitors when, presumably, both of these points were encountered.

25.30　As was noted in paragraph 25.17 above, there is a professional duty on a solicitor who has reason to believe that something may have gone amiss to warn his client to seek independent advice. There is a general impression that it is difficult to find a solicitor who will bring proceedings for negligence against another solicitor. In the past this impression may have been justified, but in 1977 the Law Society recommended that those local law societies which had not already done so should establish panels of solicitors skilled in negligence actions and willing to take on that type of work. Most, if not all, societies have responded to this recommendation. The effect of these arrangements has not yet been assessed by the Law Society but we recommend that this matter should be followed up, so as to ensure that all those who have a claim for recompense will in future have the means to pursue it.

Procedure for dealing with complaints

25.31　If the Professional Purposes Department considers that a complainant's case should be taken up, it requests the complainant's permission to send the complaint to the solicitor for his comments. If the solicitor's reply does not satisfactorily dispose of the matter or the complainant remains dissatisfied, the complaint is then referred to the Professional Purposes Committee which decides how the matter is to be dealt with in the light of all the circumstances. The majority of cases are resolved as a result of further enquiry and explanation. In some cases however, the committee may decide to take no action and if the complainant is still dissatisfied he is told that he may refer the matter to the Lay Observer; we shall revert to this aspect of the procedure later. In the remaining cases, the committee may decide to impose sanctions and for this purpose it has the powers set out in the following paragraph. The number of occasions on which the committee exercised each of the different powers in respect of complaints by or on behalf of clients during 1978 is indicated by figures in parenthesis.

25.32　The powers are as follows.

(a) The committee may, in varying degrees, reprimand the solicitor and, in appropriate cases, particularly in respect of complaints of delay, the solicitor may be required to submit monthly progress reports(23 occasions).

(b) The committee, in exercise of the power given to the Society under the Solicitors Act 1974, may impose conditions on the issue of the solicitor's next practising certificate, that is with effect from the following 1st November, the date on which all practising certificates are issued. Under this power the committee may withhold the next practising certificate from a solicitor (which in effect prevents the solicitor from practising as a principal) or may impose appropriate conditions on the way in which the solicitor practises, for example by a restriction on his practising without a partner (8 occasions).

(c) The committee may decide that proceedings before the Solicitors' Disciplinary Tribunal should be instituted against the solicitor (17 occasions).

(d) The committee may reject the complaint (5 occasions).

25.33　We should point out that, of the complaints which the Law Society at present decides to investigate, approximately 99 per cent are disposed of by the Professional Purposes Department and Professional Purposes Committee in the way we have described. It is necessary to resort to the Solicitors' Disciplinary Tribunal as described in paragraph 25.32 (c) in only a small number of cases.

Suggested changes
25.34   We had evidence of a general feeling of unease about the Law Society's handling of complaints, a feeling that "lawyers look after their own". This is damaging to the profession and we make suggestions below which we believe will be helpful in this respect. In making these proposals, we should add that some of us were able to attend meetings of the Professional Purposes Committee and to examine its papers. We were impressed by the conscientious way in which the committee went about its task and by the amount of time the members devoted to this purpose, without reward. Our proposals should not be regarded as a criticism of the members of the committee, nor of the way in which they undertake their responsibilities.

Investigation of bad professional work
25.35   In the first place we think it is necessary to bring into effect the important change of policy which we have indicated in paragraph 25.24 above. In consequence, the Law Society should deal not only with questions of professional misconduct but also complaints of incompetence or inefficiency, and such matters should be investigated whether or not the complainant has a claim for negligence in the courts against the solicitor concerned.

The investigation and adjudication process
25.36   Two other features of the system should, we think, be altered. The Professional Purposes Department which carries out the investigation process is responsible to the Professional Purposes Committee, the body which adjudicates on those complaints which are not disposed of by the department. In this way, the investigation and adjudication processes are too closely associated. We recommend that the two processes should be separated within the Law Society. The department in charge of investigation should not be the responsibility of the Professional Purposes Committee but of a separate committee of the Council.

Investigation
25.37   All complaints notified to the Law Society should first be examined by an Investigation Committee. The Investigation Committee must be given adequate powers so that it can do its work effectively and it should be empowered, amongst other things, to inspect a solicitor's practice. In some cases, complaints will be found to be ill-founded or unsubstantiated. In others, sympathetic attention can often resolve the problem and satisfy the complainant that his case has been promptly and fairly dealt with.

345

25.38   In planning the administrative work of the committee, arrangements should be made to see that complainants receive prompt replies to their letters. We observed that letters written to complainants were not always happily worded; although technically accurate, they showed a lack of understanding of the complainant's point of view and possible distress and thereby exacerbated existing ill-feeling. The effect in such cases is that the complainant does not feel that his complaint has been adequately dealt with, even if it has been. We think that steps should be taken to improve this aspect of the work.

25.39   When the cause of the complaint is an inadvertent act or oversight on the part of the solicitor, perhaps resulting from inexperience, it should often prove possible to deal with the case in a manner which is satisfactory to the complainant, without resort to formal disciplinary proceedings. The Investigation Committee may find that instead of invoking this costly and time-consuming process, the help and advice of a senior member of the profession would be more appropriate. If, at the same time, the complainant is provided with an explanation and apology, this will often satisfy him that the matter has been adequately dealt with.

25.40   We were told in oral evidence that complaints are often made direct to local law societies who resolve them locally by conciliation without resort to the Law Society in London. This is a helpful way of disposing of such problems. The Investigation Committee of the Law Society should, we think, explore the possibility of using local law societies to provide a conciliation service of this nature in appropriate cases, because personal discussion with a dissatisfied client will often dispose of a complaint which is proving intractable in correspondence.

25.41   We would expect the overwhelming majority of complaints to be disposed of in the above ways during the investigation process. Only a small number of matters would be sent forward to the Professional Purposes Committee for adjudication, or, in fewer cases, to the Solicitors' Disciplinary Tribunal (see paragraph 25.47).

Adjudication
25.42   As pointed out in paragraph 25.36, the members of the Professional Purposes Committee and the staff responsible to it should not be those responsible for the investigation process. Apart from the fact that these proposals are preferable from an administrative point of view, there is an important question of principle. The Professional Purposes Committee has a quasi-judicial responsibility to examine complaints dispassionately and to impose sanctions. It is important that its independent judgment should not appear to be prejudiced; this cannot be relied upon if its members and staff have already been concerned with the investigation process.

346

The lay element

25.43 The second feature calling for alteration is the lack of any active lay element in the bodies and procedures which deal with complaints. The Professional Purposes Committee is composed solely of practising solicitors. This is not a new point. It arose in 1974 when the Solicitors Bill was passing through the House of Commons. To meet public and parliamentary criticism of the lack of any lay influence in the handling of complaints against solicitors, provision was made in section 45 of the Act for there to be lay observers "to examine any written allegations by or on behalf of a member of the public concerning the Society's treatment of a complaint about a solicitor or an employee of a solicitor made to the Society by that member of the public or on his behalf". By virtue of this provision, the Lord Chancellor appointed a Lay Observer on 17th February 1975.

25.44 In paragraph 25.31 above, we described how a complainant who is dissatisfied with the Law Society's refusal to investigate a complaint may refer the matter to the Lay Observer. In his report for the year ended 31st January 1978, the Lay Observer then in office stated that he accepted 121 cases for examination and in 16 of these he criticised the Law Society's treatment of the complaint. In five of these 16 cases, he recommended the Council to consider, or reconsider, the complaint as an issue of conduct.

25.45 Thanks to his personal qualities, the first Lay Observer was successful in representing the public interest in the treatment of complaints. However, he lacked, and told us that he did not wish for, any direct power of intervention in the investigation and disciplinary processes. We agree with those who, in 1974, thought there was a case for direct lay involvement. Accordingly, we recommend that lay members appointed from panels nominated by the Lord Chancellor should sit on the Investigation Committee proposed in paragraph 25.37 and on the Professional Purposes Committee, when it is adjudicating on complaints. Lay members will thus participate in the decisions made by these committees on matters brought before them by their respective staffs. In this way, the lay element will be an active part of, and not a mere adjunct to, the complaints procedures. We think this will lead to increased public confidence in the handling of complaints by the Law Society. The point should be emphasised in the pamphlet on complaints referred to in paragraph 25.13. As a result, the number of cases referred to the Lay Observer may diminish to the point where there ceases to be any need for his services. Further consideration will need to be given to this at the appropriate time.

Powers of the Professional Purposes Committee

25.46 We think that the disciplinary powers of the Professional Purposes Committee set out in paragraph 25.32 should continue but they should be enlarged in the following respects. It will be seen from paragraph 25.32 (b) that the committee can impose conditions on the next, but not the current, practising certificate. It was suggested to us that the committee should be able to withdraw, or impose conditions on, a solicitor's practising certificate at any time during the course of the year. We agree that the committee's powers should be extended to allow this. We think also that where a solicitor has been shown to be incompetent in a particular field of legal aid work, there should be power to make appropriate deletion from the legal aid solicitors lists mentioned in Chapter 27. Furthermore, if the Professional Purposes Committee finds, as the result perhaps of an inspection carried out by the Investigation Committee, that a solicitor's practice is not being conducted in accordance with acceptable standards of competence and efficiency, it should have the right to impose on the conduct of the practice such restrictions or conditions and for such periods as it considers appropriate. The cost of instituting disciplinary proceedings is heavy and we think that the Professional Purposes Committee should, in appropriate cases, have the power already available to the tribunal to require a contribution to the cost from those found to be in default.

The Disciplinary Tribunal

Present powers of the tribunal

25.47 The Professional Purposes Committee has the power to institute proceedings against a solicitor before the Solicitors' Disciplinary Tribunal. This tribunal is an independent body established under the Solicitors Act 1974 and composed of practising solicitors of not less than ten years' standing and lay members who are neither barristers nor solicitors. All members are appointed by the Master of the Rolls. The tribunal is properly constituted if at least three members are present of whom one is a lay member. Any member of the public may commence proceedings before the tribunal but proceedings are normally brought by a solicitor appointed by the Professional Purposes Committee. Hearings before the tribunal are held in private and are conducted in much the same way as those before a court with the parties being present and represented if they so wish. The standard of proof required is the same as that in criminal proceedings: the evidence must prove guilt beyond reasonable doubt. The findings of the tribunal are made public.

25.48 The tribunal may find at any stage of the hearing that there is no case to answer. At the conclusion of the hearing, the tribunal may reject the charge or on finding it proved: —

(a) reprimand the solicitor (8); or

(b) impose a fine not exceeding £750 (17); or

(c) suspend the solicitor's right to practise (usually for a period not exceeding five years) (6); or

(d) order that the solicitor's name be struck off the Roll (14).

The figures in parenthesis indicate the number of orders made, under each heading, in the period 25th August 1978 to 25th April 1979. In two further cases the tribunal imposed no penalty but ordered the solicitor to contribute towards the cost.

25.49 We consider that, as at present, matters remitted to the Disciplinary Tribunal should be confined to those of a serious nature; for example those which involve the possibility of striking a solicitor off the Roll or suspension of his practising certificate for more than one year. The tribunal has the power to impose lesser penalties than the foregoing if, as a result of the hearing, this appears appropriate. Matters of a less serious character should be dealt with by the Professional Purposes Committee in the way we described earlier. At the instance of either the complainant or the solicitor, an appeal should lie to the tribunal from a decision of the Professional Purposes Committee.

25.50 The Disciplinary Tribunal of the Senate to which we refer in Chapter 35 has different powers and structure. We think that the powers of the two tribunals should, as nearly as possible, be the same. Those of the Solicitors' Disciplinary Tribunal should therefore be extended to include the following matters which are at present within the powers of the Disciplinary Tribunal of the Senate: —

(a) power to order a solicitor to repay to his client the fee received in respect of the piece of work which is the subject of the disciplinary proceedings;

(b) the power, similar to that now proposed by the Bar, to require a solicitor to undergo a course of training. The extent of this will depend upon the availability of suitable facilities and a consideration of the circumstances of the solicitors' practice.

25.51 On some occasions, though they are infrequent, a solicitor and a barrister are both involved in the same complaint. If the matter complained of is sufficiently serious to warrant proceedings before their respective Disciplinary Tribunals, we think that arrangements should be made by the tribunals for a joint hearing to take place.

25.52 The proceedings before the Solicitors' Disciplinary Tribunal are at present held in private and we have considered whether in future they should be held in public. Differing views have been expressed. There is much to be said for the proceedings being heard in public; but against this, a complainant might be deterred from pressing charges for fear of details of his private affairs being made public in the course of the proceedings and it might prove harmful to the solicitor though innocent of the misconduct with which he was charged. It is our view that the decision whether the proceedings should be held in public should be at the discretion of the tribunal, which would take into account the representations of both parties .

Appeals
25.53 A solicitor has a right of appeal to the Master of the Rolls against a decision of the Professional Purposes Committee to withhold his practising certificate or impose conditions on it, and the Master of the Rolls may make such order as he sees fit. An appeal against a finding of the tribunal that a charge is proved or against penalty lies to the High Court at the suit of the solicitor, and against a rejection of the charge at the suit of the complainant. Thereafter an appeal lies from the High Court, on a point of law only, to the Court of Appeal and thence, with leave, to the House of Lords. As we indicated in paragraph 25.49, we consider that an appeal from a decision of the Professional Purposes Committee should henceforward lie to the disciplinary tribunal. The procedure for appeals against the findings of the tribunal should remain as hitherto.

The Legal Aid Complaints Tribunals
25.54 In addition to the Solicitors' Disciplinary Tribunal, separate complaints tribunals have been established under both the criminal and civil legal aid schemes. The purpose of these tribunals is to consider complaints about the conduct of solicitors and barristers and to decide whether a person in respect of whom a complaint has been made should be allowed to do legal aid work. We have been informed that although these tribunals were kept in being when the Legal Aid Panels were abolished in 1977, they have not met for many years. In view of this and of the proposals we make above for dealing with cases of incompetence, we consider that it is not necessary to keep these tribunals in being; the authorities dealing with legal aid should, however, have the same power to bring cases to the attention of the Law Society and of the Senate as they have to refer cases to the existing complaints tribunals.

Conclusions and Recommendations

Paragraphs

Practice Rules   R25.1   The Solicitors' Practice Rules should   25.8
be amended as stated in the text.

R25.2   The procedure for approving Practice   25.10
Rules should be changed.

Complaints   R25.3   The Law Society's pamphlet about   25.13
complaints procedures should be
updated regularly.

Paragraphs

	R25.4	The Law Society should analyse and publish details of complaints received.	25.19
Misconduct and negligence	R25.5	It should be the responsibility of the Law Society to take action when cases of bad professional work are brought to its notice. The existence of a potential claim at law by the complainant or provisions in indemnity insurance policies do not absolve the Law Society from this responsibility.	25.24–25.29 and 25.35
	R25.6	The Law Society should ensure that independent legal advice is available for those who allege negligence against solicitors.	25.30
Investigation and adjudication	R25.7	Within the Law Society, the processes of investigation and adjudication of complaints should be separated.	25.36
	R25.8	The standard of correspondence with complainants should be improved.	25.38
	R25.9	Local law societies should, in appropriate cases, provide a conciliation service.	25.40
Lay participation	R25.10	Laymen should be involved in the processes of investigation and adjudication of complaints. The need to continue the appointment of a Lay Observer should be considered.	25.45
Professional Purposes Committee	R25.11	The powers of the Professional Purposes Committee and of the Solicitors' Disciplinary Tribunal should be extended as stated in the text.	25.46 and 25.50
Appeals	R25.12	Appeals from decisions of the Professional Purposes Committee should lie to the Disciplinary Tribunal.	25.53
Complaints tribunals	R25.13	The complaints tribunals established under the criminal and civil legal aid schemes should be discontinued.	25.54

CHAPTER 26

Discipline: Barristers

Rules of Conduct

Introduction

26.1 We have already indicated in this report that a profession is under an obligation to ensure that its clients receive a high standard of service; and that it is incumbent upon the profession to lay down and enforce strict standards both of professional conduct and of competence in the services it provides. The Bar has always recognised that, like the solicitors' profession, it has a responsibility not only to its clients but also to the courts to ensure that justice is done. Its members have therefore been conscious of the need to act against any abuses or failings that might bring the profession, and by implication the administration of justice, into disrepute. In this chapter we examine the arrangements made by the Bar to regulate the conduct of its members, to investigate allegations of misconduct or incompetence and to apply sanctions against barristers in respect of whom such allegations have been substantiated.

Barristers' discipline

26.2 One of the disciplines to which a professional person is subject is that his livelihood is dependent upon the quality of his work. A barrister is particularly vulnerable in this respect because he works under the surveillance of the instructing solicitor whom he knows will be unlikely to instruct him again if work is inadequately performed. Furthermore, much of his work is carried out in public before the courts where failures of behaviour or of standards of work may expect to attract judicial comment or complaint. Although the loss of clients may, in the long run, prove an effective sanction against a persistent offender, it is nevertheless no substitute for an effective professional disciplinary system.

Rules of conduct and etiquette

26.3 All practising barristers are required to observe the rulings or recommendations on matters of professional conduct which are formulated by the Professional Conduct Committee of the Bar Council and endorsed by the full Bar Council. These rulings are brought to their notice by various means including publication both in the Senate's annual statement and in the *Guardian Gazette* which is received by all subscribing members of the Bar. The rulings are also summarised in Boulton's *Conduct and Etiquette at the Bar,* a copy of which is given to every barrister who expresses the intention of subscribing to the Senate, at the time he is called to the Bar. Among the many subjects covered are the acceptance of instructions, briefs and pleadings, fees, advertising and conduct in court. At the time we were drafting our report the Bar Council had in course of preparation a code of professional conduct, with the purpose of bringing up to date and consolidating extant rulings. It was expected to be released in 1980.

26.4 We are satisfied that the existing system whereby the Bar lays down rules of conduct for its members is sound and operates in the public interest. Apart from those rules which will need revision in the light of our recommendations in other chapters, we see no need for general changes in the Bar's rules of conduct.

Complaints against Barristers

Incompetence

26.5 In Chapter 22 we analysed the volume and nature of complaints against barristers and, in some cases, suggested remedies. We also indicated both in that chapter and in Chapter 25 that the legal profession should take action if the work of its members falls below an acceptable standard. The Senate is alive to this responsibility and said in its evidence to us that—

> incompetence ought to be controlled whether or not barristers are liable at law for negligence.

We agree with this view and feel that the disciplinary procedures of the Bar should in future reflect this attitude.

26.6 This has already been reflected in practice for some years in serious cases. Thus, Boulton quotes the 1972 annual statement of the General Council of the Bar as follows : —

> Professional misconduct or conduct unbecoming a barrister can include such professional incompetence on the part of a member of the Bar as would be likely to be detrimental to the proper administration of justice or otherwise bring the profession into disrepute.

26.7 More recently, the Bar has taken powers enabling it to deal with cases of incompetence which are not sufficiently serious to amount to professional misconduct. We discuss these powers, which have already been applied in a number of cases, in a later paragraph.

The Professional Conduct Committee

26.8 Complaints about barristers are handled, in the first instance, by the Professional Conduct Committee of the Bar Council. This consists of 15 members of the Senate, at least one of whom must be a barrister in employment, together with two laymen (of whom only one is present at each meeting) co-opted from a panel nominated by the Lord Chancellor. Under a self-imposed rule, no complaint is rejected unless the lay member present agrees.

Dealing with a complaint

26.9 Until recently, the preliminary investigation of a possible breach of professional conduct, including gross professional incompetence, was carried out by a barrister member of the Professional Conduct Committee in his spare time. A solicitor was sometimes also instructed. Since October 1977 the Senate has employed a full-time investigation officer and is also reviewing the committee's procedures with the aim of completing investigations more quickly. We welcome this development which is clearly in the interests both of complainants and of barristers who are the subject of complaint.

The investigation and adjudication processes

26.10 The role of the investigation officer is limited to ascertaining the facts of the matter under complaint and placing these before the Professional Conduct Committee. The investigation officer has, therefore, no powers to reject a complaint or to declare it outside the purview of the committee; such decisions can only be reached by the committee itself. Furthermore the investigation officer only examines those complaints, usually from lay clients, where the information supplied is inadequate to enable the committee to reach a decision. The number of complaints handled by this officer is, therefore, small.

Interviewing the lay complainant

26.11 When complaints were investigated by a barrister member of the Professional Conduct Committee, information might be sought from solicitors and other barristers concerned in the case, the clerk of the court and other persons with knowledge of the case. It was however considered impractical for the barrister member of the Committee to interview lay complainants, partly because many were unavailable, in some cases in prison, and partly because the barrister conducting the investigation as a voluntary service in out-of-court hours was unable to afford the necessary time. The complainant was, however, informed of the committee's findings and had the opportunity to ask that they be reconsidered.

26.12 The appointment of a full-time investigation officer has made the interviewing of lay complainants less difficult and we understand that he interviews complainants whenever possible. We believe that if the public is to have confidence in the procedure whereby complaints are investigated, it is essential that this is seen to be thorough and that a complainant should normally be given the opportunity to explain his case, however trivial or misguided this might appear. Accordingly, we recommend that, whenever practicable, an interview with the lay complainant should form a normal part of the investigative process.

Responsibility for investigation

26.13   In Chapter 25 we recommended that, in relation to the solicitors' branch of the profession, the process of investigating complaints should be separated from the adjudication process. We think that for the reasons there given, the same principle should be followed by the Bar and that the investigation officer should be responsible to a separate Investigation Committee of the Senate and not to the Professional Conduct Committee.

Lay membership

26.14   As we observed in paragraph 26.8, another recent development is the introduction of a lay member to the Professional Conduct Committee, along with the self-imposed rule that no complaint should be rejected unless the layman present agrees. We are satisfied that the Bar has been punctilious in examining complaints and that disciplinary proceedings have always been conducted with integrity. The public, however, does not always have complete confidence in such bodies if they are open to the allegation that they protect their colleagues. Accordingly, we regard the above development as not only desirable but necessary.

Disciplinary Procedures

Powers of the Professional Conduct Committee

26.15   The courses of action open to the Professional Conduct Committee are to: —

(a)   dismiss the complaint or decide that no action is required; or

(b)   advise or admonish the barrister either informally or formally; or

(c)   in grave cases, prefer a charge on behalf of the Senate before the Disciplinary Tribunal of the Senate.

Where advice or admonition is decided upon, this may be given by the chairman of the committee or some other person such as a judge, circuit leader or head of chambers.

26.16   During the year ending 31st March 1979, the committee disposed of 179 complaints, as follows.

Rejected on grounds of no professional misconduct	80
Referred to Disciplinary Tribunal	14
Minor misconduct—admonished	6
Minor incompetence or breach of etiquette—advice given	8
Dealt with informally by the Chairman	15
Withdrawn or no action taken	13
Still under investigation	43
	179

Source: Annual Statement for 1978/79 of the Senate of the Inns of Court and the Bar.

Extended powers of the Professional Conduct Committee

26.17   In April 1977, the Bye-Laws of the Bar Council were amended to empower the Professional Conduct Committee to deal both with minor acts of professional misconduct and minor cases of incompetence or breach of etiquette falling short of misconduct. Serious cases falling under these headings remain the subject of a charge before the Disciplinary Tribunal of the Senate.

26.18   The powers now available to the Professional Conduct Committee and the Disciplinary Tribunal of the Senate to deal with matters of incompetence are important. They conform to the recommendations which we have made in Chapter 25 in relation to the solicitors' branch of the profession that, if the quality of service provided by the legal profession is to be maintained and improved, incompetence, delay and failure to meet accepted standards of professional work should be the subject of disciplinary procedures.

26.19   In paragraphs 25.25—25.29, we pointed out that such proposals raise a number of administrative problems. So far as these same problems affect the Bar they will require consideration by the Senate. In particular, if actions for negligence are brought against barristers, it will be necessary to consider the timing of disciplinary proceedings and the conditions included in barristers' indemnity insurance policies.

Training

26.20   The present powers of the Professional Conduct Committee to order that a barrister be given advice may not be sufficient to bring his performance up to a requisite standard of competence. The Senate accordingly suggested in evidence to us that a barrister who had been incompetent could be ordered to undergo further training. We agree with this suggestion. As we indicated in paragraph 25.50, the extent of such training must depend on the facilities available and consideration of the circumstances of the barrister's practice.

The Disciplinary Tribunal of the Senate

26.21 The Disciplinary Tribunal of the Senate consists of from four to six practising members of the Senate and a layman (co-opted from the same panel as the lay member of the Professional Conduct Committee) under a standing chairman, currently a Lord Justice of Appeal. The tribunal must always include at least one member of the Inn of the barrister charged and, should he be in employment, an employed barrister must also sit on the tribunal. No member of the Professional Conduct Committee who has been concerned with the investigation or adjudication of a matter may sit on the tribunal that hears the charge.

26.22 The tribunal, after hearing the case may dismiss the charge; or on finding it proved : —

(a) decide to take no action; or

(b) reprimand the barrister; or

(c) order him to repay or forgo fees; or

(d) suspend his membership of the Bar; or

(e) order that he be disbarred.

26.23 During the year ending 31st March 1979, Disciplinary Tribunals were convened on 12 occasions with the following results.

Disbarred	5
Suspended	1
Ordered to repay fees	–
Reprimanded	4
No action	1
Charges dismissed	1
	12

26.24 In paragraph 25.50 we recommended that the powers of the Solicitors' Disciplinary Tribunal and the Disciplinary Tribunal of the Senate should as nearly as possible be the same. Accordingly, we think that the powers of the Disciplinary Tribunal of the Senate should be enlarged to correspond with those of the solicitors' tribunal so that it can compel the appearance of witnesses and the production of documents; it should also have the power to impose a fine.

26.25   In paragraph 25.52 we indicated the circumstances in which we thought that the proceedings of the Solicitors' Disciplinary Tribunal should be held in public. We consider that similar arrangements should be made in respect of the Disciplinary Tribunal of the Senate.

Appeals

26.26   An appeal against the findings of the tribunal or the penalty imposed may be made to judges sitting as visitors to the barrister's Inn. During the year ending 31st March 1979, three barristers entered such appeals. One appeal was concluded before the end of that year; the finding was confirmed but the period of suspension was reduced. No changes in the present arrangements have been proposed to us and we recommend none.

Inns and circuits

26.27   The Inns of Court exercise a residual jurisdiction affecting personal conduct within the precincts of the Inn and over the discipline of students. Some circuits exercise disciplinary powers in an informal way, by admonition and advice. These cases apart, all disciplinary matters not concluded by the Professional Conduct Committee are remitted to the Disciplinary Tribunal. As we state in Chapter 32, we consider a strong regional organisation is an important element in the management of a profession and in that connection we recommend a review of the powers and functions of the circuits. Nonetheless in our opinion disciplinary matters of any substance are best handled centrally, although the circuits may have a valuable role to play, for example in investigation and conciliation.

The Senate's proposed review of disciplinary procedures

26.28   In the course of a submission made to us in August 1978, the Senate stated that it had embarked on a thorough review of disciplinary procedures; we hope that the observations made in the preceding paragraphs may be of some assistance in this regard. The submission proposed that the call declaration by barristers should be amended to include a positive declaration to abide by the rules of conduct and practice for the Bar as published by the Senate. We support this proposal.

Conclusions and Recommendations

Paragraphs

Rules of conduct   R26.1   The present rules of conduct and the   26.4
procedure whereby they are made are
sound.

358

Paragraphs

Complaints	R26.2	Complainants should whenever possible be interviewed.	26.12
	R26.3	The processes of investigation and adjudication of complaints should be separated.	26.13
Disciplinary sanctions	R26.4	The Senate should have the responsibility of taking action when cases of bad professional work are brought to its notice.	26.18
	R26.5	The Professional Conduct Committee should have power to order further training if a barrister is not considered to be competent.	26.20
Senate's Disciplinary Tribunal	R26.6	The Disciplinary Tribunal of the Senate should be able to compel the appearance of witnesses and the production of documents, and to impose a fine.	26.24

CHAPTER 27

Information for the Public

Introduction

The need for information

27.1 Among the causes of unmet needs, we identified in Chapter 4 lack of knowledge that a particular problem requires legal advice and lack of information about the availability and location of solicitors and about the type of work they are willing to undertake. Later in Part II we made recommendations intended to alleviate this difficulty. One was that general awareness of the law should be improved by teaching the subject in schools, another that access to legal services should be developed through generalist advice agencies, able to identify legal problems and to refer clients with such problems to lawyers willing and able to deal with them. No such measures will be as effective as they should be unless they are backed up with information about the services provided by lawyers in general and the specific services provided by individual solicitors in particular areas. Such information should be available not only to citizens advice bureaux and other organisations which refer clients to solicitors but also to any member of the general public who has need of them. In this chapter, therefore, we examine the availability of information about legal services, its content and quality and the way in which it is made known to the prospective client, either directly or through the medium of CABx and other bodies.

The need for safeguards

27.2 The need to inform the public about available legal services must not be allowed to conflict with the need to maintain high standards of integrity and performance by members of the legal profession. The public would be ill-served if the provision of information became an excuse for touting for business in hospital casualty departments, for making inflated claims of expertise and for deliberately reducing standards of service so as to compete in a price war or if it led to the disappearance of smaller firms. Accordingly, we shall examine not merely the need to provide information to the public but also the need to restrict advertising and touting by solicitors. The public interest requires a balance to be struck between these potentially conflicting principles so that the flow of information to the public may be substantially increased while at the same time proper control is maintained over the professional conduct of solicitors.

Means of informing the public

27.3   There are three means, each appropriate to a certain kind of information and directed to a particular purpose, by which details of the availability and extent of legal services can be made available to potential clients and those who have need of them. These are as follows.

(a)   *Corporate advertising and official publicity*
This form of advertising can be of value in informing the public about the nature and availability of legal services provided by solicitors generally and it may also be used to stimulate demand for such services.

(b)   *Referral lists*
These indicate to a prospective client where he may find a solicitor willing to handle his particular problem; their purpose would be to inform rather than to promote competition or stimulate demand. As we describe in paragraphs 27.9 and 27.10 below, the Law Society has issued referral lists for legal aid purposes.

(c)   *Individual advertising*
This form of advertising can be used by individual firms of solicitors to inform potential clients of matters such as their experience, qualifications, charges, business address and hours of opening; it may also increase the business of the firm concerned in competition with other solicitors.

27.4   We received evidence from a large number of witnesses, including members of the legal profession, other professional bodies, organisations providing advice and assistance and other users of legal services that one of the main requirements of the public was for more information about legal services that are available locally. We are satisfied that it is here that the emphasis in publicising legal services should be laid.

Corporate Advertising and Official Publicity

Advertising by the profession

27.5   At various times, the Law Society has promoted advertising campaigns to explain the role of solicitors and encourage the public to seek their services. In 1977 the Society mounted the "Whatsisname" campaign and promoted a national information campaign between April and July 1979. It issues information leaflets about the services which it provides in respect of matters such as complaints against solicitors and the compensation fund, subjects which we cover in other chapters, and has issued a number of other publications. A recent example is the magazine *Exchange Contracts*, given free by solicitors to clients instructing them in conveyancing transactions. The Society has also developed an extensive Schools Education Programme which contains information on many aspects of the law and the work of lawyers. The Society is

361

investigating a long term strategy for the teaching of law in schools. Without going into matters of timing or style, we consider as a general principle that it is a proper function of the governing body of a profession to improve public knowledge of the services provided by its members. Such publicity has the advantage over individual advertising that it promotes the services of the profession as a whole rather than those of individual practitioners.

27.6 The Law Society recently granted a general waiver from the practice rule concerning advertising so as to enable local law societies to publish in the local press at intervals of not less than one month the names and addresses of local firms of solicitors, specifying the categories of work which they are willing to undertake. This development is to be welcomed. We consider the next step should be for local law societies to make public in other ways comprehensive lists of the firms practising in their areas. This could be achieved by means of permanent advertisements or notices in, for example, the yellow pages of the local telephone directory or on notice boards in courts, police stations, local government offices, public libraries, community centres and other appropriate places. We believe, furthermore, that the information given in these advertisements or notices should give as much detail as possible of the information contained in the legal aid solicitors lists.

Official publicity

27.7 There are many aspects of the law and legal services about which the public should be kept informed but which it is not the responsibility of the legal profession to publicise. We have in mind the functions performed by courts and tribunals, services, such as legal aid, which are publicly funded, and the effect of new legislation. We receive evidence from the National Association of Citizens Advice Bureaux that information on such matters, and in particular on the effect of new legislation, was often not available to the public at the time when it was needed. We regard it as the function of government departments and other bodies with statutory responsibilities to ensure that the public is given the required information. In the paragraph following we make specific recommendations which are designed to improve the flow of information to the public.

27.8 The main weakness of general advertising, whether by the profession, the government or any other body, is that its impact is slight unless the campaign is sustained. It should, therefore, be supplemented by information which is continuously available and specifically directed to those who have need of it. Accordingly, we recommend that every private person who is involved as a party in proceedings before a court or tribunal should as a matter of routine be informed at the outset about the availability and conditions of legal aid. We further recommend that information about legal services and the means of obtaining them should be prominently displayed in all social security offices, courts, police stations and prisons. This should include, where appropriate, information about duty solicitors (see Chapter 9). This information should be backed-up by leaflets on specific aspects of the law, such as those provided by the Office of Fair Trading on consumer law, which should be freely available in CABx, public libraries and any suitable place frequently used by the public. Such leaflets should be produced and distributed as a matter of routine.

Referral Lists

The present position
27.9   The Law Society and the profession in general have a major role to play not merely in informing the public about the legal services provided by solicitors in general but also in advising anyone who has an immediate need for a specific service where this may be obtained. The Law Society has accepted that detailed information about the work done by individual firms of solicitors should be made available to prospective clients and for some time past has produced, on a regional basis, detailed referral lists of the firms who are willing to undertake work under the legal aid scheme. These are now known as the legal aid solicitors lists.

27.10   The first such lists, consisting of 28 booklets, each covering a separate area, were published in December 1976. These listed over 7,000 offices and indicated which of 14 categories of legally-aided work each firm was prepared to undertake. Over 25,000 copies were distributed to various agencies approached by the public for information about solicitors, including CABx, consumer advice centres, local authority social services departments, the probation service and numerous welfare agencies, advice centres, courts, public libraries, town halls and police stations. The second and third editions, for 1978 and 1979, are in the same format but contain a number of improvements suggested by agencies which had received copies of the first edition. The most important improvement is that the lists indicate which firms are prepared to give an initial interview of up to half an hour for a fee of not more than £5 inclusive of VAT. Each firm listed may now also choose to give one emergency telephone number at which a solicitor may be contacted outside normal working hours and may give the opening times of any office or branch office which is not open in both the mornings and afternoons from Mondays to Fridays. We include, in annex 27.1, a typical page from a current legal aid solicitors list.

27.11   The introduction of these lists has been helpful to advice agencies and of benefit to the public. The lists have yet to realise their full potential and in the following paragraphs we suggest some ways in which they may be developed. This should not, however, be taken to belittle the achievement of the Law Society in producing and distributing this source of information.

Criticisms of the legal aid solicitors lists
27.12   The main criticisms of the legal aid solicitors lists to have come to our attention are as follows.

(a) The lists are not sufficiently available directly to members of the public.

(b) The lists are not sufficiently detailed to enable members of the public in all cases to make an informed choice of solicitor.

(c) The lists indicate which firms are willing to undertake specific kinds of work but give no indication of their experience of, or competence in, such work.

Availability

27.13 We doubt whether any useful purpose would be served by increasing the number of organisations to which the lists are regularly sent. It would, however, be helpful if the existence of the lists was more widely known to the general public. We recommend, therefore, that the Law Society should advertise the issue of new legal aid solicitors lists in the national and local press, including, where appropriate, information about where the local list may be consulted. The cost of such advertisements, like the cost of producing the lists, should be borne out of the legal aid fund. The lists should be freely available in referral agencies and elsewhere for consultation by members of the public. In addition, provided the cost is not too great, copies or photocopies of extracts should be made available to organisations and individual members of the public if reasonably required.

Detailed information

27.14 We recommend that, in future issues, more information should be supplied about the firms offering their services. In particular, the names of the partners and an indication as to whether firms provide services outside normal working hours, for example in the evening or on Saturday mornings, should be given. If suitable arrangements can in future be made to identify specialists in particular aspects of the law, on the lines suggested in later paragraphs, we think that their names should be shown in the lists.

Ability to undertake services listed

27.15 It has been suggested that a defect in the existing lists is that some solicitors may hold themselves out as willing to accept certain types of work of which they have no experience or which they are not equipped to handle. This does not mean that solicitors should be limited to offering only those services in which they specialise or have expert knowledge. It is proper for a solicitor to offer services in any field in which he considers himself competent to practise; if, however, he offers a service in which he is unable to achieve a sufficient standard, this should be regarded as an abuse of the lists.

27.16 This problem is not capable of a simple solution. An independent check cannot be made on every entry in the lists; their contents must be left largely to the good sense and ethical standards of the solicitors concerned. It should, however, be made clear by the Law Society to all firms of solicitors that, because entries in legal aid solicitors lists are taken by the public as an indication that the firms listed are able to provide an adequate service in the types of work set out against their respective names, the information must not be misleading, and that, if it is established that a firm has held itself out to do work of which it is incapable, disciplinary proceedings may ensue and the name of the firm be deleted from future lists.

Specialisation

General principles

27.17 The increasing complexity of legislation and case law means that no solicitor can be competent in handling every kind of problem. As we have pointed out in previous chapters of this report, there will be a growing demand for specialisation in particular branches of the law both among solicitors and barristers. We do not, however, imply that all lawyers should be specialists; both generalists and specialists are needed in every profession, each offering complementary services.

Specialisation in other countries and other professions

27.18 There is a trend towards recognising specialist skills among certain professions both in Britain and overseas. In the United States various state Bars have adopted systems by which lawyers may claim a special qualification in certain branches of the law. In California, for example, since 1971 lawyers who have been in practice for at least five years may obtain certification as specialists by attending a course and passing an examination. Certification was originally available in three subjects but in 1976 those responsible for administering the scheme made known their intention to increase the number of subjects in which certification is possible. In Britain, members of professions who practise as specialists include not only doctors but also engineers and architects. The Royal Institute of British Architects publishes a directory of practices, in which architects are permitted to specify the work they have done.

Specialisation by solicitors

27.19 The increasing complexity of the law will encourage this trend towards specialisation in the future. Provided that the characteristics of a specialist can be defined satisfactorily, we see no reason why a solictor should not describe himself as such. It would be of assistance to the public if specialists in particular subjects were permitted to be included under suitable descriptions in legal aid solicitors lists or other referral lists and similar material.

The role of the Law Society

27.20 We consider therefore, that a move should be made in this direction and that initial action by the Law Society might proceed on the following lines. It will first be necessary to define the categories of legal work which are suitable for specialisation. We think that the number of topics chosen should, initially, be small; progress thereafter should be in stages and the list should be extended in the light of experience. Particular attention should be paid to areas of work in which there is, at any given time, a shortage of solicitors with specialist knowledge and experience, such as juvenile work.

Eligibility for designation as a specialist
27.21 We suggest that the following criteria should be satisfied.

(a) Designation should be granted to an individual and not to a firm. The solicitor concerned should have held a full practising certificate for at least five years immediately preceding his application.

(b) The solicitor should have devoted at least one-quarter of his time to the subject in question during each of the last five years.

(c) No solicitor should be designated as a specialist in more than two subjects at any one time.

(d) The claim to be designated as a specialist should be by written application to the Law Society which should satisfy itself that the work carried out by the applicant has been such as to justify the designation of specialist. The names of referees should be provided if requested by the Law Society.

(e) The applicant should be interviewed by a panel of three experienced practitioners who should investigate in confidence the professional record and work of the applicant in order to determine whether the designation of specialist would be justified.

27.22 Applicants satisfying these criteria would be entitled to describe themselves as specialists in the appropriate category of work on their firm's writing paper, in the Solicitors' Directory, in the legal aid solicitors lists and other referral lists and in advertisements. A solicitor who has been recognised as a specialist should certify on every successive application for an annual practising certificate that he has devoted at least one-quarter of his normal working time to his specialism. A solicitor who ceases to meet this requirement should no longer be entitled to claim to specialise in it. In the event of a complaint being upheld against a solicitor's conduct or competence in his specialism, his designation as a specialist should be reviewed.

Summary
27.23 We believe that the formal introduction of specialisation into the solicitors' profession will, in the long term, prove to be of significant benefit to the public. We recognise, however, that such a development cannot be introduced overnight and that a considerable period of experiment and refinement will be needed before it is fully established.

Individual Advertising

The present position

27.24   Corporate advertising and detailed referral lists are regarded as acceptable by the profession but advertising by individual solicitors or firms remains prohibited. This prohibition, with those against inviting instructions and touting for business are contained in rule 1 of the Solicitors Practice Rules 1936—1972, in the following terms.

A solicitor shall not obtain or attempt to obtain professional business by : —

    (a) directly or indirectly without reasonable justification inviting instructions for such business, or

    (b) doing or permitting to be done without reasonable justification anything which by its manner, frequency or otherwise advertises his practice as a solicitor, or

    (c) doing or permitting to be done anything which may reasonably be regarded as touting.

The position in other countries

27.25   The prohibition of advertising by individual practitioners has long been regarded as a characteristic of a profession; with few exceptions, it applies to all professions both in the United Kingdom and abroad. The International Bar Association has ruled that it is improper for a lawyer to solicit business. The Union Internationale des Avocats has said that a lawyer should rely only on the quality of service to distinguish him from others. In the EEC, the Commission Consultative des Barreaux de la Communauté Européenne (CCBE) observed that : —

. . . in the context of harmonisation of lawyers' professional rules and practices, the Commission Consultative finds that professional publicity for the individual is in principle forbidden by all the Bars and lawyers.

The CCBE set up, in October 1978, a working party on the subject of advertising and specialisation. A certain measure of individual advertising is permitted in Canada, Denmark, Norway and Sweden. In the United States in June 1977 the Supreme Court held by a majority, in *Bates* v. *State Bar of Arizona,* that it was unconstitutional to prevent lawyers advertising the availability and cost of routine legal services. The Court suggested that advertising should be controlled by specifying certain forms and methods which were unsuitable. In the light of this decision, the American Bar Association amended its Code of Professional Responsibility so as to permit lawyers to advertise both in print and on radio and television. Among the information that may be included in advertisements are details of fees, the fields in which a lawyer practises and, with their consent, the names of clients for whom a lawyer acts regularly. We understand that appropriate regulations have been introduced by State Bars but that only some three per cent of American lawyers have chosen to advertise.

The reports of the Monopolies Commission

27.26   Restrictions on advertising by solicitors were the subject of two recent reports by the Monopolies Commission. Of these the first, in 1970 (Cmnd. 4463), was concerned with restrictive practices in the professions in general. The more recent report, published in July 1976 (HOC 557), was concerned only with advertising by solicitors. In its 1970 report, the Commission suggested in paragraph 347 that restrictions on advertising should not be such as to prevent "publicity by individual practitioners that is informative in the sense that primarily it provides information about the availability of services". In 1976, the Commission went further: it remarked that advertising was also valuable for the purpose of promoting competition and found that the present restrictions on advertising by solicitors were against the public interest on the grounds that: —

(a) they prevented the public, and potential new entrants to the profession, being given information about the services offered by individual solicitors or firms of solicitors;

(b) they were likely to have a disadvantageous effect on the competitiveness and efficiency of the profession generally, on the introduction of innovatory methods and services, and on the setting up of new practices;

(c) they might in some degree enhance the importance of other less open and challengeable methods of attracting business and detract from the public confidence in the profession.

27.27   The Monopolies Commission recommended that the current rules prohibiting advertising and touting should be replaced by a rule which permitted any solicitor in England and Wales to use such publicity as he might think fit, provided that: —

(a) no advertisement, circular or other form of publicity used by a solicitor should claim for his practice superiority in any respect over any or all other solicitors' practices;

(b) such publicity should not contain any inaccuracies or misleading statements;

(c) while advertisements, circulars and other publicity might make clear the intention of the solicitor to seek custom, they should not be of a character that could reasonably be regarded as likely to bring the profession into disrepute.

27.28   The findings of the Monopolies Commission have been strongly criticised by the profession on a number of grounds. Chief among these are the following.

(a) Individual advertising might have an adverse effect on the relationship of trust between solicitors and their clients and between solicitors themselves; it might also have a prejudicial effect on the discharge by solicitors of their duties to the court.

(b) Solicitors are not free agents in their choice of working methods. Much of what they do is governed by rules of the court and the prices that they may charge are subject to independent review and taxation. The scope for innovation and cost saving is therefore limited; in consequence, the effect of competition, enhanced by advertising, would not be to raise standards but to increase overhead costs to the detriment of the smaller practice, the newcomer and the client.

(c) If advertising led to excessive competition with undercutting and unrealistic offers as to the form of the service or the time it would take, there would follow a deterioration in standards and in the reputation of the profession as a whole.

General principles

27.29 We have re-examined all the arguments both for and against individual advertising by solicitors. The most important is the interest of the client. Prospective clients should be provided with the fullest information about the availability of legal services that is consonant with the maintenance of high standards of professional work and probity.

27.30 A number of witnesses argued that the promotion of competition between solicitors for its own sake, by means of advertising compaigns vaunting the superior services provided by a particular firm as compared with those of other firms in the locality, would not be in the public interest, and that, because solicitors' prices and standards are controlled by independent judicial and administrative processes, competitive advertising could not lead to the provision either of services of a high standard or of services of the same standard at a lower price. It was also said that advertising would lead a solicitor's services to be less sensitive to the individual needs and circumstances of the client. The minority opinion in the United States Supreme Court case of *Bates* v. *State Bar of Arizona* was that advertising of professional services differed from the advertising of tangible products in that it had a greater potential for deception and was more difficult to control effectively.

27.31 This opinion has particular force in relation to advertisements seeking to promote the services provided by one individual or firm at the expense of others. We accept, therefore, that this form of advertising should not be permitted. We believe, however, that in other respects the views set out in the preceding paragraph are over-cautious; the fact that some individual professional advertising is bad does not mean that it must all be bad. Advertising is inherent in any free or mixed economy and helps the consumer exercise the choice between competing products or services which characterises such economies. The potential of advertisements to mislead or offend has long been realised; consequently, advertisements of goods and services are closely regulated. Potential clients should have a choice between those who offer the services which they require. It follows that, subject to the appropriate controls, advertising is necessary to enable the individual client to exercise a properly informed choice.

27.32   In our view, the present rule prohibiting all personal advertising by solicitors is too restrictive. There are circumstances in which advertising by individual solicitors is appropriate. Among the examples we have in mind are the newly-established firm or the recently-qualified specialist. It is in their potential clients' interests as well as their own that they should make themselves known in their locality. A solicitor who is in direct competition with non-solicitors, such as banks who are themselves permitted to advertise, should be enabled to compete on equal terms. The freedom of a client's choice should lead to competition among solicitors in offering high standards and reasonable prices; the effects are not the same as those of competitive advertising described in paragraph 27.30.

27.33   We have already acknowledged the value of referral lists and corporate advertising, and the steps recently taken by the Law Society to enable and encourage local law societies to publish in the press the names and addresses of local solicitors and the types of work they undertake. Two members of the Commission would prefer in this way to channel all advertising, including advertising on behalf of individual firms, through local law societies. We are also aware that the Law Society now permits solicitors to announce in the press the establishment of new practices and branch offices, amalgamations, retirements, changes of address, changes of opening hours and telephone numbers and that the number of announcements permitted has recently been increased. Furthermore, the Law Society has recently allowed solicitors opening new or branch offices to send a circular letter to, and establish personal contact with, the agencies who receive copies of a legal aid solicitors list, thereby enabling the agencies to keep the list up to date. We welcome all these developments, which have occurred since this Commission was first established; they will undoubtedly increase the flow of information that is available to advisory agencies and to the public. Nevertheless, despite these improvements, we are not convinced that these arrangements provide all the information that is required by members of the public at the time when it is most needed.

27.34   A proper balance may be struck between the need for the public to be adequately informed and the need for the standards of the profession to be maintained, provided that the primary purpose of advertisements by solicitors is to inform the client about the availability of legal services. We are aware that the purpose of advertising is to attract business and of the difficulty in distinguishing informative advertising from that which promotes the services of one solicitor at the expense of others. Nevertheless, the good sense of the profession, combined with detailed regulations as to the form and content of advertisements, should ensure that there is no abuse. We consider that, with the restrictions which we discuss below, a limited amount of personal advertising will be of benefit to the public.

Restrictions on individual advertising

27.35 In order that all advertising by individual solicitors or firms shall be properly conducted, advertisements should conform with the principles enunciated in 1976 by the Monopolies Commission which we set out in paragraph 27.27 above. Furthermore, the information contained in such advertisements should be restricted to: —

(a) the name, address, telephone and telex numbers, the telegraphic address and the description of the firm as "solicitors";

(b) the names, professional and academic qualifications and recognised specialisms (if any) of the partners and the dates of their qualification as solicitors;

(c) any other addresses from which the firm carries on practice;

(d) the hours of opening;

(e) the types of legal work which the firm is willing and not willing to undertake and whether it is prepared to accept legal aid work;

(f) details of any fixed charges including charges based on an *ad valorem* scale;

(g) knowledge of foreign languages including languages of ethnic minorities;

(h) if appropriate, the statement that a brochure of the type mentioned in paragraph 27.40 below is available on request.

27.36 In order to avoid claims of superiority and to forestall excessive competition, solicitors should not be permitted to advertise publicly the quality of their service, or the numbers of staff other than partners, the fee income or case load of their firms. The same prohibition should also apply to information about fees charged, unless these are of a fixed amount. There should also be prohibited, to preserve the ethical standards of the profession and the confidentiality which clients are entitled to expect from their legal advisers, any reference to other clients of the firm and the work undertaken on their behalf

371

or any mention of reduced fees in consideration of the solicitor being given other work.

27.37 The principles we have stated above carry the implication that advertising by individual firms of solicitors should be limited in scale and aimed specifically at the public in their particular locality. An appropriate medium for such advertisements is, therefore, the local press. Some of us would define this term to include London evening newspapers and also would see no reason why advertising on local radio and television should be excluded; others of us would prefer to tread more cautiously. A large majority of us consider that the public interest would not be served by the use of forms of advertising of which the cost could be borne only by wealthy firms.

The role of the Law Society
27.38 All existing methods of control over advertising would apply in the case of solicitors, but the additional detailed regulation and monitoring required in the case of professional advertising would have to be undertaken by the Law Society. We recommend, therefore, that the Law Society should formulate and introduce regulations concerning such things as the contents of the advertisements (see paragraph 27.35 above), the form of text and type face, the frequency with which they may appear and the amount that may be expended on advertising in any year. The Law Society should also lay down regulations concerning the style and contents of the brochures referred to in paragraph 27.40 below. We appreciate that detailed guidelines of this type may take some time to evolve; accordingly, we recommend that, until firm and authoritative rules can be established in the light of experience, all proposed advertisements and brochures should be submitted to the Law Society for approval as conforming with the guidelines we have suggested.

27.39 The Law Society should have the right to monitor the claims made in advertisements by solicitors. When a firm advertises the kinds of work that it is willing to undertake, it must be prepared to satisfy the Law Society, on request and at any time, that it has a partner or partners and staff who are competent to carry out such work. If such claims are found to be inaccurate or exaggerated, the Law Society should take appropriate disciplinary action. If a solicitor claims in an advertisement to be a specialist when he has not been so designated by the Law Society in the manner described in paragraph 27.21(d), this also should be treated as a disciplinary matter.

Requests for information
27.40 The Law Society permits solicitors to make available to clients or potential clients, in their waiting rooms or on request factual brochures giving the names of partners and senior staff, with a brief description of their departments, and also containing guidance for a client showing how he can assist the firm to deal promptly with his business, for example by completing a questionnaire. Such brochures are valuable and should be widely used, but

the information contained in them should be subject to the same controls by the Law Society as public advertisements. The availability of information of this kind should be more widely publicised in order that potential clients may confidently shop around and make an informed choice of solicitor.

Marking of premises

27.41 We received evidence that clients may find solicitors' offices difficult to locate and forbidding in appearance. This is because offices are often situated on upper floors in commercial centres with unwelcoming entrances in side streets or alleys. Solicitors' offices have traditionally been required to be discreet; they are normally indicated by a small plate giving the name and description of the firm, sometimes supplemented by the display in a window of the legal aid symbol and the name of the firm.

27.42 The Society has recently relaxed the restrictions on the marking of offices. Solicitors are now permitted to display a fascia board with the name, description and telephone number of the firm along with information about the type of work undertaken, the availability of a fixed fee interview, an emergency telephone number and a statement that the firm does legal aid work, provided that the board is suitable both to the premises themselves and to their location. It is desirable, for the benefit of those without access through a referral agency, that a suitable solicitors' firm should be easy to find and that its appearance should not intimidate or deter those who are not accustomed to taking professional advice. The relaxation of restrictions on marking offices is therefore to be welcomed.

Touting

27.43 The general principles expressed above also relate to touting. Touting can be distinguished from the type of advertising that we advocate in that its primary purpose is not to inform the public but to drum up business. The objective of our recommendations is to ensure that a member of the public is able, either directly or with the support and guidance of an agency such as a CAB, to find the solicitor most suitable for his particular case or problem and willing to deal with it on reasonable terms. The initiative rests with the client to make a rational choice of adviser. Touting impedes such a choice and it applies pressure to those who are particularly vulnerable to it. It may be acceptable for a solicitor to advertise that he is willing to undertake personal injury work, but it would clearly be undesirable for him to tout for business in hospital casualty departments. We consider, therefore, that the present regulations against touting are sound and should be maintained.

Barristers

General

27.44 We have concentrated in this chapter on the issue of informing the public about the services provided by the solicitors' branch of the profession, because this is the branch with which the public is directly in contact. Since a barrister can normally be approached to advise or represent lay clients only through a solicitor, we consider there is no need to supply detailed information to the public at large about barristers or about the services that they provide, either as individuals or as members of the profession. It needs to be considered, however, whether more detailed information about barristers should be made available to solicitors.

The report of the Monopolies Commission

27.45　The amount of information about individual barristers that is available to solicitors was considered by the Monopolies Commission in its report (HOC 559) published in July 1976. The Commission concluded that : —

> In view of the special relationship between solicitors and barristers, solicitors are likely from their experience to have adequate information about barristers, or to have the means of obtaining it readily. Although we recognise that such information cannot be complete we are satisfied that the restrictions on advertising by barristers do not deprive solicitors of useful information which might otherwise be made available to them or prevent them readily obtaining information. We conclude therefore that the restrictions are not harmful in respect of the availability to solicitors of information about barristers.

The Bar List and specialisation

27.46　All practising barristers are listed, along with their date of call, in the Bar List which is revised annually. There have recently been introduced "practice codes" which enable barristers, if they so wish, to indicate the categories of work which they are willing to undertake. Certain other indications may be given in the Bar List about barristers' specialisations; for example, there is a list of members of the Central Criminal Court Mess, and a list of barristers conversant with foreign laws. We welcome the introduction of the practice codes; they have increased the amount of information available to solicitors. We recognise that an entry in the Bar List indicates a barrister's willingness to undertake certain kinds of work and not the level of his experience or competence. We see no objection to this because of the specialist knowledge that is available to solicitors about the quality and experience of counsel whom they may brief. A barrister who holds himself out to do work that he is not capable of handling will rapidly be detected. In serious cases the appropriate disciplinary sanctions should be applied.

27.47　For the reasons stated above, we do not think that there is at present any need for the Bar formally to designate any of its members as specialists. Nevertheless, if it is found desirable to do so in the future we see no objection, provided that the Senate makes itself responsible for identifying appropriate subjects for specialisation, for laying down criteria and for granting recognition.

27.48　The Senate suggested to us that solicitors would be assisted if, in addition to the Bar List, there were made available to them a centrally compiled register indicating which barristers were available to accept briefs in particular courts. We welcome this suggestion and recommended that it be implemented.

Advertising

27.49 Barristers are prohibited from advertising their services, with certain exceptions. For example, barristers who form a new set of chambers, or whose chambers change address, are permitted to send a circular letter to existing clients and to issue a general advertisement in legal journals which state merely the change of address. There is at present no means of making known in what departments of the law the members of a set of new or existing chambers practise, save by the use of the practice codes in the Bar List. We believe it reasonable that information giving the general character of the work undertaken by the members of the chambers be included in circulars or advertisements relating to new chambers or to changes of address. It is also reasonable to allow a barrister of standing who joins a set of chambers in a new locality or who returns to private practice after a period elsewhere to indicate the type of work he is willing to undertake. This apart, we agree with the conclusions of the Monopolies Commission that information about the services provided by individual barristers may be obtained by those who require it without resort to individual advertising. As to the services provided by the Bar as a whole, we can see no objection to these being advertised, should the Senate so desire.

Conclusions and Recommendations

Paragraphs

Corporate advertising	R27.1	The governing body of a profession may properly publicise the services provided by its members.	27.5
Official publicity	R27.2	There should be a substantial and sustained increase in publicity for legal services provided at public expense.	27.7-27.8
Referral lists	R27.3	The existence of the legal aid solicitors lists which contain information about solicitors should be made more widely known.	27.13
	R27.4	Legal aid solicitors lists should include further information about firms of solicitors and their working hours.	24.14

375

Paragraphs

Specialisation R27.5 When solicitors have been recognised 27.19
as specialists they should be allowed
to include this information in referral
lists and other documents.

R27.6 The conditions of eligibility as a 27.20-27.22
specialist are set out in the text.

Individual R27.7 Individual solicitors or firms should 27.34
advertising be permitted to advertise subject to
certain restrictions.

R27.8 Advertisements should be regulated 27.35-27.39
by the Law Society, in accordance
with the criteria set out in the text.

R27.9 Firms should supply detailed infor- 27.40
mation about themselves to potential
clients to enable clients to shop
around.

Marking of R27.10 The easing of restrictions on methods 27.41
Premises of marking solicitors' offices is
welcome.

Touting R27.11 The prohibition against touting 27.43
should be retained.

Barristers R27.12 It is not at present necessary for 27.47
barristers to be designated as special-
ists.

R27.13 Solicitors should be provided, from 27.48
a central system, with information as
to which barristers are available to
accept briefs in particular courts.

R27.14 The present restrictions on advertising 27.49
by barristers should be retained
subject to modification in respect of
new chambers, changes of address and
return to practice.

[Extract from Legal Aid Solicitors' Lists]

(paragraph 27.10)

	A	B	C	D	E	F	G	H	I	J	K	L	M	N	O
E1															
Adler (Bernard) 59 Commercial Street E1 6BD 01-247 2271	*			*	*	*		*	*					*	
Bard & Keith Joseph Capital House 141 Shoreditch High Street E1 6JE 01-739 5977			*												
Bookatz & Co (SS) 192 Commercial Road Stepney E1 2JY 01-790 4833 Emergency tel. no. 01-790 4374	*	*	*	*	*			*							*
Edwards & Co (TV) Textile House 87 Whitechapel High Street E1 7QZ 01-377 9011 Emergency tel. no. 01-603 8303	*	*	*	*	*					*	*	*		*	*
Fail Bradshaw & Waterson (Edward) 402 Commercial Road Stepney E1 0LG 01-790 4032	*	*	*	*	*			*	*			*	*		
Kemp (Arthur W) Capital House 141 Shoreditch High Street E1 6JE 01-739 5977			*												
Morris (Dennis) 297 Whitechapel Road E1 01-377 0045	*			*	*			*	*	*			*		
Segalow & Co (DG) 125 Shoreditch High Street E1 6JE 01-739 3018			*				*	*	*			*			
Suriya & Co 277 Whitechapel Road E1 1BY 01-247 0444 Emergency tel. no. 01-551 3977	*	*	*	*	*	*	*	*	*			*		*	*
Wallace Bogan & Co Coburg House 238 Commercial Rd Stepney E1 2JT 01-790 5119 Emergency tel. no. 01-882 4104	*	*	*	*	*	*	*		*	*			*	*	*
OTHER LEGAL HELP Legal Advice Centre Toynbee Hall 28 Commercial Street E1 6LS 01-247 3633 Wednesdays 7-8.30pm Stepney Green Legal Advice Session Dame Colet House Ben Jonson Road E1 Tuesdays & Thursdays 7-8.30pm Run by the Tower Hamlets Law Centre Tower Hamlets Law Centre 341 Commercial Road E1 2PS 01-790 6311 by appointment only															

CHAPTER 28

The EEC

Free movement

28.1   The Treaty of Rome provides for the removal of any restrictions which prevent the nationals of one member state from providing professional services in other member states. The European Court has held, in the *Van Binsbergen* case [1975] 1 CMLR 298, that these provisions are in force and must be treated as having direct effect save in respect of services the reservation of which is objectively justified in the public interest of a member state.

28.2   The rights of lawyers from other EEC countries to practise in the United Kingdom are set out in the European Communities (Services of Lawyers) Order 1978 (SI 1978 No. 1910) which came into operation on 1st March 1979). Under this Order, which implements a Directive of the Council of Ministers of March 1977, a lawyer from another EEC country may provide any service in connection with legal proceedings in the UK, including representation, provided that he acts in conjunction with a British lawyer who is entitled to provide the service in question. When appropriate, the EEC lawyer may provide such services under the legal aid and legal advice and assistance schemes. So far as concerns representation, the Legal Aid (General) (Amendment) Regulations 1979 (SI 1979 No. 263), which came into operation on 6th April 1979 state "that a legal aid certificate shall not authorise representation by an EEC lawyer unless and to the extent that it expressly provides for such representation". An EEC lawyer providing professional services in this country is subject at all times to the rules of professional conduct and discipline applicable here and in his own country.

28.3   The Order and Directive mentioned above make no changes in the restrictions affecting conveyancing and probate work. Therefore an EEC lawyer may not for remuneration draw or prepare instruments creating or transferring interests in land nor prepare papers for obtaining title to administer estates. Given the differences between the legal systems of the different member countries, we think it unlikely that the Order and Directive will have the effect of causing any significant number of lawyers from other EEC countries to offer their professional services in this country.

28.4   Studies are in progress in a number of EEC countries of a right of establishment for lawyers; that is, the mutual recognition of all qualifications, enabling EEC lawyers to practise in any member state without restriction. Whatever formal measures are taken for this purpose, it must be accepted that lawyers cannot practise abroad as readily as, for example, doctors, architects or engineers. The position may change when the laws of member

378

states are harmonised, but this is not likely to happen soon. As things stand, British lawyers practising abroad are usually members of large British firms which have established offices in other EEC countries with the particular purpose of serving their large United Kingdom clients who have subsidiaries or substantial business transactions abroad. This apart, we doubt whether the movement of lawyers between the member states will significantly affect the volume of work available to the home profession and the numbers available to do it.

International courts and proceedings

28.5   Membership of the EEC has provided a number of British lawyers, both barristers and solicitors, with the opportunity to include in their practices the preparation and presentation of cases before the European Court of Justice and the Commission of the European Communities. This work is likely to become of increasing importance as the national courts make greater use of the referral procedure whereby they seek rulings from the European Court of Justice on the interpretation of the Treaty of Rome and of Community law. It seems unlikely, however, that the additional demands arising from such work will affect more than a minority of the profession.

Structure of the legal profession

28.6   Concerning the effect of membership of the EEC on the structure and organisation of the British legal profession, the United Kingdom Association of European Law said in evidence to us, referring to the views of the European Court of Justice on the separation of the British legal profession into two branches.

> . . . from the vantage point of this Court no reason can be discerned why the United Kingdom membership of the European Communities should entail any change in the basic structure of the English . . . legal profession . . . there is a very strong case for preserving the basic structure.

The impact of Community Law

28.7   Community law is now a part of English law, interpreted in accordance with principles laid down by the European Court of Justice. Its impact at first was restricted to those branches of the law, relating for example to restrictive practices, patents and consumer protection, which are affected by the integration and harmonisation of trade and commercial practices. This has now extended to other branches of the law.

Education and information

28.8   It is recognised that lawyers should be given a grounding in Community law and should keep up to date with it. Community law is included in the educational syllabus of both branches of the profession though not as a separate core subject. Study of any topic includes study of the effect of Community law on domestic law. Given an adequate grounding, it is desirable for practitioners to be able to keep up to date without having to purchase a large number of books to which only occasional reference will be required. We understand that the Commission of the European Communities has stated that traditional methods of information retrieval, such as reference books, can no longer adequately cope with the present volume of new Community law. The Commission of the European Communities has, therefore, authorised and funded a pilot study for a computerised retrieval system, initially for Community law alone. The use of computers for information retrieval may prove to be of considerable value and we discussed the possible introduction of a computerised retrieval system in Britain in Chapter 22. There are clear advantages in an accessible retrieval system for Community law, compatible with future domestic systems.

28.9 Both the Senate and the Law Society have established links with their professional counterparts in other EEC countries and have established European groups to promote knowledge of the institutions of the EEC and of the legal systems, procedures and professions in other European countries. These groups foster good relations and help to spread information about developments in the EEC.

The role of the Senate and the Law Society
28.10 The profession assists government departments in ensuring that the effect of EEC proposals for the harmonisation and reform of the law of the member countries on English domestic law is fully considered and that Directives and Conventions are framed in a way which will produce a coherent and workable result in Britain. The legal profession's contribution to the development of Community law is of value and should be maintained.

Printed in England for Her Majesty's Stationery Office by Burrup Mathieson & Co., Ltd.   S605616/AW
Dd 595218   K48   10/79